The publisher gratefully acknowledges the generous contribution to this book provided by the Samuel H. Kress Foundation and the Art Endowment Fund of the University of California Press Associates, which is supported by a major gift from the Ahmanson Foundation.

PROPAGANDA AND THE JESUIT BAROQUE

PROPAGANDA AND THE JESUIT BAROQUE

Evonne Levy

UNIVERSITY OF CALIFORNIA PRESS
Berkeley   Los Angeles   London

University of California Press
Berkeley and Los Angeles, California

University of California Press, Ltd.
London, England

© 2004 by the Regents of the University of California

Library of Congress Cataloging-in-Publication Data

Levy, Evonne Anita
    Propaganda and the Jesuit Baroque / Evonne Levy.
        p. cm.
    "Ahmanson-Murphy fine arts imprint."
    Includes bibliographical references and index.
    ISBN 0-520-23357-3 (cloth : alk. paper)
    1. Jesuit art—Europe.   2. Jesuit architecture—Europe.
3. Counter-Reformation in art.   4. Art, Baroque.   5. Propaganda
in art.   6. National socialism and art.   I. Title.
N7865 .L48   2004
303.3'75'094309043—dc22   2003017328

Manufactured in Canada
13   12   11   10   09   08   07   06   05
10   9   8   7   6   5   4   3   2

The paper used in this publication meets the minimum requirements
of ANSI/NISO Z39.48-1992 (R 1997) (*Permanence of Paper*).♾

To Emily Bakemeier
and Samuel Stein, *in memoriam*

CONTENTS

FIG. 1
Albert Speer, Courtyard of the Reichskanzlei, 1935–39, Berlin.

INTRODUCTION

> Art is so well received because it has lost its sting.
>
> EDGAR WIND, *ART AND ANARCHY* (1960)

> When all's said, we should be grateful to the Jesuits. Who knows if,
> but for them, we might have abandoned Gothic architecture for the light,
> airy, bright architecture of the Counter-Reformation? In the face of Luther's
> efforts to lead an upper clergy that had acquired profane habits back to
> mysticism, the Jesuits restored to the world the joy of the senses.
>
> ADOLF HITLER, 21–22 JULY 1941, FROM *HITLER'S SECRET CONVERSATIONS*

When faced with Albert Speer's Reichskanzlei (fig. 1) or Paul Ludwig Troost's Haus der Deutschen Kunst in Munich, few would deny that architecture functioned as a powerful form of propaganda in the Third Reich. Indeed, there is ample evidence that although Hitler had a paltry knowledge of architecture, he did understand the medium as a vital form of propaganda, a formulation made explicit in the title of a 1939 film about Nazi buildings: *Das Wort aus Stein.*[1]

But would we so *unequivocally* attach the label "propaganda" to a Jesuit church of the early modern period? In this context, Hitler's utterance about Jesuit architecture in one of his recorded evening conversations brings us right to the point. Did Hitler, the foremost practitioner of the propaganda arts in the twentieth century, the so-called architect of the Third Reich who often remarked that his political, artistic, and military ideas formed a unity, consider the "joy of the senses" that he experienced in Jesuit architecture as a model for his own architectural program? And even if this admiration, professed in a private context, was just the expression of a personal preference—Hitler's distaste for Gothic architecture is well known[2]—his articulation of the sensuous appeal of Jesuit architecture, though utterly banal, derivative, and rife with contradictions, is provocative.[3] I am not suggesting that a line be drawn from Jesuit architecture to Nazi architecture, although it would not be an exaggeration to say that the fear of demagoguery links the virulent anti-Jesuitism of the nineteenth century to the Western world's disgust for Nazism in the twentieth. Rather, I would like to offer two readings of this remark. First, and this will be substantiated in the pages that follow, Hitler's remark, surprising in its valorization of what was considered an imported non-German style,[4] was a twisted restatement of what was by then an outdated concept grounded in the art historical literature on the so-called Jesuit Style dating back to the 1840s. That Speer and Hitler self-consciously modeled the domed Great Hall (fig. 2), a key element of their grand plan for Berlin, on a Roman building like St. Peter's (fig. 3)—seeking to generate a comparable venerability for a regime building by imitating the basilica and making it known by how much they exceeded it in scale[5]—suggests that the historiography of the Catholic Baroque made it ripe for appropriation by a totalitarian regime. In the pages that follow I hope it will become evident how this could be the case.

The second point is harder to prove but must be risked nonetheless. And that is, that the formal qualities of Jesuit architecture to which Hitler—departing somewhat from opinions advanced by his advisors[6]—was attracted (and here the bright massive vault of the Jesuit St. Michaelskirche familiar to Hitler from his years in Munich comes to mind; fig. 4) are not *precisely* the qualities that led scores of travelers and later art historians to be suspicious of Jesuit architecture since the seventeenth century. But they suggest that this architecture long enjoyed a power to affect its viewers. It is this power that has supported a charged art historical discussion of Jesuit architecture and its characterization as an art of mass manipulation. Jesuit architecture specifically and the Catholic Baroque in general *have* often been considered an art of propaganda. But the legacy of Hitler and Goebbels (and to a lesser extent of Mussolini and of Stalin) has made it virtually impossible for propaganda to become a productive category of analysis. Propaganda, for good reason, is an extraordinarily loaded term whose function primarily as an epitaph in Baroque studies has gone unexamined until now.

In approaching the Baroque (and here I limit the field to the Catholic Baroque) through its most controversial builders, the Jesuits, I seek to challenge art history's neutralization of the period since World War II. This shift in art history occurred in successive stages, the result of a long historical process of neutralizing the role of the Church in Western society in general. In spite of the attack on the Church during the Enlightenment, and the major impetus toward secularization in the French Revolution and its aftermath, the institution remained in place, battling for its former position and pitting its adherents against newly formed national governments. It was the nineteenth century, age of nationalisms, that produced art history as a discipline, enlisting the history of architectural monuments in efforts across Europe to define national character. It is no wonder that the international Catholic organization the Society of Jesus and its architecture would be regarded with suspicion in this era of nation building.

It was only with World War I that the Catholic Church truly receded from its preeminent place in the controversies of European politics. With the far-reaching social changes of modernity that saw the rise of international socialism and the empire building of European nations, the pope in Rome became a far less pressing issue. With the Church thus neutralized, the Catholic Baroque could become the subject of depoliticized formal and

FIG. 2
Albert Speer, Project for a Great Hall for Berlin, 1937–40.

FIG. 3
Carlo Maderno, Facade of St. Peter's, 1607–12, Rome.

FIG. 4
Friedrich Sustris and Wolfgang Miller, St. Michael's, 1583–97, Munich.

iconographic analyses, with many historians concluding that the art of the period was the expression of a sincere religiosity. Indeed, many art historians after the world wars studiously avoided the stigma of propaganda, going to some lengths to deny that the Baroque was either ideologically suspect or ideological at all. Had the scales at last fallen from art historians' eyes? Or was this a search for alternative readings in order to reserve judgment for that which was truly threatening?

This adjustment in the place occupied by the Baroque in world and art history was marked in Erwin Panofsky's lecture "What Is Baroque?" written in 1934, one year after the Jewish art historian emigrated permanently to the United States from Nazi Germany.[7] Challenging once again the long-held tradition that the Baroque marked a "decline" of the Renaissance, Panofsky argued that it marked, instead, a second "climax." Rather, industrialization, "the forces of masses and machines," he remarked in the conclusion to the lecture, signal the real shift and, by implication, the decline of civilization: "The rise of these new forces, not the Baroque movement, means the real end of the Renaissance, and at the same time the beginning of our own epoch of history, an epoch that is still struggling for an expression both in life and in art, and that will be named and judged by the generations to come—provided that it does not put an end to all generations to come."[8] A period that had been problematic in the past, because decadent or meretricious, had become good. In view of the Nazi rise to power Panofsky makes it seem inevitable that propagandas of the past recede in the face of the present, more potent ones.

I have not quoted Hitler's views of Jesuit architecture at the outset of this study to provoke my potential critics. Unlike Jesuit architecture, the cultural production of the Third Reich has not been entirely neutralized with time and it is doubtful that it will be in the foreseeable future.[9] But in the past twenty years, studies of Nazi film, art, and architecture, the ideological novel, and other forms of propaganda have treated politically sensitive material, wedding the formal qualities of ideologically loaded works to their functions.[10]

The neutralization of the Baroque since World War II, while opening our eyes to many previously neglected aspects of the period, has also tended to wrench aesthetics from its politics. This separation has been sustained more tenaciously in Italian Baroque studies than in other areas of the discipline (especially nineteenth- and twentieth-century art, even the Renaissance) that have been the subject of Marxist criticism and the focus of the social history of art. Why the Italian Baroque has resisted such interventions has to do, in part, with the proclivities of leaders in the field in North America, some of whom were German émigrés who, in their own version of politics, tended to avoid political arguments.[11] Italian Baroque studies today, especially around the Catholic Church, remain fundamentally unaffected by political critique.[12] For instance, in spite of the balanced account of patronage of all possible classes implicated in the purchase of art in the Baroque period in Francis Haskell's pioneering *Patrons and Painters,* many specialists in the field have taken a comfortable view of papal and other ecclesiastical potentates as beacons of taste, casting a benevolent eye on the institutional dimension of their patronage with all the concomitant implications of power and discourse that might otherwise be attached to the works of art they commissioned.[13] While the study of the political uses of art is a notable strength of the field,[14] the question of what may be at stake in the deployment of art by various institutions often remains unarticulated. Several recent studies have done much to illuminate the workings of ecclesiastical institutions engaged in artistic patronage. But the tendency remains to keep the goals, ideological assumptions, and functions of artists and patrons distinct.[15] It is, however, only by joining the two that we can arrive at an understanding of the Catholic Baroque that takes full measure of the institutions that produced it and the publics to which it was directed.

It is the purpose of this study to apply the modern sense of propaganda to a key realm of Baroque representation, the art and architecture of the Jesuit order, with a higher degree of self-consciousness. The Jesuits, I believe, are a key to the problematic historiography of the Baroque. The political controversies that swirled around this powerful Counter-Reformation order in the nineteenth century coincided with the beginnings of the art historical definition of style, giving rise to a tenacious and overtly politicized rubric, the Jesuit Style. As one locus of a moralizing approach to the period (which viewed the sensuousness and the international success of identifiably Jesuit architecture as highly suspect), the Jesuit Style continues to inform our notion of the Baroque in critical ways, despite the common belief that this thesis was long ago discarded. This becomes particularly evident after World War I, when some art historians began to attach to the Catholic Baroque the term "propaganda," in essence a renaming of those morally problematic elements of the Jesuit Style that had been in circulation since the mid-nineteenth century. As I show in chapter 1, propaganda as we understand it today is already present, more narrowly in characterizations of the Jesuits but, because of their representative function, also more broadly applied to the Baroque of Catholic lands.

When first invoked as an art historical category for the Baroque in the 1910s, propaganda was not entirely negative. Indeed, one can sense that for some writers the Baroque suddenly bore a resemblance to the modern world. After the escalation of propaganda in World War II and the incommensurable moral consequences of Nazi propaganda, the term, while not neutral before, became much more inflammatory. In the postwar period, with some exceptions, propaganda has been invoked in the art historical literature as a sometimes more, sometimes less dismissive epithet. In the Cold War period propaganda became almost exclusively a term of debasement, and it is because this tradition of its use persists that it needs to be examined. A highly symptomatic example is to be found in Rudolf Wittkower's *Art and Architecture in Italy, 1600–1750*, of 1958, the standard English textbook for Italian Baroque art and architecture, recently reissued, unrevised.[16] Wittkower termed two Roman chapels executed at the turn of the seventeenth century in what he calls the "'pragmatic' style" propaganda. The works, significantly, are the sump-

FIG. 5
Domenico Fontana, Sistine Chapel, 1585, S. Maria Maggiore, Rome.

tuous papal Pauline and Sistine Chapels (fig. 5) in S. Maria Maggiore, which, by the standards of the day, were collectively produced by a group of artists who harmonized their individual manners so that the projects were stylistically unified. As Wittkower's term "pragmatic" indicates, he found the artistic quality lacking, leading him to argue that the pragmatic style "fulfilled its purpose and gratified the patron even when it sank down to the level of pure propaganda."[17] It is apparent from the contrast between the failure of the "equalizing tendencies" of works such as these and the success of works by "strong-willed individualists" (like Bernini) that for Wittkower art and propaganda are two mutually exclusive categories. Does Bernini's *Cathedra Petri* (fig. 6), the reliquary embodiment of papal authority, for example, rise above propaganda because it qualifies as great art? Remarks like Wittkower's suggest that in spite of the neutralization of the Catholic Baroque, deep-seated suspicion still persists.[18] And this suspicion—reserved for a select group of objects that preserve the rest from contamination—is revealed when the criteria for "scientific" discourse, like aesthetic quality or individual creativity, prove inadequate. Suspicion is itself a form of affect, and the disturbing feelings are channeled by creating a category of containment. To call a work "propaganda," in other words, constitutes a particular form of (art historical) response.

FIG. 6
Giovan Lorenzo Bernini, *Cathedra Petri*, 1657–65, St. Peter's, Rome.

The affective force of images so studiously avoided by intellectuals is the subject of David Freedberg's groundbreaking study of the history of response, *The Power of Images*.[19] Disturbed by the distancing of art historians (through what he calls "folklorization") from a series of historical and cross-cultural responses to images, Freedberg focused on arousal, violence (iconoclasm), and piety in his magisterial study of Western and, to some extent, non-Western images. One lacuna in his study, he noted, was that of propaganda, of the response to political images, which he chose to leave aside.[20] While I have not set out to fill in Freedberg's lacuna, this book is, effectively, a chapter in the history of response. But it differs from Freedberg's approach in viewing the invocation of the term "propaganda" itself as a form of response. That is to say, I am interested less in how "the people" viewed the monuments to be considered here (part of Freedberg's quibble with art historical scholarship is that it sets intellectuals above human, that is to say, emotional, response) and more in how and why art historians have needed to isolate only some objects by terming them propaganda. How does propaganda function in art history? This study is a subchapter in the history of the power of images: but here it is not the erotic, the mystical, or the power of images to elicit violence under examination. It is rather a power, often bound to an ethical position, that may generate fear, resistance, or a deeply felt sense of responsibility not to enjoy a work as art. And this power is so great that it, in a sense, blinds us to the object itself.

The work of art is always a site of projection, but this is, arguably, more pronounced in art that we label propaganda. Indeed, I believe that it is a characteristic of the response to works of art placed in this class by art historians that the object itself is to some extent looked past and through, that it is often reduced to a sign of something else. The work of propaganda is difficult and distasteful because it possesses a disturbing ideological indexicality: the artistry of the work can be overlooked (or considered a distracting or deceptive gloss) for its message; its author can be overwhelmed by its (institutional) patron; its originality can be compromised by its relation to a model or a style that it needs to reiterate on some level. A work of Albert Speer, for example, reads immediately as a Nazi work: Speer stands in for Nazi architecture (in spite of the stylistic diversity of Nazi-sponsored architecture), but the priority is on Nazi. Analogously, for nineteenth-century historians of architecture, a Jesuit church, whether built by a well-known architect such as Vignola or by a lesser-known Jesuit architect, was read first and last as Jesuit. There is in the work of propaganda no gradual arrival at the ideological destination; the speed and efficacy of this movement put the propagandistic work *of art* in a precarious position.[21]

The idea that art is propaganda is often resisted, in sum, because propaganda makes of art something that *cannot be seen* or is seen *past*. And such a work cannot sustain itself as art in light of its use as a vehicle for an ideological program: this is not art that is ideological, or art as a form of ideology, but ideology in the form of art. This formulation may suggest an outmoded view to Marxists, who have left behind the idea that artistic conventions do not impinge on the formal expression of ideology, that the aesthetic is a transparent bearer of ideology.[22] This is not my view, but it is my view of how propaganda (problematically) functions, in art history, or not. For a work that cedes so quickly to its ideological emplotment is often considered a failure as a work of art at some level. But of course the notion of the failure of a work of art for any of these criteria is more a reflection on our criteria for *art* than on the works themselves. In becoming aware of how calling a work propagandistic amounts to a particular type of response to the work of art, we may be able to open up the circumstances in which those works of art were produced to more fruitful and lively analysis.

It is my intention to examine the historical use of propaganda as a route into understanding why historians of the Catholic Baroque have needed it but have contained the term and its application. Even intellectuals of the postwar generations who consider themselves immune to propaganda often deploy the most reductive understanding of the term. As Hans Belting remarked, in the postwar period German art history developed a variety of strategies to keep ideology at bay,[23] but those strategies were in place well before then. The Germans were not alone, and the varieties of formalism and iconography effectively functioned similarly in North America through the 1970s and up to today.[24] In the Cold War environment there was much at stake in maintaining that art could be pure and truthful.

Since the end of the Cold War, that is to say, recently, propaganda has been invoked in a more neutral fashion, especially in studies of the art produced in the emerging early modern centralized states. A few years ago Theodore Rabb remarked that "it has become something of a fashion in recent work on Renaissance and early modern Europe to see visual images as essential and efficient weapons of political propaganda—vital components of the rise of the state."[25] The term has been used more by historians than by art historians. With few exceptions (discussed in chapter 2), these studies tend to assume the contours of propaganda without defining the term itself.[26] Invoked in this way, propaganda makes historical subjects relevant, casting a knowing eye on hegemonic subjects that are at the center of a critique by new art historians. But these studies have done little to advance the discipline's understanding of and engagement with propaganda. Indeed, one might argue that such an approach irresponsibly misuses propaganda, for by neutralizing it, one abandons its essence.

This study is intended as a corrective—both to the containment of propagandistic art and to the neutralization of the Catholic Baroque—in several ways. It seeks to discover propaganda, unnamed but already in our midst, in the early historiography of the Jesuit Style in particular and the Catholic Baroque in general. What this apparition suggests is that although art history's use of propaganda has often been reductive, the term's invocation is a symptom of the powerful identity of the institutions responsible for propagandistic monuments as well as of difficult qualities (like excessive material splendor) possessed by the objects themselves. In both of these senses the treatment of Jesuit art is a paradigmatic case in art history. In the mid-nineteenth century a public and politicized discourse on architecture and a hostile political debate over the survival of the Jesuit order converged in the concept of the Jesuit Style. The Jesuit Style has been challenged and declared dead since the beginning of the twentieth century. One could write a history of art history from all of the ink spilled over diffusing this highly politicized concept. It lives again in these pages because the nineteenth-century formulation of the problem penetrates to essential problems concerning art and ideology. The Jesuit Style, its genesis and thematics, is the subject of chapter 1, but the constitutive elements of the concept are taken up throughout this book.

In spite of the problematic nature of applying a term so defined by our modern experience of it, I will also argue that propaganda, rather than the historically justified category of rhetoric, or rhetorical persuasion, should be employed in an analysis of Jesuit art and architecture. A few art historians have elided rhetoric and propaganda in their characterizations of the Catholic Baroque, and distinctions between these two models of persuasion need to be made. The slope between these two concepts is particularly slippery and not all will be satisfied by my solution. My focus on propaganda has primarily to do with the centrality of institutions to propaganda and their far more shadowy presence in the theory of rhetoric. Propaganda is also, unlike rhetoric, a phenomenon that is deeply connected to the rise of the modern urban masses. And while in terms of sheer numbers the early modern mass is incomparable to the modern mass, the Baroque has long been perceived—and there is much evidence of such a perception in the period itself—as an art that appeals precisely to the masses.[27] The vicissitudes, interrelations, and differences between these two models of persuasion will be brought to bear on why propaganda has a place in art history.

My focus here on propaganda lies above all in its necessity to us. As I argue in chapter 2, rhetoric's traditional designation as an art of persuasion has irrevocably shifted. Propaganda has taken the place of rhetoric as the site of interested discourse, of instrumentality. The irreducible *interestedness* of propaganda is central to my own characterization of it in this study. Propaganda is produced in an institutional context to further the aims of that institution, to create subjects. For the art historian, there are troubling aspects to this. When art becomes the means by which ideological ends are achieved, that directedness is disturbing.[28] No matter how free we may feel as spectators, often embedded in our response to propagandistic art is a sense of entrapment. This *directedness,* the *interestedness* of propaganda is a key way in which it is set apart from rhetoric as well as from art, in the Kantian sense. Works of art deemed propaganda are often separated (from "pure art") because they challenge important values; insofar as the invocation of propaganda also helps us to detect and define values deeply embedded in the discipline, it serves an indispensable function.

Thus most generally this study addresses a key lacuna in the study of art and propaganda of the early modern period: namely, the problems that arise in applying the term "propaganda" to works of *art*[29]—two categories that have resisted each other most obviously in the study of arts employed by the Nazis.[30] The formulation of the issue in Hellmut Lehmann-Haupt's *Art under Dictatorship*, published a decade after the end of World War II, is typical: "To call these [Nazi buildings] good architecture would require an almost superhuman degree of detachment for anyone not in sympathy with these ideals."[31] In this and other cases, the invocation of propaganda has also allowed the art historian to express ethical reservations and to separate a professional interest in the object from personally held views of the institutions that may have originally made use of it. Because much time separates us from the Jesuit monuments examined here, a less than superhuman degree of detachment need be exercised to narrow the gap between art and propaganda. Indeed, the question I posed at the outset of this introduction points to the need for a reversal, toward attachment, not detachment.

To make propaganda a productive and appropriate tool of art historical analysis, it must be applied to specific cases, to show how it functioned. As Jacques Ellul, the foremost analyst of propaganda in the twentieth century, has argued, "[T]he primary goal of he who operates the propaganda instrument is efficaciousness. And one should never ignore this supreme rule because inefficacious propaganda is not propaganda."[32] The remainder of the chapters of this study test the means and limits of propaganda in three major aspects of propaganda that present fruitful areas for art historical investigation: the *propagandist,* or the authorship of institutions (chapter 3); the formation of a *message* (chapter 4); and *diffusion,* or reception (chapter 5).

My method is in part one of exemplification, and the examples are potent: the art and architecture of the Society of Jesus in general and, in particular, a series of projects dating to the end of the seventeenth century undertaken by the Jesuits in Rome to enhance the cult of their founder, St. Ignatius of Loyola: the Jesuit painter and architect Andrea Pozzo's corridor in the Roman Casa Professa (figs. 35–40 and 42–44, in chapter 4), his frescoes in the Church of St. Ignatius (fig. 47, in chapter 4), and the Chapel of St. Ignatius (fig. 16, in chapter 3) in the Gesù of Rome. In addition to the sumptuousness and cultic importance of these projects, the last of these, the reliquary chapel, serves as an example here because the proceedings surrounding its design and construction are preserved in an extraordinary set of documents. We know more about this chapel's genesis than virtually any work of the period. From the archival record emerges the picture of an institution crafting its own authorship, a message, and seeing to the diffusion of the imagery of the chapel worldwide. Each of these three aspects is taken up with specific reference to these projects, as well as to Jesuit art and architecture more broadly, in chapters 3 through 5.

My aim is not to provide a definition of propaganda for the art historian, a formula that will aid us in determining why one monument may be considered propaganda (as for Wittkower, the papal chapels in S. Maria Maggiore) and another may not. The need to uncover propaganda was deeply embedded in much of the literature on propaganda up until the 1960s: it is a defensive posture, based on the fear that propaganda is a masked form of communication that we must be alert to if we are not to succumb to its underlying ideological origin. There is also a legitimate fear that once a definition of propaganda is in place, it will be difficult not to see it everywhere.

My assessment of propaganda's usefulness to art history is a methodological inquiry in which propaganda sets out a path that extends from the relationship of an institution to a work of art's inception through its diffusion. Art historians deal with every aspect of this longer process through iconographic analysis, reception history and author studies, and so on. Propaganda can be put more productively into play in art history. To do so, however, we must understand its components and see how they coincide with and where they challenge the concerns of the discipline.

THE "JESUIT STYLE"

You have written a distinguished book. With your broad synthesis, beginning
ab ovo, that is from the decline of the nineteenth century and up until our
day, that blessed term "Jesuit Style" has been eviscerated by your logic, and
not without moments of exhilarating humor. With that term, the great
men of German art history and ours as well divulged and tried to accredit
(as much as it was in them) the most foolish fables of this world.

LETTER TO CARLO GALASSI PALUZZI, AUTHOR OF *LA STORIA SEGRETA
DELLO STILE DEI GESUITI*, FROM FATHER PIETRO TACCHI VENTURI, S.J.

In 1951 Carlo Galassi Paluzzi published a sharp-tongued, polemical historiography mockingly entitled *The Secret History of the Jesuit Style*.[1] Treating the art historical literature on Jesuit architecture from 1879 to his day, Galassi Paluzzi ridiculed the scientific imprecision of earlier assessments of the architecture of the Society of Jesus. He argued that the Jesuit Style—in short, a conspiracy theory that the Jesuits invented an opprobrious ornate Baroque architecture themselves and systematically diffused it worldwide—was itself a monstrous hybrid. Informed by the "spirit of levity and superficiality" of the Enlightenment, the Jesuit Style, he trumpeted, was largely the fantastical invention of a highly biased Hegelian school of Protestant historians, a form of propaganda with no basis in historical fact.[2] Bent on forever dismantling misinformed notions of the Jesuit Style (while ascribing some validity to the idea), Galassi Paluzzi rightly pointed to basic "scientific" errors embedded in the concept when judged by the standards of the discipline in the middle of the twentieth century. His study was followed in 1969 by an interdisciplinary symposium and volume edited by Rudolf Wittkower and Irma Jaffe, *Baroque Art: The Jesuit Contribution*.[3] It was this symposium, far better known among art historians than Galassi Paluzzi's book, that really sounded the death knell for the Jesuit Style.

Although no one would claim today that a Jesuit Style existed, this term and its historiography still occupy a central if hidden place in our understanding of the Catholic Baroque. From the 1840s the Jesuit Style constituted a precocious formulation—as viewed from Switzerland, France, and Germany—for seventeenth-century art, a critical precursor to the periodization of the Baroque. Following the overriding of the Jesuit Style with the term "Baroque" in the 1880s, the view of the centrality of the Jesuits to a history of seventeenth-century architecture—if not the concept of the Jesuit Style itself—nonetheless persisted, finding new meaning in the 1910s and 1920s as a historical equivalent to modern propaganda. The context in which the Jesuit Style emerged, what it meant, and why it translated so easily as propaganda following World War I are explored in this chapter.

Galassi Paluzzi's study, an ad hominen attack on German art historians, was more of a work of criticism than historiography, one that did not attempt to come to terms with the cultural and historical context from which the Jesuit Style emerged. Unfortunately, the book's conclusions have remained fundamentally unchallenged. In spite of the highly partisan nature of Galassi Paluzzi's work, which most art historians have chosen to ignore, both the charged political environment that produced the Jesuit Style and the author's petulant assessments of the literature remain unexamined. In dismissing the Jesuit Style as indefensible according to the scientific standards of the discipline, Galassi Paluzzi and those who have come after him have not fully come to terms with the challenges, especially regarding institutional interests in deploying the arts, that Jesuit art and architecture offer to the discipline. In examining the historiography of the Jesuit Style in its historical context, I aim to bring back into view the controversial dimensions of the works embedded in the concept and to reintegrate them into our understanding of the Catholic Baroque.

THE CONTEXT FOR THE EMERGENCE OF THE JESUIT STYLE IN GERMANY AND FRANCE

The term "Jesuit Style" emerged in the early 1840s, around fifty years before the first studies of seventeenth-century art and architecture used the term *Barock* in their titles. Although a precise origin of the term remains elusive—it may well have been used in a newspaper, a speech, or a lecture—the times were ripe for its invention. The Jesuit Style appears first in Germany and France, in the context of discussions under way since the 1820s about which historical style should constitute the English, German, and French national styles of architecture. Informed by the Hegelian view of the art and architecture of a nation as an expression of its spirit, architects and historians endeavored to understand and define historical styles. They were also coming to terms with the moral and political inflection that the employment of old styles anew would give to the present. Even if architects of the nineteenth century did not imagine a revival of Jesuit architecture, the corpus of Jesuit buildings attracted their attention because of pressing contemporary debates—often focusing on the Jesuits—about the roles of religion and institutions and the limits of human liberty in postrevolutionary Europe. Contemporary architectural practice and the history of architecture emerged as two interrelated sites where these ideas took visible and audible form. As such, we must understand the emergence of the Jesuit Style as a politically charged event, inextricable from both the precarious and tendentious position of the Jesuit order and the rise of a politicized architectural discourse.

The position of the Society of Jesus in nineteenth-century Europe must likewise be understood in the context of its longer history. The political tension around and antagonism directed at the nineteenth-century Jesuits were grounded in a continuous critique of the Society dating to its origins. The nineteenth-century Jesuit order was a weakened one, fighting for its existence following the complete suppression of the Society in 1773. The Jesuits had traveled far from their auspicious beginnings as a papal favorite. But the close ties to the papacy that had engendered their early success would become the most politically problematic aspect of the Society in the nineteenth century.

Founded in 1540 by the Basque Ignatius of Loyola together with a handful of his Spanish and Portuguese companions, the Compagnia di Gesù, or Society of Jesus, established a close and loyal relationship to an embattled papacy just beginning to react with seriousness to the Reformation. To state this loyalty Jesuits of the fourth and highest class took a fourth vow of obedience to the pope in addition to the standard vows of poverty, celibacy, and obedience. As Dauril Alden notes, "[B]esides the Society's appropriation of the name of Jesus, perhaps no feature of the Society became such a red flag for its opponents as the papal oath, particularly among those who feared or resented the perceived expansion of papal political authority."[4] The Society was rewarded with special privileges and, more important, encouragement to grow. As a result of explicit papal support the Jesuits multiplied at an astonishing rate, their houses spreading far and wide. Having started as a group of eight in one house in Rome in 1540, the Jesuits numbered approximately 1,500 by the time of Ignatius's death in 1556 and had grown to more than 17,600 members in thirty-five provinces in 1679.[5]

Numbers mattered to the Jesuits. Not only can their success be measured by the growth of their membership, but they seemed to have had a keen sense of their own influence, self-consciously seeking a "mass" audience for their diversified work. When Ignatius and his companions first came to Rome, where they established their administrative center, their primary mission was an urban one. As Thomas Lucas has shown in a recent study of the early Jesuits' urban mission, Ignatius sought the largest possible audience for preaching, for conversion, and for the administering of their greatest contribution to Western spirituality, the Spiritual Exercises.[6] They did not initially consider education as part of their mission, but they were almost immediately called upon as teachers. One decade after the founding, the colleges became a cornerstone of Jesuit activity, thereby enlarging their audience even further.[7] Indeed, Jesuit schools came to dominate postprimary education in many Catholic countries; in some, like Italy, Poland, and Portugal, they eclipsed any other type of school.[8] A second aspect of Jesuit activity in which they came to be a dominant institution was missionary work. Extending from Latin America to China, Jesuit missions placed the Society's members among those of all social strata and ethnicities, thereby making the Society the most international early modern institution, bar none.

Such international ambition and success, supported by a complex communications network, engendered great sophistication, along with intense hostility and criticism from outsiders. Suspicion of Jesuit imperialist ambitions seems to have been present from the very beginnings of the Society when it was still made up of a handful of energetic preachers working the streets and the courts. In 1547 Ignatius wrote to the young father Juan de Polanco: "We [already] have a reputation among some persons who do not trouble to find out the truth, especially here in Rome, that we would like to rule the world."[9] This perception of the Jesuits was reinforced by their popularity at the European courts, where Jesuit confessors were in high demand. Although a vow of secrecy bound confessors and spiritual advisors of the princes and princesses, conspiracy theorists have always imagined them as active agents of Jesuit ambitions.

By the time Clement XIV suppressed the Society in 1773 (following the expulsion of the Jesuits from Spain, France, Naples, Sicily, and Portugal between 1759 and 1767), the Jesuits numbered 22,589 men in forty-one provinces. With the suppression these men either disbanded or moved underground until Pius VII restored the Society in 1814. But the reinstating of the Society was resisted in France, Germany, and Portugal on political grounds.

The history of the Jesuit order touches on virtually every world power and colonial country, but here I focus on France and Germany as the cradles of art and architectural history. In France, from which the Jesuits were expelled again in 1830, 1845, 1880, and 1901, the Society struggled against widespread public hostility that focused on whether it should be allowed to run schools.[10] At a time of immense political instability politicians recognized that the formation of a stable set of national ideals and beliefs could only be instilled through the systematic instruction of France's youth. Permitting Jesuits to continue to run schools amounted to producing a counterrevolutionary Catholic public that promised to continue to fragment the future nation.

The first virulent wave of public attacks on the Jesuits commenced in the 1820s and peaked in the years leading up to the second expulsion of the Society from France in 1845. The public imagination was roused by the publication of Eugène Sue's wildly popular Jesuit conspiracy novel, *Le Juif errant,* which appeared first in serial form (1844–45) in a Parisian daily and was subsequently printed as a book, widely translated and reprinted into the 1920s.[11] Sue's was only one of numerous novels to feature evil Jesuits in the nineteenth century[12]—in his case the central protagonist was the diabolical Jesuit Rodin (fig. 7), who in pursuit of the goal of worldwide dominion left a trail of devastation in his wake. But it appeared at a particularly intense moment of anti-Jesuitism, coinciding with the rousing anti-Jesuit lectures given by the historians Jules Michelet and Edgar Quinet at the Collège de France, which the Parisian press described as "scenes of disorder, frantic applause and heckling." The political impact of these university lectures, inconceivable today, is best understood by their dissemination: they were reprinted in extenso the following morning in *Le Siècle,* France's largest daily newspaper, and were immediately published, translated, and repeatedly reprinted.[13] These contributions to the theme, well

FIG. 7
The Jesuit "Rodin," in Eugène Sue, *Le Juif errant* (Paris, 1845).

established since the late 1820s, elicited a particularly paranoid public response: in 1844 the *feuilleton* of the *Gazette des hôpitaux* described "jésuitophobie" as the latest malady afflicting the French people.[14] Sue's anti-Jesuit novel and Quinet's and Michelet's lectures (two examples of a soaring production of anti-Jesuitica in the period) are important because the new mass media helped them to reach an ever larger reading public and because the Jesuit question was *actuelle,* tapping into the fundamental political questions of the day. This actuality bears directly on the origin and meaning of the art historical notion of the Jesuit Style.

At stake in Michelet's and Quinet's lectures at the Collège de France were two oppositions—one moral and one political—with which the Jesuits were identified. The political opposition was between the liberal values of the Revolution and its promotion of universal religion and individual liberty versus the Jesuit position: Ultramontanist (aligned with the papacy), pro-monarchy, and intolerant of progress. As Michelet put it, "Take any man in the street, the first passer-by, and ask him: 'What are the Jesuits?' He will answer without hesitation: 'The counterrevolution.'"[15] The moral position staked Jesuitism (characterized by insincerity, deviousness, and artificiality newly reinforced by suppressed Jesuits operating covertly under disguise) against the "spirit of life" (truth, authenticity, and spontaneity).[16] Quinet went so far as to posit Jesuitism as a principle of degeneration. "I should not be much puzzled to prove," he wrote, "that every religion has sooner or later its Jesuitism, which is nothing but its degeneration."[17]

Whereas the Jesuits occupied a fairly clear if embattled position in partisan French politics, in preunification Germany the situation of the Society was even more complex. Paradoxically, at the time of the suppression, the Jesuits found refuge in Frederick II's Protestant Prussia and farther east in Catherine II's Catholic White Russia. Frederick's motives for keeping the disempowered Jesuits appear contrary to his progressive ideas and contact with the philosophes. But nothing was more pleasing to Frederick than to be able to assert his own authority against the Papal See by supporting the Society it had suppressed.[18] At Frederick's death in 1786 his successor expelled the Jesuits from Prussian territories.

With the annexation of the Catholic Rhineland to Prussia in 1815 the situation became more complex again. The Jesuits became quite powerful in the region, spreading Ultramontane views among the young clergy. For Catholics in the Rhineland, disillusioned by the occupation of the Napoleonic forces, a strong Catholic presence guaranteed a certain balance of power in the region. Far from representing the ancien régime, the Jesuits, in this context, constituted an important political minority that safeguarded freedom of worship. In incipient democracies, a Catholic body now represented a voting public, thus politicizing the Enlightenment's philosophical opposition to the Church and giving rise to the very idea of *anti*clericalism.[19] In spite of the ostensible separation of Church and State in Germany, as a voting body the Catholic Church posed a threat to the unification of the Germanic lands (only accomplished in 1870). To clear the path to unification strong repressive measures were taken against the powerful Catholic minorities in the Rhineland and majorities in Bavaria. Because the Jesuits were the leading Catholic presence in Germany, they were the principal targets of the Falk laws, resulting in their expulsion of the Society in 1872.[20]

The Jesuit paranational obedience to both the Society and the pope threatened the formation and stabilization of nations. This is the central political problem of the international Jesuits in the nineteenth century. The very internationalism that was key to their successful worldwide apostolic mission in the early modern period (and which placed fealty to both the Society and the pope over demands of political loyalty) now threatened to undermine national interests.

As the discussion of French politics showed, the alliance of Jesuits and the pope represented political conservatism. "Jesuitism," Geoffrey Cubitt writes, was understood as "an anti-Christian theory based on a false conception of the Church as an absolute monarchy."[21] If the Jesuits persisted in believing in the monarchy, then their monarch was the pope, and obedience to him placed German Catholics in an untenable position: for it was impossible to be loyal to the pope and to Protestant Prussia, where Church and State were ostensibly separated.

All of this came to a head in 1864 with the publication by Pius VII of the notorious Syllabus, which condemned Protestantism and modern science and generally placed the

Catholic Church and its flock in staunch opposition to the principles of liberty and the new philosophy put in place by the revolutions of the previous century. In 1869–70 the Vatican Council declared the Syllabus dogma with the main piece of business focused on declaring a position on papal infallibility, a venerable idea but one whose most tense political moment had arrived. European leaders awakened late to the political implications of infallibility and sought in vain to organize secular opposition to the Council's deliberations. The pope, visibly supported by the Jesuits, succeeded in passing infallibility into dogma. As a result, any Catholic who pledged allegiance to a secular leader risked excommunication. This radically politicized move forced numerous confrontations. Because the Jesuits were widely perceived as the principal promoters and beneficiaries of infallibility they were often targeted in the aftermath of the Council. Nowhere were the results of the Council more closely followed than in Germany, for in the years preceding the unification of the German Empire, to be made up of Catholic and Lutheran lands, the Council's decision stood to divide the political union. Immediately following the Council, Germany erupted in the *Kulturkampf* driven by the new minister of education and cultural affairs, Adalbert Falk.

During the tense years around the Vatican Council, the Jesuit alignment with Rome, their Ultramontanism, was increasingly thematized, and this explains in part why so much of the *Kulturkampf* was directed at the Society.[22] In a polemical history of the Society written in 1865, the German Theodor Griesinger described how, after 1850, Catholicism literally developed into Jesuitism:

> Thus have Jesuitism and the Papacy grown into one another, and in most recent times they can, indeed, no longer be distinguished from each other. Thus, as the Pope was infallible, so were the Jesuits infallible; or, as may be better said, as the Pope obtained a fullness of power through the dogma of infallibility, such as no former Popes ever possessed, so this plenitude of might tended, above all, for the benefit of the Jesuits. For they acquired the entire sway in the Catholic Church over science, literature and matters of instruction, and, above all their theology and moral philosophy were raised to be canonical.[23]

As in France, education played a major role in the German *Kulturkampf* debates. Following the publication of the Syllabus, German Catholics who rejected the reactionary policies separated themselves from the divisive encyclical, declaring the "New Catholicism" it called for heretical and distinguishing themselves as "Old Catholics." Once the Council's decrees had passed into dogma, the New Catholics provocatively required that Catholics teaching theology at German universities affirm the Syllabus. Confrontations resulted. Thus in 1872, as the German government considered the implications of the new dogmas it asked whether the so-called New Catholicism should be supported by state subsidies (for teaching and parsons), whether it should be taught, and, most important, whether the newly infallible Catholic Church should have any further claim on the State at all. The parliamentary debates that ensued put the Jesuits at the very center of the Catholic problem. In one astonishing speech delivered in June 1872, the Bavarian deputy Völk, himself a Catholic, makes evident the extent to which the Jesuits represented the larger issue of Catholicism:

> It is a question as to whether the German Empire shall become subservient to the Jesuit power, or liberate itself from the same. Were it merely a matter regarding the five or six hundred Jesuits, viewed as individuals, it would not be worth the trouble to make so much talk about it, but it is a point as to whether the whole Jesuit Ultramontanist clergy as a huge corporation, shall be allowed to comport itself like a great power. Indeed it is a question affecting the Papal power itself, which, in our days, has identified itself with Jesuitism, and it has come so far as this, that the Jesuit Ultramontane Catholics represent themselves to be the only true representatives of the Faith.[24]

Supported by both progressive Catholics and the massive Protestant population which was condemned by the Syllabus, Bismarck expelled the Jesuits from all German territories in 1872. They would not return to Germany until after World War I. These dates are significant, for it is only in the 1880s that German scholars first used the term *Barock* to describe a period style formerly designated the Jesuit Style. And it would be only after World War I that the heat would be taken off the Jesuit Style altogether.

As the above account suggests, the background to the nineteenth-century characterizations of the Jesuits varied from country to country according to the religious profile of the region and the political situation. Yet the themes of anti-Jesuitism that emerged in the first half of the nineteenth century are remarkably consistent and international in scope, like the Society itself. And although it has been pointed out that nineteenth-century anti-Jesuitism produced little original content—the critique of the Society as a distinct genre stretches back at least to Pascal's *Provincial Letters* of 1656[25]—the themes of this particularly virulent (and effective) wave of anti-Jesuit sentiment are crucial to us, for they produced the notion of a Jesuit Style. Catholic critics targeted the Jesuits in part because of their large numbers, the extent of their properties, their powerful political connections, their extensive networks of schools—in sum, because of their success and, in short, their power. It should be kept in mind that the Jesuits' visibility was far greater than that of any other Catholic group, even and especially the pope, in the age before television.

Throughout the nineteenth century a principal fear linking many of the themes of anti-Jesuitism was that of deception. While praised in missionary contexts for his adaptability, the Jesuit was widely perceived as morally corrupt for his willingness to remake himself, to use any means to achieve his imperialist ends. Fueled by the suspicion caused by the assumption of alternative names by Jesuits driven underground at the time of the suppression in France, the public associated the Jesuits generally with falsity: false appearances, false sentiments, and false beliefs. When students at the Collège Royale in Orleans were queried what "Jesuit" meant, only one replied "a priest" while the others answered that "they attached to the word Jesuit the idea of falsity."[26] What is more, the venerable tradition of critique of Jesuit casuistry, the science of false reasoning, became

canonical, entering French dictionaries of the nineteenth century under the very definition of "Jesuite": "Par dénigr.," "Personne hypocrite, astucieuse."[27] Using the confessional
as his weapon, so the critics claimed, the Jesuit priest, under cover as a watchdog of his
victim's salvation, insinuated himself into the lives of the unsuspecting, wresting away
family fortunes, influencing weak politicians, even, according to some, going so far as to
poison his enemies.[28] The Jesuit was a creature of artifice, at every turn challenging the
truth of appearances: he was capable of assuming any external appearance himself while
remaining loyal to his organization. And through his education system and the Spiritual
Exercises, he could annihilate the individual personality, making of men not live sentient
human beings but mere appearances of men, automatons.[29] Jesuitism, Quinet declared
in one of his lectures in 1843, creates "instruments not disciples."[30]

The nineteenth-century Jesuit myth was generated by a nexus of political anxieties and
historical explanations for the revolutionary period that persistently converged on the conspiratorial Society of Jesus. For those who believed that the revolutionary events of the times
could only have been driven by organized sects, the Jesuits provided a ready explanation for
the rise of powerful political forces (in spite of the fact that the Jesuits remained aligned with
counterrevolution).[31] Because the very legality of the Society was often in question, the Jesuits were at the center of the debates over the jurisdiction of the state in matters of religion,
and over the nature and limits of individual liberty. As Geoffrey Cubitt has argued, at stake
in the Jesuit question was nothing less than the limits of liberal individualism.[32]

The anti-Jesuits used a variety of compelling metaphors to describe the Jesuits. They
were likened to animals (snakes, chameleons, insidious insects, the hydra and phoenix):
like the spider, they often deployed the trap; they were imagined as dwelling underground;
they embodied the anti-Enlightenment as creatures of darkness, operating under the cover
of shadow.[33] The so-called Jesuit myth became so pervasive in the nineteenth century
that the appellation "Jesuit" was loosened from the Society, coming to refer to anyone
manipulative, deceptive, or conspiracy forging. The terms "Jesuit" and "Jesuitical" functioned in the nineteenth century like "mafia" or "mafioso" today, as descriptive terms that
can refer to anyone exhibiting the characteristics of the group that gave the terms meaning.[34] The use of the terms in literature, the popular press, and daily life speaks to the
power and pervasiveness of the Jesuit topos. One can imagine that as a result of the political and even linguistic saturation with Jesuit issues, Jesuit buildings came to occupy
an ever more looming presence in the French and German cityscapes.

THE PUBLIC DISCOURSE ON ARCHITECTURE
IN THE NINETEENTH CENTURY AND THE EMERGENCE
OF THE "JESUIT STYLE"

I am concerned, ultimately, with how the characterization of Jesuits would be projected
onto Jesuit architecture and onto the Baroque. In keeping with that aim, a comprehensive treatment of anti-Jesuitism does not concern us here. Because of the combination of

the visible achievement of the Jesuits in architecture and their political *actualité,* the Society's architecture would be accorded a place in the new discipline of architectural history. Although architectural historians only named the Jesuits explicitly in the 1840s (at which time post-Medieval architecture received little attention in the nascent discipline), the prehistoricist and early historicist writings laid the groundwork for the Jesuit Style. They did so by pointing to the importance of institutional conditions, with an emphasis on religious and political conditions, for artistic excellence and decline. As Sylvia Lavin has argued, in the aftermath of the French Revolution "architecture was transformed into one of the public sphere's most significant means of self-definition."[35]

The most influential works on architectural history of the late eighteenth century were those of Quatremère de Quincy, who inherited from Winckelmann and Mengs a highly critical stance toward post-Renaissance art and architecture as exemplifying decline in the arts.[36] The pre-Neoclassical critics—still primarily concerned with issues of individual genius—did not posit historical reasons for that decline; that is, they stopped short of a historicist outlook. But in the changing political circumstances the politically conservative idealist Quatremère and others writing at the end of the eighteenth century (following Winckelmann and the German Sturm und Drang) developed broader historical explanations with some urgency. In particular, writers on both sides of the political spectrum showed a growing preoccupation with the role that institutions play in fostering culture.[37]

While Quatremère did not touch on the Jesuits, he provided influential formulations of several fundamental ideas that would be applied by later historians to the Jesuit question. First, he, like others before him, understood the arts as products of social institutions, endeavoring himself to establish institutions of the arts in France that might set an example for society in general. Placing architecture in the public realm, Quatremère argued for its formative influence in political and social life rather than as a passive reflection of existing institutions.[38] Elaborating on the parallels drawn since the seventeenth century between architecture and rhetoric, Quatremère could envisage a social role for architecture because he understood it as constructed, as a language that could be put to use in an ideal Republic of the Arts to build a better society.[39] A few decades later Victor Hugo gave literary form to Quatremère's idea in a famous passage in *Notre-Dame de Paris* (1831), the novel that idealized the Gothic cathedral:

> Architecture began like any other form of writing. It was first of all an alphabet. A stone was set upright and it was a letter, and each letter was a hieroglyph, and on each hieroglyph a group of ideas rested, like the capital on a column. Such was the way of the first people, everywhere at the same moment, across the whole surface of the globe. . . . Later on, they formed words. Stone was superimposed on stone, and these granite syllables were coupled together, the word tried out in a few combinations. The Celtic dolmen and cromlech, the Etruscan tumulus, the Hebrew *galgal,* are words. Some of them, the tumulus especially, are proper nouns. Sometimes even, when they had plenty of stone and an extensive site, they wrote a sentence. . . . Finally, they wrote books.[40]

Although the political sympathies of Quatremère and Hugo were opposed,[41] the former's argument for architecture's communicative potential and the latter's even more explicit formulation of the idea, arising in the political contexts that they did, show a shared assumption of the rhetorical foundations if not the propagandistic potential of the arts.[42]

Given his utter disdain for nationalism—that "'false and partial interest' 'typical only of ignorants and knaves'"[43]—Quatremère did not engage in the enterprise of naming historical styles that would dominate mid-nineteenth-century writings on architecture. Rather, among other things, we find him defining character (or style) itself.[44] In the *Dictionnaire d'architecture* (1788–1825), the three specialized volumes he contributed to the *Encyclopédie méthodique,* he makes an important distinction between the "manière" of the artist, which refers to the execution of the work or the practical talent of the artist, and character *(caractère).*[45] In his definition of character, Quatremère establishes both the collective nature and the moral content of style:[46] character "designates the employment of moral qualities which determine the manner, or better yet, the result of the general qualities that influence the taste of each century, of each country, of each school, of each genre."[47] He appears to follow Winckelmann and others in locating those moral qualities in Greek architecture (the superiority of which is pointed to throughout his entries in the *Encyclopédie méthodique*). But Sylvia Lavin shows that the abstract language of Greek architecture was valued as a sign that the Greeks had overcome natural constraints to develop an abstract language of form.[48] His preference for Greek architecture was not a question of taste.

Where this moral quality is lacking, however, is in cases of *abus.* In the entry under this term, together with the entry on the greatest source of immorality in architecture, "bizarrerie" (and its related term, "Baroque"), Quatremère defines at greatest length the architectural—and hence the cultural—malaise of modern Europe. Abuses are relatively minor offenses, the result of the poor or faulty application of true principles, that inadvertently "confuse" or "misread" the spirit of true principles. But vices are more serious, for they amount to a willful attack on the constituent forms of art. And while in the field of morals, Quatremère writes, "bizarrerie" is a personal vice, in the arts it is far more dangerous, for it can (and has) become "une espèce d'épédemie," a question of public health.[49] The causes for the "epidemic" lie in the countries, the times, and the artists who adopt the taste for the bizarre, but he points mainly to an immoderate desire for change or novelty, of the tyranny of fashion, which produces the antipathy between morals and art.

Quatremère's prime example of such "bizarrerie" is modern Italy—the Baroque—from where the epidemic passed to France. The two architects that he chose to exemplify the vice are Borromini and Guarini, although their names appear under the heading "Baroque," a "nuance du bizarre."[50] On the surface of things, Quatremère's moralizing about Borromini and Guarini appears like a continuation of the Neoclassical distaste for what we now call the Baroque, part of a larger stream of eighteenth-century writings stressing the decline of the arts since the early sixteenth century.[51] But the political circumstances in which he was writing and would be read were changing. This epochal moralizing would prove important in that it is manifested as style *(caractère)* and appears next to a politically driven program for architectural reform.

Unlike later theorists and historians of architecture, Quatremère aimed to rise above national interests, favoring an abstract deployment of architectural language rather than borrowing specific historical forms for the present. In the aftermath of the French Revolution he and his contemporaries would be much more taken up with debating the role of state institutions of the arts and whether the arts thrive best in conditions of liberty than questions concerning religious institutions and the arts. Indeed, the secularizing drive of the Revolution, poignantly embodied in the designs for the transformation of S. Genevieve into the Pantheon, considered religion as a condition rather than in its institutional agency.[52] But just before the Revolution, others already applied both the institutional and the moral themes emphasized by Quatremère to contemporary religious institutions. The Hannoverian F. W. B. von Ramdohr in his *Über Mahlerei und Bildhauerkunst in Rom* (1787) seems to have been the first in the context of a treatise (as opposed to a guidebook) to designate the work of Bernini and Cortona the "church style," attributing its stylistic decadence to the unfortunate demands made on art by Christian religion.[53] The pro-revolutionary J. G. Forster of Mainz echoed von Ramdohr's sentiment in an essay of 1791, arguing that even in the Renaissance, religion was inimical to great achievement in art.[54]

In spite of this unsurprising ambivalence toward religion and its institutions in the age of the Enlightenment, in architectural histories of the period it is repeatedly asserted that churches are the most important architectural achievements of the past. As historians of architecture turned to the architecture built on their own soil, they paid overwhelming attention to churches, especially Gothic cathedrals, as the great collective works of the Middle Ages. Thus the term "Jesuit Style" emerged both in the heightened atmosphere of anticlericalism and in the rise of a historicism that linked broad historical and political conditions to the greatness or decline of the arts.[55]

Out of both of these conditions emerged a remarkable visualization of how the perniciousness of the Jesuits might be articulated through the language of architecture. The work is a fine monarch-sized print, signed though undated, probably produced sometime between 1830 and 1845 (fig. 8).[56] Its title is held aloft by a horned devil: "Monument Symbolique et Historique de la Religion et de la Doctrine Impie, Meurtriere, et Sacrilége, Enseignée, Soûtenüe, et Constamment Pratiqueé, par les Disciples de Dom Inigo de Guipuscöa Chef de la Société se disant de Jesus." This freestanding classical aedicula on a high base is an architectural parody of the Roman chapel dedicated to St. Ignatius, who reclines on a sarcophagus clutching a mock cross crowned by a devil. The architecture gives form to Hugo's history of architecture as a history of writing: "finally, they wrote books." But what kind of books? The columns supporting the edifice are bound packets—of jewels, precious stones, money, booty, in short—and the books that form their bases are the account books for the missions. In the pediment is a library of all of the theological errors of the Jesuits: their support of Chinese rites, of the quietist Molinos, their "moral" theology, and their philosophy, much cast into doubt. The crowning element is

FIG. 8

Anonymous, *Monument Simbolique et Historique de la Religion . . . ,* nineteenth century.

a two-faced idol: that the idol itself can swing the incense, the inscription notes, shows the Jesuit alliance with Balliol. The impious, meretricious, sacrilegious edifice of the Jesuits is founded on the "lucre" of the missions: chests of money. And in a parody of the actual tomb of Ignatius, rather than Faith and Religion spreading their message through the world, Ignatius's henchmen are devils masked in innocence (disguised as priests) (see fig. 16, in chapter 3; figs. 70 and 71, in chapter 4). These masked crusaders for Christ hold the cross high above them. But this is only a pretense, for they literally bear arms: a torch and a dagger. Cannons blast into the distance on both sides of the globe, and the Chinese and American peoples are represented not as converted but as subjugated peoples, chained and fearful. Below them are arranged the heads of the Jesuits' prominent victims: kings, queens, popes, princes, cardinals, all victims of suspected Jesuit regicide, conspiracies, and "troubles." Even the skull of Pascal, crowned by laurel, appears on the second step. If the history of civilization can be gleaned from the books of architecture, then this one, built on a foundation of ill-gotten riches and crowned by false doctrine, represents a most regrettable episode.

While the Jesuits had inspired their share of visual satire before the nineteenth century, a work such as this one was unthinkable before Quatremère de Quincy and Hugo. The idea of a malformed perverse "Jesuit architecture" conveyed immediate meaning once there was a public, and a historical, discourse on architecture. The print lays out an idea of Jesuit architecture, although by this is not meant a style of architecture invented by the Jesuits. The moment for that *has* arrived, but it is not represented here. Rather, this work conveys the Jesuits, practitioners of a false and ignoble "religion," literally embodied in architectural form; the idea of architecture as a symbolic form and the public hatred of the Jesuits here converge. As we shall see, architectural historians first looking seriously at Jesuit architecture were somewhat more dispassionate in their notion of a Jesuit Style.

1840s: THE JESUIT STYLE

The Jesuit Style could only be born once historians directed their energies away from the pursuit of the antique toward recognizing historical achievement in the arts at the national or local level. The most sustained expression of this new historicist outlook was the European Gothic revival movement, initiated and driven by the semischolarly Ecclesiologists in England and highly active in France and Germany as well.[57] This scholarly activity, which supported intensive historical investigation of Medieval architecture, laid the ground for the emergence of the Jesuit Style in two ways. First, the Gothic revival, driven by nationalism, linked morality with specific historical styles, arousing suspicion of non-native forms, especially imported styles.[58] Second, it developed a much more sophisticated lexicon for historical period styles, pointing the way to refined chronologies and the designation of regional styles.

In architectural histories, dictionaries, and journals of the first half of the nineteenth century, "modern" (post-Medieval) architecture was decidedly neglected for the architecture of antiquity and the Middle Ages. While Ecclesiologists debated the precise lexicon for various phases of Gothic architecture, a chaotic vocabulary was in use for what we now refer to as the Renaissance and Baroque periods.[59] In many publications Romantic designations—grand, sublime, and so on—persisted through the 1830s,[60] while increasingly thereafter, post-Medieval epochs were termed "modern"[61] or "Italian"[62] (emphasizing the importation of a foreign style in England, Germany, and France), "Renaissance"[63] or "Cinque-Cento" style.[64] The terms "Baroque" and "Rococo" became operative in this period as well, although they resisted periodization to a certain extent, retaining the eighteenth-century sense of "decadence" and "abuse" formulated by Quatremère, among others.[65] The Baroque would subsequently take on a more explicit definition as a period style, although it would not be until the 1880s that its parameters would move toward those agreed on today.[66]

Thus both the political and art historiographic contexts out of which the term "Jesuit Style" emerged were complex and in flux. On the one hand, the years around 1843–45 marked the peak of anti-Jesuitism in France (as well as in Switzerland). On the other hand, in architectural history the 1840s were the decade in which historians, though still influenced by eighteenth-century periodization schemes, sought more precise though still inchoate terms for the modern era.

The term *Jesuitenstil* is mentioned as early as 1842, but it is first fully defined in an encyclopedia entry in Brockhaus's *Allgemeine deutsche Real-Enzyklopedie* in 1845. The unsigned entry was written by young Jacob Burckhardt on his return to Basel (via France) after four years of study in Berlin; until now the idea of the Jesuit Style has been unattributed in the literature on the subject.[67] While the implications of Burckhardt's buried authorship of this term and concept for his own work will not occupy us here, it is crucial to know that he wrote the entry at the height of his own liberal views and support for a greater Germany and precisely at the moment that controversy over the Jesuits in Lucerne brought Switzerland to the brink of war. Moreover, because this definition, which appeared in a German publication known for its Protestant perspective,[68] was the first in a long string of subsequent refinements of the definition, Burckhardt's entry established the parameters of the Jesuit Style that would be repeated up until World War I:

> The Jesuit Style in architecture and decoration designates the method of handling forms in Jesuit churches and houses which had become preeminent since the middle of the seventeenth century. The Jesuits were as insincere in their architecture as they were in every other aspect of the spiritual life of the people; they wished only to dazzle them. Initially, until even the middle of the seventeenth century the German Jesuits held fast—with an affected sincerity—to the Gothic and even the Byzantine style, as their churches in Koblenz, Bonn and Cologne demonstrate. The interiors of their buildings are decorated at times with playful splendor, full of gilding and carving. Their altars are especially colossal, mostly gilded ensembles of flowers, figures, angels, saints and architecture, with often three very bad paintings stacked up. From the middle of the seventeenth century they practically reached the apex of church architecture and the degenerate Italian style would now be their

own realm. At the time of the height of their power they built their largest churches and they were for the most part made with great solidity and pomp. Very costly materials, jasper, porphyry, lapis lazuli and so on, would be preferred for decoration above all in Italy; ceilings, vaults, pilasters and so forth overloaded with the richest coffering, foliage, and festoons. But the unimaginative composition of the whole remained impoverished even though towers and cupolas can be such wonderful flourishes. The great pomp of their church style with its inner poverty brought all of church architecture of the time down with it, following the lead of the Jesuits, sacrificing everything, even the highest goods, to achieve raw effects.[69]

The definition here of style is both less historical and altogether less systematized than later art history has led us to expect. Since the German Jesuits built in the Gothic, Byzantine, and "Italian" styles, and all of these are included under the rubric "Jesuit Style," we cannot understand this style as a function of a historical period. Style means the "method of handling form," and that method has mostly to do with sumptuousness. There is a deeply rooted discourse against ornament as license that flourished in Renaissance treatises on architecture.[70] In the nineteenth-century assessment, this sumptuousness is more psychological, recalling the long-standing critique of rhetoric as artifice. Since the Jesuits were themselves associated, especially in France, with the sumptuous Asiatic style of rhetoric, a topic of perennial debate, the Jesuit Style rings as a direct projection of the moral degeneration identified with the form-makers themselves. That is, the insincerity of the Jesuit and his desire to control the viewer are posited as a *style* of form-making. It is in the spirit of Quatremère's moral notion of style, *caractère,* that the *ends* that these forms served define style. It is not surprising that in the search for stylistic coordinates, institutions like the Society of Jesus, which possessed what were perceived as clear goals, could anchor stylistic designations.[71]

The Jesuit Style was in the air in France right around this same time, issuing forth from the pen of Léon Vaudoyer, a politically engaged architect in the circle of the historian Edgar Quinet. A fervent believer in the political and social potential that architecture held for the reform of society—the phrase coined by Hippolyte Fortoul, "l'architecture est la véritable écriture des peuples," became his motto[72]—Vaudoyer wrote of a style of architecture imported by the Jesuits from Italy to the rest of Europe in an article on seventeenth-century French churches published in 1846. Characterizing Jesuit architecture by its "luxe"—the Jesuits always "attached great importance to the exterior pomp of the cult"—Vaudoyer stops short of naming the Jesuit Style.[73] But within five years this text, probably supported by others, had been reread and the term *architecture jésuitique* derived from it in the final volume of Jules Gailhabaud's *Ancient and Modern Architecture,* a work to which Vaudoyer contributed.[74] Because this latter work was organized around detailed descriptions of important buildings, the issues are treated somewhat differently than in Burckhardt's Brockhaus entry, although both authors characterize Jesuit architecture as one of excess: a "profusion and superfluity of ornaments" (as well as magnificence of bad taste) is "one of the peculiar features of the Jesuitical architecture" shared by the facades of Jesuit churches in France and the interiors of Jesuit churches in Rome.[75] With a closer knowledge of chronological relationships between buildings and their authorship, the authors also make a precociously judicious assessment of the Jesuits' dissemination of their architectural style:

> The imitations, more or less successful, of the works of Vignola, modified according to the country, sometimes in form, at others only in detail, as they passed under [sic] the hands of different architects, soon covered all Europe with buildings that betrayed a common origin. This kind of architecture, of which the principal type is the Jesuits' Church at Rome, begun by Vignola, and finished by Jacopo della Porta, his pupil, was distinguished by the name of Jesuitical Architecture, and it is characterized by certain peculiarities to be remarked in all the religious edifices erected at that epoch in the different cities of Europe, where members of that Company were established. This kind of architecture, which is no less curious than interesting to study as one of the pages of the history of art, deserves to be particularly noticed here.[76]

There are a couple of important ideas here. A historical explanation is given for the existence of a recognizably Jesuit architecture: namely, that it originated with Vignola and spread to the rest of Jesuit buildings in Europe. But Vignola is not ultimately held responsible for Jesuitical architecture. For while the design of the (lower half) of the much imitated Gesù facade may have been Vignola's, "it is in a type of style which one *could call* that of Vignola, *but to which one gives the qualification of jesuitical.*"[77] We see the author here overriding Vignola's authorship for that of the corporation, where blame is to be laid for encouraging excessive ornament. In arguing for the priority of patron over architect, the author echoes the convictions of Vaudoyer's circle that too much emphasis had been placed by the Romantics on individual genius.[78] At the same time, it reinforces the growing case for the Jesuits as having directed the creation and dissemination of an aesthetic identified with the "Italian" style of architecture. The implication of this Jesuitical style of architecture invented in Italy and exported to northern Europe is that the Jesuits themselves invented and diffused the Baroque. The coherence of Jesuit architecture occupied other authors and in other countries around the same time.[79]

In subsequent decades the definition of the Jesuit Style was elaborated in various encyclopedias. The Brockhaus "Jesuitenstil" entry was paraphrased in abbreviated form in the second edition of Meyer's *Neues Konversations-Lexikon* issued in the 1860s. In the third edition of the same encyclopedia (1876), the definition keyed in to an incipient though still uncertain art historical vocabulary, designating the Jesuit Style a "degeneration of the Renaissance" (instead of the earlier and more general appellation "Italian style") and falling "under the concept of Baroque style."[80] In the fifth edition of 1895 the definition takes a decidedly negative turn. The Jesuit Style is now "the degenerate Baroque style which the Jesuits followed in the churches on the grounds of the aims of Borromini and Pozzo, and which . . . through the emancipation of forms from structure, through the rule-less pile-up of decoration, through sensationalism in the composition of the whole space, they intended to intoxicate the senses towards the accomplishment of the order's aims."[81]

Hippolyte Taine summed up well the views of his contemporaries, and the context from which they emerged, in his famous description of the Roman Gesù in his *Voyage en Italie* (1866):

> The cathedral of the Middle Ages suggested grand and sad reverie, the sentiment of human misery, the vague divination of an ideal realm where the impassioned heart finds consolation and ravishment. The temple of the Catholic restoration inspires sentiments of submission, of admiration, or at least of deference to that person so powerful, so established, above all so accredited and so well furnished, that one calls the Church.[82]

THE THEMES OF THE JESUIT STYLE

The encyclopedia entries, syntheses of learned and popular opinion, established the parameters of the Jesuit Style. From these and other accounts of the Jesuit Style emerge three major themes familiar from the themes of anti-Jesuitism discussed above: I call these the *Jesuit Ur-Author, Jesuit Architectural Imperialism,* and the *Conquest of Minds and Spirits through Visual Intoxication.*

The *Jesuit Ur-Author* rests on the assumption that the Society of Jesus was the "author" of all of its productions. That the society put its stamp on its members and all those connected to it echoes the widespread invective in the nineteenth century against the Jesuits for producing automatons who would blindly and obediently act out the Society's programs.[83] The Society-as-Author idea was an extension of pervasive (and idealized) discussions in the nineteenth century of Medieval architecture as collective national productions of an era that produced few known individual authors. Victor Hugo, passionate purveyor of Gothic architecture's eclecticism, eloquently conveyed this positive view of the collective nature of Gothic buildings in *Notre-Dame de Paris*:

> Great buildings, like great mountains are the works of centuries. . . . Indeed, many a massive tome and often the universal history of mankind might be written from these successive weldings of different styles at different levels of a single monument. The man, the individual and the artists are erased from these great piles, which bear no author's name; they are the summary and summation of human intelligence. Time is the architect, the nation the builder.[84]

When the idea of the Jesuit Ur-Author emerged in the 1840s, the collective aspect of its authorship was less problematic than its Jesuit nature. Indeed, in the circles of Quinet and Michelet, of Reynaud and Leroy, architecture was viewed largely as a product of impersonal forces such as climate and building technologies; reacting against the apotheosis of individual genius in Romanticism, this new generation of intensely historically minded writers called for a "social art" in which the architect played the role of a helpful handmaiden to history.[85] But in contrast to the era of the cathedral, whose architects, in part by accident of history, remain mostly anonymous, in the early modern era the figure of the architect *had* emerged. That the creative independence of the well-known architects who worked for the Jesuits (Vignola, Giacomo della Porta, Bernini, for example) could be absorbed or set in the background of a corporate authorship must be accounted for by the overwhelming power of the corporation's identity.

There was also material evidence of Jesuit corporate control over design that, when brought out by scholars later on, reinforced the Jesuit Ur-Author established by Burckhardt and Gailhabaud. As I discuss further in chapter 3, the Jesuits closely controlled the design of their international building campaigns from Rome and even made an early attempt—which failed—to provide (most say, to impose) standardized designs for Jesuit buildings. The significance of the Jesuit Ur-Author for art history was in its collapsing of any distinction (in an era in which such distinctions were becoming paramount) between the Society (which had its own internal rules), external patrons (who had their own "taste"), and artists (through whom, many claimed increasingly toward the end of the nineteenth century, the inner laws of art unfolded). Who is the "author" of a Jesuit building paid for by an external patron, guided by the Society's advisors, and designed by a Jesuit or, for that matter, a non-Jesuit artist? In creating a category of corporate authorship for an age otherwise dominated by titan individuals, the early proponents of the Jesuit Style made the Jesuits the author not only of their own massive building output but also of the Baroque in general. It seems no coincidence that Quatremère's assessment of the Baroque as a principle of degeneration or decline converges with Quinet's of Jesuitism as the same principle in religion. The degenerate Jesuit Ur-Author, to whom responsibility was attributed for the entire epoch, provided a new historical explanation for a historical Baroque as the decadence of the Renaissance.

Jesuit Architectural Imperialism, or the premeditated plan of conquest, essentially argued that the Jesuit Style of architecture constituted an artistic means invented by the Jesuits to achieve their "imperialist" ends. The idea that the Jesuits were intent on worldwide dominion was a conspiracy theory grounded in the undisputed success of the order worldwide and fueled by Jesuit involvement in virtually every sphere of social, cultural, and political life. Architectural historians, for their part, needed to come to terms with the existence of what seemed to be paradigmatic buildings or designs, often Roman, that were imitated or copied outside of Rome, Italy, and Europe. The presence of Gesù-like churches all over the world—even those that by today's standards of resemblance would no longer be considered of the same design—lent force to the imperialism argument. The much imitated Mother Church of the Society became central to the art historical narrative of the Jesuit Style, and later the Baroque.[86] Even though easily disproved, the idea that the Jesuits invented and imposed a Roman style of architecture on the rest of the world became a central topos of and source of debate over the Jesuit Style, and of the

Baroque style as organized *by* the Jesuits. Jesuit architectural imperialism essentially translated the fear of Jesuit political influence into architectural terms, taking Quatremère de Quincy at his word in believing that the language of architectural style was a powerful and formative one, which could, in this case, "impose" the Jesuit will on its users.

The implicit psychological basis of the architectural imperialism topos is made explicit in the idea of the *Conquest of Minds and Spirits through Visual Intoxication*.[87] A persistent theme in the Jesuit Style argument is that the emphasis the Jesuits placed on sight—from the *imagination de lieu* of the Spiritual Exercises to the dizzying material splendor found in some Jesuit churches—constituted a calculated strategy to manipulate the masses with the aim of bringing them into the order's purview. Quinet's description of the Spiritual Exercises, in which the exercitant was called on to imagine in detail the sites of Christ's passion, as making "use of the sensations as a decoy to attract souls" typified the adjudication of Jesuit artifice.[88] The characterization by architectural historians of Jesuit churches as sensually overwhelming has much to do with the general sense that the Jesuits used whatever means were at their disposal to entrap souls. Later historians easily disproved this generalization through a cursory survey of Jesuit buildings. Ornamental excess is certainly found in some of their churches (and of course is not exclusive to Jesuit churches, as many authors eventually pointed out) but not in all. The idea persisted because it *is true* of important Jesuit churches in Rome, in particular the Gesù (fig. 9) and the Church of St. Ignatius (see fig. 47, in chapter 4), whose rich ceiling decorations acquired canonical status in histories of Baroque art. Drawing on the deeply seated Western tradition of mistrusting the senses, the nineteenth-century idea that material splendor could conquer the souls of viewers expressed a widespread belief that the Jesuits had a spiritual hold on the Baroque epoch because of the fear of a Jesuit hold on their own.

As historians in several countries increasingly turned their attention to the "modern era," the Jesuit Style, soon reaching a wide audience through encyclopedia entries and a specialized audience through histories of architecture, was taken up immediately, though it was not uncontested.[89] This moment in the history of art and architecture would not have occurred had the Jesuits not been considered such a representative organization of the entire Catholic Church at the time the term was invented. The Jesuit Style proved to be a tenacious idea because of its political currency.

Historians invoked the Jesuit Style several decades before they consistently invoked the Baroque as a period designation.[90] For a brief time, between the 1840s and the 1880s, the Jesuit Style provided a definition for what would later be named the Baroque, a fact that is an important and overlooked aspect of the historiography of this subject.[91] The Jesuit Style provided the first historical explanation for the Baroque as viewed from France and Germany (where Jesuit architecture was an imported style). Although it emphasized the degeneration of the Renaissance, it was based less on particular forms than on the aims and character of the Jesuits. The term would be dismissed when it was later interpreted as the style of architecture invented by the Jesuits rather than the style of archi-

FIG. 9
Giovanni Battista Gaulli, *Adoration of the Name of Jesus*, 1672–75. Il Gesù, Rome.

tecture that embodies and represents the Jesuits. But at the time of its inception, the Jesuit Style aptly described the architecture of a period largely thought to have been dominated by the order, just as the Age of the Cathedral was romanticized as the product of a collective national body.

THE JESUIT STYLE IN GURLITT'S
AND WÖLFFLIN'S BAROQUE

The Jesuit Style emerged in the 1840s, driven by German, Swiss, and French anti-Jesuit-ism. Ironically, it was expelled from art history by German art historians fifteen years after the expulsion of the Jesuits from Germany. At this time, two major art historical stud-ies appeared that definitively established the Baroque as a period scheme.[92] In the first book of a three-volume corpus on European Baroque architecture (1887–89) Cornelius Gurlitt argued that the "Jesuitenstil" had been superseded in art history because what were understood as its qualities are in fact the characteristics of the style of seventeenth-century architecture in general.[93] There was, nonetheless, still a prominent place for the Jesuit Style in Gurlitt's Baroque, though he was loath to allow it to define the entire period, especially for Germany. In an effort to claim the Baroque for Germany Gurlitt included chapters not only on the "Jesuit Style" but on the "Catholic Baroque style," the "Huguenot style," and the "Protestant style" as well.

In Heinrich Wölfflin's far more widely read *Renaissance and Baroque* (1888) the term "Je-suit Style" as such never appears.[94] This book also marks a turning point for the fortune of the Jesuit Style; but far from putting an end to the idea, it marks the real beginning of the debate. Like Gurlitt, Wölfflin questioned the role of the Jesuits in the formation of the Baroque. As something of a summa of the literature to date and a powerfully influential study for the next generations of scholars, it merits more detailed examination here.

Wölfflin's project in *Renaissance and Baroque* is to characterize and to explain why a radical change in the style of Italian architecture occurred between the sixteenth and sev-enteenth centuries. Most of the book is given over to establishing a corpus of Baroque works and their formal qualities (massiveness, movement, etc.), as they emerged in three building typologies (Church, Palace, Garden). These chapters provide primary evidence for the key chapter of the book, "The Causes for the Change in Style."[95] For Wölfflin con-sidered the driving question of the art historian: *why* does change in style occur? Re-sponding to art historians such as Franz Kugler and Carl Schnaase (and even his much admired mentor, Burckhardt), Wölfflin lamented the vagueness of his predecessors' attri-bution to the Jesuits of a central role in the emerging Baroque as weak cultural explana-tions. But as Michael Ann Holly has rightly pointed out, far from arguing that the forms of art evolved autonomously, Wölfflin was interested in the "theoretical relationship be-tween extrinsic factors (spirits of the age, cultural ideals, social milieus, etc.), and the in-trinsic history of form."[96] In this early work Wölfflin asked, "[W]hat can be expressed by means of architecture at all, and what are the factors which influence artistic imagination?"

> What has Gothic to do with the feudal system or with scholasticism? What bridge connects
> Jesuitism with the Baroque? Can we be satisfied with comparison with a vague movement
> towards an end that totally disregards the means? Is there aesthetic significance in the fact
> that the Jesuits forced their spiritual system on the individual and made him sacrifice his
> rights to the idea of the whole?[97]

Wölfflin never actually answers the rhetorical questions posed here. And although he questions the "aesthetic significance of the Jesuit conquest of the individual," throughout the book he suggests that the submission of the individual to the whole, which he attributes to Jesuit practices, was a fundamental aspect of the Baroque. So although he never names (and therefore appears to reject) the Jesuit Style, it lurks in the shadows. Bypassing Jesuit *forms,* Wölfflin posits Jesuit *psychology* as the primary historical explanation *for* Baroque forms. As such, he defines Baroque form as *evidence* of Jesuit techniques.

Wölfflin's early writing relied on empathy theory to explain that we relate to external forms through the body. Accordingly, what distinguished Renaissance from Baroque architecture was the relative independence of forms. Renaissance forms remained individual and distinct (fig. 10), while in the Baroque parts would be subsumed into a whole (fig. 11). This explanation (inherited from Burckhardt and shared by Gurlitt) of the formal shift between Renaissance and Baroque was politically inflected. The independent Renaissance form is identified with the individual exercise of reason, the basis for democracy.[98] In Wölfflin's view of the Baroque, which bears distinct similarities to the Romantic sublime as well as to the Nietzschean Dionysian, reason is eclipsed, the individual overwhelmed:

> [The Baroque] was only able to manifest itself on a grand scale. It is therefore in the church alone that it finds full expression: the pathos of the post-classical period is in the desire to be sublimated in the infinite, in the feeling of overwhelmingness and unfathomableness. The comprehensible is refused, the imagination demands to be overpowered. It is a kind of intoxication with which Baroque architecture fills us, particularly the huge church interiors. We are consumed by an all-embracing sensation of heaviness, helpless to grasp anything, wishing to yield totally to the infinite.
>
> The new religious fervor kindled by the Jesuits finds a perfect outlet in the contemplation of the infinite heavens and countless angels and choirs. It revels in the imagining the unimaginable, it plunges with ecstasy into the abyss of infinity.[99]

While Wölfflin is careful not to ascribe to the Jesuits alone the role of having invented this "uncontrolled enthusiasm" of forms,[100] his notion of the Baroque was highly indebted to those vague historical generalities about which he himself complained. Wölfflin equates the Baroque subsuming of the part into a whole—with the accompanying admixture of media that retained their independent identities in the Renaissance[101]—to the spiritual possession of the spectator. The polemical characterization of the Jesuit Style precisely in this way points to its persistence in Wölfflin's Baroque. Even though *Renaissance and Baroque* is, overall, the most systematic appraisal of the period to date, as others have noted, it is not the purported recuperation of the Baroque that many have claimed it to be, for about the period Wölfflin remained deeply ambivalent.[102] While he recognized that the Baroque shared affinities with his own age, his insistence on the perfection possible in Renaissance art seems to have corresponded more closely to his own deeply felt political beliefs about human liberty.[103]

FIG. 10
Filippo Brunelleschi, Nave of S. Spirito, begun 1436, Florence.

FIG. 11
Jacopo da Vignola and Giacomo Della Porta, Nave of Il Gesù, begun 1569, Rome.

Wölfflin's association of the Baroque with the eclipse of the individual in a crowd was initially influential. Both the political implications and the psychological means of architecture's influence for which he argued were taken up with the introduction of the term "propaganda," a significant shift in the vocabulary describing the Catholic Baroque and Jesuit art after World War I. The term achieved widespread currency in art history and elsewhere as a result of the manipulation of public opinion (through radio and other new mass media) during World War I. As the first *Encyclopedia Britannica* entry on the term reported in one of the postwar *Supplement* volumes, even though wartime propaganda had slackened, "there still exists a propaganda state of mind which differs from anything experienced before the war."[104]

Though propaganda was recognized as a powerful new tool as a result of the war, it did not assume entirely negative connotations in its early employment in art history. For example, in a study of late Renaissance painting, Hermann Voss argued neutrally that architecture played a representative role as religious propaganda during the Counter-Reformation. Drawing directly on Wölfflin, Voss implied that this is a function of the absorption of individual architectural elements into a unitary system.[105] In his influential study, *Der Barock als Kunst der Gegenreformation* (1921), Werner Weisbach repeatedly described the artistic and spiritual means of "Jesuitismus," a central force of the Counter-Reformation, as forms of propaganda, a view that would stimulate Emile Mâle's magisterial book on the iconography of the Counter-Reformation.[106] Without decrying the ends or the means used by the Church, Weisbach emphasized the Counter-Reformation Church's need "to satisfy the masses, to win them and to bind them."[107] The means used by the order "with talent and effectiveness," he writes, were the "satisfaction of taste and of sumptuousness."[108] While enumerating material splendor—a classic topos of decline or decadence since Vitruvius picked up by Winckelmann and countless others thereafter[109]—and complex forms of illusionism as key visual techniques of persuasion, Weisbach conceptualized Jesuit propaganda as a multimedia campaign that used the Spiritual Exercises, preaching, theater, and the schools alongside the visual arts.[110] Nikolaus Pevsner drew on both Wölfflin's view of Jesuitism as oppression of the individual and Weisbach's formulation of Jesuit propaganda as a multimedia campaign in his study "The Counter-Reformation and Mannerism" (1925). Pevsner's article has been influential not least because he first challenged the Jesuit Style on a chronological basis, questioning the fit of the Jesuit Style to Mannerism or the Baroque.[111] This line of questioning played out later in the discussion of the distinction between an early, austere Jesuit Style and the later more bombastic work that Burckhardt's conception, with its emphasis on profusion of form, had in mind.

I have called the invocation of propaganda a shift in vocabulary for the Baroque in general and Jesuit architecture in particular because propaganda, in essence, absorbed all of the themes of the Jesuit Style discussed above while avoiding the discredited term. For propaganda, in its popular definition, makes the state an author, is driven by psychological manipulation, and is designed to enlist the masses in a struggle for worldwide dominion. The new term encapsulated decades of historiography that characterized Jesuit art—and later, the Baroque—as manipulative, aggressive, and designed to persuade a mass audience. Out of this glimpse of the historiography of Baroque art emerges, then, an important observation. Propaganda was recognized as a central aspect of the art of the Catholic Baroque, and it was already present: embedded in the notion of the Jesuit Style and taken over for the Catholic Baroque in general once the Jesuit Style had been rejected.

In the early 1900s studies of Jesuit architecture outside of Italy by Louis Serbat and Joseph Braun provided material evidence that called the Jesuit Style seriously into question.[112] At the end of the 1920s and into the 1930s the term was either noted as incorrect or cycled out of encyclopedias altogether.[113] And yet, since then, historians have nonetheless felt compelled to both dismiss and then redefine the Jesuit Style, again and again.

This outline of the Jesuit Style is, admittedly, fragmentary. The subject is deserving of further attention, not least because it is a highly symptomatic concept in the historiography of art, a clear case in which art history is inextricable from contemporary politics. The themes of the Jesuit Style will be taken up again in the chapters that follow. My account provides a corrective to Galassi Paluzzi's distorted historiography of the subject, which failed to address what was at issue in the persistence of the Jesuit Style, beyond the Protestant Hegelian spirit that he blamed for an undifferentiated anti-Jesuitism. By looking at the political and historiographic contexts out of which the rubric emerged (and my account identifies Burckhardt as its author and pushes back the origins of the concept more than thirty years before Galassi Paluzzi's), an institutionally driven version of this history, one closely tied to the political vicissitudes of the embattled Jesuits, emerges. Every insult hurled at Jesuit architecture was consistent with insults hurled in other arenas of European cultural and political life at the time. Architectural historians were entirely in step with their times in their characterization of Jesuit architecture and are not to be faulted for a lack of scientific rigor. On the contrary, it is crucial to know that here, as elsewhere, architectural history traveled on pathways inextricable from the political and religious issues of the day.

This account of the Jesuit Style has also shown that the concept emerged because the writing of architectural history served political needs. The themes of the rubric also render legible its logic in the burgeoning discipline of art history. For in all the discussion of why the term should be rejected, it has never been noticed that the Jesuit Style has also served art history well: it pointed to issues of authorship because the Jesuit corporation so dominated individual authors; it provided a new historical explanation—centered on the controversial order—for the eighteenth-century decrial of the degeneration in taste in the seventeenth century; it helped to articulate national styles since the Jesuits were perceived as having exported a paranational style of building.[114] The Jesuit Style, in sum, was a lightning rod for many of the pressing issues of the early discipline, as defined by political exigencies. In the past fifty years the standard line about the Jesuit Style is that it was wrong. My account suggests that, given the context in which the criteria for style developed, the Jesuit Style was, in fact, not only quite right, but an extraordinarily fertile idea.

In spite of the denial of the Jesuit Style in the twentieth century, like a succubus, it returns again and again, if only for its defeat to be declared once again. The Jesuit Style provides a piquant example of the art historical repressed. This, I argue in subsequent chapters, has much to do with the response to Jesuit art and architecture as a form of propaganda. Its Jesuitness, in sum, is the source of both its fascination and its affliction.

2

RHETORIC VERSUS PROPAGANDA

In short, we are stuck with our magical, premodern attitudes toward objects,
especially pictures, and our task is not to overcome these attitudes but to
understand them.

W. J. T. MITCHELL, "WHAT DO PICTURES *REALLY* WANT?" (1996)

The nineteenth-century notion of a Jesuit Style designated architecture as a system of
persuasion, treating built forms as evidence of the manipulative methods of the Jesuits.
The invocation of propaganda after World War I to describe the Jesuit and the Catholic
Baroque was a shorthand, a trace of the troubling aspects of the institutions and architecture of this historical period. But should propaganda operate as more than a sign in
art history? Above and beyond the historiographic overdeterminations that place Jesuit
architecture in the realm of propaganda, how can our modern sense of this term help us
to understand the art of the past?

I am compelled to question the question. Why use propaganda, a distinctly modern
category of persuasion, rather than rhetoric, the classical form of persuasion that was operative and indeed one could say in some measure was systematized by the Jesuits themselves in the Baroque period? The histories of both rhetoric and propaganda intersect at
critical moments with the vicissitudes of the controversial Society of Jesus, with propaganda eventually eclipsing rhetoric as the term that accounts for twentieth-century forms
of persuasion.

To build an interpretive framework around propaganda for the Baroque period, it is
essential to try to come to grips with both categories of persuasion. There is, strangely,
not much crossover between the study of rhetoric and propaganda, although the two
categories are deeply interrelated.[1] Here I provide a schematic history with an eye to
some of the traditional debates that have plagued rhetoric, especially in relation to philosophy. My emphasis is on rhetoric's characterization as persuasion, but its constitu-

tive elements and the institutional contexts in which they received elaboration are also important. The rhetorical tradition is complex; hence my remarks prepare us to address two general problems: first, the art historical engagement with historical rhetoric, which inevitably focuses on specific aspects of its history and traditions and, thus, which illuminates some aspects of Baroque art and not others; and second, the meaning of rhetoric today.

Rhetoric has become particularly prominent in the historiography of Baroque art and architecture, and we need to understand the deployment of rhetoric as distinct from that of propaganda. In the past fifty years, historians have come to understand the early modern period as a rhetorical culture,[2] in which this overarching system of discursivity touched all of the visual arts from Alberti onward. Art historians have reestablished the links between rhetoric treatises and uses of rhetoric and the art theory of the period. Rhetoric has also been used as a framework for the Baroque as a whole by Giulio Carlo Argan. In Argan's work rhetoric functions as the symbolic form for the Baroque as perspective does in Panofsky's Renaissance.[3]

Because it has received cursory treatment by art historians,[4] the history of propaganda, its use, and the vicissitudes of the term are outlined here. My purpose in doing so is twofold. First, a historiography will help us to sort out a context for its invocation at various moments (and in various countries) in art history since definitions of propaganda have always arisen in response to specific uses and protagonists. Second, it will help us to move away from using a historically contingent definition of propaganda for a discussion of the Baroque today, to see, rather, the need for the category of propaganda in society in general and in art history in particular.

Since Argan's work on the Baroque, rhetoric has been significantly repositioned in postmodern thinking, playing a pivotal role in the reshaping of the humanities and the social sciences. Alongside this new "rhetoricality"—not an overarching theory of discourse but rather the impossibility of such—propaganda has an important and specific function, one that we cannot do without. For the new thinking on rhetoric points in the direction of propaganda as occupying the site of "interested discourse" previously occupied by rhetoric. Propaganda as it has functioned in art history up until now reiterates that role and should continue to do so. Hence here I am not searching for a definition of propaganda that will suit the Jesuit Baroque. Rather, I am trying to understand how propaganda already functions in the discipline and how it can do so more fully. In showing how interrelated propaganda and rhetoric are, but also how they function as distinct interpretive frames, I hope to move beyond previous discussions.

RHETORIC

Rhetoric first appeared as an art of public speaking in the fifth century B.C.E., in the context of the expectation in the Greek city-states that a free male citizen be able to speak in the public domain on his own behalf. Throughout antiquity rhetoric remained a civic tool, indivorcible from the vicissitudes of public life;[5] the institutional dimension of rhetoric is critical to an understanding of its history.[6]

The first handbooks of rhetoric were composed by the Syracusan Corax, who invented a system of argumentation necessitated by the flooding of the courts with land disputes following the overthrow of a tyrant.[7] Rhetoric would inherit from this early sophist (in antiquity sophist meant "teacher of rhetoric")[8] the suspicious practice of "making the weaker argument stronger," which it never succeeded in shaking off. Gorgias, the Sicilian-born sophist of the fifth century B.C.E. who entranced Athenians with his figurative language, opened rhetoric up to further criticism by characterizing words as a *pharmakon,* a drug capable of powerfully affecting the emotions of the spectator. Gorgias's approach proved particularly threatening because it reflected his philosophical skepticism: in one of his philosophical writings he called into question the very possibility of finding or communicating truth. Thus, he argued, the orator can only stir his audience through emotion, to a *will* to believe.[9] For Gorgias, rhetoric is not staked against truth-seeking philosophy but is that which is left in the void of philosophy's own inability to produce truths. Thus Gorgias's rhetoric was no empty technique but a philosophical position based on a deep skepticism about the limitations of human knowledge. Rhetoric as practiced by the sophists did not lack a civic function; indeed, it was the "main tool of politics in Athenian democracy."[10] But because sophistic rhetoric made no claims to be a (disinterested) truth-seeking form of discourse, it appeared a self-serving one and hence posed a threat to democracy itself.

Perceiving the danger of Gorgias's relativism, Plato attacked rhetoric in the *Gorgias.* This dialogue, together with the *Phaedrus,* gave canonical status in Western philosophy to the opposition between distracting and entertaining rhetoric (which Plato banned from his Republic, along with painting and poetry) and a logocentric philosophy that strives toward truth. For Plato, the sophists erred not in having provided tools for men to defend their freedom but in their willingness to present a persuasive argument convincing us of mere opinions *(doxa)* rather than truth, which alone produces real knowledge *(episteme).* So while Plato was not disputing the role of speech in Athenian democracy, he was intent on wresting power from those who did not serve the higher good.[11] For Plato, the Socratic dialogue—spoken one-on-one—was the only way to arrive at truth. Vickers has argued that Plato's pessimistic view of the power of the (misguided, pleasure-seeking) crowd in fourth-century Athens—which had perverted the role of public speaking—led him, paradoxically, to imagine a far more tyrannical model of public life than the one he decried.[12]

Aristotle (and later Cicero, Quintillian, and the Renaissance humanists) rescued the art of oratory from Plato's adjudication of sophistry as empty and misleading by emphasizing the ethical and logical bases of its practice. Responding to the critique of the sophists as having taught mere commonplaces, providing students with examples to memorize rather than principles to help them learn to think for themselves, Aristotle systematized rhetoric. He defined three distinct types of rhetorical practice and their arenas of deployment—the judicial (court cases), the deliberative (determination of the best future action, mostly political or military), and epedeictic (praise or blame). Each would receive different emphasis in later ages, although epedeictic would consistently be the most vulnerable to the accusation of emptiness, of its emphasis on form.[13] He defined the three principal modes of persuasion as *ethos* (establishing the good character of the speaker induces trust), *pathos* (creating a suitable disposition in the audience facilitates persuasion), and *proof* (or *logos*, by means of a thorough definition of which he brought rhetoric in close connection with logic).[14] While Aristotle placed equal emphasis on these three modes, rhetoric would be problematized again and again by the prioritization of one part over the other, of *logos* over *pathos*, or *pathos* over *logos*: of rhetoric as moral argumentation (or primary rhetoric) versus style (or secondary rhetoric).[15] This process has been described as one of *letteraturizzazione*, or the tendency, after Aristotle, for secondary rhetoric to define rhetoric itself.[16] For while rhetoric has often been synonymous with its secondary aspects (broadly termed persuasion), *logos* was never the defining element of rhetoric; it lent a helping hand but never succeeded in defining rhetoric, for it belonged to philosophy.

Aristotle was also the first to argue that rhetoric's three elements—speaker, subject, and person addressed—are an essential unity. Picking up on Plato's argument that rhetoric must influence men's souls,[17] Aristotle wrote the first comprehensive treatment of the passions, establishing rhetoric's psychological foundations. In so doing, he broadened the almost exclusive concern of the sophists with the speaker's art to the audience.

Aristotelian rhetoric received further elaboration by Cicero and Quintillian. Because the Roman authors remained in circulation, their works became the fundamental sources for rhetoric through the Middle Ages. Cicero reaffirmed Aristotle's reconciliation of philosophy and rhetoric with a scathing critique of Plato's separation of philosophy from rhetoric, and hence from politics.[18]

The Romans are attributed with having focused on rhetoric as the foundation for humanistic education and for having developed certain areas in particular. Cicero drew on the Aristotelian triad for his definition of the three aims of rhetoric—as *movere, docere, delectare*—the formulation repeated in later centuries as Aristotle's texts were lost sight of.[19] Significantly, while these Roman orators acknowledged the necessity of instruction and delight, both emphasized the preeminence of the orator's skill in *movere*.[20]

Both Cicero and Quintillian, following the pupils of Aristotle (Theophrastus and Demetrius), considered *elocutio*, or eloquence, one of the five components of rhetorical composition *(inventio, dispositio, elocutio, memoria, pronuntiatio)*. The concern for eloquence, comprising qualities of style (clarity, ornateness, appropriateness, etc.), constituted a concern for the artifact alone and thus is a new poetic dimension of rhetorical composition.[21] I point this out because later attacks on rhetoric as "empty style" have in view this aspect of rhetoric, one that was elaborated after the golden age of rhetoric, that is, the period of its most democratic application in the fifth century.

The Middle Ages were a low point in rhetoric's history. Although Augustine and others made important contributions, rhetorical form was so deeply associated with pagan thought that Augustine asked whether Christian truths could or should be expressed through a pagan set of figures that appeal to the senses. Moreover, because of reduced activity in the public realm, the importance of rhetoric declined. It became, rather, mostly a textual art, only reemerging as an oral form and as an important subject in humanist thinking with the renewal of civic life in the communes of late Medieval Italy.

Rhetoric's status rose in the fifteenth century, when humanist scholars sought to define their own activity as orators in the public realm by rethinking the relative roles of eloquence (rhetoric) and wisdom (philosophy).[22] Whereas the humanists, if such a generalization may be made, were more concerned to define their activity as rhetors in terms of their own intellectual identity, in the Counter-Reformation a new emphasis would be placed on the *ends* of rhetoric. What was its purpose and its value? It was in the area of preaching that there emerged a clear sense that although the civic forum—the traditional site of the orator—was dead, the Church provided the new site in which great speaking could effect good for society.[23] In the late sixteenth century arguments for the use of ancient rhetoric revolved around the new content for which it was to be employed. Echoing Aristotle's (and Cicero's) insistence on the importance of *ethos,* the orator was to be the very embodiment of his message: a man of virtue and humility. He was to embody the content of his message.[24]

Intent on reaching a diverse mass audience, the new rhetors were among the most important agents through which the Catholic Church aimed to reform society. But preaching itself also had to be reformed. Two changes are remarkable. First, the Church disciplined its own members: it was now prohibited to criticize the clergy or the Church in a public sermon. Evidently this prohibition was strictly enforced.[25] Second, the new oratory was to avoid the scholastic form of sermon that consisted of a proposition and a defense of it. Sermons were now to assume the truth of Catholic doctrine (rather than defend it), to glorify the Church and its doctrines.[26] Thus epedeictic rhetoric was preferred over other forms.

Rhetoric flourished in the seventeenth century in large part owing to the interest that new institutions (the academies and religious orders that ran schools) took in codifying rhetoric for their constituencies.[27] Rhetoric was allied with new, national interests. The Académie française established the norms of French eloquence for the court; its definition of the forms of discourse (and official instatement of French over Latin) was positioned in contradistinction to an "eloquence sacrée" established by the Church (but on which it was nonetheless dependent).[28] The institutional control of discourse was indeed profound, but the way the situation played itself out in France, it was a vying for institutional power that generated different forms of discourse above all.[29] So while institutions were deeply embedded, indeed determinative of the history of rhetoric, what was at issue was the institutional control of the form of rhetorical style rather than the content of those messages themselves. Control of form brought power.

The Jesuits themselves were deeply engaged in the Counter-Reformation revival and transformation of rhetoric. In their schools, they led in according rhetoric a prominent place in a fixed college curriculum. But, as Fumaroli has shown, rhetorical instruction was not necessarily prestigious: rhetoric became as prominent as it did in French Jesuit schools because the universities succeeded in blocking the Jesuits from granting degrees in the higher subjects of theology and philosophy. Hence students came to the Jesuits for grammar and rhetoric, then departed for higher studies. This explains in part the deep association of rhetoric and the Jesuits and the special focus of critique on their style of rhetorical expression. As both teachers and members of court, they contributed to the courtly direction of rhetoric of the period, especially in France. This new rhetoric, with its emphasis on style and figures, developed in full recognition of the profound difference between the ancient forum and the court, the new site for the exercise of the art.[30] Fumaroli has shown that the Jansenists were already critical of the abundant "Asiatic" style of rhetoric the Jesuits employed in their oral and written publications (as opposed to the more constrained Attic style practiced by Port-Royal).[31] This would come back to haunt the Jesuits in the nineteenth century when the school debates saw the hallmark of the Jesuit curriculum, rhetoric, debunked. The tenacity of the French tradition is evidenced by its imprint on the Jesuit Style in architecture, which was expressed in remarkably similar terms.

Rhetoric's fortune declined with the rise of aesthetic theory in the late eighteenth century, becoming the linguistic victim of the Revolution. Kant's and Shelling's argument for art as good and disinterested, the product of unteachable genius, gave rise to the new category of the aesthetic in general and specifically to the distinct category of "literature." The nineteenth century saw the separation of literature (along with religious, philosophical, and scientific discourse) from rhetoric, which had previously been the category of discourse that did not distinguish qualitatively between them. With truth-value now attributed to some disciplines but not to others (theories of rhetoric always maintained that truth was the ethical responsibility of the orator but, unlike philosophy, never aimed to *produce* truth) and with the rise of the aesthetic ideology, starting with Kant, rhetoric became the locus of "fraudulent discourse."[32] Focusing on the persuasive possibilities of the art, of its privileging of form over the production of content, rhetoric's critics (including utilitarian philosophers) cast it as not only fraudulent but also *interested* discourse, that is, a discourse interested in persuading its audience of some*thing*. The renewed politicization of rhetoric, in terms of both its role in education and its internal aims, was brought about in part by the reorganization of public education. The way Hayden White presents it, the suppression of rhetoric in the age of democracy was the product of a willful misreading of rhetoric because of the insights rhetoric yielded "into the relation between political power and the control of language, speech and discourse, which political élites have always recognized as a necessary basis for effective rule." Recognition of this in the public realm resulted, first, in rhetoric's condemnation and, second, in its marginalization from the public schools, while it resurfaced as the humanities for the children of the elite.[33]

The characterization of rhetoric as faulty persuasion offers an irresistible parallel to the condemnation of the Jesuits in the same period. For though dressed as priests, Jesuits belied their robes with their silver tongues: in the terms of the day, the Jesuits were rhetorical figures themselves, living embodiments of the deceptive nature of form, like Eugene Sue's lizard of a Jesuit, Rodin:

> The cadaverous countenance of M. Rodin, his almost invisible lips, his little reptile eyes, half concealed by their flabby lids, and the sordid style of his dress, rendered his general aspect far from prepossessing; yet this man knew how, when it was necessary, to affect, with diabolical art, so much sincerity and good-nature—his words were so affectionate and subtly penetrating—that the disagreeable feeling of repugnance, which the first sight of him generally inspired, wore off little by little, and he almost always finished by involving his dupe or victim in the tortuous windings of an eloquence as pliant as it was honied and perfidious. . . .[34]

With rhetoric as their weapon, the Jesuits spread only lies, and in their rhetoric-dominated program of instruction they promised to train new generations of manipulators and liars.

The demotion of rhetoric in the nineteenth century accomplished two things. First, the two following strands of rhetoric, often separated in the past, were now definitively separated. The technical applications of rhetoric were absorbed into basic training in literacy while the goal of persuasion marked rhetoric as pure form and, as such, the antithesis of truth-seeking discourses.[35] Second, because the production of beauty now belonged exclusively to the domain of disinterested art, aesthetics and rhetoric became mutually exclusive. The centuries-long foundation of artistic, musical, and poetic theory in rhetoric was torn asunder.[36] The new polarization between rhetoric and other "truthful" discourses, like art, helps to explain how aesthetics and politics could become so removed from each other.

RHETORIC AS EXPLANATORY MODEL FOR BAROQUE ART

Since Giulio Carlo Argan first characterized the Baroque as rhetorical in a key essay published in 1955,[37] the rhetorical basis of Baroque art in theory and practice has been a commonplace in the literature on the period. Indeed, rhetoric has been promoted by Baroquists as, if not peculiar to the era, then particularly renewed in it, this in spite of the continuity of rhetoric throughout the early modern period.

The rhetorical has been situated in relation to several interrelated aspects of the artistic culture of the Baroque. Rhetorical theory continued to shape art theory in the seventeenth century.[38] As Rensselaer W. Lee and Michael Baxandall have shown in their influential studies of Renaissance art theory, starting with Alberti, early modern theory was fundamentally dependent on rhetorical theory for both the means (expression, composition) and ends *(movere, docere, delectare)* of the visual arts.[39] Rhetorical figures such as *contrapposto* and *difficoltà* have been discussed in connection with sixteenth-century art and architecture.[40] Other studies have focused less on tropes and more on the persuasive dimension of rhetoric as it played out in theory and practice. Jacqueline Liechtenstein has shown, for instance, that the debates in the sixteenth and seventeenth centuries over the seductive character of *colore* versus the rational basis of *disegno* are contiguous with the debate between philosophy and rhetoric.[41] In these rhetorically informed debates in Baroque art theory, rhetoric did not always have a positive value. *Colore* corresponded to one of the most problematic dimensions of rhetoric, the coloring of speech unique to live performance. For those who favored *disegno* as the principle of *ratio*, *colore* functioned virtually as a figure for rhetoric, absorbing the anti-Platonic view of color/body as threatening the metaphysical priority of rational discourse embodied in *disegno*.

The *disegno/colore* debates in the seventeenth century were not particularly novel in approach or in substance. But where the reframing of the visual arts in rhetorical terms gave fundamental impetus to Baroque art, many have argued, was through the reprioritization of the goals of art in the Counter-Reformation. Alberti's argument in *De Pictura* (1435) that art should have as its goal the representation of the *historia* was now embarrassingly unspecific and insufficiently directed to the Catholic *historia* for the embattled Church. The connection between rhetoric and the religious reform of the visual arts is made explicit in two key documents of the Counter-Reformation. The decrees on art issued at the Council of Trent (1563) stressed the traditional emphasis (since Gregory the Great's defense of images as the Bible of the unlettered) on the instructive use of images— *docere*. The decrees were elaborated in the Bolognese reform bishop Gabriele Paleotti's *Discorso intorno alle immagini sacre e profane* (Bologna, 1582).[42] In the first of two completed books (of a projected five), Paleotti offered a Catholic alternative to the increasingly secularized discourse and use of the arts. The fundamental message of the *Discorso* is that while it would be "inane" to deny that images provide pleasure, such cannot be the goal of art. Affirming the tripartite rhetorical function of images *(movere, docere, delectare)*,[43] Paleotti seizes on the passage in Cicero's *De Inventione* (in turn directly drawn from Aristotle's) as one that may have led artists and their audiences astray:

> The function of eloquence seems to be to speak in a manner suited to persuade an audience, the end is to persuade by speech. There is this difference between function and end: in the case of the function we consider what should be done, in the case of the end what result should be produced.[44]

While both Cicero and Aristotle tied rhetoric closely to politics and to ethics, this literally open-"ended" definition clearly left Paleotti unsatisfied. And so, Paleotti says, while the ends of art "are always to persuade," and following Cicero, this can cover a variety of needs, "for Christian images there is one end: to persuade to piety and bring people to God." Within this goal there can be more specific ends, such as bringing men to penitence, to charity, to virtue. But "these are all instruments of uniting men with God, which is the true and principal end of images."[45]

Paleotti recognized the breach that the revival of ancient rhetoric opened up to the Church's traditional justification of the arts as the Bible of the illiterate. It is notable that he arrived at the same conclusion that his contemporaries writing about rhetoric for orators also came to: namely, that the ancient theorists left uncomfortably open the relationship between the function of rhetoric and its end, which is not in the control of the speaker.[46] In proscribing an end, he responded much as Aristotle had done in tying rhetoric explicitly to ethics. In spite of Aristotle's pleading for the production of truth as one of the principal subjects of the orator, ancient rhetoric had opened up the possibility of separating the ends and means of persuasion. Aristotle could leave this question open in his treatises on rhetoric, as his philosophical writings addressed the ethical question of the good. But he could also leave this aside as there were no serious alternative ideologies of the good. By virtue of being the political tool crucial to Greek democracy, rhetoric was practically synonymous with it.[47] But by the end of the sixteenth century, with both competing religious ideologies and the rise of the European monarchs challenging the Church, just *who* was writing on rhetoric mattered a great deal. Paleotti was writing not only in this larger political context but also in the context of the reintroduction of rhetoric by the Renaissance humanists. In reopening the possibility of pleasure, the humanists had led the ethical foundations of rhetoric into dangerous territory, one that demanded disciplining, and a clear definition of the ends aspired to by all arts.

The history of the figurative arts in Catholic lands can be written as a consequence of Paleotti's fundamental reorientation. In particular, the highly communicative language of gesture and an intensification in the expression of emotion in Baroque art are explained as a function of a rhetorical turn in the figurative arts, explicit evidence that artists strove to move the spectator.[48] While entirely based on the Renaissance foundation in rhetorical theory, the heightened interest in the Baroque in communicating distinct emotional states is a defining feature of the period. Another indication of the preoccupation with making expression legible (and teachable to artists) were Charles Le Brun's efforts to designate definitive physiognomic characterizations of emotional states in the series of drawings of the passions that he used to illustrate his famous lecture on expression delivered in 1668 at the French Academy (fig. 12).[49] Thus the figurative arts of the Baroque period exercised one of rhetoric's fundamental goals: to communicate distinct emotional states to the spectator, who was thus to experience them himself. The connection between rhetoric and the renewed sense of mission in the Baroque to achieve a convincing representation of the passions is, by now, taken for granted.[50]

The broadest application of rhetoric to the Baroque period is to be found in the writings of Argan. He first explicitly emphasized the foundation of Baroque art in rhetoric and characterized the period as a whole as an art of persuasion. Argan in part located this in a turn in the period itself from Aristotle's *Poetics* to his *Rhetoric,* from the Cinquecento concern with painting as *poesia,* to the Seicento concern for painting as eloquence.[51] He argued, in far greater detail than had been done in the past, that the visual arts assumed the character of "a technique, a method, a type of persuasion" that leveled the stylistic

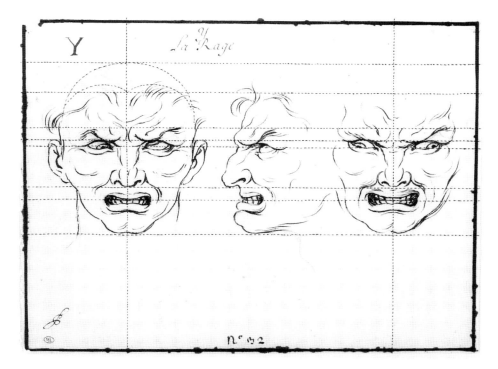

FIG. 12
Charles Le Brun, *Y: Rage,* from the album, *Expressions des passions de l'ame.*
Représentées en plusiers testes . . . , ca. 1668.

dualities of the period and reduced any theme or subject that one may have been tempted
to read as social mirror to their affective possibilities.[52]

Argan expressed a renewed interest, shared by some of his Marxist contemporaries such
as Meyer Schapiro and Arnold Hauser,[53] in the role of institutions in shaping the artistic
output of an era. Insofar as Argan's reading of the Baroque as rhetorical aimed at an all-
encompassing characterization of the period, he was led initially to question the dominance
of the Church as the institution that most shaped the period. If Baroque art, he wrote,

> configures discourse with a method of persuasion, it is legitimate to ask what the subject
> and ends of that persuasion are. . . . It is not contested that, in Baroque art, religious and
> moral motives prevail nor that this was used largely, and precisely for its intrinsic force of
> persuasion, by the Catholic Church for its propagandistic ends; but it would be simply absurd
> to reduce the entire Baroque theme to the religious foundation of the Counter-Reformation.[54]

Argan's positing of art as persuasion, or rather as communication and "relazione," depends not so much on the great religious ideologies as on the new mode of social life and

principally on the progressive affirmation of the European bourgeoisie in the great monarchical states.[55]

Although Argan viewed Baroque culture as rhetorical in the largest sense, he resisted defining the ends of this Baroque rhetoric, positing a "persuasione senza oggetto." In viewing the Baroque as rhetorically driven, he emphasized the advent of the Baroque bourgeois spectator not as a victim of religious power but as the objective of a new civil subject in a social and political world. In basing his interpretation on the positive Aristotelian sense of rhetoric as a technique of social and political life—rather than as the degradation of poetry—Argan steered clear of Benedetto Croce's universal condemnation of the rhetorical Baroque as the exclusive and repressive product of the Catholic Church.[56]

Argan's rhetorical Baroque had a swift impact. Wittkower immediately promoted the idea in one of the most widely read books on the Italian Baroque.[57] What is more, he seems to have been able to discard the Jesuit Style thesis in light of precisely this new cultural-historical explanation.[58]

Ten years after "La 'rettorica' e l'arte barocca," Argan reassessed his denial of the dominance of the Catholic Church in his essay "Rettorica e architettura." In overcoming the apparent difficulty of applying a concept based in the narrative arts to the nonfigurative arts, Argan argued that the (rhetorically based) principle of art as persuasion has "a relationship to the religious program of the Catholic Church and this program must refer also, and perhaps mainly, to architecture."[59] But even here Baroque persuasion does not derive its raison d'être from specific ends. For example, Bernini's metaphor of the Piazza of St. Peter's (fig. 13) as the Church embracing the faithful, he argued, persuades the viewer not to enter the Church as much as to "enter into the *concetto*."[60] For Argan, Baroque persuasion is about persuasion itself: it is a meta-art, not tied to any specific ideology, but to the task of persuasion itself. According to this view, the Baroque is the first modern era because it foregrounds the technique of persuasion as such, rather than persuasion of some*thing*.

Argan is attentive to the distinction so important in rhetorical theory between means and ends. In characterizing the entire Baroque period as rhetorical, he does not define those ends. Rather, art is a means of reaching as well as of reflecting the new role of the spectator. The unity of message and audience established by Aristotle lies at the heart of Argan's thinking. It is thus the new dependence of those institutions *on* their audience rather than what may be at issue in adherence for the institutions that occupied Argan.

Thus understood, Argan's rhetoric can be readily distinguished from propaganda. In his earliest essay (quoted above) Argan distinguishes between the articulation of discourse (through rhetoric) and the ends of such discourse as propagandistic. That is to say: rhetoric was the suasive means used by the Church for its propagandistic aims.

Propaganda was a corollary for Argan, but of course it is the central concern here. And propaganda urges us to investigate the areas left aside by Argan: what the institution's intentions may have been, what it hoped to accomplish through the use of persuasive arts; how the institution, in its relation to the artists who executed these works, may have actually achieved its goals.

FIG. 13
Giovan Lorenzo Bernini, Piazza of St. Peter's, begun 1656, Rome.

CROWD PSYCHOLOGY AND RHETORIC
AT THE END OF THE NINETEENTH CENTURY

In the background of the attack on rhetoric in the last quarter of the nineteenth century was a new concern about persuasion in political thought. While the fear of the persuader drove anti-rhetorical movement earlier in the century, in the last three decades of the nineteenth century social scientists and psychologists turned their attention to the susceptibility of the audience in the new study of crowd psychology. This scientific turn to the audience displaced the old psychology of the passions, providing a new psychological foundation for the modern form of persuasion in the offing, propaganda. It also unleashed a wave of interest in rhetoric on the part of some progressive thinkers and laid the ground for propaganda to replace rhetoric as the dominant theory of persuasion. Crowd psychology was not limited to intellectual circles but swept the popular imagination. This had, I believe, an echo in art history as well.

Crowd psychology emerged in the 1870s (especially in Italy and France) in the attempt to explain the unprecedented popular uprisings that characterized the political upheavals of the nineteenth century, threatening the bourgeois democratic order of the day.[61] The fundamental impulse for the development of crowd or mass psychology was Hippolyte Taine's revisionist history of the French Revolution, *Les Origines de la France contemporaine* (1875–93). In this widely read work, Taine, a professor of art history at the Ecole des Beaux Arts who worked in a variety of disciplines, countered Michelet's argument that the enlightenment of the Third Estate had brought about the French Revolution and that "outside parties" were responsible for all violent disturbances. Taine and his contemporaries, braced by recent mob action, attributed to the mob far greater responsibility for the Revolution, turning their attention to crowd behavior in order to explain—and in the hope of controlling—the destabilizing actions of the growing urban mass.[62]

The increasingly worrisome crowd behavior that the psychological theories attempted to explain stressed the suggestibility of the mass. Research of the 1880s and 1890s explored hypnotic suggestion (attributed by the famous Jean-Marie Charcot to hysterics alone, by Hippolyte Bernheim in 1884 to all men), a state in which credulity, obedience, and excitability could be accentuated. In the mid-1880s in France especially, but all over Europe, magnetism, hypnotism, and related phenomena were widely debated, not just in scientific circles, but in popular journals, reviews, and drawing rooms.[63] Anticipating Freud's psychology of the unconscious, Taine, Charcot, Scipio Sighele, and the best known of the group, Gustave Le Bon, brought attention to the uncontrollability of the psyche in mob situations, fueling public fears of political, religious, and other forms of persuasion. Indeed, several of these authors had to soften their early emphasis on the delinquency of crowds, realizing that crowds could also function positively, generating good social action and not just violence.

Even though some historians today hesitate in comparing the mass society of industrialized Europe to early modern society, these early psychologists of the mass agreed that all great movements, especially religious ones, began with mass movements led by strong leaders. Citing exorcisms and healings at holy sites as precedents for the secular scene of mass suggestion, they were well aware that what they were experiencing in their own times was the secular equivalent to religious experience in the past.[64] Indeed the displacement in nineteenth-century France of the clergy by medical doctors, the psychologists of the late nineteenth century, as the "most influential group in parliamentary circles" is suggestive of the continuity between these two historical types of experience.[65] It would therefore not be surprising at all to find the new suspicions projected back onto historical persuaders like the Jesuits with a new vehemence.

I believe that this shift in psychology heightened the suspicion of visual persuasion that was constitutive of the Jesuit Style. Because these newly recognized forces act on us unbeknown to us (and to all of us), they threatened to level the class distinction implicit in one of the traditional critiques of rhetoric as dangerous because it appealed to the "marketplace," to the crowd. The new psychological techniques of persuasion and psychosocial theories inaugurated a new age of suspicion of persuasion that was less centered on specific public enemies and more on the enemy within us all, even intellectuals, that can be awakened in particular situations by particular types of agents.[66] In art history, visually induced intoxication, the topos embedded in the Jesuit Style, provided an artistic equivalent to the mob leader. So when Wölfflin writes in *Renais-*

sance and Baroque in 1888 that in the Baroque empathic reaction to form breaks down, that it "lacks the wonderful intimacy of empathic response to every single form which was characteristic of the Renaissance" (fig. 10), he echoes the idea then in circulation that individual reason gives way in crowds. His binary oppositions between Renaissance architecture as calm/fulfilled, controlled/disciplined versus the Baroque as restless animation and loss of control (fig. 11) also correspond to characterizations of crowd behavior in this period. Our response to Baroque architecture is analogous to the response of the crowd ("The comprehensible is refused, the imagination demands to be overpowered. It is a kind of intoxication with which Baroque architecture fills us. . . . We are consumed by an all-embracing sensation of heaviness, helpless to grasp anything"), suggesting that Wölfflin's views on the Baroque reflect this shift in psychological theory.

The ground on which Wölfflin's thinking was based is beginning to come into focus. He wonders aloud how to draw a line between the Jesuit priest and the forms of the Baroque church. The psychologists of the crowd may have turned Wölfflin's attention to the spectator, in the Baroque not an individual but the crowd, on which the effect of persuasion was visible and legible. He then reads and characterizes the work of architecture not as the mirror of the preacher and his method but rather as the mirror of the persuader's effects. Wölfflin understands form as the embodiment of a psychological effect that acts on the crowd but is also like the crowd, an undifferentiated mass: the crowd as historical form.

I have dwelled on the new and politically driven psychological theories because their invocation, though quite indirect and uncited,[67] marks a critical turn in our view of the Catholic Baroque. Wölfflin may seem to have given up on the idea of the Jesuit Style, but his thinking was fundamentally shaped by it. The Jesuits remained a malingering ghost in his text as the organizers of mass persuasion, and the forms associated with them become the forms embodying the persuaded mass. Wölfflin's path of inquiry shifted attention from the Jesuits as authoritative agents of style to the forms as an embodiment of the history of their audience. In his absorption of mass psychology over the psychology of the passions on which rhetoric was traditionally based, Wölfflin set up a Baroque that would be easily understood later, once the term had acquired new meaning, as propaganda.

The crowd psychologists of the 1880s and 1890s provided the new psychological basis on which the great twentieth-century topos of persuasion would be based, namely, propaganda. Because of the emphasis in this moment on the helpless audience, over and above the persuader, propaganda's early course would be particularly marked by the vulnerability of the crowd. It is important to understand that both propaganda and rhetoric depended on audience psychology and that propaganda only entered when rhetoric, with all its former connections with psychology and poetics alike, had been killed off. For the era of the crowd a new category of persuasion had to be invented that was distinct from previous forms of persuasion because of the conditions of modernity.

PROPAGANDA

The original term "propaganda" comes from the Latin *propagare,* a biological or agricultural term that means "to sow." This meaning, which the verb retains, was picked up by the Catholic Church in its name for its missionary organization, the Propaganda Fide, or Propagation of the Faith. Founded by Gregory XV in 1622 and based in Rome, the organization coordinated missionary activities of the various religious orders (including the Jesuits), especially in the New World.[68] The term was not limited to the institution but was freely used in Catholic contexts.

Though the term "propaganda" was fully institutionalized by the Catholic Church, initially it was not associated exclusively with the propagation of the Catholic faith. On the contrary, from the seventeenth century until the early Enlightenment, when it became most strongly associated with the Catholic Church, both Protestant and Anglican organizations with similar missionary activities used the term.[69] By the time of the French Revolution, the early confession-blind use of propaganda had given it the connotation of some institution of conversion.

Propaganda's use came into new prominence and broadened to politics at the time of the French Revolution. Importantly, propaganda also became something that could be made. Coined by the antirevolutionary forces to arouse suspicion against the "revolutionary propaganda," propaganda's meaning nonetheless remained elastic in the French context: for the antirevolutionaries, the term carried with it the scent of conspiracy that characterizes it to this day.[70] But the revolutionary forces also used it for their own purposes. Just as they appropriated symbols of the Church and religion to endow their own movement with legitimacy, they also argued that though propaganda was bad, it could be destroyed and rise again as a force of good.[71]

Propaganda first took on explicitly negative connotations in Germany around 1780. Used by enlightened Protestants to bring out their anti-Roman sentiment, "propaganda" joined terms like *Proselytenmacherei* (proselytizing) and *jesuitische Verschwörung* (Jesuit conspiracy), anti-Catholic terms coined in Prussia, which expressed fear of an anti-Enlightenment offensive of the Catholic Church.[72] In this German context, propaganda meant antirevolutionary and connected to Rome, and the latter would remain the dominant meaning in the next century.[73] As the several Jesuit-related corollary terms and the close association of the Jesuit to Ultramontanism suggest, the early-nineteenth-century German use of propaganda was linked closely to the Jesuits. It is not surprising that, like rhetoric, propaganda would have such close associations with the Jesuits, though with different connotations. Propaganda practically meant ideological content, whereas rhetoric was largely understood as a technique of discourse, the forms of discourse capable of holding an audience captive. This distinction is important: there has never been a poetics built into propaganda in the same sense that there is in rhetoric.

The French Revolution widened the application of propaganda to political activity in general. German lexicons up until 1830 define the term as the activity of an institution dedicated to conversion, carrying the institutional origins of the term into its current forms. New institutions and journals used the word "propaganda" in their names around the July Revolution of 1830, compelling one commentator to precociously enunciate the twentieth-century refrain that they lived in an age of propaganda.[74] This institutional connection, which would remain with the term, is a critical way of distinguishing propaganda from rhetoric.

In the course of the nineteenth century propaganda continued to accrue negative connotations. In the 1840s Marx had no use for it, going so far as to argue that the word should be banished. The worker cannot be given superficial propaganda but rather concrete teaching and scientific ideas. Nonetheless, beginning in 1848, negative associations with propaganda would be shifted to the communists.[75] Under German Social Democracy in the 1860s, the term was avoided, and "agitation," a closely allied term since the French Revolution, was used instead. Propaganda reemerged around 1872, in the first years of the new German Republic. In the 1890s the term's employment was relatively neutral, referring to the spread of ideas and active engagement and work for political parties.

At the turn of the century in Germany the term experienced the moment of its greatest neutrality. It could be more strongly invoked in politics due to the widespread use of the term in business and trade with the rise of *Reklame* (advertising). Before World War I concern about German isolation resulted in new efforts to spread German ideas, marking the new use of propaganda with specific regard to culture *(Kulturpropaganda)*. Similarly, the *Nouveau Larousse,* published at the turn of the century, carried the historical definition of *propaganda fide* but also noted, rather neutrally, that the term was used by analogy as an "association that has as its goal the propagation of certain opinions."[76]

World War I marked the turning point in the practices and reputation of propaganda. Modern conditions (the growth of cities, elective politics, universal conscription) and modern warfare (requiring massive troops and organization of civilian populations to support the war) created an unprecedented need for the effective use of the media at home as well as in warfare itself.[77] With an increasingly influential mass media at their disposal, the coordinators of the war effort extended their message into schools, clubs, the workplace, even the burgeoning cinema. Propaganda quickly became pervasive: as a term, a concept, as a fact of daily life. And even though it has been argued more recently that because of the overwhelming consent of the publics that participated in this war the actual effectiveness of propaganda has been grossly distorted, propaganda was widely perceived as crucial to the war's outcome.[78]

England, Germany, and the United States established propaganda ministries during the Great War. And although Germany's attempt to influence public opinion abroad by buying U.S. newspapers first gave propaganda a bad name (as dishonest communication), it is widely agreed that the English made the most effective use of propaganda. British methods, which included radio, pamphlets, and printed posters, were considered so successful that after the war the Germans saw their own insufficient use of propaganda as having been decisive to their defeat. In the United States propaganda efforts were coordinated by the Committee on Public Information (CPI; its leadership referred to the organization in private as America's propaganda ministry) run by George Creel, a former newspaperman who used sales techniques in what he termed the "battle for men's minds."[79]

At the conclusion of World War I propaganda was hotly debated in the United States, England, and Germany. Initially the public reacted against propaganda with disgust as the manipulation of news during the war was revealed: the suppression, exaggeration, and outright falsification of facts (in particular, the misleading use of atrocity stories on both sides) aroused general awareness of the need for critical reading of government and press communications.[80] But the critique of propaganda following the war was even more far-reaching, encompassing growing concerns about the power of the new mass media and the vulnerability of democracy to its use by special interest groups.[81]

In this postwar period of open debate social scientists and political commentators continued to be occupied by the definition and analysis of propaganda, spawning an enormous literature on the subject. In the United States two distinct points of view emerged in the 1920s. On the one hand, optimistic accounts by leaders in the advertising and newspaper industries argued that propaganda was a neutral practice, a necessary technique to organize behavior and opinions in mass society. The figurehead of the "professional response," Edward Bernays, former CPI official and pioneer in the advertising field, remarked, "I am aware that the word 'propaganda' carries to many minds an unpleasant connotation. Yet whether, in any instance, propaganda is good or bad depends upon the merit of the cause urged, and the correctness of the information published."[82]

On the other hand, the opposing view of propaganda as a sinister and dishonest force dominated the popular press.[83] The "humanist perspective" feared that propaganda capitalized on the captivity of the mass audience to the media, menacing traditional democratic participation.[84] While many argued that propaganda should be abolished, the majority voice countered that it was a necessary force in modern society. Leonard Doob argued that society had entered into an era of competition and conflict that was unlikely to end; propaganda was with us to stay.[85] It needed, however, to be understood and put to use. Walter Lippmann took an extreme and cynical view of the current situation in his *Phantom Public* (1925), arguing that those who believed that democratic systems enacted the public will operated under a deep illusion. The mass was neither prepared for nor accorded a role in public affairs and the propaganda machine was itself responsible for the illusion that it was.[86] So successful was the leveling of propaganda and so saturated had the public become in the postwar period that, as one writer put it, "in the 1930s people threw down their newspapers and echoed the familiar refrain, 'it's all propaganda, anyway.'"[87]

With the rise of Hitler (not to mention Stalin), the dangers of propaganda became pressing once again, giving rise to an alarmist literature. The political circumstances under which the new wave of propaganda studies emerged stimulated a variety of approaches—

sociological, psychological, political[88]—but as the Second World War approached, analysis of propaganda was forced to become less a disinterested science and more an urgently needed political tool. On the one hand, O. W. Riegel's *Mobilizing for Chaos* (1934) exposed the political and technical communications infrastructure that created the condition of possibility for the new propaganda. Riegel viewed with great pessimism the convergence of new and fast media technologies (especially radio and news), a technical and professionalized propaganda driven by dangerous national interests.[89] Serge Chakotin's *Rape of the Masses: The Psychology of Totalitarian Political Propaganda* (1939), which came out in Paris just a few weeks before German troops marched into Poland, used Pavlovian psychology to analyze "Hitlerian" propaganda, making analysis of propaganda the first step in political action.

As World War II approached, a school of quantifiable propaganda analysis arose based on polling practices begun in peacetime. These studies operated under the optimistic belief that the enemy's propaganda program could be outwitted through statistical analysis.[90] Along these lines Harold Laswell was a pioneer in statistical content analysis. Ernst Kris, a Viennese anthropologist, art historian, and psychoanalyst, together with the social scientist Hans Speier conducted a massive study for the Rockefeller Foundation on Nazi radio propaganda, providing training in the analysis of propaganda in anticipation of the U.S. entrance in the war.[91]

Perhaps the most widely influential publications around and after World War II were those aimed at self-defense. In 1936 a Boston merchant, Edward Filene, concerned that the public, bombarded by propaganda, was unable to make its way unassisted, provided a grant to found the Institute for Propaganda Analysis (IPA). Dedicated to the education of the public in the analysis of propaganda, the short-lived IPA (which disbanded when the United States entered the war) gave impetus to the pedagogical thrust of a new generation of texts.[92] The IPA's purpose was to introduce scientific methods of analysis that would help the public to distinguish truth from falsehood (without producing skepticism, which "destroys belief in everything") and to develop an "emotionally-detached consideration of controversial problems."[93] The rational evaluation of propaganda, they argued, was the key to the functioning of democracy. The IPA's seven-point analysis of propaganda became standard in textbooks, and by 1939 their materials were in use in five hundred high schools, colleges, and adult civic groups in the United States.[94]

Although criticized at the time, the how-to manual that emerged in the 1930s lived on into the Cold War period. For example, "The Propaganda Game" for "clear thinkers" (first manufactured in 1964) repackaged the IPA's message of the late 1930s. In the publicity for the game the actor Lorne Greene ponderously warned: "In a democratic society such as ours, it is the role of every citizen to make decisions after evaluating many ideas. It is especially important then that a citizen be able to analyze and distinguish between the emotional aura surrounding the idea and the actual content of the idea. It is to the goal of clear thinking that THE PROPAGANDA GAME addresses itself" (fig. 14). The depiction of propaganda as a menace became a basic component of civic instruction (what a later

FIG. 14

The Propaganda Game, 1966. Wff 'N Proof Publishers.

generation would recognize as propaganda about propaganda). In an age of heightened patriotism (in the United States), this attitude toward propaganda cannot but have influenced the generations of intellectuals reaching maturity from the late 1930s through the mid-1960s.

In Germany, where the term "propaganda" first appears in studies of Baroque art and architecture in the 1910s and 1920s in relatively neutral terms, the reputation and future prospects of propaganda were even more ambivalent than in the Allied countries in the aftermath of World War I. German social scientists, like their Anglo counterparts, undertook important studies of propaganda (like Stern-Rubarth's *Die Propaganda als politisches Instrument,* which was crucial for Germany's future use of cultural propaganda, and Wilhelm Bauer's 1930 history of public relations, *Die Öffentliche Meinung in der Weltge-*

schichte). But propaganda as a political practice was discouraged. The Weimar Republic preferred the term *Aufklarung,* and some argued that in the future propaganda should not be used for foreign relations.[95] The political retraction on the subject is clear in the first postwar edition of the *Meyers Lexikon,* whose entry for propaganda (published 1928) defined the term neutrally as the spreading of certain teachings in a religious and political context, extended in commerce to advertising. In stark contrast to the postwar *Encyclopedia Britannica* entry that revolved around the emergence of propaganda in the war, the *Meyers* entry makes no reference to recent events.[96] The entry in *Der Große Brockhaus* in 1933 is even shorter and more restricted.[97]

In 1933 the Nazis officially reserved the use of the term "propaganda" for politics. But the Third Reich's propaganda minister, Joseph Goebbels, expressed the most telling ambivalence about the term. Shortly after his rise to power, Hitler appointed Goebbels Minister of Popular Enlightenment and Propaganda, which included the departments of press, radio, film, theater, and propaganda. However, Goebbels wrote in his diary that the word "propaganda" "left a bitter aftertaste," and he proposed an alternative: Reich Ministry for Culture and Popular Enlightenment. When Hitler rejected the name Goebbels "talked himself out of his objections to 'propaganda,' transforming it into a political art, a creative process, a question of productive imagination—in short, something entirely positive."[98] To ensure that his own determination to exclude the negative semantics of the term also became a public one, Goebbels issued directives that "propaganda" only be used positively. Goebbels put propaganda to work for itself. That he was successful is evidenced by Doob's comment in 1935 that "Goebbels does not hesitate to have himself called 'Minister of Public Enlightenment and Propaganda'—evidently the word possesses or has to possess different connotations in German."[99]

With moral victory so clearly residing on the Allied side after the discovery of the concentration camps, it was possible for propaganda to be morally polarized, as it had been in earlier moments but now more definitively. We can see the shift in how Leonard Doob, a leader in propaganda analysis with an empirical perspective, defined propaganda before and after the war. In his *Propaganda: Its Psychology and Technique* of 1935, it was "a systematic attempt by an interested individual (or individuals) to control the attitudes of groups of individuals through the use of suggestion and, consequently, to control their actions."[100] Here the emphasis is on the propagandist's purposefulness and control. In his *Public Opinion and Propaganda* of 1948, propaganda, he writes, is not education but rather "the attempt to affect personalities and to control the behavior of individuals towards ends considered unscientific or of doubtful value in a society at a particular time."[101] By putting equal emphasis now on the means (control) and the ends (by definition of dubious value), Doob eradicated the neutrality that marked his earlier approach.

The scientific literature that grew up around propaganda before and during World War II did nothing to lessen its negative connotations after the war. "Psychological warfare" (coined by German psychologists in World War II and picked up in the Anglo world) was often substituted, though not without some objections.[102] With the occupation and divi-sion of Germany and the commencement of the Cold War, the sense of perpetual un-armed conflict deepened and propaganda strategy intensified, as did the connection be-tween analysis of propaganda and policy.[103] Because the Cold War challenged traditional definitions of war and peace, propaganda, already a slippery term, became an even more potent player on shifting semantic grounds.

Before World War II it was generally acknowledged that propaganda was produced in all political systems, in democracies as well as in totalitarian states. After the war, among the same group of (largely German émigré) intellectuals, the terms of analysis changed somewhat, though the spirit remained the same. But in the next generation, those on the side of the Allied forces in the war denied that all political systems produce propaganda. The American public now perceived Communist Russia as more expert and willing to use propaganda than democratic societies. The reliance on appeal to emotion and the fundamental dishonesty of Russian propaganda were contrasted to U.S. propaganda, which "tries to be scrupulous with the facts." The term "propaganda" reverted to its ear-lier popular definition as manipulation by the enemy and was avoided in any reference to U.S. policy tools.

By the early 1950s, accompanying this moral paradigm shift was the sense that U.S. policy makers had to adjust to propaganda fatigue. "The psychological resistances of a skeptical, propaganda-weary world must be respected and intelligently taken into account," wrote Ralph White in 1952 in a special issue of the *Public Opinion Quarterly* dedicated to communications research.[104] White recommended masking propaganda techniques in "high journalistic standards." Propaganda would be dissociated from the government to encourage the ideological split between propaganda and truth. The use to which propa-ganda has been put in art history shows that we are the heirs to the Cold War moral po-larization of propaganda.

The most important work on propaganda in the twentieth century, *Propagandes,* pub-lished by the French sociologist Jacques Ellul in 1962 and subsequently widely translated, was written in the wake of this dissociation of propaganda from democracy.[105] Like the analysts of the 1920s, Ellul insisted that propaganda was a phenomenon of the modern world, an instrument, a technique indispensable to our "technical civilization," which he defined in another influential book in 1954.[106] Indeed, one of Ellul's most resisted ideas was that all societies, especially democracies, *need* propaganda.[107] In insisting on the es-sential similarity of all propagandas, regardless of specific ideological program, Ellul ar-gued that propaganda itself is the mother ideology, of which Nazism, communism, and democracy are merely epiphenomena. Intent on eliminating the "judgmental character" of propaganda studies in his day, Ellul nonetheless insisted that propaganda cannot be studied entirely in theory but must be studied in real practice.[108]

In outlining a sociological type (similar to Doob's "unintentional propaganda") distinct from overtly political propaganda, Ellul made propaganda a far more inclusive category than his contemporaries were willing to embrace. In Ellul's view, sociological propaganda, which creates new habits, is not produced intentionally but penetrates through existing structures. An example of sociological propaganda is the American filmmaker who makes a film that expresses the American way of life, though he has no intention of making propaganda. Particularly difficult was Ellul's argument that the intellectual is most vulnerable of all to propaganda because of his own function as opinion maker.

And yet Ellul himself would insist on the distinctness of propaganda from education and preaching and rhetoric, all embraced by propaganda, the most encompassing technique of modernity. He agreed with recent publications' emphasis on the *intention* to indoctrinate as key to distinguishing propaganda from education and other practices. But whereas previous authors, especially in the 1920s and 1930s, emphasized the psychological functioning of propaganda on a passive mass (Stalinist propaganda based on Pavlov's conditioned reflex; U.S. propaganda based on Dewey's theory of teaching; Hitler's based on Freud's suppression of the libido),[109] Ellul shifts the attention back to the propagandist as the key to defining the phenomenon.

Because propaganda must be "continuous and durable," it requires an administrative organization:

> Every modern state is expected to have a Ministry of Propaganda, whatever its actual name may be. Just as technicians are needed to make films and radio broadcasts, so one needs "technicians of influence"—sociologists and psychologists. But this indispensable administrative organization is not what we are speaking of here. What we mean is that propaganda is always institutionalized to the extent of the existence of an "Apparat" in the German sense of the term—a machine. It is tied to realities. A great error, which interferes with propaganda analysis, is to believe that propaganda is solely a psychological affair, a manipulation of symbols, an abstract influence on opinions. . . . As long as no influence is exerted by an organization on the individual, there is no propaganda.[110]

This is a particularly important way of distinguishing propaganda from rhetoric. And it begins to explain, in part, why historians are more apt these days to speak of the art produced under Louis XIV as propaganda (rather than discourse) and to speak of the discursive structures of (the far less powerful) artistic academies and the theorists that supported them.[111]

Ellul occupies a key place for having emphasized propaganda's ideology-blind practice. Once it becomes undeniable that democratic societies use propaganda as much as totalitarian societies, no discourse theory, even the aesthetic, can be maintained as the realm of truthful, or, more precisely, disinterested discourse. Rhetoric had to be challenged so as to allow for the emergence of the aesthetic ideology. Propaganda rose up in rhetoric's place to preserve the truth claims of democratic societies' definition of propaganda as the lies told by the "other." With Ellul's exposure of this fallacy, the politico-scholarly interest in propaganda waned.[112]

In the 1960s, with Ellul's work, a shift in thinking about propaganda occurred. It is at this moment, contemporaneous with a renewed discussion of rhetoric, especially in

France, that popular opinion, more or less consistent with scholarly views, now diverged from Ellul's relativist view of propaganda.[113] A long line of popular publications, some more neutral than others, continued to reproduce an essentially Cold War view of propaganda. But in the specialized literature, propaganda could no longer be morally polarized as it had been.

NOTES ON ART HISTORY AND PROPAGANDA

Cold War attitudes toward propaganda are palpable in the work of the generation of art historians who lived through the war. Rudolf Wittkower's use of propaganda as a supplement (see introduction) is, I believe, representative of his generation. Wittkower admitted to some propaganda in the Baroque, but he strategically reserved the epitaph for certain objects, so that the rest of the Baroque might remain pure. Thus he preserved the judgmental character of the term. Writing at the same time as Wittkower, Walter Friedlaender, also a German émigré to the United States,[114] used Jesuit propaganda as a negative foil in a revisionist study of Caravaggio's mature work as the expression of a *sincere* spirituality. Because Friedlaender found affinities in Caravaggio's work to Ignatius of Loyola's Spiritual Exercises, he felt compelled to distinguish between a close engagement with a legitimate spiritual source and the entrenched negative view about the Jesuits:

> The affinities between Caravaggio's mature religious conception and the Exercitia [Spiritualis] by no means prove or even suggest a direct affiliation of the artist with the Company of Jesus. The kind of art which the Jesuits were later to use as a special kind of *propaganda fidei* is closely connected with the flamboyant Baroque style of Rubens and Bernini, of Baciccio and Padre Pozzo, and hardly adapted to the expression of the sober and mystic realism of Saint Ignatius and Caravaggio.[115]

Did Friedlaender struggle over the term *propaganda fidei,* softening and neutralizing the isolated word "propaganda"? This question cannot be answered, but it appears that in arguing for Caravaggio's spiritual purity against the usual accounts of his impious, murderous life, Friedlaender needed to distance Caravaggio from impious Jesuitism. Rubens, Baciccio, and Pozzo could be sacrificed for Caravaggio.

One can understand why a generation with direct experience of Nazi propaganda would want to contain or reject outright the use of the term "propaganda" to describe historical art. Paul Zanker (German, b. 1937) in his *Power of Images in the Age of Augustus* (1985) refuted the idea that the establishment of a monarchy in Augustus's time and the "new method of visual communication" that accompanied it amounted to a "propaganda machine."[116] Zanker's discomfort with the category is made apparent throughout the book but specifically in his argument that Augustan imagery spread through the Empire spontaneously, that the imagery reproduced itself instead of being imposed by imperial administrators. Zanker substituted for the top-down imposition of propaganda that informed previous work on the subject the idea of a flexible dialogue. Did his personal experience press his reformulation of the subject? A reviewer of the book pointed out the following remark that appeared in the German edition: "whoever has experienced the architectural politics of the National Socialists and fascists knows that the emotional effect of built form can scarcely be underestimated."[117] Apparently the English translator of the work was uncomfortable with Zanker's remark, for he bizarrely omitted the crucial part of the sentence ("whoever has experienced the architectural politics of the National Socialists and fascists"), rendering the autobiographical overdeterminations that lie behind the careful argument of the book indecipherable to the reader of the English edition.[118] For some, propaganda may, for now, still remain cordoned off, just as the study of the art and architecture of the Nazi regime remains to some extent isolated from the rest of twentieth-century art as well.[119]

A generational split can be detected in more recent invocations of propaganda, especially in subfields of the discipline in which a state structure (empire) or use of a mass media (print) is under examination. Several scholars have used propaganda in a neutral fashion, searching for definitions to suit their subjects. So, for instance, in a study of Roman coins, sculpture, and other media, Jane DeRose Evans created a hybrid definition of propaganda (somewhat misleadingly attributed to Ellul) as "the educational efforts or information used by an organized group that is made available to a selected audience, for the specific purpose of making the audience take a particular course of action or conform to a certain attitude desired by the organized group."[120] Similarly, in a study of Reformation imagery, Carl Christiansen employed the term "in a neutral or non-pejorative sense, that is, as referring to the use of visual or verbal symbols for the purpose (whether good or ill) of influencing public opinion."[121]

It is striking that these (and other studies) that have used propaganda as a dispassionate category of analysis are often not invested in the aesthetic status of the works of art.[122] In these studies, art is seen through and past. And for these scholars such an operation is unproblematic (art is evidence), in a way that it would not be for an art historian (such as Zanker). What this suggests is that propaganda, in a sense, remains art history's problem. When it is set against a category—art—that, for all of its demystification, still retains a privileged sacral status in our thinking, propaganda asserts itself as every bit the live category as art itself. When invoked by some of the historians I have pointed to, propaganda denies artistry, but in doing so, it affirms it. Our effort must be not to diffuse but to understand, as W. J. T. Mitchell's remarks cited in the epigraph to this chapter suggest, how propaganda works.

THE NEW RHETORIC AND PROPAGANDA AS "SUPPLEMENT"

The first effort must be to understand propaganda in relation to art history. To this end, the function of rhetoric today can help us to sort out why propaganda is a critical category in art history.

Rhetoric has been habitually, but especially since the eighteenth century, broken down into two areas: forms of expression (tropes) versus persuasion. Its demise occurred over the course of the eighteenth and nineteenth centuries on two fronts. With the rise of the scientific method (Locke, Bacon, the Encyclopedists), a type of transparent writing—that did not try to persuade, that was free of style—brought about the separation of rhetoric from truth-seeking forms of writing. The Enlightenment project of establishing realms for the transparent use of language, as well as supplanting oral with written communication in the public realm, witnessed the first important marginalization of rhetoric. The second related front was that of aesthetics. The Romantics established literature as the realm of imaginative expression, one in which rhetoric had no part.[123] Kantian aesthetics set rhetoric (associated with non-truth-seeking or "interested discourse") against literature, a new and free "disinterested" form, which (together with the fine arts) also had the status of a truth-revealing form. By the nineteenth century rhetoric thus belonged to two ghettos: to the study of tropes and schemes, tied to grammar and "empty" style; and, as persuasion, to the realm of "interested" discourse.

The modern revival of rhetoric has likewise occurred on two fronts: in both the critique of metaphysics in philosophy and in literary theory the revival of rhetoric has been at the base of the fundamental interdisciplinary turn. In the writings of Northrop Frye and I. A. Richards, and as part of a larger movement of questioning the assumptions of positivism, rhetoric was reconciled to literature.[124] Frye in particular began to break down the claims to truth of scientific discourse by pointing to the discourse of truth as a rhetorical strategy all its own. Perhaps more fundamental for the "rhetorical turn" of the past decades were Nietzsche's lectures on rhetoric and writings on language, which have had their greatest impact in France since the 1970s.[125] Not first but at a critical juncture, Nietzsche (the consequences of whose thought were played out by Kuhn, Barthes, Foucault, and others and in deconstruction especially) pointed to the artificiality of distinctions between truthful and non-truth-seeking discourses, opening the way to a revival of rhetoric as the broadest possible system of discourse. In postmodernism the discursivity of all human language in all disciplines leveled previous distinctions about the relative truth-seeking statuses of the sciences, social sciences, or humanities. Hence Plato's fundamental dismissal of rhetoric—which can neither produce truth nor know itself—in favor of philosophy is called into question and, for some (especially in literary theory), overturned. Upheld since Plato as the locus in Western thought of truth-seeking discourse, of a metaphysical truth outside of history, philosophy can no longer maintain this position once it is seen that philosophy does not simply use language but is produced through language. In postmodernism rhetoric is the condition for the production of philosophy rather than an effect out in the world.[126] Philosophy, which has traditionally battled rhetoric for a privileged position as the encompassing discipline, has had to cede to rhetoric.[127]

But which, or whose, rhetoric is this? The rhetoric of tropes or rhetoric as a system of persuasion? Rhetoric as the ends of speech or the rhetoric that sets out means? Barthes and others (following Saussure) base their linguistic turn on tropes as the constitutive elements of rhetoric, speaking of all linguistic function as fundamentally metaphorical and metonymical (and hence rhetorical or, in Hayden White's term, "tropical"). But more relevant here (and I think the more important strain of the revival of rhetoric) is the emphasis on rhetoric as the overall model for the inescapable discursivity of all language, of all forms of expression, of writing, of text, of speech, in short, of all forms of expression.

Refining the phrase "the rhetorical turn" coined by the Iowa School, Dilip Parmeshwar Gaonkar has referred to an "implicit rhetorical turn," that is, the broadest possible understanding of the epistemological function of rhetoric, as opposed to the explicit remodeling of classical rhetoric's actual components.[128] Similarly, John Bender and David Wellbery argue that the new rhetoric is distinct from its historical forms: it is rhetoric "with a difference."[129] They call the new necessity for this category "rhetoricality," taking their cue from Nietzsche, who showed that rhetoric has lost the sense of a rule-bound approach to discourse, that it points to the "rootlessness of our being." Rhetoric is what is left when the illusory nature of positivist "truth" is revealed. And rhetoricality gestures to the institutional rootedness of all discourse, scientific or otherwise: Kuhn's location of scientific discovery in previous paradigms, Foucault's location of discourses in their institutional contexts. So the new rhetoric is not "a specialized technique of instrumental communication" but rather a "general condition of human experience and action." And that condition, rhetoricality, cannot, as before, posit rhetoric as a governing system that encompasses all others. For rhetoricality is the condition of the *impossibility* of any "single governing discourse."[130] With this pronouncement, rhetoric is not only neutralized, but leveled: its previous distinctiveness as the locus of "instrumental discourse" is made untenable. All forms of discourse are by nature embedded in power relations, and "rhetoric" now signals this fact rather than pose as its foremost iteration. But are we to abandon the idea of instrumental discourse altogether? Here Derrida's subtle reading of Plato, the inaugural moment of rhetoric's marginalization, can be of some help.

For Derrida, in Plato's dialogues on rhetoric and in the *Republic* rhetoric stands in a "supplementary" relation to philosophy.[131] The status of the supplement in Derrida is quite changeable, but in this case a useful analogy is to that of the encyclopedia supplement, that which is added but without which the previous work would be incomplete. Hence the supplement appears both as an addition, that which was not imagined in the original scheme, and as necessary: it is that which points to the previous state of incompleteness. Thus when Derrida posits rhetoric as the supplement to philosophy, rhetoric is not the discourse of all discourses. Rather, in Derrida's reading of Plato, rhetoric bears the stigma attached to writing as the orphan of *logos*, the form of expression that only comes about when the father of *logos*, the living being that must be present to respond in order to produce philosophy, truth, has been left behind as a mere trace. Rhetoric appears in the Platonic dialogues, the *Gorgias* and the *Phaedrus*, not as speech (which produces philosophy through dialogue) but as *writing* (Gorgias's manuals for speaking, or speeches written by one but delivered by another): it points, paradoxically, to the very embeddedness of writing within Plato's very conception of the living *logos,* which he always comes back to refer to in terms of inscription, impression, writing.

The ambivalent figure this rhetoric qua writing takes on in the Platonic dialogues is that of the *pharmakon,* the term familiar from the sophistic tradition. And here is where Derrida's analysis of the Platonic dialogues is particularly important to us. Derrida argues that even though Plato is openly against the art of rhetoric/writing, his ambivalence is belied by the ubiquitous appearance of writing around the production of *philosophy,* which Socrates believed should take the form of spoken dialogue, an argument Plato must take responsibility for writing down. And so, Derrida argues, the *pharmakon* (which, he points out, means remedy *and* poison), this highly multivalent term, stands in for rhetoric/writing. Why? In part because it is not just writing (in the form of manuals of rhetoric or written speeches) but also living speech/the good/*logos* in which the *pharmakon* is operant. The sophists themselves describe persuasive speech as a *pharmakon,* as a drug that can unwittingly captivate its audience, that can act on the soul as the *pharmakon* (drug) acts on the body. But the ubiquitous analogies to writing in Plato's own discussion of dialectics point to the fact that this truth-producing form of speech itself is also infected. In a gesture of deflection, Plato attacks the sophists on the very site of writing.

What are the implications of Derrida's argument concerning rhetoric's status in Plato (and by extension to the long history of logocentrism in Western thought) as a "supplement" for rhetoric today? The ambivalence Derrida notes in Plato's critique of rhetoric suggests that accompanying the explicit condemnation of rhetoric was considerable anxiety: rhetoric *had* to be present in the *polis,* Derrida argues, even though Plato decried it. In spite of the ambivalent status of both speech and writing, in Christopher Norris's words, "the *polis* seems able to sustain its identity only by allowing a certain admixture of the alien, the 'debased' or useless. And as metaphors of writing invade the very discourse of logocentric reason, so the scapegoat becomes that indispensable 'other' by which the Greek city-state defines its own powers and constitution."[132] This comprises another Derridian inflection of the supplement: the supplement is also an other, an outsider residing inside, necessary to that which it supplements. But it is often cast in shadow, the denigrated, the debased: it is that which, as so much of Foucault's work points out, constitutes the rest by its difference.

I would like to take a historical turn here. There are two strains in the history of the rejection of rhetoric. First is the philosophical rejection of rhetoric that dates back to Plato's time and which resurfaced periodically up to and during the nineteenth century. In the face of all challenges, rhetoric remained firmly at the center of philosophical discourse. Second is the actual rejection of rhetoric, its elimination from school curricula in the late nineteenth and early twentieth centuries. Here Plato's wish was granted. Or was it?

If we follow Derrida, rhetoric played an indispensable role in the *polis:* as the supplement, rhetoric was critical to the definition of the *polis* itself. And thus we are left with two questions. At the end of the nineteenth century has the *polis* sufficiently redefined itself that rhetoric is truly no longer necessary? To this one could answer that it is striking that it was precisely the democratic societies of the nineteenth century, which for the first time most closely approximated the ideal of the Greek city-state, that saw rhetoric as a threat. It is equally striking that rhetoric's demise was immediately followed by the emergence of an alternative form of persuasion: namely, propaganda.

What to make of this emergence? With rhetoric now cast out of schools, where the formation of the nation was taking place, what message did this send to the educated masses about how to communicate in the public realm? Is it possible that this public, no longer trained in rhetoric, was left more vulnerable to a new form of communication that had persuasion as its principal goal?

Ellul's work brought propaganda and rhetoric as discussed since the 1960s closer together. His notion of a sociological propaganda is quite close to the everywhereness of rhetoric. Although he describes a type of sociological propaganda that seems to lack intentionality, Ellul disagreed that virtually everything in the economic and political worlds can be seen as driven by propaganda. To abandon the study of propaganda to the notion that "everything" is propaganda is an unforgivable intellectual surrender, because propaganda exists.[133]

Distinctions must be made. And here is where the crux of the matter lies: while all propaganda, as a particular strain of persuasion, can be said to be rhetorical (that propaganda partakes in the "rhetoricality" described by Wellbery and Bender and others), the same cannot be said in reverse: not all rhetoric is propaganda.

So when I say that propaganda took over for rhetoric it took over for a particular aspect of rhetoric: namely, rhetoric as persuasion, that aspect of rhetoric which was criticized from antiquity but especially in the nineteenth century with the rise of positivism, the rise of the disinterested aesthetic. In the new rhetoricality, propaganda is but one aspect, one manifestation of the manifold forms of rhetoric—history, science, speech in the public realm, advertising, literature, and so on.

Propaganda, in my view, has taken over an important function in the Western metaphysical debate. With the diffusion of the debate over rhetoric's competition with philosophy for the upper epistemological position, a slot is left open for a (dangerous) form of discursivity defined as instrumentality. This is what was at stake for Plato in his critique of the sophists: this was the foundation for Aristotle, Cicero, and the Renaissance humanists' attempts to wed rhetoric to philosophy, to knowledge, to responsible and virtuous civic activity. Whether their pleas for the rhetor as *homo philosophus* were absorbed or not, the transformation of rhetoric into rhetoricality has left a place open for a new supplement: for pure instrumental discourse. Indeed propaganda, arguably, has provided the condition of possibility for the new rhetoric.[134] It might bear suggesting that the new rhetoric could only emerge once propaganda was in place.

If understood as pure instrumentality without an eye to the *need* for this instrumentality, propaganda, like rhetoric before it, will appear pernicious. Here is where Ellul's work is important. Ellul extended the psychological importance of propaganda to the human drives, arguing that the certainty of the propaganda message has a necessary function: to placate the ideological insecurities of man, to provide ready-made truths and adherences that take man beyond his fears and insecurities, and his unknowingness in the face of a complex and uncertain world. Ellul argued that propaganda replaces the reassuring function of religion. Hence, propaganda cannot be seen as a one-way imposition by an elite and crafty few who, with psychological techniques at their disposal, take advantage of a passive mass. Rather, propaganda is necessary to man himself, determining the "religious" character of propaganda.[135] The significance of this argument cannot be overstated. The idea that instrumental discourse—in all forms, including the arts—does not just happen but is necessary to man must be taken seriously. Propaganda, in sum, is neither good nor bad but necessary. It is thus easier to understand why propaganda has become an art historical scapegoat, a figure that we need, that we must include in our discursive *polis,* but one that we will at times abhor.

While propaganda has taken over for rhetoric as instrumental discourse, it is not simply a modern form of rhetoric. For the rhetorical tradition was far more complex, aligned at times with logic and also encompassing a poetics. Rhetoric's troubles often stemmed from its pliability, and from its attention to its audience. For here is where the abuses seemed most dangerous. It was rescued time and again by those who insisted on its positive social and political function, on its basis in reason, on its use for the good.[136] Propaganda keeps its eye on its primary goal: efficacious persuasion. And it does so without recourse to a legitimating discourse of either logic or poetics. Indeed, both truth and beauty are equally important means—not ends—of certain forms of propaganda; they possess psychological rather than metaphysical value for the propagandist.

Propaganda already has a place in art history. It is a supplement that enables art history to consider its activity a positive if not a redemptive one. The work of art as a work of propaganda—the work that points incessantly, uncomfortably to its signified, at the expense of the signifier—redeems the discipline's attention to form. The work of art as propaganda is transparent, invisible, pointing incessantly to its faulty god (Nazism, Fascism, Jesuitism, in short, ideology). Propaganda is a difficult subject in art history insofar as the aesthetic is merely a guise that can be stripped away. What is so bothersome about it is that it is easy to strip away the art to see the ideological substructure but nearly impossible to operate the process in reverse. Speer's work will always be read as Nazi architecture but never unambiguously as good architecture.

One might protest that the new art history often looks around the object (context), back at the spectator (psychoanalysis, reception), that the object is not always central. But with the recent "pictorial turn" (W. J. T. Mitchell), the visuality of art history's objects, their opacity, has been reasserted as the center of the discipline. Art history is an idolatrous practice insofar as it cannot do without its Golden Calf; as a discipline it is incapable of seeing that calf not as an object. The twentieth-century museum, with its galleries filled with objects separated from the altars of their original gods, is sufficient evidence of art history's glorification of its objects.

Until now art history has *needed* propaganda—the objects set before the people by a false god, objects that fool their worshipers into believing in pernicious ideology—to be cordoned off. The object deemed propaganda is accused of idolatry, of a misdirected use of the image: misdirected because the object is seen past to the false god. In propaganda one worships the prototype rather than its iteration. Though in the case of the work of propagandistic art we may deem its god a false one, this is, in the Christian tradition, a "correct" use of images. But if the viewer of propaganda is engaging in a licit form of viewing, what is the status of the view of art history?

In making the *image* the god, is art history not a modern form of idolatry? For what is idolatry if not the worship of the thing itself rather than the thing represented? Has art history not labored mightily to focus on the object, at the expense of that which lays behind, under, and over it? Our eyes are filled with the glow of the Golden Calf. We are the discipline that has performed the longest dance around it. So that the dangers of art history's own idolatrous practice remain concealed, the work of propagandistic art is cast as a dangerous supplement. But just as writing infected the living *logos* in Plato's *polis*, so too our sacred "art" is infected by false gods, by ideology. And so too is propagandistic art infected by art. The rapid movement through the work of art to its ideological basis that I have described as a response, covers over, is a denial of another experience of the object as art. I hope to have convinced my reader as to what is at stake in this response. But having described the response, we must also move beyond it. The artistry of propaganda needs to be brought back to bear on the phenomenon.

Here lies the challenge: is it not possible to both see and see past (beyond) the visible, the work of art? We must endeavor to look at once at and past, lest our eyes be burned. "You are requested to close an eye."[137]

3

THE PROPAGANDIST

The presence of the organization creates one more phenomenon: the propagandist is always separated from the propagandee, he remains a stranger to him. Even in the actual contact of human relations, at meetings, in door-to-door visits, the propagandist is of a different order; he is nothing else and nothing more than the representative of the organization—or, rather, a delegated fraction of it. He remains a manipulator, in the shadow of the machine. He knows why he speaks certain words and what effect they should have. His words are no longer human words but technically calculated words; they no longer express a feeling or a spontaneous idea, but reflect an organization even when they seem entirely spontaneous. Thus the propagandist is never asked to be involved in what he is saying, for, if it becomes necessary, he may be asked to say the exact opposite with similar conviction. He must, of course, believe in the cause he serves, but not in his particular argument.

JACQUES ELLUL, *PROPAGANDA* ([1962] 1965)

Master Lorenzo used to say that Our Blessed Father [Ignatius] taught him how to obey, and he did it in this way. With his walking stick Our Blessed Father drew a window that he was to make in a large old wall: –and make it neither too large nor too small.– In the meantime the Father Procurator of the Casa passed by and said to him: –Master Lorenzo this window is too small, make it a little larger.– He simply enlarged it. When he was done, Our Blessed Father returned and saw that it was larger than the window he designed. He said: –Brother, what have you done? It's larger than the one that I designed for you.– He responded: –Father, the Father Procurator told me to make it larger.– He made him redo it and make it small. When he was done Our Blessed Father returned and said. –Brother, undo it again and make it as you had it before.– And he redid it in this way, without saying a word. And from then on he obeyed blindly.

FROM THE NECROLOGY OF THE JESUIT BROTHER LORENZO TRISTANO (1586)

One of the most striking aspects of the literature on propaganda—both in theory and in historical practice—is that the "propagandist" is an anonymous figure. With few exceptions (like Goebbels, who is accorded more of the role of theorist of propaganda and author of the Third Reich than author of propaganda in its specific productions), the propagandist remains a hidden character. Ideology, or the institution that embraces and enforces that ideology, is the apparent author of propaganda. As such, propaganda as a "work" is inimical to a Kantian notion of art, dependent as the latter is on the authorship of free individuals. Thus, with specific reference to authorship, when considering art as propaganda we are immediately faced with a formidable obstacle. How can an institution produce art?

The inimicability of corporate authorship to the very notion of art has long stood at the center of debate about the Jesuit Style and was extended to the Catholic Baroque. The most pointed and influential articulation of this thesis was the centerpiece of Benedetto Croce's work on the Baroque, which was widely influential for generations of intellectuals, including art historians. Without invoking the word "propaganda," Croce argued that the domination of the Church in the Counter-Reformation was inimical to the development of aesthetics, for art cannot be produced by an institution. Linking the Baroque directly to the Jesuits ("il 'secentismo' o 'barocchismo' non è altro che il 'gesuitismo nell'arte'"), Croce characterized the Baroque as an anti-aesthetic because institutions are incapable of the "eternal spiritual and moral moment" necessary to the production of an aesthetic.[1]

Croce's view is marked by long-held beliefs about the domination of the Baroque period and its art by the Jesuits. As I argued above, Jesuit corporate authorship—a prime product of the "Jesuit myth"—was a key theme of the Jesuit Style. This topos, which I term the Jesuit Ur-Author, presumed that the Society of Jesus "authored" all works produced for the Society, although these early histories did not call into question the status of Jesuit productions as "art." For art historians writing in the nineteenth century, the Jesuit corporate identity overwhelmed individual artists' work, allowing the Jesuit Style to signal that art and architecture were expressions of ideology.

This early idea of Jesuit corporate authorship, advanced in ignorance of archival sources that show how Jesuit works actually were built, would be debunked over the course of the first decades of the twentieth century. The notion of the corporate author became increasingly difficult to sustain as art historians investigated the careers of artists and architects, tracing their development. The discovery of individual stylistic trajectories was greeted with relief, for once deemed the creative products of individuals, key works for the Jesuit Style argument (such as the Jesuit Mother Church, Il Gesù) comfortably took their place in a history of art comprised by works of individual genius.

The persistent denial of the Jesuit corporate author, even now, brings forcibly home how much rests on style as the direct manifestation of, among other criteria, including time and region, individuality.[2] At a famous conference on the topic of the Jesuits and the arts held in New York in 1969, Rudolf Wittkower, assessing the past seventy years of scholarship, concluded by affirming the autonomy of the artist in the employ of the Society of Jesus. He remarked that in spite of the Jesuits' interest in controlling design, "insofar as style is concerned, it was the artists who influenced the Jesuits and not vice versa."[3]

Wittkower here generates an image truly worthy of the Enlightenment: Art History assists the Artist in the capitulation of Religion.

Because of the premium placed on artistic freedom in the twentieth century, it is fair to say that Wittkower and many other art historians who have written about Jesuit architecture have viewed this specific artist-patron relationship as strained.[4] Indicative of the tension surrounding the authorship issue is Luciano Patetta's comment on an article by Diego Angeli of 1908 that portrayed the Jesuit artists as cogs in a larger administrative machinery. Angeli writes:

> Most of these artists were creatures of the Company of Jesus, many of whom wore the cloth, and all of whom worked in their churches and palaces. And they worked following the instructions of the [Jesuit] generals who called competitions, selected amongst models, changed plans, against which the artists did not even think to protest.[5]

As we shall see below, Angeli's portrayal is not in fact inaccurate. Perhaps only the assumption that a Jesuit should want to protest might have struck a Jesuit architect as misplaced if ultimately realistic. In an important essay on Jesuit architecture, Patetta responded to this passage symptomatically mistranscribing the last phrase as "potessero" ("were unable") instead of "pensassero" ("did not even think"):

> This last assertion [that the Jesuits were unable (*sic*) to protest] is entirely false. When artists like Bartolomeo Ammannati, Pellegrino Tibaldi, Jacopo Vignola, Giacomo della Porta, Girolamo Rainaldi, Gian Lorenzo Bernini, Francesco Maria Ricchini, Filippo Juvarra, Carlo Fontana, Alfonso Torreggiani, Luigi Vanvitelli worked for the Jesuits, they worked for them with full liberty of expression, as is proven by the diversity both amongst their works and between the work of these artists and those internal to the Society.[6]

For Patetta (who countered Angeli's comment about *Jesuit* architects with a statement that refers exclusively to prominent *non*-Jesuit architects), what is at stake in the Jesuit Style is whether architects working for the Society were at liberty to express themselves freely. Were we to apply the same criteria to artists and architects working for pope or prince, of course we would have precisely the same kind of doubts that these artists exercised full liberty of expression.[7] The architect Vincenzo Scamozzi (1548–1616) articulated something of the early modern architect's quandary when he wrote that serving a "principe assoluto" was viable if that prince were virtuous and generous. But it was preferable "for man to live freely."[8] For Patetta, part of the postwar generation invested in individualism,[9] the liberty of the artist proved the nonideological nature of Jesuit architecture.

The lay or Jesuit identity of the architects plays a critical role in debates over the Jesuit Style. The Jesuit Style argument has survived as long as it has in part by polarizing the evidence of who produced Jesuit architecture. Some who argue against it emphasize the work of prestigious non-Jesuit architects (whose Jesuit buildings are stylistically indis-

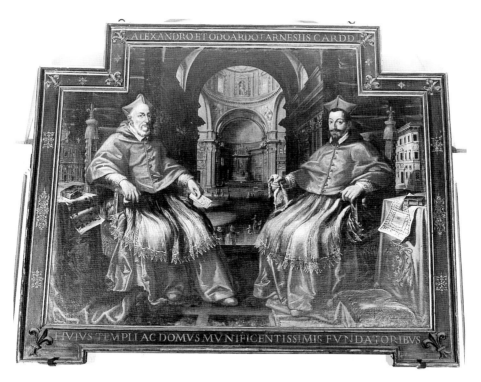

Anonymous, *Cardinals Alessandro and Odoardo Farnese,* ca. 1615–25. Ante-sacristy, Il Gesù, Rome.

tinguishable from their *non*-Jesuit works) as evidence that the Jesuits were not masters of style. Jesuit architects present different problems.[10] Giovanni Tristano, for example, was responsible for a series of buildings in a stripped-down style, in keeping with the modest financial resources of the early Society. Not surprisingly, these buildings—built by a member of the Society, comparatively simple and hence apparently consistent with a stated belief system, and because of their homogeneity creating an impression of seriality—lend themselves readily to characterization as "Jesuit." The consistency of a Jesuit architect's work, whether attributable to the Society's program or to the unity of individual style, makes the Jesuit Style argument hard to dismiss.

At times a prominent non-Jesuit patron further complicated the relationship between the Society and its architect. The dispute over the vaulting of the Gesù, with the Jesuits preferring a flat roof for its acoustic superiority and the patron Alessandro Farnese (see fig. 15, left) insisting on the barrel vault that was eventually built, is a prime example. The episode has received much play in the literature because the patron's priority in the decision-making process poses a serious challenge to the Jesuit Ur-Author thesis.[11] Clare Robertson, echoing Haskell, neatly summed up the opposing view: "if we are to speak of a style for the Gesù in Rome, it is surely a Farnese style rather than a Jesuit one."[12] Robertson's conclusion suggests that while Jesuit authorship of a Jesuit Style is still unpalatable, the impulse to attribute a stylistic designation based on the similar though more palatable criterion of taste remains in place. Not surprisingly, Manfredo Tafuri's reading of this episode as demonstrating Vignola's "obsequious conformity" is little discussed.[13]

The idea that architects operated independently from the institution produces a distorted picture of the Society's complex architectural planning. Marxist art historians have written extensively of the imbrication of patrons in the production of architecture.[14] The history of Medieval architecture, for example, less fettered by knowledge of names and the oeuvres of individual architects, often must be written as institutional history. The study of Jesuit art is a symptomatic chapter in the history of art in which some distortion of artistic autonomy has been tolerated. I believe this is fueled in part by the political and historiographic background of the Jesuit Style, which reminds us that the autographic aspect of artistic production must, for important reasons, remain fundamental to art historical explanation.[15] As Meyer Schapiro wrote in the early years of the Cold War of the diversity of styles in avant-garde art, they reflect the "individual's freedom of choice," which is one of the "the most cherished values of our culture."[16] Though understandable, this resistance is difficult to reconcile with the overwhelming evidence that the Society of Jesus was the most controlling of artistic production of the early modern religious orders.[17]

While art historians who reject the Jesuit Style often rely on the argument of artistic liberty, a second line of explanation accounts for the evidence of institutionalized building practices. Since the beginning of the twentieth century Jesuit scholars sustained that while no Jesuit Style can be said to have existed, the Jesuits did have a clear way of proceeding in building, a "modo nostro."[18] This phrase, used widely from Ignatius onward to describe a Jesuit way of doing things, most often referred to the functional rather than the "aesthetic" aspects of architecture. In arguing that the Jesuitness of Jesuit architecture was all about practicality, these historians (Braun, Duhr, Ackerman, and others) also diffused the ideological meaning attributed to Jesuit architecture by the term "Jesuit Style."[19] It is an indication of art history's investment in style that practicality could divert attention from ideology. Thus while the "modo nostro" argument is essentially sound, it also bypasses crucial issues. By arguing that the Jesuits were only interested in how their buildings worked, leaving the question of form to architects, those who favor the "modo nostro" explanation downplay ideological content.[20] I too am interested in the *modo nostro* but will show how the path of design taken by the institution, whether to practical or "aesthetic" ends, has everything to do with the ideology of Jesuit architecture.

The scholar who has taken the lead in shifting the terms of the debate is Richard Bösel, who has made the most thorough study of the corpus of Jesuit architecture and its documentary sources to date. Focusing on the Society's Italian churches, Bösel has found abundant examples to support his claim that the Society did have an architectural culture expressed through self-conscious typological citations.[21] From generation to generation Jesuit architects built new versions of buildings of central importance to the Jesuits: the Gesù in Rome, the Collegio Romano, S. Fedele, among others. Their corporate culture made these exemplars known and provided a motive for keeping them in the institutional repertoire. At the same time, this culture allowed for and encouraged new solutions. Hence the "prime objects" (as Kubler termed them) provided what Bösel terms "primary material" that was always present and conscious but which did not prevent adaptation to contemporary needs, both practical and stylistic, as use and taste changed. Putting to one side the question of style in favor of a notion of an architectural culture, Bösel broke down the function-aesthetic polarity. In its place he provided a positive explanation for the coherence of Jesuit architecture based on the use of architectural typologies.

For Bösel, authorship is not a central issue. Yet the tension between art and institution that marks the debates outlined above had already taken root in the early modern period. While the corporation and the architect may not have been as inimical to one another as imagined in modern times, it is important to take note of how the Jesuits negotiated this tension in the process of making architecture. I view Jesuit projects as tapping into two mutually reinforcing aspects of authorship: Jesuit authorship as a propagandistic activity that advanced the interests of the Society and the artist's design of the project as a means to that advancement.

THE JESUIT CORPORATE CULTURE OF ARCHITECTURE

The Jesuit corporate author failed in art history for one principal reason. It assumed that the Jesuitness of Jesuit architecture is legible at the level of style: that the Jesuit control of architecture amounted to the dictation of specific forms; that individuals who were Jesuits designed Jesuit forms because they were Jesuit forms themselves. In insisting on style as that which drove and thus defined the organization's architectural interests (even after no Jesuit Style could be found), we are destined to misunderstand the Jesuitness of Jesuit architecture.[22]

Far from designing a recognizable Jesuit Style, the Jesuits wished above all for the desirable effects of the success of their building projects: enhancement of their reputation and adherence.[23] Success is essentially a political category that looks outward rather than inward. It amounts to the articulation of a public ambition, of a concern for how the Society was perceived and listened to by the outside world. The Jesuit desire for success and the effects that flowed from it dictated the control of their architects and a rule-bound process of design and construction, the same hallmarks of Jesuitness in architecture that led earlier historians to posit the existence of the Jesuit Style.

Jesuit control was far less regimented and far more fraught than usually presumed. For control—a defining aspect of Jesuitness generally in the anti-Jesuit tradition—is but a symptom of Jesuit anxieties about the possibility of the public failure of their enterprise. Jesuit documents on architecture should be read with this in mind. Reassessing Jesuit control as a symptom rather than the defining quality or aim of the organization reveals the productive aspect of institution and author as forces that vie with or against each other.

Two interrelated aspects of Jesuit institutional practices bear directly on the nature of the authorship of buildings in the Jesuit architectural enterprise. First, with the rapid expansion of the Society's building infrastructure within decades of its founding, the Jesuits put in place administrative rules for building. Starting in the 1560s, the administration centralized the coordination of projects in Rome rather than leave such decisions in the hands of the Jesuits on the site. The Society was certainly not the first religious order to have created *policies* for its buildings.[24] But it was, to my knowledge, the only order to systematically control design of every building it paid for through its central administration in Rome. Just why this took place, it has recently been inferred, may have been the legacy of Ignatius's own tenacious interest in building the Society as much brick by brick as soul by soul.[25] Circumstances also played a role: with faster means of communication,[26] the now well-established practice of using paper for drawings, and the rapid and international expansion of the order, the coordination of building was at once possible and, in the minds of the Jesuits necessary. The Jesuits of the early modern world had new means and arguably greater interest—and success—in systematizing their building practices than had their monastic and mendicant predecessors.

Ignatius himself controlled building projects closely in the last years of his life. Following his death in 1556, at the first General Congregation of 1558, the Jesuits articulated the administration's need to have a building policy to control both quality of construction and conformity with the Society's modesty.[27] The 1558 decree stated a principle of control; in 1565 general Francis Borgia established a concrete procedure in decreeing that the Society's general was to be conferred "with regard to the form and manner" of all buildings.[28] The next year he sent out a circular specifying that—for important buildings— a drawing be submitted to Rome, together with an evaluation by local "consultores."[29] Once approved, the drawings, one of which was archived in Rome, became authoritative and no departure was allowed without permission. The consultant reviewing the projects in Rome whose opinion most mattered was that of the *consiliarius aedificiorum* (or *revisore romano*)—an architect when available but usually the mathematician of the Collegio Romano—whose official duty was to review plans for the general.[30] In addition to their in-house *consultore,* the Jesuits often conferred with local architects, although the general remained the final arbiter in matters of building.

Once these basic practices were put in place they remained, although an important attempt to revise them advises us of their limitations. In 1593 the Jesuit architect and painter Giuseppe Valeriano wrote a memo recommending tightening the organization of building supervision, which he hoped would be discussed at the meeting of the fifth General Congregation.[31] By that date Valeriano had spent twenty years in a supervisory capacity for Jesuit buildings in Spain and Italy and had designed several buildings himself. He knew well what the problems were. Valeriano was disturbed by the interference of Jesuits, "pseudoarchitects," who, stepping out of their assigned occupations, found personal delight in architecture and insinuated their opinions to the detriment of the project. To remedy the situation, which often brought about unnecessary expense and resulted in buildings that were "mal fatte," Valeriano proposed that the Society's hierarchy of design be strengthened (not diminished). He wanted to ensure that once "un Superior assoluto" in Rome approved a design it could not be altered; that an architect choose a designer (presumably a Jesuit himself) who might create designs suited to the Society's special needs; and that one or two secular architects be consulted in difficult cases. Jesuits on the site should be chosen to administer projects but not to supervise them if they were not qualified. *Capomaestri secolari* were preferable to incompetent Jesuits. Although Valeriano's recommendations do not appear in the acts of the Congregation, and no new legislation resulted, his concerns were addressed directly by reinforcement of existing rules.

There is, of course, virtually no client, private or institutional, who does not engage at some level in planning a project, from its program to its budget. But Jesuit control of their building projects exceeds the ordinary controls exerted by patrons in its self-consciousness. To cite an early example, in 1561 the Roman administration wrote to the rector of the Jesuit establishment in Loreto, eager to build in nearby Macerata: "Beginning to build seems a matter requiring much thought, not so much beginning to build but the way of beginning, since this is a college to be built from its foundations, and therefore it will need to be planned with regard not only to the present, but also to the future."[32] This prudence persisted. Listen to the cautious beginning of the project to renovate Ignatius's chapel in Rome sounded by one of the general's assistants in late 1694:

> Because the good conduct of such a work requires not only particular attention and care, but also some real prudence so that errors are not made on the essential things, errors which can result in irreparable mistakes, or when reparable, changes that wouldn't be made because they would be so expensive, and that perhaps would bring the work to a halt instead of bringing it to completion. Therefore before beginning the project it is expedient to seriously examine the whole project, with the opinions of the most expert, to be able to move forward with sureness.[33]

Care was always taken to avoid mistakes that cost money, but money was not all that concerned the Jesuits.

Time after time Giuseppe Valeriano wrote from his posting in Spain to his superiors in Rome of the importunities to the Society of bad architecture. First, though perhaps not above all, poor planning meant wasted money. Second, poor construction posed physical danger ("In Leone di Spagna after the first mass and sermon in our church, with the doors closed while our brothers were resting, the church fell down, which frightened and shocked the entire population who had been there"; "In the casa professa in Naples the corridors fell in: the architect advised the superior in the presence of many [50] fathers who now live in great danger of being killed").[34] Third, and this is perhaps the most important point, Valeriano pointed to the disgrace of poor design and the risk that embarrassment posed to the Society (the "poor edification of others"; causing "disquiet, rumors amongst our own and the dis-edification of the non-Jesuits who serve us, who, sooner or later, make note of our imperfections"; "In Seville . . . the church was built poorly by our own members and it opened and in many parts of the city there were bad signs: this contributed little to the edification of the city, because it was built by us with the great liberality of our friends and it is not a durable building"; "In Bavaria it was the idea of one of our own to build a church and tower, and because of the defect of a rector and a brother who designed the building, the tower fell and ruined part of the church with a loss of approximately 80,000 scudi: and with great damage to the honor of the most Serene Duke of Bavaria who spent the money; and the dis-edification of our friends and the exultation of the heretics, as the Duke himself recounted to me").[35]

The comments of Valeriano (and others) point to a clear awareness of the dual meaning of "edification" for the Society, a Pauline play of words drawn on by Michelangelo in his self-representation.[36] Strong, stable, and beautiful buildings provided both the physical place and the metaphor for the improvement of the soul. The disturbing incidence of quite the opposite, bad building, was literally "disedifying." Poor architecture worked against the Society's goal of building a community of faithful, of supporting faith, whether that of the ordinary man or woman of the congregation or the wealthy and powerful patron of the order. In consoling his fellow Jesuits in Zaragossa about their own difficulties, Ignatius referred to the Society of Jesus itself as a "splendid and distinguished spiritual edifice," whose foundations were as deep as they were for having been built on "contradiction [opposition]."[37] When Ignatius pored over the plans for the Casa Professa in Rome and spent hours corresponding with Jesuits in others cities about their new buildings, he was indeed "building" for the Society and for the Church: a brick for every soul. We need to look more closely at the aims for their buildings, at the aspirations and the insecurities that drove this sort of control.

The second, related aspect of the institutional architectural practices of the Jesuits concerns why and how the Society employed Jesuits as architects. They preferred to do so when they could, and as a result Jesuit architects designed many of the Society's buildings, from well-known works like the Collegio Romano to much less architecturally distinguished ones.[38] While the notion that a Jesuit architect is the bearer of Jesuit form has been exaggerated, it is true that the Jesuit architect was not as "free" as his lay counterpart, that his appurtenance to the organization in some way shaped his practice. If we are to consider Jesuits who were members of and worked for the Society in a special class, what makes a so-called Jesuit architect to begin with? Here I refer not to conventional training: most Jesuit architects of note received their training before they became Jesuits, in the secular world; some, like Valeriano, were autodidacts.[39] If membership is a principal criterion, does Giovanni Tristano's entrance into the order as a forty-year-old man, twenty years later than Andrea Pozzo took his vows, make him any less Jesuit as an architect than Pozzo? Or, if being bound to the Society at the moment in time in which a design is made is the criterion, in what does that boundedness consist? A distinctive Jesuit spirituality as expressed in the arts has been argued by other historians but mostly for Jesuits working as painters or sculptors.[40] Here I wish to focus on obedience, the leitmotiv of Jesuit membership. What is the place of individual creativity in a culture of obedience?[41] We must rethink Jesuit discipline, principally the vow of obedience, as the site of a central tension in the Society: obedience as a form of discipline and a generative force.

Though a foundational element in all religious vocations, the vow of obedience received particular emphasis in the Society of Jesus. Ignatius made it the cornerstone of the Jesuit life, writing in a famous letter, later summarized in the Jesuit *Constitutions,* that he intended it to be the characteristic virtue of the Society.[42]

> We should perform with great alacrity, spiritual joy, and perseverance whatever has been commanded to us, persuading ourselves that everything is just and renouncing with blind obedience any contrary opinion and judgment of our own in all things which the superior commands. . . . We ought to be firmly convinced that everyone of those who live under obedience ought to allow himself to be carried and directed by Divine Providence through the agency of the superior as if he were a lifeless body which allows itself to be carried to any place and to be treated in any manner desired, or as if he were an old man's staff which serves in any place and in any manner whatsoever in which the holder wishes to use it. For in this way the obedient man ought joyfully to devote himself to any task whatsoever in which the superior desires to employ him to aid the whole body of the religious Institute; and he ought to hold it as certain that by this procedure he is conforming himself with the divine will more than by anything else he could do while following his own will and different judgment.[43]

Blind obedience, the lifeless body, the "stick," the "corpse": these are among the most threatening and parodied aspects of Jesuit spirituality.[44] But the practice of obedience is more complex than blind obedience suggests. The mere execution of a command cannot be considered an act of true obedience unless one surrenders one's will in so doing. But such a surrender—a great sacrifice since "this disposition of will in man is of so great worth"—is but a first stage. Far more difficult than obedience of the will is obedience of the understanding. If the latter is not mastered obedience will eventually fail altogether, for "in the long run the will cannot obey without violence against one's judgment."[45]

Obedience governs two types of relations among members of the Society. Ignatius recognized that the obedience required by the superior of all Jesuits was practical, playing an important role in the maintenance of hierarchies of all sorts, earthly and heavenly: "the better this subordination is kept, the better the government."[46] As we will see played out in the superiors' correspondence, obedience was an organizational necessity. But above all, it is a governing virtue, an internal practice whose reward is the perfection of the individual will in conformity with divine will. In the moment the individual allows himself "to be carried by Divine Providence," obedience releases the individual from his own will to become God's willing servant. In this respect, obedience also has a transcendent purpose. In its ideal form obedience can be, paradoxically, at the same time a binding and a liberating practice. According to this way of thinking, the Jesuit architect's design, whatever form it might take, becomes a drawing out or a manifestation of Divine Providence—

not a denial of individual expression but rather the only route through which it can reach perfection. This view of obedience allows for the possibility of creativity within a culture of obedience.

Nonetheless, it *is* difficult to understand obedience as a creative principle because in order to be reborn into obedience "as a walking stick, a lifeless body," a death seems to be required. The astonishing incident recounted in the eulogy of the Jesuit lay brother and builder Lorenzo Tristano (quoted in an epigraph to this chapter) exemplifies the extreme reading of obedience as erasure of the individual. In this anecdote the Jesuit practicing obedience gives over his judgment. The parallel to the propagandist is irresistible, for any institution that produces propaganda requires of the propagandist that he put aside his individual strivings for that of the cause.

Jesuit letters document graphically the obedience demanded of its architects by the superiors. Cases of insubordination reveal anxieties that obedience was intended to keep at bay. For example, general Thyrsio Gonzalez warned the rector of the Jesuit college in Dubrovnik (1699), "Brother Enrico [Laloyau, the architect] should not make any changes [to the design] awaiting my orders, that he should execute exactly and to which he should be completely subordinate."[47] Drawings such as Laloyau's were to bear the approval of Rome; as many documents attest, these approvals had authority. Incessant references in correspondence to past approvals kept straight the decisions made when designs were in process. At times, insistence on this procedure had to do with protecting the building process from the unpredictable outcomes decried by Giuseppe Valeriano in surveying the Society's building projects in Spain. Given the wide range of talent among the architects working for the Society, the Jesuits wished to avoid the bunglings of incompetent architects, the incursions of individual initiative, and the fantasy of the overly ambitious.[48] For example, in 1681 general Gian Paolo Oliva wrote to the provincial of Naples that the design for the ceiling of the church in Catanzaro had been decided on by various unnamed "experts" but that under no circumstances should it be executed by padre Carlo Quercia, whose "ill-formed architecture" ("malregolata architettura") had already "maimed more colleges."[49] Regarding the Jesuit college in Ancona, general Franz Retz wrote to the vice rector Giuseppe Vanuzzi (1739):

> I am displeased that in the construction of this church you are working more from your own caprice than from the ideas that were already established and agreed upon and you have thus loaded the college with debts.[50]

When mistakes were made or obedience was violated the Jesuits required penance. An egregious case of disobedience on the part of the rector of the Sulmona college elicited the following censure from the general Michelangelo Tamburini (1717):

> Before receiving your letters, I received news that certainly amazed me, that is that you ordered work begun [on the building], having the foundation of the church laid before re-

ceiving approval of the design: this is a matter which, other than being itself very imprudent, is also contrary to my orders. Such an attempt, so lacking in consideration and full of irreligiosity made me contemplate sending you a final and grave order to remove yourself from the project and to cease work on it all together. And you would force me to make this order, but also further and greater resentment, if you were to continue to fail to demonstrate the requisite obedience.[51]

In matters of building, it was as much the local administrators as the architects who were subject to obedience and to strict control. For Vibo Valentia (Naples), padre Carlo Quercia designed a residence far too large for the number of Jesuits ever expected to live in the town. The ambition and expense of the scheme were revealed in 1668 when general Oliva, who knew well who the architect was, wrote to the rector of the college:

[T]he unconsidered vastness of the idea of the project, which has uselessly cost the college so much money and so much trouble for you, pains me. How is it possible that the person who designed the building planned 36 rooms for a house that will never be inhabited by more than 12 or 14! The architect, if he is one of our own, would merit a great penance, and the same for whoever approved the plan.[52]

While a principal danger of such mistakes was financial, these documents allow a glimpse into the Jesuits' fear of failure, of their whole enterprise of construction.

The authoritative air of admonitions coming from Rome does not always mask insecurities that could appear at every level of the design hierarchy: not just the general but also those specifically appointed to judge designs. It comes as something of a surprise that at least some of the seventeenth-century *revisori* were insecure about their judging ability. For example, in response to a complex plan submitted for the small Jesuit church in Montepulciano, the *revisore* appears unwilling to take a risk on a novel and ambitious plan: "Since Montepulciano is not so far from Rome, where there are so many small and very beautiful churches, I would think it much more expedient to follow a design that one can see has succeeded [*ben riuscita in opera*], than to risk falling into errors that very often do not appear in plan."[53] At times the *revisore* and others involved in the process of approving designs (such as the father provincials) relied less on their own judgment and more on what they referred to as "shared opinion," or approval "by use." The Jesuit church in Castellamare (Campania), whose plan was approved in 1624, would serve ten years later as model for their church in Chieti (Abruzzi): "This plan is the same as the church of Castellamare, approved by experience by shared opinion [*approvata dal'esperienca per la commune opinione*]."[54] Padre Giles François Gottignies (1630–89), *revisore* in the late seventeenth century, wrote in 1679 on the plans for the new church in Termini (Palermo): "[T]his [design] seems good; moreover, I feel that this same plan has been followed with satisfaction in other locations in Sicily and therefore is approved by use [*approbata dal uso*]."[55] The Jesuits' repetition of their own forms—also to be understood as an expression of the institution's drive to replicate itself—turns out to be a mark of their insecurities as well.[56] New designs posed rewards as well as risks. Some Jesuits assigned to evaluate those risks mistrusted their own judgment, relying on collective opinion and on what had already been proven successful by use.

This is, admittedly, a selective review of the Society's buildings practices, but it is also a revealing one. In stressing the practice of obedience in its psychological complexity, I wish to emphasize a different aspect of a familiar image of the Jesuits exerting strict control over their architects and their building projects. The Jesuits did shape design as a consequence of their intimate involvement in the process. Yet because their design aims revolved more around the process than around a specific type of design, neither style nor control is a marker of Jesuit ideology in architecture. Arguably the opposite is true on the issue of style: Jesuit control over their architectural production makes style an *untenable* category for analysis. For, dependent as it is on the (however dubious) unity of the individual, style cannot easily be understood as a collaboration between an organization and an individual. This is not to say that there is no struggle: the individual, in spite of his vow, cannot easily submit his judgment to that of his superiors. But it is, I argue, precisely in that struggle—whether within the individual or between him and the organization—that ideology is at work. The Jesuitness of Jesuit architecture lies in the process in which design takes shape. In Jesuit culture obedience—complex and difficult as it was—cannot be considered coercive. For to assert that the Jesuits controlled an individual who in reality submitted willingly to a vow of obedience is to misconstrue the nature of the religious vocation and as such, is surely more of a reflection on us than on the Jesuit architect.

I wish to reorient our understanding of Jesuit control in architecture. The documents cited here suggest that control was not the aim of Jesuit culture but a means employed to create a positive public image through a work of art. This will become clearer in the detailed discussion of the genesis of one Jesuit project that follows.

THE DESIGN OF THE CHAPEL OF ST. IGNATIUS

In the design process for the Chapel of St. Ignatius (fig. 16), the most important Jesuit architectural project of the late seventeenth century, many of the themes discussed above are played out in exemplary fashion. As will become clear, the design of the chapel was a deeply collaborative affair between the Jesuits and their architect as well as a group of critics and the public at large. We need be attentive to what desires drove that collaboration. A crucial issue that unfolded in the public realm was whether Andrea Pozzo (fig. 17), a Jesuit, should design the chapel or whether non-Jesuit architects should be invited to submit designs. The proceedings reveal that the competition, the selection of an architect, and the subsequent development of the final design became a public spectacle. While such publicness may seem precisely the opposite of the invisible and anonymous context for the production of most propaganda alluded to at the beginning of this chapter, it was a directed strategy by which the Jesuits controlled the work's reception. The at-

FIG. 16
Andrea Pozzo, Chapel of St. Ignatius, 1695–99. Il Gesù, Rome.

tention paid by the Jesuits to public opinion from the chapel's inception to its unveiling was part and parcel of the chapel's function as propaganda. Yet an analysis of the copious surviving documentation shows that publicness was fraught with tension as internal organizational practices and obedience were put to the test.

FIG. 17
Caredus Allet, *Andrea Pozzo,* 1717.

The analysis of the design process that follows is made possible by the survival of two key documents. Both are unsigned but surely authored by the Jesuit coadjutor Carlo Mauro Bonacina, Lombard by birth and the general's personal assistant. Entrusted with the administrative direction of this project, Bonacina produced two lengthy narrative accounts that merit brief description before detailed analysis.

The first document, the "Diligenze," forty pages in manuscript, is written in diary form over a six-month period.[57] The entries extend from the first presentation by Pozzo of a design to the general (20 February 1695) to the rental of work space from a neighbor for construction (4 August 1695). The "Diligenze," recording day by day the submission of drawings—at first by Pozzo alone and then by other architects—followed by the construction of models—several terra-cottas and then one expensive wooden model of the agreed-upon design—provides the most detailed account in Jesuit records of the interaction of architects and Jesuit and lay experts. The document makes extensive use of quotations from other letters and documents written by architects and consultants who commented on the plans at various stages of the decision-making process. In spite of its appearance, the "Diligenze" is a considerably biased account of the proceedings. For reasons that I discuss below, Bonacina wrote the "Diligenze" in order to justify the choice of Andrea Pozzo, the in-house architect, for this project.

The second document written by Bonacina, the "Ristretto," seventy pages in manuscript, in narrative form, is a quirky personal account of the highlights of his administration of the project.[58] The "Ristretto" opens with Bonacina arriving in Rome and catalyzing general Gonzalez to begin the long-desired renovation of Ignatius's chapel. Moving between the practical aspects—procuring of stones and materials, organization of five hundred artists and builders—and the public life of the construction project—a competition for the statue of St. Ignatius, an unveiling at midpoint of construction, the dramatic raising of the columns, a papal visit, and candle-lit unveiling—the "Ristretto's" main task is to justify Bonacina's role as director of the project.

Our narrator's position was controversial at the time for reasons that may seem strange today. But in the showy court culture of Rome in 1695 Bonacina cut a rather poor figure. Many detractors believed that he, a mere brother, not even a priest, would be incapable of bringing the project to a successful conclusion. As a result, the procurator of the Society, Pier Francesco Orta, officially held the position of director, although Bonacina filled the position in every sense.[59] Given the publicness of the insult it is no wonder that Bonacina wrote the "Ristretto." And though the document is filled with demonstrations of his own modesty and complaints about the vanity of others, the "Ristretto" from beginning to end vaunts Bonacina's success. He even attaches a set of instructions for administrators of other, like projects. It is safe to assume that in proscribing the qualities of the ideal administrator—"better a bit bilious than too phlegmatic, or the project will never get done"—Bonacina was describing himself.[60]

Why Bonacina composed the "Ristretto" and the "Diligenze" in the first place and what their functions might have been remain matters for speculation. The "Ristretto," the far more personal account, exists in a fine manuscript copy with a portrait and dedication to Clement XI on its first page. Whether Clement XI—who while still Cardinal Albani, in 1695, anonymously submitted the drawing by Pozzo that eventually won universal favor—solicited a copy of the account, we do not know. Of the two copies of the manuscript that survive, one is dated 1706, a year before Bonacina's death and seven years after the unveiling of the project. Was Bonacina just getting around to writing his memoir, which is so full of quotes and eyewitness accounts that it has the freshness of a document just dashed off on the moment? Or might there have been a specific reason to curry the pope's favor at that time? We do not know. But the instructions Bonacina attached to the document "for he who would direct a similar project" point to his or his superiors' intention to circulate the document within the Society if not beyond.

Bonacina certainly composed the "Diligenze" as the design of the chapel proceeded in 1695, and this document functioned as an internal if not also an external one. A payment for two copies of some incomplete form of it in May 1695[61] confirms the well-documented concern around the proceedings within the Society; three of the last entries record the circulation of the "Diligenze" together with other letters among Jesuit superiors.[62] The "Ristretto" was composed, it appears, post facto, at the very least as a form of self-justification, at the very most to glorify the glorious project of the chapel. But should a Jesuit have been so interested in earthly glory that he would create what appears to be such a self-serving document? The tension between these two aims is apparent in Bonacina's use of the third person throughout the "Ristretto," although it is abundantly clear from the personal nature of several of the accounts that only he could have been its author. The intention, however, to circulate both of these documents is important, another mark of the self-consciousness that marks the Chapel of St. Ignatius as a work of propaganda.

The richness of Bonacina's texts is such that several stories can be told from them. Pio Pecchiai and Bernhard Kerber already narrated the construction of this chapel based on these accounts.[63] What follows is a very different sampling with an eye to the role of the Society and its interaction with architects and the public in the process of design.

The Chapel of St. Ignatius, located in the left transept of the church of the Gesù in Rome, houses the relics of the Society's founder. The Basque Ignatius, who died in 1556, was canonized in 1622 (together with one of his original companions, Francis Xavier), at which time his relics were moved from a tomb flanking the high altar in the apse to his own altar. With the canonization of the first two Jesuit saints, the dedications of both transept altars would be changed to receive them. The right transept chapel of the Resurrection, with an aedicula erected provisorily in wood only at this time, became the altar of Francis Xavier. The left transept, previously the Savelli Chapel of the Crucifixion, erected in the 1580s, became the altar of Ignatius. When the Jesuits took the chapel over for Ignatius, it had only a marble aedicula of far smaller scale than the current altar. Some Ignatian imagery had accrued in the chapel between 1622 and 1695: a few paintings that have not survived and above all the precious bronze urn modeled by Algardi that is still below the altar today (fig. 18). But the ambitious scheme of colored marble revetment walls originally planned by the Savelli and designed by Giacomo della Porta in the 1580s, remained incomplete.[64] Given the cultic importance of the site and the provisory nature of the setting for the relics, it is not surprising that by midcentury the Jesuits were already discussing a major renovation of the chapel.

New impetus to renovate Ignatius's chapel came in the 1670s during the generalate of Gian Paolo Oliva, who was behind a master plan for both the architectural and the pictorial renovation of the public spaces of the church, including a new Chapel of St. Ignatius.[65] At this time Baciccio, directed by Bernini, frescoed the entire vault of the church. But the painted decorations were only one component of a larger plan to unify and finally

FIG. 18
Alessandro Algardi, *Urn of St. Ignatius*, 1629–37. Chapel of St. Ignatius, Il Gesù, Rome.

finish, a century later, the incomplete embellishment of the apse and transept altars. Carlo Fontana, Bernini's pupil, made plans for new transept and apse altars of the same scale, a plan (fig. 19) that would unite three altars originally radically different in scale: the two-story sixteenth-century high altar by Della Porta rose high above the entablature, while the two transept altars, typical of altars built at the end of the sixteenth century, floated far below the entablature of the church against the wide transept walls. Fontana designed a four-column aedicula for all three spaces that reached just to the entablature. The height of the proposed aediculas was crucial, for Fontana's design would have increased the scale of the aediculas in the transepts while allowing Vignola's entablature to run uninterrupted around the entire space, thereby visually unifying the Latin cross form of the church. I have argued elsewhere that Bernini's admiration of the Gesù's unbroken entablature and his attention to the continuity of the entablature in other churches help to account for this feature of the renovation project.

Included in Fontana's master plan were designs for either an open confessio or a crypt chapel (fig. 20) below the high altar for Ignatius's relics. A controversial proposal that generated much discussion (and much opposition) among the Jesuits, the project would be revived again in 1692 by some in favor of it.[66] It would be reconsidered, briefly, in 1695 as well. But the Farnese family, who still controlled the apse of the church, objected to the excavation entailed by an open confessio, and many Jesuits feared that a closed crypt would

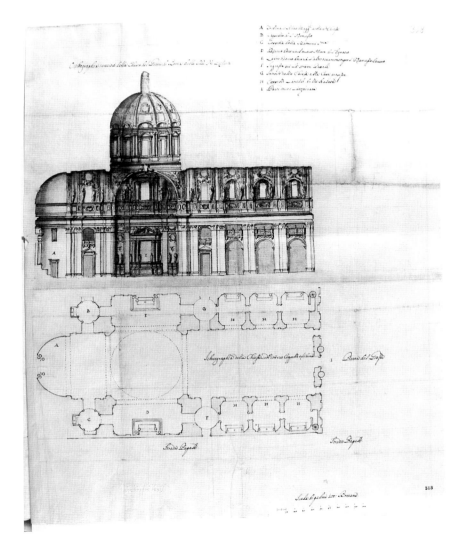

FIG. 19
Carlo Fontana, *Project for decoration of Il Gesù*, ca. 1672.

compromise Ignatius's cult. Since the project was designed to bolster Ignatius's cult by placing him at the high altar of the church, the crypt project seemed counterproductive.

For those who know the church today with its transept and apse altars all of different design, it is obvious that Oliva's master plan was foiled. Unable to organize financing for the entire project, only the vaults would be executed as planned. The Farnese were unwilling to commit to the architectural renovation. Oliva did manage to find in the prelate Gianfrancesco Negroni a patron to rebuild the right transept chapel of St. Francis Xavier.

FIG. 20

Carlo Fontana, *Design for a crypt chapel of St. Ignatius below the high altar of Il Gesù*, ca. 1672.

But Negroni, too imperiously for the Jesuits, hired his own architect and painter for the vault, thus compromising the scheme for unified transepts and apse. The Jesuits' dissatisfaction with this chapel (completed in 1679)—some thought it a "waste of money"— would influence how the Jesuits envisioned the new Chapel of St. Ignatius in the left transept. The Negroni chapel debacle may also have helped the Jesuits resolve to pay for the project themselves. Their control of the Chapel of St. Ignatius, following the official cessation of the Savelli family's rights in the chapel in 1695, was unique in the Church.[67]

The Chapel of St. Ignatius began like many other Jesuit projects. The general solicited a design from Andrea Pozzo, a Jesuit coadjutor holding the rank of brother who worked in Rome for the Society as a painter and architect (fig. 17). Pozzo submitted his first idea to the general with humility, "supplicating him to have it examined, to be amended and improved as deemed necessary."[68] The general subsequently ordered Pozzo to the Casa Professa to explain the drawing to Jesuits in high administrative posts: the general's assistants, the secretary, and the vice preposito, as well as to others considered knowledgeable about architecture, such as the mathematicians who taught architecture at the Collegio Romano. He also asked Pozzo to show the drawing to three prominent senior lay architects: Carlo Fontana, Matthia de'Rossi, and Giovanni Antonio de'Rossi, whose opinions were to be reported to the general, who would then "come to some prudent decision."[69] The extensiveness of the list of experts, internal and external, signals the importance of the project.

The kind of plan Pozzo devised in that first drawing (like all the drawings and models mentioned in the documents, it is lost) concerns us less than the responses it generated. But in brief, the major problem with the project was its scale, far too great for the shallow left transept. Pozzo's plan called for four or six freestanding columns with their bases resting directly on the floor and mounted by angels carrying a crown. Four bronze statues on corbels were to flank the pilasters on the side walls. His design included a statue of Ignatius inside a niche as the altarpiece, but some complained that, given the scale and disposition of the columns, it would not be visible from many points in the chapel.[70] Pozzo had also proposed, problematically, to raise the urn containing Ignatius's relics above the altar.[71] A quick bit of research (probably accomplished by surveying their own members) proved that for such an arrangement many precedents existed in churches all over the world.[72] But they deemed the idea risky, since experts in ritual voiced objections. As Bonacina noted, it would be better to drop the idea, beautiful as it was, than leave themselves open to the accusation by other orders of trying to set precedent. For the "actions of the Company are always the most observed and while others get away with this, the most severe criticism is displayed against our own."[73] Bonacina shows an awareness of Jesuit visibility.

Almost everyone who saw Pozzo's first drawing commented favorably on the plan, though there were also consistent recommendations for changes. These were summarized six days later in six points.[74] Of the Jesuits asked to evaluate the drawing, three came down heavily against it, although Bonacina minimizes their recommendations in the "Diligenze." The highly critical comments of two Jesuits, Antonio Baldigiani and Filippo Bonanni, seem to have influenced what happened next. Dissatisfied with the perspective view Pozzo had submitted because it failed to convey space accurately, Bonanni requested in a written note that Pozzo make a "disegno geometrico" of the same plan. In the "Diligenze" Bonacina altered Bonanni's statement, reporting, quite misleadingly, that he recommended that Pozzo pass to what was understood as the next stage in the process: making a model.[75] While neither Bonanni nor Baldigiani rejected Pozzo out of hand as the architect, both recommended that the Jesuits consider more than one drawing. Baldigiani called for "other drawings if there [already] are any and which could be easily had according to the usual practice on these occasions of having many, or rather any architect who wants to submit a design so that we can then choose the one which we think is the most appropriate." Bonanni also recommended that not one but many "experts" should make designs.[76] In spite of these clear indications of ambivalence about Pozzo's designs, in the entry in the "Diligenze" for 28 January Bonacina singled out Bonanni and Giovanni Antonio de'Rossi (among the lay architects) as having approved passing to the model stage on Pozzo's first submission as well as his second.[77] According to Bonacina, these two experts (contrary to the entry of the previous day) "in conformity with opinions already given by many other men of intelligence" considered it best that Pozzo make two models after the two drawings submitted thus far. In the "Diligenze," Bonacina clearly suppressed evidence of internal discontent with Pozzo, his early drawings, and, above all, with the presumption that he should design the chapel. All of this suggests that Bonacina wrote the "Diligenze" to justify the choice of Pozzo as architect.

Here things get murky. In the entry in the "Diligenze" for the same day Bonacina notes that drawings by two young lay architects, Sebastiano Cipriani and Giovanni Battista Orrigone, "were brought in by the vice preposito."[78] The opening up of a competition to external architects is slipped in without a note of explanation. In the "Ristretto," by contrast (which was composed with some distance from the early controversy over who should design), Bonacina refers openly to early objections—by Jesuits *and* non-Jesuits—to the de facto choice of Pozzo as architect (and Bonacina as administrator).[79]

Soon after the submission of plans by lay architects events accelerated around the young Sebastiano Cipriani's drawing. For reasons that remain unstated in the "Diligenze," the vice preposito Luigi Restori suggested (March 1) that all drawings and models be shown to "people with expertise," specifically proposing prince Agostino Chigi.[80] In the meantime Pozzo continued to make new plans and began a third model, which he was unable to complete in time for Chigi's visit. Bonacina documents this last point in detail: he notes when Pozzo was told to have the project ready and shows that Chigi came to the Casa Professa—together with the ambassador to Malta, Sachetti, and marchese Teodolo—earlier than expected, before Pozzo was able to finish his latest drawings.[81] Then it turned out to be too "crowded" for the *cavalieri* in the Gallery where the models were on display, and they had the drawings (though not the models—thereby excluding Pozzo's latest project) sent to Chigi's palace. Bonacina implies that Pozzo's plans were not represented when Chigi made his choice. In the privacy of Chigi's palace, the noblemen examined the plans and selected Cipriani's. The vice preposito reported their choice to the general, as well as the pledge made by the three men to "get involved so that the project could be helped by the [choice of an] architect."[82]

It is quite likely that the Jesuits showed the drawings to Chigi and his entourage because of the prospect of receiving their financial assistance on the project. What is curious, though, is that they referred to these noblemen as "persone periti," that is, people who know something about design. Did the Jesuits believe that these gentleman had expertise, or was this flattery? Whether motivated by money or other benefits of soliciting their expert advice, the Jesuits immediately accorded the gentlemen's decision authority. We know this because Giovanni Battista Orrigone, the third architect who submitted a proposal, protested the swift decision. He lamented the unfairness of the procedure in a letter to his protector, Cardinal Barbarigo, who forwarded the architect's letter to the Jesuits. Orrigone's main point is that Cipriani's plan was not chosen on the basis of its virtue. Rather, influenced by their architect Giovanni Battista Contini (Cipriani's teacher), Chigi and his cronies selected what was to their own taste. The drawings, Orrigone wrote, should be examined not only by gentlemen but also by "more experts, publicly and privately, and models should be ordered of those projects esteemed the best, because otherwise they will potentially move precipitously on this work, which they are thinking to make so grandiose."[83] In other words, Orrigone complained that the gentlemen were biased, that they exercised their taste rather than their judgment. The distinction is important. Taste, personal and political, has little virtue. Judgment, based on knowledge and study, transcends taste.

The vice preposito, Luigi Restori, who ushered the designs through the field of experts, immediately investigated Orrigone's claims. In a long note to the general he offers a very different picture from that described in either the "Diligenze" or Orrigone's letter. First, Restori points out that Cipriani's design found favor not only with Chigi and friends but also with the Jesuits: in-house it was in fact universally approved.[84] Restori solicited further opinions on the plans from other unnamed "experts" who preferred Cipriani's design as well and, in the process, revealed the "very grave defects of the other [by Pozzo]."[85] Second, he wrote, it is a calumny against Chigi and the others to claim that they have "no intelligence" in architecture. Restori clearly asked around town, for he reports that these gentlemen have the reputation of possessing a modest knowledge of architecture "on a par with the top rung of professors" in the city.[86]

The Jesuits' lack of semantic clarity about their expert *cavalieri* points to a significant theme throughout the "Diligenze" and the Jesuit architectural correspondence in general. The flash fire over the gentlemen and their judgment highlighted Jesuit insecurities about who was in the position to judge design. The situation they found themselves in—the general's first inclination toward Pozzo contested by some Jesuits as well as by supposedly knowledgeable gentlemen—challenged the system of design approval intended to guarantee the successful outcome of a project.

It suited Bonacina's narrative in the "Diligenze" that many of those asked to view the plans ultimately deferred to the opinion of those who everyone could agree were the most qualified experts, namely, the secular architects. Thus he is sure to report on the Jesuit Italian assistant's qualification of his positive opinion of Pozzo's design, which he "liked"; nonetheless, the assistant said, he would "base his opinion on that of the architects and those of the profession."[87] Similarly, the Society's secretary, Francesco Guarino, said that although he had an opinion on limiting the amount of bronze in the chapel so as not to appear to compete with St. Peter's (i.e., the Cathedra), architecture was "not his profession."[88] Bonacina also reported that when Cardinal di Goes was asked his opinion on Pozzo's first design, he answered appropriately that while he might have something to say about a "theological point," which he would "discuss with the general or other fathers," "in this matter what is needed is experience and not speculation and that the Jesuit fathers should consult with architects."[89]

By calling attention to each Jesuit's hesitation to judge, Bonacina built his case for privileging the expertise of lay architects. In the reports on consultations with the latter there is also the inevitable disparaging remark about the inexpert ideas in circulation. The architect Giovanni Antonio de'Rossi criticized a suggestion made by one Jesuit that a large model be made, remarking that expensive wooden models should not be made for every design put forth but only after a terra-cotta model had been made and corrected. "For a chaste and intelligent eye in the profession," de'Rossi said, this is all that is necessary.[90]

The culminating moment of Bonacina's "Diligenze" comes when Carlo Fontana, the most esteemed of the lay architects, approves Pozzo's drawing on "carta turchina." As reported by Bonacina, the selection has all the ring of an annointment ceremony. He viewed each drawing twice and, in the presence of three witnesses, declared that Pozzo's design should be executed. Echoing a phrase familiar from the correspondence about design approvals, Fontana pronounced that from it there should be no departure. Moreover, he confirmed for the Jesuits that Pozzo, the in-house candidate, was not just a choice of convenience: "If P. Pozzi had been in India you would have had to call him, and if he had done nothing other than the marvelous cupola in [the Church of] St. Ignatius it would suffice to quell any doubts about his work."[91] Fontana then named all of the other architects who had submitted projects (proving that, unlike Chigi and friends, he had seen all submissions). And while he was still at the Casa Professa, the general, final arbiter in matters of design, returned and heard Fontana's opinion himself.

In the meantime, Cipriani's drawing had to be rejected, and with it Chigi and his friends' reputations as experts. In the "Diligenze" Cipriani's plan is summarily dismissed for flaws as major as those in Pozzo's designs. Bonacina's omission of the identity of the authors (presumably Jesuits) of a scathing critique is significant given his concern to establish the authority of the positive opinions of Pozzo. Also suspicious is the fact that the plan by Cipriani described in the "Diligenze" does not correspond to the design preserved in an engraving that Cipriani had made after what was clearly the winning entry (fig. 21). It appears that Bonacina suppressed this design and the praise heaped on it by recording only the critique of another design submitted by Cipriani that the Jesuits considered untenable.

But Cipriani fought back, bringing to public attention the discord over who should judge the project drawings. In his dedication inscription to Agostino Chigi, Cipriani focuses on the insult to his patron's expertise:

I return to the gaze of Your Excellence the design for the altar of the glorious patriarch St. Ignatius to be erected in the sumptuous Temple of the Gesù of Rome, which amongst other more developed and beautiful drawings, was exposed to the critique of many qualified gentlemen, who, for the clarity of their sublime judgment, were in complete agreement with the choice of Your Excellence, and it was also initially liked by the Reverend Fathers of the Company, who, to my embarrassment, gave the design their full approval. But the applause was ephemeral and in being admired, the design was stolen. So as not to succumb to the fate that would condemn the design to oblivion, I wanted the lamentations of oppression to awaken the fame of its defects to make them visible to the world. Who is discerning has judgment, and he who has judgment shows himself to be a good judge.

All' Ill.mo et Ecc.mo Sig.re Principe
D. Agostino Chigi

FIG. 21
Girolamo Frezza after Sebastiano Cipriani, *Project for the Chapel of St. Ignatius in Il Gesù*, 1696.

In this paean to his patron, Cipriani clarifies an issue for us. The insult to the patron's judgment resulted in the diminishment of his influence. In late-seventeenth-century Rome, judgment of a work of art is, effectively, power. Hence the investigation of Orrigone's insulting comments about Chigi's expertise; hence all of the fuss the Jesuits were making about who should decide which design was best.

While Bonacina's narrative includes some surprisingly incriminating statements about nonexpert opinions in play in the process, these have a purpose: to prove that the experts chose Pozzo's design for its artistic merit. But just why the Society of Jesus felt obligated to justify its appointment of an internal architect deserves further comment.

While Pozzo was respected as a painter (his spectacular vault in the Church of St. Ignatius was complete by 1695), his reputation as an architect was not secure either inside or outside the Society. Bonacina tells us that controversy swirled around both him and Pozzo from the very beginning of the project:

> As soon as it was known [that Pozzo and Bonacina had been assigned the chapel project], almost as if from the sound of a trumpet, everyone took to arms. You cannot believe how much raving went on in every circle, in every corner, and not only by our own but also amongst the lay community, disapproving openly that a work of such engagement and such expectation and expense should be managed by a Pozzo and a Bonacina, that is, two brothers of low rank and born foreigners. . . . Brother Pozzo, who was brought to Rome from the Province of Milan, a man of religion as much as of art, and singularly virtuous, but very humble, and not one who cared about appearances, who did not know how to make his own case for his work, nor when it was criticized did he defend it, and he was held in some esteem as a good painter, but was not credited as a great architect.[92]

Both Fontana and Giovanni Antonio de'Rossi acknowledged that the Jesuits preferred to work with an in-house architect; their remarks reassured the Jesuits that even though Pozzo was a Jesuit who would work for free, he was worthy of the task. De'Rossi addressed this issue quite directly when he said that "brother Pozzo should be the architect not only because he was of the Company [of Jesus], and suited the general's taste, but because he was of merit and capable."[93]

If the lay architects supported Pozzo, why did Pozzo face such opposition among some of his fellow Jesuits? Did they truly doubt his abilities? Did they feel that more prestige would accrue to the project if designed by a lay architect? And if so, why should prestige matter to them? Sometime during the "competition," Pozzo sent a note to Bonacina revealing another aspect of the issue, namely, that Pozzo's interest in the project bordered on the inappropriate:

> Yesterday father Durazzo came to see me and got me very upset about his intentions and those of all the others. . . . [H]e told me that everyone was in agreement in wanting more designs and models from other, more famous architects, who would have submitted them if they had not been prevented from doing so by you and me. They are terribly against us

and against all of those who have written opinions [on the designs]. I answered that I have impeded no one from designing and making models, on the contrary, it would please me very much if finished painted and gilded models were made, for in that case I would like to finish and gild mine too.[94]

Although Durazzo would praise Pozzo's designs at a later date, now he represented those calling for designs by famous architects. Pozzo, finding himself accused of being competitive with lay architects, is driven to renounce the project. He wrote thus to the vice preposito, Luigi Restori, the Jesuit who led the group in favor of Cipriani's designs:

Given my own tenuity and incapability, it would have been greatly rash and presumptuous on my part to have interfered in making designs and models for the Chapel of St. Ignatius, as a highly notable work as much for its location as for its cost, if I had not been called and prayed and ordered to do so by the father general, by yourself, by the father procurator general, and by father Grimaldi. Therefore, seeing that after [producing] various designs I have not hit the mark, I renounce this project altogether. It would please me if others more capable than myself would employ their talents for the greater benefit of this work, for the greater glory of God and honor to St. Ignatius, and I would be pleased that, if nothing else, my efforts might serve at least to stimulate the genius of the *virtuosi* to make a work worthy of our holy founder. I therefore pray that you accept this message with good intentions, having earlier offered them to the Blessed Lord in the course of my efforts and all of the debates. In addition, I pray that you show this to all so that they know that it is not my intention to prevent others from making designs, and that I have neither ambition nor desire for glory or fame.[95]

In pursuing the project, Pozzo is accused by his brothers of demonstrating an unholy, an un-Jesuit interest in earthly glories. In Pozzo's letter of renunciation he initially justifies himself, pointing out that in making his first designs he obeyed his superiors. It is slightly disturbing that these words ring of wounded pride. Bonacina would write later that Pozzo did not know how to defend himself. But he knew as well as Pozzo that the vow of obedience was binding. Bonacina responded to Pozzo's note informing him of his intention to give up the project with the following encouragement:

Don't listen to gossip, concentrate on making your angles and let them sing; already you and I for the glory of God are dead to the world; let us therefore be truly dead: without hearing, without speaking, without moving.[96]

Bonacina invokes the metaphor of the dead body to bring Pozzo back to the inner attitude if not to the deed of obedience. But even Bonacina's call to obedience has the ring of a strategy: "Indeed if we look to the peace and quiet of mind of him who obeys, it is certain that he will never achieve it who has within himself the cause of his disquiet and unrest, that is, a judgment of his own opposed to what obedience lays upon him," wrote St. Ignatius.[97]

Pozzo becomes dead. He renounces the work, releasing the project into the hands of Divine Providence. In this moment of renunciation the project is delivered to him.[98] In renouncing the project, which came dangerously close to bringing him earthly glory, the Jesuit architect became its ideal executant. Might we come to understand something of the Jesuitness of Jesuit architecture in this very paradox? As political as it appears on the surface, the process of choosing Pozzo also seems like an episode out of the *Spiritual Exercises*. The Exercises form the subject through progressive renunciation. In the process by which Pozzo submitted his will to that of a higher authority, he advanced in a process of subject formation. The "work" of the design process (like the work of the Exercises) does not merely result in the production of an object, but in the shaping of a subject: the architect. We cannot ignore the tension in these documents. They show that even within a culture that required obedience, the individual is always present, being formed: obedience was an anxious practice.

Obedience, as fraught as it was in reality, was a central practice, a default if you will, on which the success of this project depended. The recourse to obedience in the atmosphere of a highly contested competition helps to explain how the Jesuits, so divided among themselves over whose design was best, came to their decision. A pivotal letter written to the general by p. Filippo Guarnieri suggests that, given Carlo Fontana's approval of Pozzo's design, the decision should ultimately be determined by the Society's relationship to the architect.

> In clarifying my opinion I esteem that Our Father [General], having spent enough time considering the designs should unequivocally select that of brother Pozzo on the approval alone of Cavaliere Fontana, who is the only person who could do something good for this chapel; to commit to such a design by means of such a decorous approval will always act to assist the felicitous execution of this chapel. This occurred with the recommendation and approval of Baciccia by the Cavaliere Bernini [for the decoration of the vaults of the Gesù] to father Oliva, who, without considering the designs of others, under the sole direction and approval of Cavaliere Bernini had Baciccia do everything. This is a noteworthy advantage that this design has, that the design of no other author of reputation will have, since he will not want to work under the direction of Fontana nor of the general, and the latter will no longer be master of this once he has approved it.[99]

Guarnieri's letter sums up virtually all of the themes developed here. But above all, he calls attention to the premium that should be placed on controlling the design of the chapel. Guarnieri is really saying that in the process of opening the selection of the design to the public, the Jesuits risked losing their way in guaranteeing the chapel's success. For Guarnieri, this hinged as much on the design (and he assumes Fontana is sincere when he approved Pozzo's design for its excellence) as on a process directed by the right people. In saying this, he demonstrates how uncertain the Jesuits had become about who possessed the expertise to judge and then to see a design to its completion. Harkening back to the 1670s when Bernini guided general Oliva in the spectacular completion of the Gesù vaults, Guarnieri envisions Fontana playing the same role as guarantor for Ignatius's chapel. Guarnieri's letter and others like it clinched the commission for Pozzo. Fontana became the director of the work, as Guarnieri suggested, although his role soon turned very problematic for Pozzo.

After the approval of the drawing on *carta turchina,* Pozzo, evidently required to consult with Fontana, began to render the design in models: first a terra-cotta and then, after a round of alterations, an expensive large wooden model. In September 1695, as the model reached completion, Pozzo sought out Fontana.[100] But in notes from the latter we learn that he refused to look at it, claiming that other Jesuit fathers who wanted to obstruct Pozzo's project were trying to sway him to do so as well. Moreover, Pozzo had already taken too much of the project into his own hands, having given out many of the commissions for the sculptural components. Rather than be caught in the middle of the internal politics of the Jesuits and with his hands tied (and fees lost) by what Pozzo had already arranged, Fontana demurred.[101]

Pozzo tells a slightly different story in a note to Bonacina, in which he focuses on the power struggle between the two:

> Let us suspend our visits to Fontana, proceed with the model, and stop this so that we involve him no more and then [later] we will let him have his say. If our father [general] wants me to work under such an insincere architect who, under the pretext of giving opinions wants to insinuate himself as a brother and exclude me entirely, it is better to give him the entire project and throw me into the sea that this great storm be immediately quelled. You have tolerated this up until now and will continue. I beg of you to speak of it with the father general and inform him of what is going on, and present to him my renunciation [of the project] that I offer freely in the hands of the will of God of St. Ignatius and of the Superiors.[102]

Fontana refused to see the model because he could not control the project. It seems that the Jesuits, though wanting his advice, were ultimately unwilling to have the project truly directed by someone outside the Society. The way this is articulated is in itself significant: Pozzo describes Fontana trying to wrest control of the design from him as an attempt "to insinuate himself as a brother," that is, to be a Jesuit. It is generally presumed that a Jesuit architect is a creative soul striving toward release from his shackles. What of this lay architect looking to be bound? The internal-external politics of the Society are more complicated than we have presumed.

The choice of Pozzo as a great architect was the most important point of Bonacina's promotion of the Chapel of Ignatius. The debates over his merits and the quality of his design fueled gossip, thrusting the project into the public realm. Indeed, one of the most remarkable aspects of the chapel's design is how very public the process seems to have been. From the initial solicitations of architects and patrons for their opinions to the final unveiling, the Jesuits actively involved their own members and the public, far in excess of their usual practice of evaluating designs by a small committee of Jesuits and non-

Jesuit architects. I have already mentioned some aspects of this, but as the process continued, the public dimension became more open and complex.

We must come to terms with the publicness of the work. "It is not easy to remember," Bonacina writes,

> a project that was, more than this one, cast more in doubt because of conflicting opinions, more embattled outside the Society because of the pretensions of non-Jesuits, and because of the disagreements amongst Jesuits more agitated within. Both the multitude of builders who competed [for work] and the engagement of people of rank who aspired to be the arbiters, conspired to make the work notable. Above all the reputation of the project was heightened by the ambition of the architects, who used all means to become its director, moved by the two greatest stimuli of human nature, which are honor and [self-]interest, in the hope of acquiring renown for a work of such fame, and on the certainty of having good earnings in a project of such expense.[103]

It was not just the interest of interested parties, the competition for the commission, that made the project public. Even after Pozzo's design was elected and the model made, "the general, seeing that rumors still circulated sotto voce, ordered that the model be displayed to the eyes and for the comments of the public." He set aside a room accessible to both Jesuits and non-Jesuits and appointed someone to take down "judgments, reflections and objections."

> This being made known around Rome, it is unbelievable how many ran from every part of the city to see it, stimulated by curiosity which had been aroused by the shrill tones of earlier that had already spread around the city. Innumerable cardinals, bishops, prelates, princes, gentlemen, architects, painters, priests, monks, and laymen of every sort came. There was, in sum, a continuous flow of people, almost a fleet on the sea. Nor was the brigade of deputies rounding up news for the *persone intendenti* a small one.[104]

The notes from that public viewing survive. Difficult to read, including the names of numerous nobles, artists, and religious alongside names that mean nothing to us now, some of the comments of the public probably found their way into the work.[105]

The Jesuits even opened the site to the public during construction, according to Bonacina to "satisfy the great stream of people." On one occasion the chapel, usually blocked from view by a large curtain, was left visible for three days "during which time the sentiments of the public were heard" and on the basis of which several design changes were made. The comments mostly concerned adjustments of materials and sculptural components: to make the rays around the Holy Spirit larger, add cherubini below the Trinity group and angels to the pediment, raise the statue of Ignatius higher, tone down the reflection of the gilded bronze on the lapis lazuli columns, and so on.[106] But the public dimension does not end there. After the Jesuits decided that the central niche above the altar should accommodate a statue, they opened a public competition for that commission. Far less controversial than the choice of an architect, this competition was judged by the sculptors themselves, each of whom was required to cast a vote for one of the others.[107] While the Jesuits may not have initially organized the process as such a public one, it became that. This was no accident.

We need to take gossip seriously. The Jesuits took the talk around town so seriously that one could say it drove the project. Gossip started because the expense and visibility of the chapel immediately aroused public expectations of a great work of art in the making. Initially loose talk seems to have been regarded negatively. Bonacina recounts a visit paid to him and to Pozzo by Cardinal Dadda, who came out of concern for what was being said:

> One morning Bonacina together with brother Pozzo went to see the Cardinal, who declared to him how sorry he was to hear the bad news that circulated around Rome about this expensive and demanding project, that was so badly managed and which had so little hope of meeting expectations; and that such would happen in a city, where the greatest *virtuosi* of the world come to study, and where even the most perfect works are criticized.[108]

Several points emerge from this anecdote. First and above all, Rome held special status as a city of art. Rome, Bonacina notes elsewhere, had a court culture, clearly a competitive one, with its own system of patronage and values. It is implied that the patron had a responsibility to uphold the reputation of the city, for any major work would immediately be seen and publicly discussed. That public discussion, the Jesuits fully realized, would increase the reputation of their project. Even malicious gossip could raise the profile of the work—like on the occasion of Innocent XII's visit to the construction site in 1696, when the pope, turning to the general, reported rumors that the Jesuits had been snookered in their purchase of fake marbles. "No adversary lost an opportunity," Bonacina wrote, "to discredit this Chapel[,] . . . but it all served to bring it praise in the end, in the sense that the criticism stimulated people from all over the world to come see it."[109] The public display of the model aimed to bring the talk around town into Jesuit quarters, where it could be heard and controlled. Look at the lists (fig. 22) kept by a Jesuit assigned to scribble down names and comments.

When it came to gossip within Jesuit ranks, not all talk could be tolerated. Indeed, Bonacina tells us that as the design issues neared resolution the general circulated two directives aimed at bringing talk under control. First, after deciding on the official director of the project (Orta, assisted by Bonacina), he prohibited Jesuits to

> insinuate themselves either directly or indirectly in the project except if they were asked to, and that no one should criticize, or censure any of the works to be made, nor speak disapprovingly about them in any place, or at any time, especially during recreation periods, and even less amongst non-Jesuits, who, as it is well known, receive little or no edification from hearing so many contradictory opinions without subordinating them, as is suitable, to the sentiment of the superior.[110]

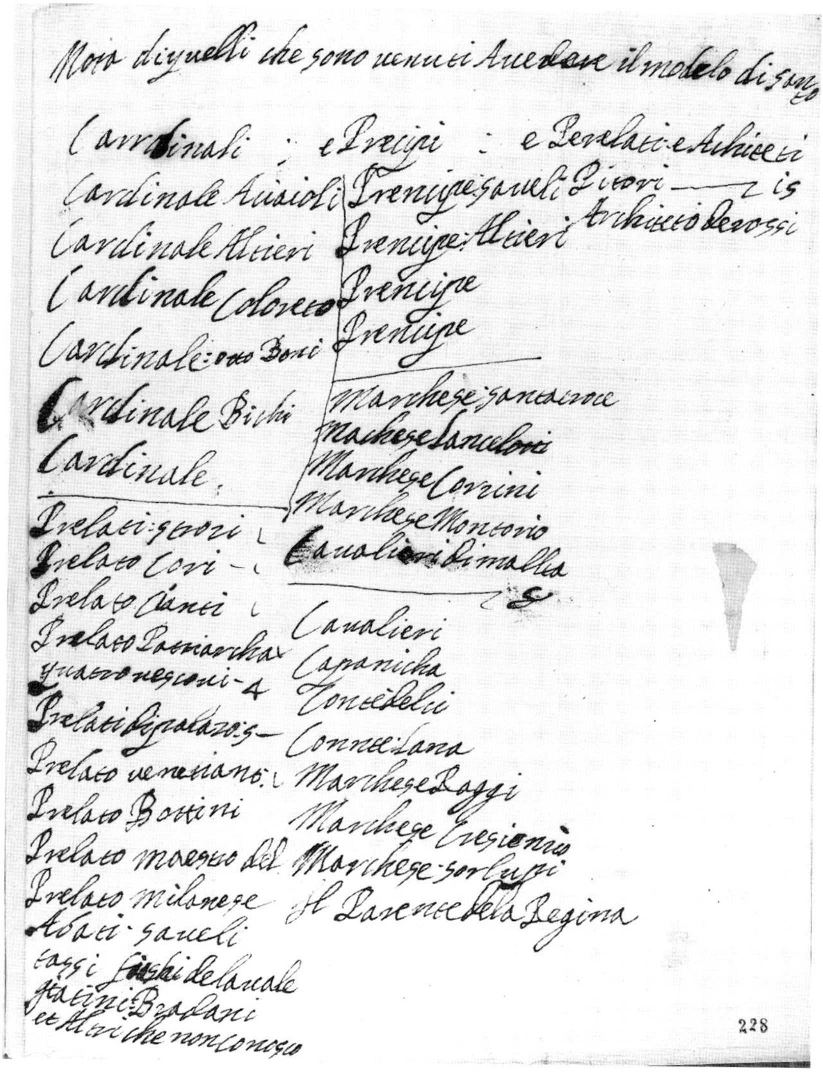

FIG. 22

"List of visitors to the model of St. Ignatius" ("Nota di quelli che sono venuti A vedere il modelo di santo"), 1695.

The general ordered the model displayed for ten days during which time anyone was free to state his opinion freely. Further comments supporting the "most perfect completion" of the work could be brought personally or in writing to the general or the procurator.

While all architectural projects evolve in response to the programmatic requirements of a client, in this case the constellation of commentators is so extensive that it is difficult to fully attribute the work to Pozzo with complete confidence. Indeed, the comments played such a significant role in shaping the final work that to understand the chapel as the progeny of a single man is an impoverished view. Let us look for a moment at the kind of recommendations made by the phalanx of Jesuits, external architects, and the public in the course of Pozzo's design process.

Pozzo produced several designs that came to naught before elaborating the final design. Both Jesuits and the architect Giovanni Antonio de'Rossi agreed that the first design, with its six massive freestanding columns (two apparently twisted), should be discarded. During this early discussion, the scale of the columns and the relationship of the aedicula to the entablature would be established, thus shaping in a fundamental way the final design.

After Pozzo produced a series of additional designs, the lay architects and several Jesuits elected one drawn on *carta turchina*. Bonacina quoted Fontana as stating that there should be "no departure" from that drawing. But, in fact, very little of that project (which had alternative designs on the sheet's left and right sides) seems to have survived the critique to which it was subjected. The comments of more than twenty Jesuits, lay architects, artists, and builders who saw the designs are recorded. And in almost every one of the letters written by the Jesuits and the prominent senior lay architects who consulted on the project (Matthia de'Rossi, Giovanni Antonio de'Rossi, and Carlo Fontana), the authors made recommendations for changes to the design.[111] General Gonzalez ordered Pozzo to make a terra-cotta model after the design once "expiated," or "cleansed" *(purgato)*—the choice of term here seems to carry a dual meaning—of its errors.[112] The Jesuits and their advisors then demanded further refinements of the corrected design. In his summary of the written critiques, Bonacina listed sixteen points for Pozzo to take into account.[113]

It is difficult to know to what extent Pozzo responded to the recommendations in his next design. But with these comments in hand he probably added the row of gilded bronze reliefs located, unusually, on the pedestals of the columns, pulled the large relief below the niche back, deepened the niche itself, added the bronze ornaments at its crown, and adjusted the position of the Trinity group that is cradled in the pediment of the altar. But even with these and other changes, the design was clearly very different from the final solution. At this stage the chapel still included statues of four Jesuits saints, probably two between the columns and two on the flanking wall. The elimination of those four figures was apparently a response to one Jesuit's argument that other Jesuit saints should not appear in Ignatius's chapel. The substitution of the two multifigured allegorical groups flanking the aedicula radically altered the profile of the built form and no doubt brought about changes to the plan of the aedicula as well.

Once the terra-cotta model of the emended design had been approved, a large and expensive wooden model was built over the summer. By this time, Fontana had become the official advisor to the project, although, given the notes exchanged between Fontana and Pozzo, it is unclear how much he had to do with final decisions on the plans.

When the model was complete the Society invited the entire Jesuit community and the public at large to view and comment on it. One long document records visitors' comments, mostly recommendations for changes.[114] Visitors like prince Chigi (the only visitor to the model on the second day of viewing) and monsignor Fanti, who had been con-

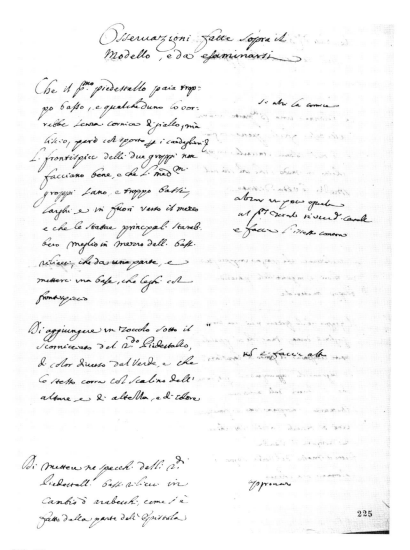

FIG. 23
Carlo Mauro Bonacina, "Observations made about the model and to be examined"
("Osservazioni fatte sopra il Modello, e da esaminarsi"), 1695.

sulted early on about the location of the reliquary urn, were among those who left no comments. Duke Salviati, who mixed in with artists and artisans, came incognito. Others, mostly artists and architects, identified themselves. The comments at this stage in the design proceedings focused on the choice of materials and the scale and detailing of the main sculptural elements, the statue of Ignatius, the Trinity, and the reliefs.

The results of the public viewing were brought together with the further comments of Jesuit advisors and summarized in one final set of recommendations for Pozzo to digest (fig. 23). This time the main points were listed in the left column, and in the right column the status of the suggestion—accepted, rejected, or to be tried out—is noted. Some of the recommendations represent the choice of one of two alternatives proposed by Pozzo on the model itself. In other cases, new ideas were given to the architect to develop.

Without any of Pozzo's drawings or models before us to compare to the comments and suggestions, it is difficult to know the full extent of their impact. But one thing is clear. Pozzo had not just one patron but dozens of critics to answer to. He resisted the interference in some fashion (his complicated relationship with Carlo Fontana is testimony to this). But it is certain that both the general outline and the detailing of his designs emerged from this process. The remarkable nature of this collaboration may be better appreciated set against a different dynamic between architect and patron. By contrast, the great Virgilio Spada went to some lengths to protect Bernini from the humiliation of having his designs (for the bell towers of St. Peter's) subjected to the ideas of others. A new proposal for Bernini's project backed by Spada was to be made. Anticipating Bernini's reaction, Spada wrote: "[I]t will not be difficult to find the means to make Cavalier Bernini appear to be its author, so that he will not be annoyed that others want to improve his designs."[115] The Jesuits had no use for subterfuge for they did not have to worry about Pozzo's vanity.

CONCLUSIONS

I began this chapter with the view commonly held in the social sciences of the propagandist as an anonymous figure acting on behalf of an organization. Assuming that the propagandist's personal views are consonant with the organization's, he need leave no mark of himself since he works to advance the organization's interests. With no deliberate trace of the individual left on the most common forms of propaganda—print, radio, posters, and so on—the organization becomes their apparent author. That historians scarcely have been tempted to make stylistic distinctions, to separate hands or authors within a regime's propaganda production, suggests that the organization-as-author adequately describes the producer of many forms of propaganda.[116]

While most social scientists consider the fine arts (and film) as forms of propaganda, it would be misleading to apply the propagandist's anonymity to artists and architects. Modern regimes that successfully employed the fine arts as propaganda achieved success insofar as they used the apparent independence of the modern system of the arts—in which the artist, his reputation, and status play an important role—to bolster their own prestige. Thus, for example, the participation by artists in competitions organized by the Italian fascists served to legitimate the regime.[117] And while Hitler had his own pretensions as an architect, he made no attempt to lessen the contributions of his professional architects. On the contrary, the Reich actively promoted them and their works. Thus the *anonymity* of an architect cannot be considered a criterion for architecture that is to be designated as propaganda. Let us not confuse the architect with the propagandist, even though in the case examined here, the obedient Jesuit architect may bear some resemblance to the propagandist.

There is, nonetheless, in a work of propagandistic architecture self-consciousness about the architect's relationship to the organization. In this respect the early modern Jesuits were quite analogous to modern producers of propaganda when they employed their own members. We can assume that an artist-architect who was at the same time a Jesuit had the kind of allegiance to the Society expected of the propagandist. As we have seen, the Jesuit emphasis on the vow of obedience compelled the Jesuit architect to articulate his own creativity in relation to the aims of and demands made on him by the Society; and this becomes exemplary of the self-renunciation proscribed in the Spiritual Exercises.[118] Although obedience was a fraught practice, the architect's battle with obedience of judgment took place in the context of an intensely collaborative design process that only superficially resembles other early modern patron-architect relationships.

Bonacina's accounts, along with other preserved documents, offer a rare glimpse into how a Jesuit as a creative individual worked in a state of tension. The Society sought expert opinion to shore up its judgment of its own architect's work and sought collective agreement on his designs. The Society cannot be seen as having imposed its own preconceived notion of design, because it simply did not have one. Moreover, it took no pains to discipline the artist for the sake of discipline alone. Rather, the Society's main interest was that the project be successful. The controls, the checks and counterchecks, the use of outside people, the solicitation and implementation of opinion, were all organized because of a basic uncertainty about what would work. As we have seen, this continuous solicitation of opinion had a great impact on the built design. In demanding that the architect suspend his own will and judgment, the Society kept him on the verge of renouncing the project. Ignatius's "obedience of understanding"—in which individual judgment is perfected through its perfect conformity with a higher judgment—helps us to understand how the Jesuit architect's creativity can operate within the Society's architectural culture.

The collaborative nature of design within the Society did not prevent Jesuit architects in general and Andrea Pozzo in particular from leaving an individual stamp on their work. But historians have erred by looking too exclusively at the contributions of the Society *or* of the architect to explain the final work as the product of ideology *or* of individual creativity. I believe the crux of the matter lies in between, in the public and institutional realm where for a moment the two met and worked together. The Jesuitness of Jesuit architecture is not, I submit, in forms themselves (Jesuit Style) but in the *process*—organized and controlled by the Society—through which forms emerged.

The Society of Jesus took a very wide view of making architecture, ultimately claiming for itself the authorship of "the work." Even in the apparent chaos of soliciting public opinion on design, the Jesuits considered the administration of the project, with its chain of command ending in the Christlike general, key to a project's successful outcome. In the end, the Jesuits disciplined the multiple voices invited to express opinions into a design that could be attributed to the Society as a whole. In this larger context of "making" architecture, the actual design as penned by a single individual played an important role but was merely one of many. More was at stake in the design of the chapel than that with which we as art historians are generally concerned. Because the reputation of the Jesuit order seems to have been on the line, it is above all in the way that the Society controlled the process that the design proceedings resemble the production of propaganda. The work, then, is viewed here not so much as the final product, one that can be subjected to stylistic analysis. Rather, the chapel is the *trace* of *working*. And in this working, the architect himself, as a subject, is produced. The author and the work are both *effects* of Jesuit work.

It is tempting to view the competition for the Chapel of St. Ignatius as a moment when the Roman public, with its concern for the "aesthetic," loosened the Jesuit grip on the process. One might be tempted to say that the Jesuits risked losing institutional control over their project. Although the public competition aroused the Jesuits' insecurities about judging design, this is far from what happened. In opening the institution to public opinion, the Society harnessed public opinion for its own purposes. An antithesis between art and propaganda cannot be maintained, for the Jesuits actively cultivated the public discourse on art.

To this end, the Society of Jesus was highly wrapped up in establishing the reputation of Andrea Pozzo as an architect. The Jesuit architect is bound to the institution, at the level of both the manifest content of the work and his working process. But the institution at the same time has learned that the autonomous artist—whose talent wins him fame—has a public value, here I would say a propagandistic value.[119] The Jesuits, through a public competition and public display of their designs as well as through Bonacina's documents, constructed their artist as possessing talent for the greater glory of God.

Even before the chapel was built, the public reception of the monument mattered to the Jesuits. Otherwise, they would have had little incentive to open themselves up to a public process. Aside from the specific message of the chapel (discussed in chapter 4), at the end of the seventeenth century, part of the monument's effectiveness hinged on its participation in a public discourse on the arts, a discourse that Argan identified as characteristic of the new social function of art in the Baroque age.[120] Bernini actually quantified the public for architecture during his sojourn to the court of Louis XIV (1665), estimating that in Rome "there were a good two hundred people who were concerned with architecture."[121] Artistic projects, followed with interest by so many, were news, as is evidenced by their prominence in the early modern *avvisi,* which circulated around Europe beginning in the middle of the sixteenth century.[122] That the Jesuits effectively controlled the public process of design should come as no surprise to us. But that that public process itself became something to be controlled is what makes it productive to think about this work in terms of propaganda.

Once the Jesuits decided to open themselves to public scrutiny they inscribed the public into the work of the chapel. The ordinary routes of tying the public to such a space were through prayer and votive donations, the lighting of candles, kneeling before the altar, the hearing of a mass outside its gated precinct. Now the competition, the public viewings of the model and construction site, and the dramatic unveiling effectively brought the public, through a quite different but analogous process, to kneel before Ignatius's new altar. The Jesuits recognized that the process of judging the work as art could be coextensive with their devotional aims for the work; for some, judgment of the chapel as a work of art offered an alternative to devotion. Far from a loss of control, the Jesuits took an alternative route to control.

The distinction between the Jesuit corporate control of discourse and the "free" play of opinion in the public discussion of the arts is crucial. We know of many such discussions of the arts in the public realm since the Renaissance. The debates over the placement of Michelangelo's *David* and the design of the facade of the Duomo of Milan come to mind, as does Baldinucci's remark in his *vita* of Bernini about the naysayers of the *Baldachin* before its triumphant unveiling: "So the tongues of the fools wagged."[123] The public discourse was no doubt far more extensive than historical records allow us to know. But what the Jesuits did with this practice is something, I believe, quite important, and it brings us around once again to propaganda. What distinguishes the Jesuit practice from these others is the valorization and use of the public discussion precisely *because* of its apparent freedom from institutional control.

In the process of treating the question of the authorship of a work of architecture as propaganda, I have emphasized the process of design—the work as the trace of working—over the design itself. The idea of the authorship of the institution is rendered more palatable by this interpretation of what constitutes the "work." What is more, in evaluating the design *process* (rather than the final work from the perspective of individual style), the architect's authorship of the work becomes something of a moot issue. For it is in the working (of which the work is the trace) that the architect himself, as subject and as author, is produced. Here the Society of Jesus, which coordinated the designs, their alterations and execution, which organized Pozzo's critics and generated a public for the work, was "at work." In fashioning the design process, it was doing something that is akin to propaganda. But even this appears tidier than I intend it to be.

What is important is that in thinking about these works in terms of how propaganda is produced, we are compelled to rethink how authorship functions in an institutional setting. The example of the Chapel of St. Ignatius shows how the individual himself was formed in the web of Jesuit designs—here I mean in the sense of intentions—and this is highly symptomatic of a broader Jesuit way of proceeding. And this way of proceeding had everything to do with negotiating a successful outcome through an institutional set of rules, an architect, a group of advisors, and the public at large. It was complex and messy, but—and this is the final point—very pointed.

4

MESSAGE

I shall then suggest that ideology 'acts' or 'functions' in such a way that it 'recruits' subjects among the individuals (it recruits them all), or 'transforms' the individuals into subjects (it transforms them all) by that very precise operation which I have called *interpellation* or hailing, and which can be imagined along the lines of the most commonplace everyday police (or other) hailing: 'Hey, you there!'

LOUIS ALTHUSSER, "IDEOLOGY AND IDEOLOGICAL STATE APPARATUSES" (1969)

Having examined the authorship of propaganda, here I turn to the core of the matter: what can be said about the nature of the propaganda message (in modern times and in the past)? My answer to this question brings us again to subject formation. For the propaganda message has one essential quality: its directedness. It is in this directedness, in the anticipation of the message's reception, that propaganda's aim to form subjects is apparent. The French Marxist Louis Althusser's description of the functioning of ideology, quoted above, sets the stage for a reading of Jesuit propaganda.[1] The proximity— if not the dependence—of Althusser's models of ideology on Christian models of subject formation points to its appropriateness for understanding visual propaganda in the Jesuit milieu in particular and the Catholic Baroque in general. Visual propaganda is to be seen here as a means by which Catholic subjects were, to use Althusser's term, interpellated.

In using the word "message" for the title of this chapter, I wish to emphasize a specific aspect of communication via images. The core of modern art historical practice is the interpretation of the meaning of objects, whether generated by the artist or in the work's reception. In its hermeneutical focus on the object, art history's trajectory is parallel to modernist literary criticism, which, in equating language with signification, broke with the ancient tradition of reading texts as guides to action.[2] Messages, which are exchanged between two parties, always imply a direction and an effect on their hearers or viewers.[3]

The difference between meaning and message, as I intend it here, can be illustrated by restaging an encounter staged previously by W. J. T. Mitchell (to another end):[4] Panofsky's iconography meeting Althusser's ideological interpellation. In Panofsky's version a man greets another man on the street by doffing his hat.[5] From the incident Panofsky develops three levels at which the encounter can be understood: perceptually as a motion (the pre-iconographic meaning), as a polite greeting (iconography), and as a socially inscribed form of politeness with implications for education, class, and so on (the iconological sense, which entails detailed knowledge of social relations). In Panofsky's description of the interpretive event, the focus is on the greeting. The greeted man is a blank to us; Panofsky does not reflect on what happens to the person addressed in the act of recognition (although interpretive models, less impervious to the social, do).[6]

Althusser's version of the encounter, by contrast, focuses on the effect on the greeted person as one of interpellation, or subject formation. As Mitchell has pointed out, to illustrate interpellation Althusser uses an example similar to Panofsky's: a policeman hails someone on the street, saying, "Hey, you there!" Althusser's interest is in what happens to the listener when he hears this, knows it is directed at him, and shows that understanding by turning around. In acknowledging that "Hey, you there," Althusser argues, the man on the street is inscribed as a subject: he is "interpellated."

Althusser's notion of interpellation has, I believe, fruitful application in thinking about art and propaganda. It is axiomatic that propaganda shapes subjects, or reinforces our already defined subjecthood. How, then, we might ask, can a *work of art* interpellate a subject?

THE NATURE OF THE PROPAGANDA MESSAGE

Most theorists of propaganda would agree that a message's specific content is less important to a definition of propaganda than its goal. But there are two critical points of disagreement on the nature of the propaganda message that warrant discussion. First, there has been widespread disagreement among social scientists as to whether propaganda's main goal is to inculcate *belief* (or, in Lasswell's words, "traditional value attitudes") or to move men to *action*.[7] In the eyes of those who make this distinction, the former, worthier goal is shared by educators, the Church, and other such "neutral" organizations.

Ellul argues that the distinction is, rather, a historical one: modern propaganda seeks to obtain an ortho*praxis* while historical forms sought adhesion to orthodoxy.[8] His view differs entirely from perhaps the best known distinction in Marxist and Leninist thought between agitation—or superficial inculcation—and propaganda, a serious pedagogical effort to train people in depth.[9] American propaganda analysts resisted this distinction through the Cold War, identifying all forms of ideological "manipulation" coordinated by the Communist Party as propaganda, including and especially Soviet-style "education." There has been disagreement on the difference between propaganda and education for decades,[10] although more recently, in the United States at least, the distinction between the so-called neutral forms of propaganda and dedicated propaganda agencies has been, to some extent, leveled.[11]

A resolution to both polarities is to be found in Althusser's argument that ideology has a material, performative manifestation. In a brief history of what he calls nonrepressive Ideological State Apparatuses (ISAs) Althusser argued that education is fundamentally ideological, the most pervasive nonrepressive arm of the State Apparatus since the Enlightenment.[12] If, as Althusser believes, education is inevitably ideological in function, it cannot serve as a neutral foil to propaganda. Propaganda must consist of more particular forms. We will return to Althusser's ISAs below.

A second point of debate concerns whether the propaganda message can be characterized as by nature truthful or deceptive. The technical terms "white propaganda" and "black propaganda" (or "disinformation") refer to propaganda that openly identifies its sources and uses the truth versus propaganda that uses false or veiled sources and is based on lies.[13] As is typical of much of the literature on the subject, debates over truth-value have been based on specific examples. The widespread use of false information in World War I helped to generate the popular belief at the beginning of the century that propaganda messages are lies.[14] Subsequent writings on propaganda and its practice in World War II overwhelmingly came down on the side of truthfulness (although Ellul would later insist that it need use both techniques).[15] Neither Joseph Goebbels nor the U.S. government argued for the truthfulness of propaganda from an ethical perspective. Rather, they reasoned practically that on a mass scale lies, with their potential to undermine their source, were too difficult to maintain. So, as Ellul puts it, propaganda like that produced by Hitler may be based on individual facts, but falsehood may lay at a much deeper level. It is at the level of intention that propagandas like Hitler's may be profoundly deceptive. So while propaganda often *connotes* deception, the latter is not one of its constitutive elements.

A third, related point of disagreement arising from the Marxist emphasis on education concerns the rational or irrational engagement with the message. In keeping with the view that propaganda is a fundamentally educational effort, Marxists emphasized rational engagement through serious study of the historical and theoretical bases of Party dogma. By contrast, Ellul and others argue that propaganda is by nature irrational—even if the form, the *style* of its content, as was increasingly the case during and after World War II, is factual.[16] Because the aim of propaganda is to exert emotional pressure, even a message based on fact is received by the viewer or listener in an irrational fashion. Facts add up to myth, generating an emotional feeling in the listener/viewer; the actual form of the message is thus spontaneously transformed.[17] This is a reception-based characterization of propaganda, which, by focusing on a desired effect rather than on the "nature" of the message, levels the distinction between propaganda and information. This is a model to which I also adhere.

The emotional appeal to the spectator is familiar from the rhetorical tradition. But there is an important difference. While rhetors were urged to aim at the hearts of their listeners, their appeals were not intended to eclipse reason. It has been argued that what distinguishes propaganda from other forms of messages or teachings is that, in its presentation, it *"dis-*

allows critical reflection." The critical process may be undermined by presenting information in a partial way, or wildly out of context, or by presenting too much information so that a synthesis offered up by the propagandist is quickly assimilated. For Ellul, a characteristic aspect of modern propaganda is its employment of an overwhelming amount of what is often factual data. This "surfeit of data," the "mechanisms of modern information induce," he argues, a "form of hypnosis."[18]

From these remarks about modern propaganda emerge two central qualities relevant to its historical forms. First, propaganda should be distinguished by its intended effect on the subject rather than by its rational or irrational, truthful or untruthful character. Second is the too-muchness of propaganda. Although this quality is not always present, in this potentially irrational situation it produces an effect (whatever its style may be) that shapes the individual, controls him, and deprives (or frees) him of himself.[19] Whether overwhelming or not, like other rational processes, propaganda aims to make him a subject.

Ellul's characterization of propaganda in its tendency to confuse or overwhelm the propagandee readily lends itself to comparison to the Baroque. We have seen that Wölfflin characterized Baroque architecture for its tendency to lose the spectator in infinity.[20] Arguably, the too-muchness, the hypnotic, is more endemic to the visual than to the textual forms of propaganda.

In the first sustained study of a single visual medium as propaganda, formal "trickery" was a defining element. In his groundbreaking essay "Propaganda and the Nazi War Film," the German Jewish émigré Siegfried Kracauer characterized Nazi newsreels in these terms:

> There is hardly an editing device they did not explore. . . . They were bound to do so, for their propaganda could not proceed like the propaganda of the democracies and appeal to the understanding of its audiences; it had to attempt, on the contrary, to suppress the faculty of understanding which might have undermined the basis of the whole system. Rather than suggesting through information, Nazi propaganda withheld information or degraded it to a further means of propagandistic suggestion. This propaganda aimed at psychological retrogression to manipulate people at will. Hence the comparative abundance of tricks and devices.[21]

Kracauer's profoundly pessimistic view of Nazi film propaganda was critiqued in private correspondence by the Russian art historian Meyer Schapiro.[22] The latter found Kracauer's perspective far too limited to the German phenomenon, insisting that the Nazis were not alone in their exploitation of the medium:

> Almost everything you say about [Nazi] pseudo-reality and propaganda vs. information seems to me to describe a fully-developed or extreme case of situations which we see clearly enough already in our own society. . . . When I read your beautiful account of the Nuremberg film and the congress [in Leni Riefenstahl's *Triumph of the Will*], I imagine that the

same thing might happen here [in the United States], that a big parade or festivity might be staged and designed partly for reproduction in film; the Catholic Church has done this in a film of its liturgy and ceremonies.[23]

Schapiro went on to point to historical precedents for one of the most characteristic formal motifs Kracauer identified in Weimar cinema and subsequently in Nazi propaganda, namely, repetition of forms, the subject of Kracauer's famous essay "The Mass Ornament."[24] Citing the counterexample of modern abstract art, whose "first principle is randomness," Schapiro notes that repetition is "notoriously a device of absolute power," giving as examples the "endless rows of columns in Egypt, India, Baroque Italy, Versailles."[25] What is important about this exchange for us (in addition to the inevitable comparison of Catholic Baroque to modern totalitarian forms) is that Kracauer, assuming the transparency of the documentary film genre, read artistry as motivated trickery. Schapiro pointed out that because all political systems used these techniques Kracauer's analysis was not based on a *technique* that is characteristic of Nazi film but rather was Kracauer's projection of Nazi motives.

That the "factual" is also a self-consciously employed style of visual propaganda was recently argued in a comparative exhibition of Soviet and U.S. photography of the 1930s.[26] The exhibition showed that in both systems there was a high degree of self-consciousness about the style of official photographs. In the Soviet Union the issue came to the fore when authorities censured the Muscovite photographer Alexander Rodchenko's formal sophistication (radical, emotionally provocative camera angles). In spite of the censure, Rodchenko's style caught on and became neutralized.[27] By contrast, American photographers consistently favored "straightforward" views. The exhibition showed that officials in both countries preferred very apparently unmanipulated camera angles, for stylelessness lent credibility to visual propaganda: the viewers believed that in viewing the photograph, they discovered the truth themselves.

The backlash to Mannerist art in the sixteenth century, when the autonomy of the artist's style threatened the abuse of the religious image, presents virtually the same problem.[28] Various measures were taken during the Counter-Reformation to correct the intrusion of the subjective. To cite one example, Cardinal Federico Borromeo's museum in Milan privileged works exemplary for their authentic content rather than for their exemplary style.[29] In both the early modern and twentieth-century cases, the apparent autonomy of style (and hence the artist), dangerously permitting an enjoyment of the picture independent of its content, resulted in the demand that artists subordinate form to content.[30] As both the Counter-Reformation and twentieth-century examples suggest, artistry, the place where human creativity and subjectivity burst forth, has often been the site of institutional censure in moments of ideological strife. In these moments opposition forces easily viewed art as a tool of deception. In these cases, art's capacity to please us through formal means alone distilled the essential *falseness* of propaganda. As Schapiro pointed out to his dear friend Kracauer, it was not the style of the film but the motives that determined his reaction to the work. The very definition of propaganda is, likewise, an effect of context.

THE CHURCH AS PRODUCER OF PROPAGANDA:
ALTHUSSER'S ISA AND PROPAGANDA

As striking as the parallels between modern and Baroque propaganda may be, a formalist reading of Baroque art as propaganda is not sufficient to account for the message of propaganda. What of the content, specifically, the content of art produced by the Catholic Church? Has it not always been fundamental to the Church's activity that it spread its message, whether through the mass, preaching, or the "Bible of the illiterate"? In light of the persistent distinction between education and propaganda, or between the authentic bursting forth of spirit and calculated politics, do we doubt the sincerity of the Church if we call its message, one whose truth is self-evident to *believers,* "propaganda"?

The idea that the Church be considered a producer of propaganda troubled Ellul, himself a devout Christian.[31] In his view, because the Church is pure spirit, propaganda is anathema to it. Nonetheless, in his opinion there have been moments—very unhappy ones—in the Church's history in which propaganda has been employed and indeed has been an important factor in de-Christianization over time. Among the intensive periods in which propaganda helped to transform Christianity into yet another ideology, based in institutional interests, is the Counter-Reformation.[32]

To view the Church as a producer of propaganda is to consider the Church like any other institution that is pressured to preserve its interests (both material and spiritual). One of the lessons the Catholic Church learned from the Reformation was that the institution needed to project its image through a variety of media out into the world to all social groups. The Northern Reformers' use of the print media (mostly pamphlets but images as well) to break apart the hegemony of the Catholic Church is an often-studied precursor to modern forms of propaganda.[33] A much more positive view of the Church's use of propaganda has, paradoxically, helped to cast a more positive light on propaganda itself.[34]

We can take it for granted that the Church produced propaganda. But propaganda—as directed communication—is so deeply embedded in the Church's mission that we must draw out the ideological dimension of its messages, rituals, and goals. Here I follow Althusser's outline of the history of Ideological State Apparatuses (which serves as a historical framework for his analysis of capitalism). The Church, the school, the family, he argues, are all ISAs, and they are nonrepressive expressions of ideology (in contrast to the State, which relies more heavily on repressive means). As Keith Moxey has pointed out, Althusser's principal revision of the Marxist base-superstructure reading of ideology lies in his emphasis on the dominant class's control of the institutions of *communication* over Marx's emphasis on the ownership of the means of *production.* (It is in the attribution of a material being to ideas, collapsing the Marxist distinction between the materially produced and the realm of ideas, that Althusser's scheme can be spoken of as having made ideology "material.")[35]

ISAs have a history (ideology, by contrast has no history, he argues, as like the unconscious, it is eternal, outside of time).[36] In precapitalist society religion was the dominant ISA; it held the function of education and communication that was later taken over primarily by schools. It is striking that in defining ideology, Althusser, a devout and activist Catholic in his early adulthood,[37] outlines only one example ("accessible to all"): the "Christian religious ideology," whose formal structure, he maintains, applies to all of ideology's iterations. Because I extrapolate a subject-forming function of visual propaganda from Althusser's definition of ideology, it merits a brief summary.

First, ideology pertains not only to explicit enunciations (the Testaments, sermons, etc.) but also to practices: rituals, ceremonies, and sacraments. The religious ideology is based on the existence of God, a unique Other Subject (capital *S*), who, through the scriptures directly, and through ritual indirectly, addresses each individual, making him a subject (small *s*). God makes him a subject by setting out his Commandments and establishing the subject's destination (heaven or hell) "according to the respect or contempt they show to 'God's Commandments.'" This "interpellation" (or call) of subjects by God to his Commandments is exemplified by Moses, to whom God gave his law, and who, in return, recognizes the Subject by being his subject: "God is thus the Subject, and Moses and the innumerable subjects of God's people, the Subject's interlocutors-interpellates: his *mirrors,* his *reflections.*"[38] This mirror function is "constitutive" of ideology; it "ensures its functioning by creating a center to which all subjects look to find the Subject," and, because they are themselves defined as subjects in his image, they also find themselves.[39]

Althusser's notion of the functioning of ideology draws on two key Christian concepts, a genealogy scarcely noted in the considerable discussion of this essay.[40] Althusser's speculary interpellation is an astonishingly fluent application to ideology of the idea of the *imago Dei* (of man made in God's image), as W. J. T. Mitchell previously pointed out.[41] The *imago Dei* is in turn foundational for the Christian tradition of mimetic reform, a process of subject formation whose origins lie in Greek philosophy.[42]

In Christian thought, man, created in God's image, lost his resemblance at the time of the fall. Through the logos, Christ, man could regain his divine likeness (Philo). Hence Paul's idea of the unity of the believer with God in Christ, hence his famous statement that "we reflect as in a mirror the glory of the Lord, thus we are transfigured into his likeness" (2 Cor. 3:17–18). In more than one passage Paul envisioned reconciliation with God as a matter of becoming His image. These are the roots of the *imitatio Christi,* a later mimetic practice of spiritual reform.

The Church Fathers widened the scope of Paul's notion of man, associating Christianity with humanity and the process of reforming man as one of becoming Christian. Encompassing the entire world of Christians and non-Christians, mimetic conformity became a historical process, an eschatological teleology. History was a corrective passage from estrangement (through sin) toward wholeness (toward the reformation of man through grace) to the final transformation of heaven and earth.[43] In *The City of God,* Augustine characterized the human race as one collective person and the conversion of the world as a process of moral education. The worldwide Jesuit mission descends from Augustine's universalist project, whose central technique was mimesis: the progressive approximation of man, through love, to a likeness of God.[44]

The Christian tradition of reform of the soul through mimesis also established the critical importance of exemplars: Christ first and foremost, and later, the saints. In spite of the critique of mimetic strategies by Luther and Calvin (not to mention the empirical philosophers), it was in the revivification of mysticism in the early modern Catholic Church (by figures such as Ignatius of Loyola) that mimesis hung on tenaciously into the Enlightenment.

The basis of Althusser's speculary structure of ideology in what became, in the early modern period, an identifiably *Catholic* form of interpellation is striking. But Althusser moves beyond the Catholic model of mirroring the soul in arguing that in making man in God's image, God needed men too. For Althusser ideology is a dialectic between mutually calling and responding subjects. Hence his statement that men are not only reflections of God, but His mirrors, in which the Subject sees Himself. While Althusser has been criticized for preserving a determinism in his thesis—that is, a shift from the Marxist emphasis on control of production to the far more nebulous, almost unconscious everywhereness of the control of discourse—it is precisely this quality of directedness that captures the pointedness of propaganda. The latter does not enter into Althusser's discussion of ideology, and so what follows is an extrapolation.

What is the relation between propaganda and ideology? Propaganda is often termed "an expression" of ideology, risking collapsing the distinction between the two. What does the "expression of" ideology actually *mean*? For not all rituals, acts, enunciations that, as Althusser puts it, "reproduce the illusion of our condition of existence" should be termed propaganda. There must be a play of difference. I advance my own definition here with regard to art. The work of art/propaganda is motivated; at times it makes ideology visible. By this I do not mean that *ideology* is illustrated. Rather, such a work is a call to the subject. In Althusser's view of ideology as functioning everywhere, unconsciously, expression is open-ended; it calls the subject but does not necessarily make explicit that it is calling. Propaganda, by contrast, is pointed. It makes demands of its subjects. It is the annunciatory, the self-reflexive moment of ideology: in saying "I am," propaganda demands that "you are" as well. Art that functions as propaganda is the making visible of the *call* of the subject to the mirror. Thus propaganda often entails a recognizable structure in the work and the interpellation of the viewer in seeing/reading.[45]

The propaganda message is also a necessary one. Ellul views propaganda as ordering our world, placating man's insecurities before a chaotic set of choices. But given the pointedness of propaganda, we must ask a specific set of questions before an instance of propaganda: Why is any *particular* message necessary? Why *this* message? Why this message *now*? For the production of propaganda is in some ways analogous to rules or laws formulated as responses to real circumstances. These forms arise not as a spontaneous affirmation, a bursting forth of spirit (the essence for Ellul of Christianity), but in response—perhaps a preemptory one—to a threat. Propaganda is often the mark of insecurity: when other ideologies compete for subjects (during democratic elections; during the period of *Konfession-*

alizierung, to bring us back to the current example); or when there are higher demands placed on being a subject (economic depression, wartime). It is an assertion and a demand: to be seen and mirrored. It is a message that demands to be read in a certain way.[46]

In the pages that follow, a chain of motivated representations that aim to form subjects are analyzed in light of this definition of propaganda as self-conscious, speculary, and necessary. In order for propaganda to be a meaningful category in art history, it must be tied to specific examples, whose necessity, and hence pointedness, can be demonstrated. My example is the Jesuits' primary exemplary figure for the interpellation of Catholic subjects, St. Ignatius of Loyola.

The ideal form of Ignatius's reformed soul was made visible in his hagiography and in visual images starting in the 1580s in the effort to fix his image for the future and to secure his canonization. The Jesuits reformed his image starting in the 1670s in Rome. The resurgence of Jesuit propaganda around Ignatius's cult culminates in the ceiling of the Church of St. Ignatius and the Chapel of St. Ignatius in the Gesù, the most ambitious and cultically significant sites in their program. Both of these major waves of image-making have distinctive motives and shapes. The motives are crucial. Both waves of imagery, I argue here, constitute propaganda insofar as they are clearly motivated and make visible the speculary, interpellative structure of ideology itself.

MIRROR IMAGES:
ST. IGNATIUS AND HIS BIOGRAPHER P. PEDRO DE RIBADEYNERA

When Ignatius of Loyola founded the Society of Jesus he professed a modest aim: to help souls.[47] But behind this simple statement stood a massive edifice. Distinguished by a special fourth vow of obedience—to go whither the pope sent them for the purposes of the Church—the Society was deeply committed to the universalistic project of uniting all men in the Church. In its willingness to work the gritty streets as well as to cross oceans for Christ, the Society of Jesus offered up hope for the unification of the woeful asymmetries— of pagan and Christian, of heaven and earth—brought on by the fall of man.

The eschatological nature of the Jesuit project is just a point of departure, not our destination. But it is critical insofar as it establishes the stakes of the mimetic (or specular) processes that I am ultimately concerned with here. As Marjorie Reeves has shown, the Jesuits, like the Franciscans and Dominicans earlier, laid claim to Joachim of Fiore's prophecy of an order that would come before the end of time to aid in preparing the way for the second coming. Well into the seventeenth century the Jesuits viewed themselves as chief protagonists in the augmentation of the Church before the end of time.[48] With Europe confessionally divided and a new world of souls to be converted, the worldwide Jesuit mission was one of the Church's primary instruments for the creation and maintenance of Catholic subjects. Joachim of Fiore's prophecy became deeply tied to the hagiography of Ignatius, the God-sent founder of the Society who set that plan in motion.

As one of God's ideally reformed subjects, the founder became an imitable prototype for others to copy. After his death, it was in reading about him that others could discern and conform themselves to his ideal form. Ignatius's imitability was made legible to potential subjects above all in two key texts: the so-called 'Récit' and an early biography, produced, respectively, as Ignatius and those who had known him neared their deaths, when writing was itself a process by which the Jesuits defined themselves, by which they became Jesuit subjects.[49] The 'Récit' is Ignatius's account of his own life, not an autobiography proper, but rather a written narrative composed by the Jesuit Goncalves de Camara based on notes taken from Ignatius's oral account.[50] The second text—on which I focus here—is the expanded version of the first official biography of Ignatius by the Spanish Jesuit Pedro de Ribadeynera (1526–1611). The Jesuits commissioned both texts for the Society, and the latter in particular, the first of many accounts of Ignatius to be published, was subject to intensive scrutiny.[51]

In both narratives Ignatius's "life" begins at the moment of his spiritual conversion.[52] This took place at the age of thirty, in 1521, following his vainglorious actions in a battle at Pamplona where he received disfiguring wounds to his legs. He spent the period of his convalescence in the family home in Loyola reading. At first he continued in his vain pursuit of worldly glory (he had been a page at court before going to battle), reading Medieval romances that inspired him to devote himself to the service of a lady. He also took up the lives of the saints, discovering that these narratives gave him more lasting consolation (fig. 24). So in the 'Récit':

> Reading the life of Our Lord and [those] of the saints, he ended up thinking, reasoning to himself: "How would it be if I were to do what St. Francis and St. Dominic did?" And in this way he reflected on many things that he found good, always proposing great and arduous undertakings for himself, and when he proposed them it seemed to him that it would be possible to do the same. In his reasoning, he always returned to saying to himself: "St. Dominic did this; and well, I should do so as well. St. Francis did this; well, I should do so also." These thoughts lasted a long time.[53]

The imitative formula is disarmingly simple. In both the 'Récit' and Ribadeynera's *vita* we are clearly apprised that mimetic desire was just the first step toward Ignatius's spiritual conversion. Ribadeynera glosses this moment, noting that in wanting to imitate the saints, Ignatius was coming to feel a "change in heart."[54] This initial ray of light intensified and he gained in his conviction to "imitate good Jesus, our captain and master, and the other saints equally; who, having imitated Christ, merit to be imitated by ourselves."[55] This passage occurs early on in Ribadeynera's *vita*. It constitutes an explicit instruction to the reader that although Ignatius was still far from spiritually formed, his imitation of the saints, and then Christ, is in itself imitable.[56] And that pertains to any reader of Ribadeynera's text, although initially he wrote to Jesuit readers whom he addressed directly in a moving preamble.[57] Though just the beginning of Ignatius's reform, this entrance into a new spiritual life, through a book, was crucial in establishing the speculary premise of the biography: in reading Ignatius's life, one already imitated Ignatius (whose conversion through reading, in turn, imitated Augustine).

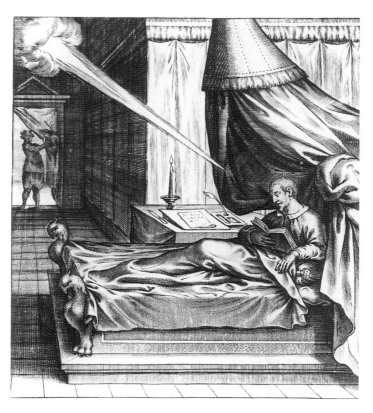

FIG. 24

Jean-Baptiste Barbé after Pieter Paul Rubens, *Ignatius reading the lives of the saints imitates them and is converted to God,* 1609.

Ignatius's progress in mimetic activity moves from the saints to the more important imitation of Christ. His reading of Thomas à Kempis's *Imitation of Christ* at a later moment, when he began to study in Alcalá, marked an important step forward.

> The spiritual book that he had in his hands most frequently, and whose lesson he commended more than any other, was the Disprezzio del mondo, entitled *De Imitatione Christi,* by Thomas da Kempis, the spirit of which he gathered [*raccolse*] and which penetrated him to his bowels in such a way that the life of Ignatius (as a servant of God said to me), was nothing else than the most perfect exemplar [*essemplare*] of all that which is contained in that little book.[58]

Having established Ignatius's exemplarity in his *imitatio,* Ribadeynera provides evidence that others perceived and enacted this as well. Ignatius soon attracted followers in Alcalá, at first three men who, "moved by the example of Ignatius, were attracted to him, as imitators of his life."[59]

Ignatius could only become a form to be imitated once he himself had been spiritually reformed. Ribadeynera treats his entire body, or to be precise, the inside of his body, as transformed, with the new internal images implanted once the previous images (*especies*) of his former life of the flesh had been erased from his soul.[60] Ignatius's form (that is, his spirit, his soul), drawing on Medieval tradition, is at various moments visualized as a sculptural form—both as a wax-receiving surface for the divine imprint and as a mold into which the divine substance penetrated and melted. Ribadeynera depicts his soul as a work of art in order to make it visible to us, for Ignatius's reformed form is internal. It is this form of the reformed man, rather than Ignatius's external form, that Ribadeynera is setting out as the imitable form of Ignatius. Thus Ribadeynera's biography is itself a critical act of discernment, to use an Ignatian term, a making visible of an invisible form.

Having received the imprint of the divine form, Ignatius is prepared to imprint other souls. And here we must understand the larger scheme of Ribadeynera's biography. The central drama in his depiction of Ignatius is the founding and expansion of the Society during his lifetime, which occupies a significant portion of the text.[61] Although Ignatius is shown to have possessed the requisite virtues of sainthood—the last of the five books is dedicated to his obedience, discipline, ardor, compassion, and so on—Ribadeynera considered the founding of the Society so important that it should be considered a miracle. The phrasing is important. Ribadeynera knew well that at the time of writing Ignatius had no conventional miracles to his name and this could stand in the way of the canonization. General Claudio Aquaviva and other Jesuits also had doubts. But Ribadeynera, marshaling an arsenal of patristic sources, argued that miracles were not a necessary sign of sanctity.[62] In his later *vita* of Ignatius included in his popular *Flos Sanctorum*, a compendium of saints' *vite*, Ribadeynera narrated a series of conventional miracles performed by Ignatius. Nonetheless, he still insisted on his earlier argument:

> But even though there are many and very certain miracles recounted and many others pending, which I will leave out here to be brief; nonetheless, the greatest miracle in my judgment, is that God the Father elected the father to institute, govern and expand a Society that amongst Catholics and heretics, and amongst the infidels, in such a short time has reaped much fruit in the world. And this miracle is so great, and so manifest, that if the other [miracles] were to be lacking, this one alone should suffice to know and esteem the sanctity that God gave to this father.[63]

The Society's form was also an ideal one. Ignatius's direct communication with God during the composition of the Society's *Constitutions* provided evidence of this. Ignatius was repeatedly subject to visions and mystical experiences while shaping the principles and forms of Jesuit activity.[64] In the cycle of images painted under Ribadeynera's direction by Juan de Mesa for the Society's house in Madrid (and preserved in a suite of engravings), the composition of the *Constitutions* is seen in close relation to the founding of the Society (fig. 25). This is not intended as a temporal sequence. Ribadeynera compares the Society to a spiritual edifice of which Christ is the cornerstone and Ignatius the chosen architect, executing God's will.[65]

A *Paulus Tertius Pontifex Maximus, anno salutis* B. *Constitutiones ac regulam S. Pater, scribit.* C *Filios suos ad prædicandum euangelium in*
1540. Societatem Iesu confirmat. Lib. 2. c. 16. Lib. 4 c. 2. *uarias mundi plagas dimittit.* Li. 3.

FIG. 25
Charles de Mallery after Juan de Mesa, *Paul III confirms the Society of Jesus* (A); *Ignatius composes the Constitutions* (B), 1610.

Through the course of Ribadeynera's *vita,* Ignatius becomes virtually synonymous with the form of the Society of Jesus itself: "It will not be far from my purpose to explain the institution of the Society with the Bull of Pope Julius III as in the *vita* that we are writing of Our Father [Ignatius] it is well that the form and image that he made of the Company be known."[66] The introductory passages to Ignatius's 'Récit' asserted that Ignatius's *life* provided the *literal* foundation for the Society. Goncalves de Camara wrote: "When father [Jerome] Nadal came, he was very happy because we had started [the 'Récit'], and he ordered me to inconvenience the father [Ignatius], telling me more than once that in no other way could the father do more good for the Company; and that this thing signified *the real founding* of the Company."[67] Over a period of four years Nadal had repeatedly asked Ignatius to recount how God had "formed" his spirit from the moment of his conversion because that story could "be of use to us."[68] As Louis Marin has emphasized, Nadal asked for a testament, a guide to those to come after Ignatius's death, not simply a record of his life.[69] I have begun my account of the mimeto-speculary functioning of propaganda with these two written narratives because their purpose was to set in place a mirroring function: the discernment of one ideal form (Ignatius),

PETRVS RIBADENEIRA TOLETANVS
SOCIETATIS IESV PRESBYTER THEOLOGVS:
B. IGNATIO CARISS. EIVSQ. VITAE TESTIS
ACCVRATVSQ. SCRIPTOR : DE VITIS QVOQ. SANCTOR.
TRIVMQ. GENERALIVM PRAEPOSITT. ET A.SALMERONIS.
VITA DECESSIT AETATIS AN. LXXXIV. RELIGIONIS LXXI.
CHRISTI VERO CIƆ.IƆC.XI. A.D.X. KAL. OCTOB.

Theod. Galle excudit.

FIG. 26
Theodor Galle reengraved after anonymous engraving, *Pedro de Ribadeynera.*

which begot another (the Society), which will beget many more (Jesuits and Catholics).

The speculary process discernible in the texts plays out in images as well, where art's natural mimetic properties replace the work of reading. This is made evident in a portrait of Ribadeynera that draws together the author's discernment of Ignatius's form in two media. The painted portrait of Ribadeynera by Juan de Mesa is lost, but it is recorded, with a significant alteration, in an engraving (fig. 26). Descriptions of the painting tell us

FIG. 27
Jacopino del Conte, *St. Ignatius*, 1556.

that his pen and ink pot and three of his books about Ignatius appeared.[70] In the engraving the inscription (which stresses the accuracy of Ribadeynera's written accounts of St. Ignatius) does the work of the books and objects of the writer's craft. It makes the viewer also a reader.

Ribadeynera's portrait is an image of an image-maker. In different ways, the original painting and the engraving captured Ribadeynera's parallel projects of discerning Ignatius in written works, and visually through the production of an authoritative portrait, a "true effigy," of Ignatius. In the latter regard, we know that he was so dissatisfied by Jacopino del Conte's portrait of the saint, produced in Rome (fig. 27), that he supervised what he considered a more accurate portrait painted by Alonso Sanchez Coello in Madrid (fig. 28).[71] Ribadeynera was also responsible for the cycle of narrative scenes

Alonso Sanchez Coello, *St. Ignatius*, 1585.

from Ignatius's life commissioned for the Jesuit house in Madrid from Juan de Mesa in 1600. The sumptuous engraved edition of the paintings (all but one is lost) produced in Antwerp in 1610 accompanied Ribadeynera's reissued *vita* of 1609 with the images keyed to the text. These prints provided the first real canon of Ignatian images, repeated over and over in various media through the precanonization years and also thereafter.[72]

The "image" of Ignatius, the portrait argues, is comprised by Ribadeynera's writings and the portrait he oversaw. The writings are made manifest to the *reader* of the inscription, while the visual image is made manifest to the *viewer* in the picture of the saint, which this mute Ribadeynera shows to the viewer. But whose is this image of Ignatius on the print? The portrait of Ignatius that we see barely approximates the *vera effigia* of

Ignatius that Ribadeynera so doggedly pursued with Coello and then saw disseminated (see fig. 28). Why would that *exact* image not appear as the true effigy to which the inscription refers? What this suggests is that the "true" effigy of Ignatius is, in its composite, what Ribadeynera offers to us (and the offer is made explicit in his gesture). In setting up the complementary claims of visual representation (the print) and hagiographic representation (the books, referred to in the inscription) of Ignatius's "true effigy," Ribadeynera himself emerges as Ignatius's Veronica, capturing the true effigy on "his cloth," that is, on his person. In other words, given these two instantiations of Ignatius's *vera effigia*—the book and the image—it is rather a third instantiation, Ribadeynera himself, as a Jesuit, who is perhaps the best effigy of Ignatius.

The specular relation of this image-maker to the person represented would remain mere inference if Ribadeynera's own portrait were not so strikingly similar—in dress, pose, expression, even the features of his face—to that of Ignatius in the print he holds in his hand. Moreover, the entire print itself, with its portrait of the writer ruled over by the Jesuit monogram of Christ and a distinct zone for the inscription, echoes the print of Ignatius he holds in his hand, with two crucial differences. First, Ignatius and Ribadeynera are posed slightly differently: Ignatius is seen almost frontally (and this is how the engraved representation differs from that original painting), whereas Ribadeynera turns to address the viewer and gestures to us: "I present you Ignatius." "He is," so "I am."

The altered position of the IHS monogram, the most pervasive symbol of the Society, is also important. This element probably did not appear in the original painting of Ignatius, in which he looked up with rays of light issuing toward his face. The original painting, interpreted in later versions with the addition of an inscription,[73] suggested the divine illumination, the unobstructed view to the heavens that brought about Ignatius's interior transformation. In adding the name of the Society (the choice of which Ignatius made after the famous vision at La Storta), placing it above Ignatius's head, the entire meaning shifted: from Ignatius's communication with God to Ignatius as namer, that is, as founder of the Jesuit order. Ribadeynera, who lived under but did not invent the Society's name, could not appear in the same relation to the monogram as Ignatius and, accordingly, it has been moved to the corner of the image, more of a coat of arms than an act. As the banner under which Ribadeynera lived, the IHS literally showed Ribadeynera's interpellation as a Jesuit subject.

How to read this image? At first appearance the print argues that Ignatius, the subject, was made *by* Ribadeynera's image. But this would emphasize Ribadeynera's role over that of Ignatius: that Ribadeynera interpellates Ignatius rather than the other way around. Is it not also the case that Ribadeynera, like all Jesuits, cannot *but* be made in Ignatius's image? Was Ribadeynera not only Ignatius's Veronica, the imprinter, but himself another effigy of the true effigy of Ignatius? As we have seen, the cornerstone of Ignatius's hagiography was his founding of the order and the making of the image of the Jesuit itself. It was Ribadeynera who created a likeness of Ignatius to which he, in the spirit of the

Society that he himself defined, could liken himself. The engraving enacts the *imitatio ignatio:* the Jesuits as an endless stream of likenesses of Ignatius.

Ribadeynera's discernment of Ignatius's form was, in other words, itself a mimetic production. Through it Ribadeynera discerned his own, and hence the Jesuit form, after Ignatius's reformed form. The Subject (Ignatius) also needs the subject (Ribadeynera, the Jesuit).

IMAGES AND INTERPELLATION:
IMAGES PRODUCING SUBJECTS, PRODUCING SAINTS

What was at stake in Ribadeynera's biography of Ignatius was the hoped-for canonization. For it is with canonization that the Jesuits gained a powerful tool of interpellation, of subject formation. Canonization brought the dedication of altars, the call to mass in Ignatius's name; it endowed corporal sanctity, heightening the possibilities for miraculous intervention through the power of relics; it created subjects through naming, as either out of devotion or accident of birth, more children would receive the name of Ignatius. As Ribadeynera noted in the dedication of Ignatius's *vita*, with the biography, his "heroic and clear virtue will become more known, esteemed by many more, and imitated."[74] Biography, or life writing, was a necessary and licit form of making Ignatius's virtue widely known.[75]

Prior to canonization, images were another matter. It was prohibited to represent Ignatius at his tomb, on altars, in processions, and already in a saintly light. The temptation to do so, however, was clearly strong. A print campaign for Ignatius began in the 1590s; it exploded in 1609, the year of Ignatius's beatification, extending through 1622, the year of the canonization. But before the beatification—the new step on the way to canonization—and canonization, restraint was necessary. The Jesuits undertook the promotion of the official cult at a transitional moment, when new and more stringent beatification and canonization procedures were being worked out. These new procedures were launched in principle at the Council of Trent (1563), made bureaucratically feasible with the institution of the Congregation of Rites (1587), and finally made official by Urban VIII in 1634.[76] Responding to Protestant criticism of the cult of the saints, the Church aimed to test spontaneous cults before they became sanctioned ones, to ensure that all candidates for sainthood met the Church's rigorous standards of heroic virtue. Canonization thus became far more difficult than it had been previously. Although the new regulations were not officially in place until 1634, in the period of Ignatius's proceedings the pope already exercised control over the public circulation and display of images.

General Claudio Aquaviva (1581–1615) maintained strict obedience with regard to the representation of Ignatius through the 1590s, fearful that even a pious misstep could jeopardize canonization. It was not a Jesuit but the Oratorian cardinal Cesare Baronio who broke the taboo in 1599 when he placed votives and a portrait above Ignatius's modest tomb in the apse of the Gesù. In 1602 Clement VIII ordered investigations of the visible signs of veneration accorded the uncanonized, marking new circumspection particularly around the tombs of possible saints but in other locations as well. Clement did not single out Ignatius; the advocates of Carlo Borromeo and Philip Neri received warnings too.[77]

But news of Baronio's bold stroke traveled, inciting public demonstrations of Ignatius's cult across Europe. In 1602 papal representatives in Spain wrote to Cardinal Aldobrandini (who was responsible for granting papal printing privileges in these years):

> The Jesuit fathers have erected an altar to father Ignatius here [in Valladolid] and at Saragosa, to the astonishment of many. They told me that he had been beatified by the Holy Father, and that the same had been done in Rome, and that the portrait of the said father [Ignatius] is sold publicly with the permission of His Holiness.[78]

Aldobrandini replied that it was "completely false" that Ignatius had been beatified and that the pope warned the Jesuits of his displeasure at the news of their "excessive demonstrations" around Ignatius's image at his tomb. Moreover, they had been ordered to cease printing images of Ignatius surrounded by "various figurines representing the actions of Ignatius."[79] In the meantime, he received further notice from another nuncio:

> I see that Your Eminence has written to me on the subject of the altar that the Jesuit fathers here [in Valladolid] have erected in honor of father Ignatius. I beseeched these fathers to remove it themselves without scandal. They have already suppressed the diadem and certain rays crowning the head of the said father, who had been painted kneeling in the center of the painting, his hands joined, gazing at one side at God the Father from whom descended towards him other rays.[80]

Although there was a new enforcement of cultic honors and the Jesuits had policies to control the latter, especially around the tomb, the most important site for the "cultivation" of a public following, there is much evidence that the Society broke its own rules before the canonization.[81] Many of these images (like the portrait of Ignatius included in Ribadeyneras *vita*) were licit. What was problematic was any hint of saintliness: halos, diadems, interior illumination, or any inscription calling Ignatius "beatus" or "sanctus."[82]

Like the public altars, engravings put into circulation that improperly anticipated beatification did not always slip past the papal censors.[83] In June 1601 Clement VIII told the Jesuits to stop printing "images of Ignatius with miracles." But the rules were loosely applied: the Jesuits were to cease and desist printing further sheets but were left free to distribute what they already had.[84] Clement's prohibition has been connected to Francesco Villamena's sumptuous engraving of Ignatius surrounded by events from his life, with an emphasis on apparitions and miracles. Published for the jubilee year 1600, the print was conspicuously dedicated to Herzog Wilhelm V of Bavaria (fig. 29).[85] Clement should have objected to the depiction of Ignatius, literally, in a holy light. Shown kneeling on top of a sarcophagus-like base, he is bathed in light, with a nimbus, and called "beatus" in

FIG. 29

Francesco Villamena, *St. Ignatius*, Rome, 1600.

the inscription below. But the image provoked the pope because it included numerous unapproved miracles among the narrative scenes. The papacy reserved its right to approve miracles *before* they were represented.

Why, we should ask, were the Jesuits challenging papal authorities? Why did they insist on representing Ignatius's *sanctity* when they could have stopped at promoting his virtuous life? And why were *images* a point of contestation? Why was a textual representation of Ignatius not only licit but required? This double standard regarding representation points to anxiety that an image is attributed with a truth-value that a text, far more demanding of the viewer's attention, is not. This anxiety suggests the image's ability to form subjects in advance of the Church's declaration of him as saint.

The Jesuits needed to mount a canonization campaign for Ignatius in order to produce the miracles necessary for canonization. As Pierre Delooz has pointed out, miracles are *revealers* of sainthood.[86] They had to be produced. But how could they if there were no signs of Ignatius's sanctity in the places—the cult sites—where miracles most often occurred? The pressure for images suggests that they were crucial in *producing* the public cult, which in turn generated the posthumous miracles necessary for juridical approval of sanctity. The circularity of the canonization proceedings is stunningly apparent: to produce a saint one needed to have *already* produced his subjects.

As Jean-Michel Sallmann has put it, "To be canonized, a servant of God had to enjoy the fame of sanctity, which could not be constituted except by external manifestations of sanctity."[87] In strictly controlling the representation of sanctity, the papacy asserted its authority in creating a saintly subject.[88] The new procedures demanded something that was common enough before canonization became such a tightly controlled juridical process— that the cults of saints arise spontaneously. But the looseness in carrying out prohibitions against representation points to some recognition of the need for images to produce sanctity. If, as Sallmann suggests, the ecclesiastical authorities needed the testimony of miracles in order to confirm their theological certainties,[89] then in cases like Ignatius's, when miracles were slow in coming, there was good reason to allow images of some candidates for sanctity to slip through.

Canonization provided the motive for the wave of representation of Ignatius before 1622. This may seem self-apparent. Indeed, it has been the subject of a study that was organized around the presumed function of images as propaganda.[90] But there is more to be said about why canonization produces propaganda in general and visual propaganda in particular. It is not just that the Jesuits desired that Ignatius be made a saint, to confirm his interpellation as one of God's chosen subjects. More important to the mission of the Society and the Church Universal, once canonized, Ignatius would become a subject who interpellates other subjects. I am simply restating traditions of imitation of exemplary heroes and intercession in ideological terms. Where images come in is in creating the condition of possibility for cult, and hence canonization, and hence the interpellation of further subjects as the cult, it is hoped, grows over time.

ST. IGNATIUS'S CULT: THE CRISIS OF THE 1670s

After the heady celebrations surrounding the canonization in 1622 Ignatius's cult did not appear to have increased with time, at least not where it should have been most spontaneous and where it mattered most: at the site of his relics in the Roman Gesù. By the 1670s, when general Gian Paolo Oliva commenced planning for the renovation of all of the public spaces of the church including Ignatius's reliquary chapel, the argument was being made that Ignatius did not have a popular cult.[91]

The renovation of the Chapel of St. Ignatius, located since 1622 in the left transept but never more than provisorily set up for the saint, was a priority of the campaign of the 1670s. Complaints about the altar, "so undignified" for the stature of the founder, had been mounting for decades.[92] The discussions over the renovation of the altar in 1671–72 turned on one main issue: how to distinguish the altar in richness and importance in the context of a unified scheme for the church. One radical idea—to move Ignatius to a crypt below the high altar—appeared to satisfy these criteria. The architect Carlo Fontana drew up several schemes, initially conceiving an open confessio (like the tomb of St. Peter). When such a scheme was deemed untenable—for compromising Vignola's plan, for disturbing Alessandro Farnese's tomb—he devised an ingenious alternative, a closed crypt that nonetheless made the relics visible from the nave (fig. 20).

The general's advisors debated the plans to move Ignatius's relics extensively. In their discussions one unidentified Jesuit in favor of translating the relics to the apse stated clearly what was at stake in the renovation of Ignatius's tomb to begin with. Here is the motive for all that follows:

> The reason why we should move the relics [of Ignatius] to the high altar is very clear, because St. Ignatius is not like St. Anthony of Padua, nor like St. [Francis] Xavier and similar saints, to whom divine providence ordained, that the people run: but in this lack of devotion our Great Patriarch is similar to other Great Patriarchs of the Church, who, although in themselves great, and stars of the highest greatness, nonetheless do not have the large popular following that other Saints of minor titles possess. For example, what great popular following do a St. Basil Patriarch of Asia, a St. Benedict Patriarch of Europe, a St. Anthony Abbot Patriarch of Africa have? The very Apostles on the feasts of whom so few communions are seen? For this therefore is also a motive to create for St. Ignatius a necessary, continuous and suitable flow of devotees, which he does not have, it was judged best to transfer him to the high altar where masses are performed for all feasts, and on vespers with noble music. In addition, Friday mornings frequent communion for the *buona morte,* and in the evening many people assemble for the same. In addition, on holidays at every mass there is always communion, and since a number of the masses are so crowded, on longer days, up to fourteen can be held as they begin an hour before dawn. With the said translation you increase, not decrease devotion to the Sacrament because of the greater magnificence of the Tribune, and with the greater number of lights [which are] to be held by a number of angels of gilded bronze, all of these are things which entice the common people, as well as the more refined.[93]

Not only does our anonymous Jesuit state, quite boldly, that Ignatius does not have a popular cult, but he also argues, equally explicitly, that to generate a cult people must be brought physically to his altar. Critical in drawing people to the site is magnificence: music, candles, and, not least, visual splendor. The importance of this document in establishing a *motive* for the redecoration of Ignatius's tomb, and indeed for the whole series of new decorations of Ignatian sites that followed, cannot be overstated.

The document quoted above reveals how a chapel might function to create subjects. The Jesuit's comments give notice to a series of arguments made on both sides of the issue, addressing the crypt idea as well as the cult. Those in favor of moving the relics thought about the symbolic hierarchy of the church plan. As the most important site in the church the high altar was appropriate for Ignatius's tomb. Those opposed considered the spatial dimension more phenomenally, arguing that distinct and uniquely dedicated spaces were more honorific. Two additional points emerge from the debate. First was a concern for visibility, for keeping Ignatius's *image* constantly before the faithful, underscoring the crucial role of the image for interpellation. Analogously, they worried about the power of linguistic habits, of the need to keep Ignatius's name in the *ears* of the faithful. One interlocutor worried that the Jesuits would refer to the apse altars collectively as the "altar of St. Ignatius," thus detracting from its actual dedication to the Circumcision and its role as a chapel of the Sacrament. The opposite was likely argued by the other side. Distinct *audibility* was also important: the same Jesuit imagined an acoustic Babylon with voices from masses on both altars, above and below, intermingling, making both inaudible. He may have been thinking practically, but from all of these arguments emerges a clear concern that Ignatius's new altar could not bear fruit unless the subject could hear the saint's name and see his face. Girolamo Muziano's *Circumcision* on the high altar celebrated the first enunciation of Christ's name. Some feared that, contrary to the enunciative moment celebrated above, the Ignatian crypt would end up literally drowning out and "burying with it the cult of the saint himself."

The discussion of the renovation of Ignatius's tomb as a function of cultic considerations resonates with the skirmish over the precanonization prints. Particularly striking is the degree to which visible and audible utterances—votives, illumination, iconic imagery, the name of the chapel, the celebration of his mass—were deemed critical to the interpellation of subjects. The internalization of Ignatius is insufficient. The mirror, Ignatius, must be made highly visible, distinct and audible, for his subjects to hear themselves called to—and see themselves reflected in—him.

IGNATIAN CULT SITES IN ROME, 1680s–1690s

Although the discussions of the renovation of Ignatius's chapel came to naught in the 1670s,[94] from all appearances, the concern voiced over the cult set off a campaign of decoration in Ignatian Rome.[95] Between the 1680s and the Holy Year 1700, Ignatian cult sites in addition to the chapel in the Gesù (renovated 1695–99) were newly adorned: frescoes for the corridor outside the rooms of St. Ignatius in the Casa Professa, a chapel on the site of Ignatius's final retreat at a Jesuit villa near the Baths of Caracalla, and the vault

FIG. 30

Jacob Frey, *Notizie della Cappella di S. Ignazio, situata in mezzo della Storta*, 1700.

of the Church of St. Ignatius. For the Jubilee of 1700 the small chapel outside Rome at La Storta, where Ignatius had his celebrated vision of Christ and God the Father, would be renovated by a minor Jesuit painter (fig. 30). With the exception of the chapel at La Storta, all of these projects were executed by the Jesuit painter and architect Andrea Pozzo, newly arrived in Rome in 1681. This prominent group of Roman monuments should be understood as a coherent and motivated redress of Ignatian cult sites.[96] When viewed as a group and in the context of the history of the hagiographic project as well as the anxiety over Ignatius's cult, it becomes clear why these projects emphasized two major themes:

4b   3b

4c   4d   4a   3c   3d   3a

FIG. 31 (THIS PAGE AND OPPOSITE)

Scheme for Borgognone paintings on the right wall, Corridor of St. Ignatius

1a. St. Ignatius playing billiards with a French theologian, who in losing takes the Spiritual Exercises

1b. St. Ignatius prevents an injustice

1c. While studying St. Ignatius is protected from an intruder by an angel

1d. St. Ignatius cures an amorous man by throwing himself into a frozen river

2a. Penitent St. Ignatius and his deprivations in the wilderness

2b. St. Ignatius's vision at Manresa?

2c. St. Ignatius in rapture appears dead

2d. Virgin and Child appear to St. Ignatius while writing the Spiritual Exercises

3a. St. Ignatius the pilgrim has a vision of the cross

3b. Unknown scene, men on horses

3c. St. Ignatius gives his clothes to a pilgrim in Montserrat

3d. St. Ignatius chooses his path for Montserrat guided by the Virgin

4a. St. Ignatius takes leave of his family

4b. St. Ignatius before the Virgin and Child (by Andrea Pozzo)

4c. St. Ignatius before a painting of the Virgin and Child

4d. St. Ignatius in battle at Pamplona

Ignatius as founder, central in the earliest hagiography, and the more problematic but cultically charged image of Ignatius as miracle-maker.

    The first site to which the Jesuits turned their attention was the corridor in the Casa Professa, which let onto the rooms in which Ignatius lived and died. Those four small irregular chambers were considered relics in and of themselves. This was articulated when, following the disastrous flood of Rome of 1598 that ruined the original building in which Ignatius lived for over two decades and Odoardo Farnese undertook a new building for the Society, the decision was made to preserve the original rooms.[97] Three steps higher

2b

1b

2c 2d 2a 1c 1d 1a

than the second story of the new house, the rooms encased in the new building were brought closer to their sixteenth-century modesty in a recent restoration.[98]

Outside the rooms was a long, uninterrupted, window-lined corridor, of which the Ignatian rooms spanned the last five bays. In the window bays in a section of the corridor a painted cycle of Ignatius's life had been begun by Giacomo Borgognone, around 1661 (fig. 31).[99] Drawing in part on engravings from earlier in the century, his series depicts scenes from Ignatius's early life, four sets of four images around the windows, which commence with Ignatius's service as a page and soldier and emphasize the exercise of his postconversion virtues before coming to Rome to found the Society.

The decision to mark the section of the corridor as belonging to the cult site by enclosing the decorated space came under the generalate of Carlo de Noyelle (1682–86). Urged by one of his assistants (in consultation with Andrea Pozzo) to erect a wall, the general was advised that this alteration would relieve the complaint that the Jesuits often found laypeople (not necessarily the devout—*cortigiani* and waiting servants were cited) underfoot.[100] These *secolari* overheard private Jesuit affairs and rites, blocked passage, made noise, and often wandered into the infirmary. A new wall would contain them as well as the pungent smell of onions and cauliflower that rose unimpeded to Ignatius's rooms from the kitchen below. How could the sweet perfume of sanctity be smelled in this olfactory Babylon?

The argument for the enclosure of the corridor was not just a strategy of containment. Pozzo had a closed perspectival scheme in mind for the space in which he would complete what Borgognone began, now covering the entire corridor: the walls (figs. 32, 33), ceiling (fig. 34), and entrance facade to the new space, uncovered in the 1990 restoration.[101] The scheme comprises five interrelated themes: Ignatius's early life (by Bor-

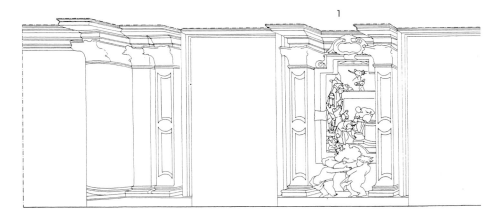

FIG. 32 (THIS PAGE AND OPPOSITE)
Scheme for Pozzo frescoes on the right wall, Corridor of St. Ignatius
1. St. Ignatius puts out a fire in Florence
2. St. Ignatius cures a nun
3. St. Ignatius frees prisoners

FIG. 33 (THIS PAGE AND OPPOSITE)
Scheme for Pozzo frescoes on the left wall, Corridor of St. Ignatius
1. Healings by the oil hanging before St. Ignatius's tomb
2. St. Ignatius exorcises a man possessed in Rome
3. Virgin and Child
4. An angel disguised as a pilgrim completes a portrait of St. Ignatius

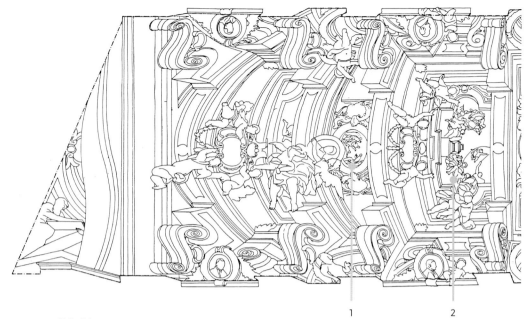

FIG. 34

Scheme for Pozzo frescoes on the vault, Corridor of St. Ignatius

1. St. Ignatius appears to a dying man

2. Glorification of the tomb of St. Ignatius

3a. Death of St. Ignatius

3b. St. Charles Borromeo at the tomb of St. Ignatius

3c. St. Philip Neri recognizes St. Ignatius's radiance

4. St. Ignatius in Glory

5. Resurrection of a dead man?

gognone); the early Jesuit companions (in gilded roundels lining the upper region of the corridor walls); Jesuit saints (on the exterior of the entrance wall); and miracles of and devotion to Ignatius. The latter dominates the cycle, and it is the aspect on which my remarks will be focused.

This new imagery about devotion appears throughout the scheme. On the terminal wall[102] (fig. 35) Ignatius is raised on a pedestal, holding a book (his attribute), and crowned by angels, he appears a statue over an altar. Yet he is a lively, naturalistic Ignatius (fig. 36). As a syntactic type, it is, perhaps, the perfect Counter-Reformation form: at once alive, real to us, able to invoke our human empathy but also in a form—a statue on an altar—worthy of veneration. The "live" statue helps us to turn an image of a "real" historical Ignatius into a cult image before our very eyes. This pictorial logic is not, of course, unique to this image.[103]

In addition to the representation of a cult-type image, Ignatius's body and his relics, the most precious source for devotion, also appear in numerous scenes. The relics are

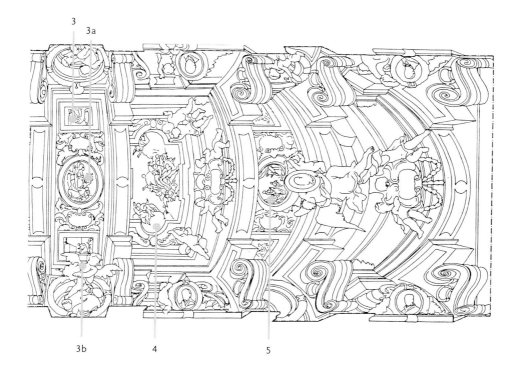

encased in a glass urn adored by angels just beyond the scene of his death, located at the center of the vault (fig. 37). This glass urn is a notable departure from the actual bronze reliquary urn contained in the church next door (see fig. 18). Is the glass front a metaphor for a renewed sense of purpose in making Ignatius's saintly body visible? A making visible of the making visible? The relics appear again in one of the small grisaille scenes along the curve of the vault. In the bay of the vault in which the scene of Ignatius's death is painted, Carlo Borromeo kneels before the altar of Ignatius in adoration of the relics (fig. 38).[104] Opposite, another small grisaille shows Philip Neri[105] recognizing Ignatius's internal illumination, his "super splendore vultus": the corporeal sign of Ignatius's sanctity (fig. 39). There will be more said about this latter scene in its elaborated form in the Chapel of St. Ignatius; its primary purpose in Pozzo's corridor, as elsewhere, is to show an authoritative witness of Ignatius's sanctity, legible during his lifetime *on his body*. The two small grisailles argue for saintliness recognized in Ignatius's bones. And they show the interpellation of renowned subjects to Ignatius's cult.

The vault narrative stresses the fate of Ignatius's body: it moves from his death (fig. 40) to his reception in heaven to his glorification as a saint, culminating with the privilege of celebration at his own altar on the terminal wall (see fig. 35). The scenes in the two end bays of the vault represent miracles enacted by Ignatius, one an appearance at the moment of a man's death, the other a rescue from death's hands. They suggest the interpellation of his subjects arising from Ignatius's own death and departure from his body, the scenes that these two miracles bracket.

FIG. 35
Andrea Pozzo, *St. Ignatius,* ca. 1682–86. Corridor of St. Ignatius, Casa
Professa, Rome.

The cumulative evidence of these scenes of bodily sanctity and cultic display points to
a narrative *about* devotion to Ignatius's corporeal sanctity. There was no more appropriate place than the Casa Professa corridor for such a narrative. Ignatius wrote the *Rules*
for and ran the Society from these rooms and he died here. As the site where he lived
and breathed his last breath, it is impregnated with the bodily presence of the living and
dying man.

The second major theme developed, or rather, redeveloped, in the corridor is that of
the Ignatian miracles. As the account of the tense years around the canonization showed,
Ignatius's miracles were not the primary basis for either his canonization or his reputation as a saint (although the requisite number were approved for the canonization). It has

FIG. 36

Andrea Pozzo, *St. Ignatius,* ca. 1682–86. Corridor of St. Ignatius, Casa
Professa, Rome.

been suggested that Ribadeynera's argument *against* miracles marked a progressive trend
in hagiography, a move toward a humanist framework for sacred history, rather than a
sign of deficiency.[106] This may well have been the case, but the revision of the Ignatian
vita in the second half of the seventeenth century suggests that if Ribadeynera's had been

FIG. 37
Andrea Pozzo, *Urn of St. Ignatius,* ca. 1682–86. Corridor of St. Ignatius, Casa Professa, Rome.

FIG. 38
Andrea Pozzo, *St. Charles Borromeo at the tomb of St. Ignatius,* ca. 1682–86. Corridor of St. Ignatius, Casa Professa, Rome.

FIG. 39
Andrea Pozzo, *St. Philip Neri recognizes St. Ignatius's radiance*, ca. 1682–86. Corridor of St. Ignatius, Casa Professa, Rome.

FIG. 40
Andrea Pozzo, *Death of St. Ignatius*, ca. 1682–86. Corridor of St. Ignatius, Casa Professa, Rome.

a humanist experiment, it had in some way failed. The traditional hagiographic narrative, suffused with miracles, served an important function: promoting the cult. With the evidence of miracles from the beatification and canonization proceedings at their disposal after 1622, the Jesuits undertook a new official *vita* to replace Ribadeynera's.

The work that established the new though deeply traditional perspective on Ignatius's sanctity was Danielo Bartoli's *Della Vita e dell'Istituto di S. Ignatio, fondatore della Compagnia di Gesù* (1650).[107] Bartoli conceived Ignatius's *vita* as the introductory volume to an ambitious universal history of the Society—"not so much a history as an apology"— although he only completed this introductory volume and five parts of the series.[108] His *vita* shares Ribadeynera's premise that Ignatius the founder was the exemplary Jesuit, his life "the form of living, and his examples a rule for conduct." And yet it is also clear that this work was written at a greater distance from Ignatius's life. Accordingly, Bartoli shifts his emphasis to how the providential narrative that Ignatius set in motion played itself out in the subsequent history of the Society.

While Bartoli reiterates Ribadeynera's thesis that Ignatius's life was indistinguishable from the history of the Society, he does not posit the founding of the Society as a miracle. Rather, where Ignatius's miracles are concerned, this is a revisionist account:

> Whereas it is true that while he lived, Ignatius prayed to God, that he not operate miracles through him, where others would believe him to be and venerate him as a Saint, and father Ribadeynera in the first *vite* that he published about him, wrote, that God had led him more by internal virtues than external marvels: but the truth is (and this was seen and Ribadeynera corrected this) that St. Ignatius performed no few miracles in his life, and not ordinary miracles.[109]

To revise Ribadeynera, Bartoli composed a corpus of one hundred miracles comprising the final lengthy chapter of the book.[110] Ignatius's miracles had not been suppressed prior to Bartoli's account. Once approved by the Congregation of Rites, they were quickly publicized, the subject of at least one print dating to around the canonization (fig. 41).[111] But until Pozzo's corridor, miracle scenes were given neither permanent nor highly visible form in Rome. The reassertion of Ignatius's miracles at the end of the century went against a trend, noted by Emile Mâle, of deemphasizing miracles in favor of visions or other signs of heroic virtue.[112] The case of St. Ignatius suggests that the effects on the cults of the saints of this shift away from miracle imagery were notable. Not only was Bartoli's account needed to redress the situation. Images would bear fruit as well.

Bartoli's history was followed by spin-offs, such as Virgilio Nolarci's abbreviated compendium of Bartoli's encyclopedic account, a synthetic work useful to priests and brothers actually out working among the devout.[113] A work such as this one—breaking Ignatius's miracles down into types like those performed in life, in nature, in childbirth, miracles performed by images of Ignatius, and so on—could well have inspired the typologically diverse examples chosen for the corridor frescoes: a healing (of a nun); re-

FIG. 41

Jan Galle, *Wonders and miracles of St. Ignatius*, 1622 (?).

versal of a natural disaster (a fire); an exorcism (this, the only miracle from Ignatius's life; fig. 42); freeing of prisoners; a miraculous image (fig. 43); a healing by Ignatius's tomb (fig. 44).

The six miracle scenes, three on the left and three on the right, dominate the scheme. Moreover, the shift from Borgognone's representation of Ignatius's virtuous life to Pozzo's miracles also marks a shift toward imagery that is more explicitly interpellative. It is well understood that a saint's virtue is to be taken two ways. Virtue provided *evidence* of sanctity. The first wave of imagery of Ignatius had to *prove* sanctity (in a society that demanded proof); in doing so convincingly, in the moment the viewer recognized that imagery as proof of sanctity ("I recognize that image as an image *of a saint*"), they were interpellated as Ignatian subjects. But once Ignatius's saintliness was proven, the Christian subject would have to know the code: to read Ignatian images as evidence of virtue that he or she was *to imitate*. The work of interpellation rests, to some extent, in the hands of the subject.

Miracle images are efficacious for subject formation because they actually represent the interpellation of subjects: they show Ignatius acting on the man on the street. Moreover, in the instant the act is acknowledged as a miracle, the interpellation of a subject has occurred. Although based on specific testimonies, with the exception of the miracle that occurred in Ignatius's lifetime (fig. 42), the miracles were represented as types rather than specific historical instances. Ignatius is thus represented, not as the saint who extinguished *a* fire, but as a saint who can extinguish *fires*. In the diversity of types of miracles, the corridor cycle suggests that Ignatius will act for you whatever danger you face.

The miracle image is more than a document of a past *event*. The representation of the miracle is also a document of the first *interpretation* of that event as a miracle: in being believed a miracle (and becoming a subject for representation), it has already shaped Christian subjects. To look at a representation of a miracle, and to identify it as such (in Panofsky's sense), is to be shaped as a subject (in Althusser's sense). Miracles are one of the most naturally interpellative categories of images.

Two scenes thematize the miraculous potential of Ignatian images in general and the corridor images in particular. Farther down the corridor, next to the spectacular anamorphic angels, Pozzo departed from the typological scheme in depicting a specific episode: *An angel disguised as a pilgrim paints a portrait of Ignatius* (fig. 43). The image is based on a sixteenth-century legend to which a thick volume had been dedicated in 1669.[114] In Munebrega (Spain) a patron commissioned a cycle of portraits of order founders. While the project was being executed, a pilgrim came through town telling of a new order and its founder in Rome. He was asked to do a sketch for the painters to execute. But while they were at lunch the pilgrim himself finished the painting, and so well they "were persuaded that he had been sent by God."[115] The canon placed the work in the parish sacristy and, following Ignatius's canonization, placed it on an altar where numerous miracles subsequently took place. This Emmaus-like narrative, in which the pilgrim is revealed to be God-sent, suggests the miracle-working potential of Pozzo's Ignatian cycle.

FIG. 42
Andrea Pozzo, *St. Ignatius exorcises a man possessed*, ca. 1682–86. Corridor of St. Ignatius, Casa Professa, Rome.

The second example is a conventional miracle that took place at Ignatius's tomb (the fourth appearance of the relics in the cycle). A woman is healed by the oil of a lamp hung before a portrait of Ignatius on top of his tomb (fig. 44). Like all the miracle scenes on the corridor (and this is typical of miracle imagery in general, not just in the case of Ignatius), there is no inscription to indicate a specific episode. Once the testimonies of the miracles for the canonization proceedings had been approved, the scenes are generalized,

FIG. 43
Andrea Pozzo, *An angel disguised as a pilgrim completes a portrait of St. Ignatius,* ca. 1682–86. Corridor of St. Ignatius, Casa Professa, Rome.

to be understood as types rather than proofs provided by specific events. The miracle of the oil is the key to the rest, for it points to the efficacy of both the relics and the image of Ignatius.

That Pozzo was engaged in an effort to create a new and recognizable set of images of Ignatius as a miracle-maker is suggested by his adaptation of the corridor scenes for a second cycle. At the Vigna Antoniana, where Ignatius spent his last days before dying

FIG. 44

Andrea Pozzo, *Healings by the oil hanging before St. Ignatius's tomb,* ca. 1682–86. Corridor
of St. Ignatius, Casa Professa, Rome.

in his rooms at the Casa Professa, Pozzo decorated a small chapel.[116] The precise date
of Pozzo's activity there is undocumented, but two of the Casa Professa corridor miracles are repeated, with precision (fig. 45). Below them two of the minor scenes are likewise executed in monochrome in slightly expanded format. Although the altar image
is different, as at the Casa Professa, live statues of Jesuit saints are posed on fictive corbels
around the space. Pozzo did not lack for inventions. The repetition of the decoration

Andrea Pozzo, *St. Ignatius exorcises a man possessed*, 1680s. Vigna Antoniana, Rome.

of one Ignatian shrine in another suggests that a new canon of images was desirable. That miracles happened to be the focus of both makes apparent the shift in the visual hagiography.

POZZO'S FRESCOES IN THE CHURCH OF ST. IGNATIUS

In Pozzo's next major work, the frescoes of the Church of St. Ignatius, both themes developing in his revised hagiography come into play. A somewhat neglected part of the program is the fresco in the apse (begun 1685), which represents Ignatius as a miracle-maker (fig. 46).[117] Unlike the corridor, where miracle types were developed in separate fields, here Ignatius appears in the heavens, a miraculous healer. Compared to the miracle typologies of the corridor, this fresco is generic in its subject, akin to the miracle scene in the center of the small engraving of Ignatian miracles from 1622 (see fig. 41). In both cases the cumulative evidence of the specific miracles produces the central image: Ignatius the miracle-maker. Given the concern for Ignatius's cult and the revisionist argument made by Bartoli about Ignatian miracles, this fresco is a bold affirmation of the miracle-working Ignatius.

Pozzo's fresco for the vault of the Church of St. Ignatius (1688–94) has long been recognized as a monumental exposé of Ignatius's role in spreading the name of God worldwide (fig. 47).[118] Pozzo himself explained the iconography of the ceiling:

FIG. 46

Andrea Pozzo, *St. Ignatius as miracle-maker*, 1685–88. Church of St. Ignatius, Rome.

My idea in the painting was to represent the works of St. Ignatius and of the Company of Jesus in spreading the Christian faith worldwide. In the first place I embraced the entire vault with a building depicted in perspective. Then in the middle of this I painted the three persons of the Trinity; from the breast of one of which, that is the Human Son, issue forth rays of light that wound the heart of St. Ignatius, and from him they issue, as a reflection spread to the four parts of the world depicted in the guise of Amazons. . . . Those torches that you see in the two extremities of the vault represent the zeal of St. Ignatius, who in sending his companions to preach the Gospel said to them: *Ite, Incendite, Inflammate omnia,* verifying in him Christ's words: *Ignem veni mittere in terram, et quid volo, nisi ut accendatur.*[119]

The work is, first of all, a monumental visualization of the passage in Luke 12:49, when Christ said, "I have come to cast fire on the earth; would that it were already kindled!" The central theme here is the diffusion of Christ's spirit and his Name through Jesuit intermediaries, a common enough iconography used by the Jesuits in prints, in theater sets for the colleges, and in altarpieces. But the phrase from Luke had become liturgically connected to Ignatius quite recently: it was chosen as the *communio* portion of Ignatius's mass, which finally entered the Roman missal in 1687, one year before the Jesuits began discussing the frescoes for the church.[120]

FIG. 47
Andrea Pozzo, *The worldwide mission of the Society of Jesus*, 1691–94. Church of St. Ignatius, Rome.

Text within the engraving:

COELO AFFIXVS SED TERRIS
OMNIBVS SPARSVS
Minut. Fel. in Octa.

S.IGNATIVS LOYOLA
SOC.IESV FVNDATOR.

Ioan: Miel del.   C Bloemaert

FIG. 48

Cornelis Bloemart after Jan Miel, engraved frontispiece to Danielo Bartoli, *Della Vita e dell'Istituto di S. Ignatio, fondatore della Compagnia di Gesù* (Rome, 1659).

    We have seen that from the beginning of Ignatius's hagiography his identity was collapsed onto that of the Society, but we must remember that the church is dedicated to Ignatius. And the Jesuits were concerned about his cult. As Wilberg-Vignau rightly observed, Pozzo's vault is tied to Bartoli's new life of Ignatius, whose engraved frontispiece shows Ignatius deflecting light to the corners of the world, represented in the form of allegorical figures (fig. 48).[121] Beyond the citation of the frontispiece, the fresco keys in to the prophetic vision of the end of time into which the Jesuits inserted themselves.

Andrea Pozzo, *The worldwide mission of the Society of Jesus*, detail, 1691–94. Church of St. Ignatius, Rome.

On this vault the relationship between Christ and man is made visible as an interpellative structure. Christ's spirit passes directly to Ignatius, who in turn passes it to other Jesuits, foremost the most "reformed" Jesuits, like him saints. From them it passes to the world. The light and the fire are the spirit of God, which does not reach the corners of the earth unaided. Ignatius is closest to Christ and his body acts like a mirror directing the light (fig. 49). The mirror borne by the angel below and inscribed with the name of

Andrea Pozzo, *Ignem veni mittere in terra*, detail of *The worldwide mission of the Society of Jesus*, 1691–94. Church of St. Ignatius, Rome.

Jesus conflates the light or spirit with the Name of Christ (fig. 50).[122] Ignatius, here literally a mirror, mirrors Christ and in turn interpellates further subjects all over the world. In this respect Pozzo's ceiling was only the most monumental of Jesuit images that posed Ignatius as specular, as an interpellated and an interpellating subject.[123]

But let us focus on how Pozzo represents exactly what is transmitted. The passage in Luke refers to fire—a widely used visual metaphor for spirit, although on the vault there are two variants of the material of spirit. From the wound in Christ's side emanate rays of light that strike Ignatius, who, in turn, deflects that light through his followers (other Jesuit saints) to the four corners of the world, the light warming the breasts of the four great Amazons. By the time the light reaches the cornice it has ignited: it is fire (fig. 51).

The conflation of light and fire, while quite common in the early modern period,[124] has an Ignatian specificity, one that adhered to his very name. Baptized Iñigo, he adopted the name Ignatius (which is not a Latinized version of Iñigo) sometime after his arrival in Paris (1528), although he used both names (in different contexts) thereafter. Although Ignatius does not derive from any Latin word, the Jesuits nonetheless "found" in it the Latin word *ignis:* a fire, a fire intentionally lit, the fire of the sun, a luminous object, a gleam, a radiance, a glow. While historians have shown that Ignatius chose to adopt a more uni-

FIG. 51

Andrea Pozzo, *Et quid volo nisi ut accendatur*, detail of *The worldwide mission of the Society of Jesus*, 1691–94. Church of St. Ignatius, Rome.

versal name after leaving Spain, hagiographers post-Ribadeynera interpreted the two names as distinguishing the pre- from the post-conversion persona.[125] In 1645 the idea spawned a new legend attributing a miraculous, a divinely ordained origin, traceable to his birth, of the more etymologically charged name Ignatius.[126]

The new name, Ignatius (or the Spanish Ignacio, which he used interchangeably), interpreted according to the mystical theory of names, was seen as capturing Ignatius's fiery essence.[127] While Ignatius's most recognizable attribute is a book (the *Constitutions* or the *Spiritual Exercises*), his radiance was the most widespread and the deeper iconography that runs through the entire early modern Ignatian corpus (fig. 52). For radiance was considered a corporeal sign of sanctity.

Was Ignatius radiant? There was compelling evidence, for Philip Neri, Ignatius's rival and one of the most charismatic saints of the Counter-Reformation, attested to having seen such a radiance. The Jesuits did not fail to promote the etymological connection as well as Neri's preeminent testimonial: in texts, epigrams, emblems, in the Casa Professa corridor, the Church of St. Ignatius, and later in Ignatius's chapel.

In the Church of St. Ignatius, emblems of fire (Pozzo calls them "symbols of this divine fire drawn from Holy Scripture") ring the vault (fig. 53). Fifty years earlier, four such emblems were executed in stucco for the sacristy, the first part of the church to be com-

Ignatius sæpe diuino lumine circumfusus, et facies
eius cælesti luce radians a diuersis adspicitur.

Hieronymus Wierx fecit et excud. Cum Gratia et Priuilegio. Piermans.

FIG. 52
Hieronymous Wierx, *Radiant Ignatius*, in the series *Vita B. P. Ignatii de Loyola . . .* , 1609.

pleted. The fire emblems there (fig. 54), accompanied by citations from the Old Testament, surround a large canvas on the vault of a miracle that occurred when a ball of fire appeared above the head of Ignatius as he said the mass on the Feast of the Pentecost (fig. 55).[128]

A host of other sources reinforced this radiant image of Ignatius. In the Jesuit Claude Menestrier's compendium of emblems of 1682 Ignatius appears ablaze numerous times: he is a mountain spurting flames generated by his zeal; the incendiary fire powering the cannonball sending Xavier and other missionaries into the world; the fire impressing its

FIG. 53

Andrea Pozzo, *Emblems of fire,* detail of *The worldwide mission of the Society of Jesus,*
1691–94. Church of St. Ignatius, Rome.

FIG. 54

Emblem of fire, ca. 1650. Sacristy, Church of St. Ignatius, Rome.

FIG. 55

Pierre de Lattre, *A flame appears over the head of St. Ignatius while saying mass*, 1650. Sacristy, Church of St. Ignatius, Rome.

image on wood just as the love of God impressed on his heart is impressed on those around him, and so on.[129]

As a surface that gathered and deflected light, the mirror was a perfect figure for Ignatius. Filippo Picinelli reported in his *Mondo Simbolico,* a great seventeenth-century compendium, that the concave mirror struck by rays of light, then deflected and catching fire, was a figure used to honor St. Ignatius: "as this great saint was a chosen instrument of the divine Sun to distribute the fire of his Holy Love in the vastness of a world. And well by means of Ignatius the hearts of sinners were to be warmed while Ignatius, receiving and uniting in his breast the rays and illuminations of the heavens was truly all Ignatio, that is all of fire."[130] Menestrier cited two further mirror emblems for Ignatius, a concave mirror that gathers light and turns it to fire and an ardent mirror, "for a man filled with the spirit of God who communicates it to others."[131] It is not surprising that in his illustrations of optical devices Athanasius Kircher chose Ignatius as the figure reflected in a mirror and projected into a camera obscura.[132]

All of these references to fire served the argument that if Christ's "fire" is to be spread throughout the world there could be no better intermediary than Ignatius. Fire adhered to him, in name and in body: it was his very essence. Ignatius-*ignis* reinforced the prophetic vision that the Jesuits were the group that would bring God to man before the end of time. With Ignatius literally imaged as a mirror on the vault, and his subjects struck by his radiating light, there could hardly be a clearer mise-en-scène of the speculary structure of ideology and the interpellation of God's subjects.

Some Jesuits initially resisted Pozzo's proposal to paint the vault of the Church of St. Ignatius. It appears that some feared the darkening of the previously whitewashed space.[133] But for their sacrifice of brightness Ignatius compensated them with light, a light that descended from Christ through Ignatius and struck the viewer with the force of a cannonball.

THE CHAPEL OF ST. IGNATIUS (1695–1699)

The Jesuits knew well that where the cult was concerned the site of Ignatius's tomb bore the most weight. Accordingly, at this site the Jesuits produced the costliest and most concerted scheme to redress the cult. The renovation of the Chapel of St. Ignatius, which I discuss here with an eye to its interpellative strategies, is a summa of the preceding revisionist projects.[134]

The chapel that Pozzo had to work with was to be renovated almost entirely. The only components of the previous chapel that were to be reused were the urn and the vault, the latter decorated to match the rest of the church in the 1670s and 1680s. Pozzo had to work with four stucco reliefs with monumental scenes from Ignatius's life and miracles and Baciccio's fresco of Ignatius ascending to heaven (fig. 56). The latter was easily incorporated into the design, and he does not seem to have been hampered in his choices of narrative scenes for the aedicula by the existing stucco reliefs.[135]

Giovanni Battista Gaulli, *Ascension of St. Ignatius*, 1685. Chapel of St. Ignatius, Il Gesù, Rome.

I begin with the two historical reliefs, carved in marble floating on oriental alabaster flanking the aedicula: Angelo De Rossi's *Paul III confirms the Society of Jesus* (fig. 57) on the left and Bernardino Cametti's *Canonization of St. Ignatius by Gregory XV* (fig. 58) on the right. These two reliefs, distinguished from the gilt bronze miracle reliefs below by their material, provide keys to the chapel's two interrelated themes. For the reliefs represent two instaurational moments for the providential goal of the Society: its founding and Ignatius's canonization.

The striking ubiquity of the scene of the *Confirmation* in Ignatian cycles was a product of Ribadeynera's characterization of the founding of the Society as Ignatius's greatest miracle. Members of the College of Cardinals voting for Ignatius's canonization unanimously cited the founding as evidence of his saintly virtue. The historical nature of the event is emphasized by the inscription "SOC.I.A. PAULO III CONFIRM.MD.XL." But with the heavens opening above and angels pushing back the clouds to witness Paul III's commanding gesture of approval, the founding is also cast as a miraculous event. The atectonic surrounds of both this and the canonization relief endow them with the quality of a celestial event while the tectonic frames around the miracle narratives below endow them with the quality of hard fact.

The *Canonization* scene shows Gregory XV receiving a taper from a kneeling Jesuit. The

FIG. 57

Angelo De Rossi, *Paul III confirms the Society of Jesus in 1540*, 1695–99. Chapel of St. Ignatius, Il Gesù, Rome.

relief compresses different moments of canonization ceremonies. In the first half a procurator asked for the saint's canonization and a decree was made by the pope. A mass was performed in the second part of the ceremony with a special offertory made to the pope, a feature unique to canonization ceremonies. The procurator figure (in real life Ludovico Ludovisi), the standing figure here, was typically the focus of canonization scenes.[136] Several parties offered gifts, but the secular group who petitioned for the canonization was al-

FIG. 58
Bernardino Cametti, *Canonization of St. Ignatius by Gregory XV,* 1695–98. Chapel of
St. Ignatius, Il Gesù, Rome.

lowed to offer "spontaneous" and "congratulatory" gifts considered "demonstrations of the
soul." These always included tapers and a gilded cage containing turtledoves, doves, or other
birds. The taper at the center of Cametti's relief had numerous meanings, but one was particularly apt for Ignatius: it demonstrated that the saint kept in mind the following precept
of the Lord: "And you, like the lamp must shed light among your fellows, so that, when they
see the good you do, they may give praise to your Father in heaven" (Matt. 5:16).[137]

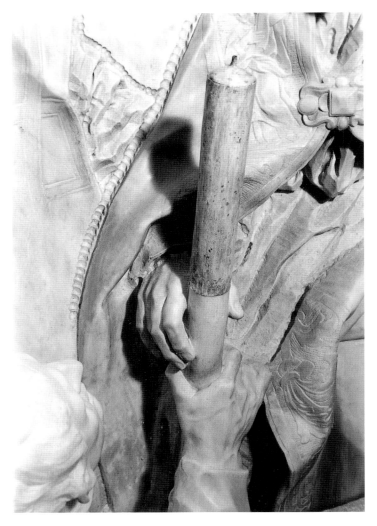

Bernardino Cametti, *Taper handed to Gregory XV*, detail of *Canonization of St. Ignatius by Gregory XV*, 1695–98. Chapel of St. Ignatius, Il Gesù, Rome.

Although Ignatius's canonization was a historical event the inscription below the relief, "IGN.A.GREG.XV.ASCR," omits the date. Space was limited, but the omission may have been quite purposeful. During the restoration of the chapel, it was discovered that the taper at the center of this relief is a hollow metal canister that seems to have been designed to contain a real candle (fig. 59). With the taper burning, the canonization event could be perpetually reenacted. By situating the viewer as witness at the moment the Church declared Ignatius's sanctity, the viewer was interpellated.

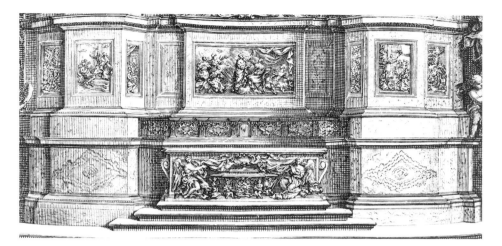

FIG. 60
Row of gilt bronze reliefs, detail from Vincenzo Mariotti, *The Chapel of St. Ignatius,* 1697.

Having established in this relief the juridical approbation of sanctity, several other elements of the chapel argued further for Ignatius's saintliness. The fulcrum in this respect is the relics themselves, encased in Alessandro Algardi's gilt bronze urn since 1637 (see fig. 18).[138] In this earlier work Ignatius's saintliness is argued by further example, for he appears surrounded by other Jesuit saints and *beati:* Ignatius interpellated other Jesuit saints.

At the site of the relics, more critical to the new image of Ignatius's saintliness were his miracles, which line the base of the aedicula in a spectacular row of gilt bronze reliefs (fig. 60). The use of this material for the lower precinct of the altar, the area most visible to the chapel visitor, visually links relics to miracles. Of the seven scenes represented here, five are taken directly from the corridor frescoes in the Casa Professa.[139] Pozzo provided designs to the sculptors, and in four of five cases, like that of the *Healings by the oil* (fig. 61), they are fairly faithful renditions of those scenes.[140] The reiteration of Pozzo's compositions points again to the revisionist plan behind the late-seventeenth-century projects as a whole.

Of the seven reliefs, only one of the scenes is new to Pozzo's repertoire. The Florentine sculptor Lorenzo Merlini's relief is the largest and is the only one to represent a miracle that graced Ignatius (fig. 62). The scene is usually described as *St. Peter appearing to Ignatius,* but the subject is Ignatius's spiritual conversion, the inaugural event of his own spiritual reformation.[141] By representing Ignatius in (anachronistic antique) military garb, Merlini makes visible Ignatius's former self, the soldier whose wounds brought him home to Loyola. The book of the lives of saints shows Ignatius's entry point into spiritual life. But before his conversion began, his life was at risk, and it was on the vigil of the Feast of Sts. Peter and Paul that his health improved after the appearance of St. Peter. Merlini's

FIG. 61
Renato Frémin, *Healings by the oil hanging before St. Ignatius's tomb*, 1695–96. Chapel of St. Ignatius, Il Gesù, Rome.

relief thus conflates three moments of Ignatius's biography: the wound incurred in battle, the healing through divine intervention, and his subsequent conversion brought about by reading. The compression of events before and after the conversion suggests that we are *witnessing* Ignatius's spiritual conversion, a process described by Ignatius as internal, here made visible. The "event" has such a prominent role at the tomb because it marks the day that Ignatius was himself interpellated as one of God's subjects, suggesting to the devout that whether through miraculous healing or the reading of the saint's lives, you too could be spiritually reformed. The Jesuits deemed the "event" so important that they

FIG. 62
Lorenzo Merlini, *St. Peter appearing to St. Ignatius*, 1695–96. Chapel of St. Ignatius, Il Gesù, Rome.

designated May 20 the feast of his conversion. Although the scene differs from the five scenes of miracles performed *by* Ignatius, it establishes the first interpellation, from which all others follow.

Francesco Nuvolone's scene, *Philip Neri recognizing Ignatius's radiance* (fig. 63), significantly elaborated the corridor grisaille (see fig. 39). Though this encounter had been represented occasionally in engravings[142] and in a large and splendid canvas attributed to Maratta,[143] this relief is the most complex known version of the subject. Although Neri, founder of the Congregation of the Oratory, was an authoritative witness to this crucial aspect of Ignatius, controversy surrounding their relationship is reflected in the relief.

Ignatius and Neri probably met in Rome in the late 1530s.[144] At that time both were involved in similar charitable and catechetical works. Ignatius, the elder of the two, was surely the more established; he was on the verge of having his Company confirmed by Paul III and was already ordained as a priest. Neri acknowledged that Ignatius had introduced him to interior prayer, and he may have encouraged some of his own companions (the first Italian Jesuits) to join Ignatius's growing group.[145] Above all, one source, corroborated by numerous others, reported in separate support of the canonization of both men that Neri had "once seen the countenance of the holy father Ignatius flooded with a supernatural brightness, and that it was therefore his opinion that no creation of the painter could represent him as he was in reality."[146]

Neri's testimony of Ignatius's radiance, seconded by others, served the Jesuits well in their campaign for their founder's canonization. The Oratorians played on Neri's ability to *see* the radiance[147] (Neri saw Carlo Borromeo's radiance as well, and the Oratorians made

FIG. 63
Francesco Nuvolone, *St. Philip Neri recognizes St. Ignatius's radiance*, 1695–96. Chapel of St. Ignatius,
Il Gesù, Rome.

engravings of that scene)[148] but certainly did not place the episode in the foreground as did the Jesuits.

Neri was also famous for having resisted joining in with Ignatius's followers. Nuvolone's relief, populated by the poor and several companions of the two saints, also addresses this thorny question of interpellation. The Jesuits claimed that Neri desired to join in with Ignatius but was not accepted. The Oratorians argued it was the other way around: Ignatius asked him to join, but Neri declined.[149] It is possible that Neri encouraged some of his companions to follow Ignatius, but his own reluctance to enter "religion" became a persistent source of controversy.[150] There are really two issues here. The first is the issue of Neri joining the *Company* and the second is his reluctance to join the *priesthood,* having founded a congregation of secular priests who lived in a community without taking vows. Ignatius may have been referring to the latter when he benevolently nicknamed Neri "la campana," the bell. The nickname seems to have been well known. At least four testimonies for Neri's canonization attested that Ignatius called him "la campana" because Neri continued to bring people to the Church, and to the Jesuits, but did not enter himself.[151] The Jesuits understood the name as that of a man only ordained in 1551, after having called others to religion before entering himself.[152]

In Nuvolone's bronze relief the distinctive bell tower of the Oratorio complex designed by Borromini appears behind the heads of Neri's followers, one of whom seems to lift his head as if he is listening. And indeed the bell appears to be tolling. The appearance of the bell tower (built a century after the purported encounter) was not a homage to the Oratorians and their noble buildings but a reminder of Ignatius's ironic nickname for a man who, like the bell, called many to religion, even to Ignatius's Society.

While the Neri relief did not represent an Ignatian miracle, its inclusion and placement below the statue of the saint was a strategic one, pointing to the corporal sign of his sanctity. Ignatius's radiance received material embodiment in the central image of the chapel: Pierre Legros's over-life-sized silver statue of Ignatius (fig. 64), a statue whose silver hands and head were melted down and remade in the 1820s. The base of the statue and disposition remain the same, although the work lacks the emotional quality the original no doubt possessed.[153] Dressed in liturgical robes, raised high on a base in a niche swimming in lapis lazuli and gilt ornament, Ignatius appears, arms flung open, looking to the Trinity in the pediment. The silver statue of the saint must have been among the most surprising elements of the chapel to the Roman public. For although silver was, after gold, the quintessential precious material, the metal preferred for the encasement of relics and widely used for church accessories,[154] no other altar in Rome in the seventeenth century could boast an over-life-sized silver statue that was permanently installed on an altar.

The Jesuits were likely to have felt that Ignatius had a special claim to be represented in silver. He was described in Picinelli's *Mondo Simbolico* as one of only two saints whose very nature was akin to silver. Recalling an episode from Ignatius's life in which he threw himself into a frozen pond to still the passions of an amorous man, Picinelli likened Ignatius to silver: gelid on the outside but burning on the inside with "flames of charity."[155] The entire tradition of Ignatius-*ignis* also stood behind the choice of silver.

FIG. 64

Pierre Legros, *St. Ignatius*, 1697–99, remodeled by Luigi Acquisti, 1803–4. Chapel of
St. Ignatius, Il Gesù, Rome.

To make materially manifest Ignatius's radiance, the Jesuits represented him in silver.
To enhance the brilliance of the metal, Pozzo cut a small window into the niche, directly
behind the head and gilt halo (fig. 65). Mirrors were originally placed on the sill and walls
surrounding the window so as to reflect more light onto the head and halo of the saint.[156]
Although the window no longer throws any light onto the statue today, imagine yourself
in the chapel at a moment when clouds parted and light suddenly shone through windows one cannot see, onto Ignatius's face. Would one in that moment not feel like Philip
Neri, like a firsthand witness of a miracle, of Ignatius's divine radiance? In this chapel

FIG. 65
Niche window. Chapel of St. Ignatius, Il Gesù, Rome.

the mise-en-scène of recognition of the radiance and hence of saintliness is another technique of subject formation.

The Jesuits reinforced the theme of Ignatius's radiance once more. As the chapel neared completion, they decorated the round chapel to the left of the transept, converted into a vestibule for the transept chapel. The decorations created an entroit for a thematic of the chapel. Here, as in the sacristy of the Church of St. Ignatius, four fiery emblems accompanied by passages from the Old Testament greet the devout.[157]

Beyond its materiality, the statue also participated in a narrative that developed the second theme of the chapel: the founding of the Society. Specifically, the statue represents a vision that took place in 1539 when Ignatius was en route to Rome to request permission for a pilgrimage to the Holy Land to be undertaken with his companions already bound by a common vow.[158] In a small roadside chapel just outside the city, at the crossroads at La Storta, where Ignatius stopped to pray before entering the city, he had a propitious vision. God appeared together with Christ bearing his Cross, who told Ignatius, "Ego vobis Romae propitius ero" (I will be propitious to you in Rome).[159] Ignatius interpreted the Vision at La Storta as a sign that he was meant to remain in Rome to found the Society. As a result, he decided to give to the Company the name of Jesus. Hence the Vision at La Storta represented a critical step in the founding of the Society: the moment of Naming.

The Vision at La Storta was represented in the chapel before Pozzo's renovation in the altarpiece, now attributed to Gerhard Seghers (fig. 66).[160] The painting shows Ignatius in his black robes holding the *Constitutions*. In a secondary scene Christ appears to Ignatius at La Storta; in subsequent representations of the scene the Trinity or God alone is usually present. In their deliberations in 1695 over the new altarpiece for the chapel, the Jesuits expressed the desirability of the Storta narrative, for its power to console in

FIG. 66
Attributed to Gerard Seghers, *St. Ignatius,* 1622 (formerly on the altar of
the Chapel of St. Ignatius).

moments of tribulation. Although in this sculptural mise-en-scène the setting is jettisoned,
Ignatius appears in relation to the Trinity in the pediment; the monogram of Christ, the
IHS that serves as the standard of the Society of Jesus, appears between them, a blazing
form of lapis lazuli and rock crystal (fig. 67). Pierre Stephan Monnot's spectacular angels
appear to have arrived with the escutcheon, heaven-sent (fig. 68). The angel on the left,
originally furnished with a pen, has just finished writing the Name, the result of the vision reenacted before our eyes. The founding of the Society was not one but a series of
miracles here enacted.

FIG. 67

St. Ignatius's vision at La Storta, 1695–99. Chapel of St. Ignatius, Il Gesù, Rome.

FIG. 68

Pierre Stephan Monnot, *Angel composing the Name of the Society,* 1696–97; Lorenzo Merlini, *Escutcheon,* 1696; Lorenzo Ottone and Bernardo Ludovisi, *Trinity,* 1726. Chapel of St. Ignatius, Il Gesù, Rome.

FIG. 69
Andrea Pozzo, *Christ handing the banner of victory to St. Ignatius*, 1699. Chapel of St. Ignatius, Il Gesù, Rome.

But there is more. While the silver statue is permanently displayed on the altar today, originally it was only intended to be displayed on feast days. A painting by Pozzo hangs behind the altar base, and a system of pulleys that raise and lower the painting is still intact, accessible through a panel to the right of the altar mensa. The painting, by Pozzo, represents *Christ handing the banner of victory to Ignatius* surrounded by allegories of the four continents (fig. 69). Like the vault of the Church of St. Ignatius, the painting expresses Ignatius's

FIG. 70

Jean-Baptiste Théodon, *Faith trampling heresy with the king of the Congo rising converted*,
1695–99. Chapel of St. Ignatius, Il Gesù, Rome.

and by extension the Society's triumph in spreading the Name of Christ through the world.

The two allegorical groups flanking the altar give dramatic form to the providential
narrative of the Jesuit order. The left group, carved by Jean-Baptiste Théodon, represents
the Jesuit missions among non-Christians (fig. 70). Toward Faith, raising her chalice high,
and stepping on a serpent, rises the king of the Congo, converted.[161] With that conversion, it is implied, idolatry, gnashing her teeth, pulling at her hair, is dispelled. Faith's feet
crush a book inscribed "CAMES FOTOQUES AMIDA ET XACA," the Latinized versions of
Portuguese translations of the terms for and names of Japanese and Chinese gods.[162] On
the right side, the Jesuit mission among the heretics was given form by Pierre Legros (fig.
71). Religion, the true religion, bolt of fire in hand, casts out heresy and the books of the

FIG. 71
Pierre Legros, *Religion triumphing over heresy*, 1695–99. Chapel of St. Ignatius, Il Gesù, Rome.

heretics, inscribed "LUTHER," "CALVIN," and "ZWINGLI." She is aided by a putto, who gleefully tears pages out of a heretical text.

Allegories, staples of early modern tombs, usually embodied the virtues of the deceased. These allegories express the virtues of the *Society* that Ignatius had the virtue to have founded, for the expulsion of heresy and conversion of kings in Africa was carried out by Jesuits, not by Ignatius himself. As in Ribadeynera's and Bartoli's narratives, the chapel allegories collapse Ignatius's life onto the activities of the Society he founded. It was, after all, his greatest miracle and a miracle, these works argue, felt all over the world.

FIG. 72
Camillo Rusconi, *Angels,* 1696–99. Right overdoor. Chapel of St. Ignatius, Il Gesù, Rome.

The diffusion by the radiant Ignatius of light worldwide is also enacted elsewhere in the chapel. Across the space of the transept four angels, two pairs each over the doors on the lateral walls of the chapel, capture and diffuse that light from radiant emblems of the Name of Christ (fig. 72). Elaborate bronze lamps hang over these doors and stand at the interstices of the balustrade (fig. 73). The lamps, bearers of light, were the symbolic and literal representation of the diffusion of the Jesuit order, of the light of Catholicism, for each was to be paid for by a different province of the Society.

The convex bronze balustrade formed of arabesques that encloses the altar precinct marks the final expression in the chapel of the Society and its worldwide mission. With putti holding books of the *Rules* of the Society (fig. 74), the *Spiritual Exercises* (fig. 75), and the *Constitutions,* the Society is again emphasized as Ignatius's most important edifice. The form itself, probably devised by Pozzo, is significant.[163] Pozzo accommodated this massive, fifty-eight-foot-long structure to the shallow chapel with a curvaceous form, a radical departure from the usual rectilinear plan. The curve was determined by the plan for the aedicula, which it follows, or rather, to which it conforms. That conformity is a theme of the balustrade is suggested by the gate (fig. 76). In the abandonment of the architectural form for the natural form, the balustrade made reference to a Jesuit emblem, "A FLEXU FORMA," that appeared in Carlo Bovio's *Ignatius Insignium, Epigrammatum et Elogiorum* of 1655 (fig. 77).[164] The emblem is a vine that has been trained to take on the form of the IHS monogram. As the inscription explains, Ignatian obedience (to the *Rules* and the *Constitutions,* held in the hands of the putti) and flexibility (embodied in the me-

FIG. 73
Francesco Maglia, Balustrade lamp, 1697–99.
Chapel of St. Ignatius, Il Gesù, Rome.

andering form of the work) went hand in hand. The natural forms of the balustrade, obedient to the hand of the artist, to the form of the altar that sets the path, are figures for
the Jesuits themselves: of the flexibility that enabled the Jesuits to adapt to what they found
in the world, *A flexu forma*. The Jesuit worldwide mission spread light through the chapel
in the forms of the lamps; four small bronze figurines on the Four Parts of the World (fig.
78) with antique triumphal imagery embedded in the lamps flanking the gate make explicit the balustrade's iconography of the triumph of the Jesuit mission. In establishing
the obedience that stood at the center of Jesuit life, Ignatius provided the subject-forming principle from which this form was generated.

One final note on the gate, on the Jesuits, and on the chapel. Two toothy dolphins curl
around the bases of two lamps flanking the central gate (fig. 79). Symbols of persuasion,[165]
the dolphins make evident that the means of Jesuit forming and reforming of souls, of
the propagation of the Name, of the spreading of the light of God through the world are
not hidden. Their appearance at the entrance of the altar precinct is an explicit sign to us
of the directedness of this chapel's message. In the multifarious ways in which the chapel
inscribes the viewer, it constitutes propaganda.

FIG. 74
Domenico Melussi, *Putto with book inscribed* "REGVLAE SOCIETATIS IESV," 1697–99.
Detail, balustrade. Chapel of St. Ignatius, Il Gesù, Rome.

FIG. 75
Domenico Melussi, *Putto with book inscribed* "EXERCIT. SPIRIT. S. IGNATII SOC. IESV FUND. DOCENTE MAGISTRA RELIGIONIS," 1697–99. Chapel of St. Ignatius, Il Gesù, Rome.

FIG. 76
Pietro Papaleo, *Gate,* 1697–99. Chapel of St. Ignatius, Il Gesù, Rome.

FIG. 77
"A FLEXU FORMA," in Carlo Bovio, *Ignatius Insignium, Epigrammatum et Elogiorum Centuriis Expressus* (Rome, 1655).

FIG. 78
Giovanni Battista Antonino, *Allegories of parts of the world,* 1697–99.
Chapel of St. Ignatius, Il Gesù, Rome.

FIG. 79
Francesco de' Vecchi, *Dolphins*, 1697–99. Chapel of St. Ignatius, Il Gesù, Rome.

CONCLUSIONS

What I am trying to do here through the example of St. Ignatius and the Society he founded is simple enough: to bring Althusser's ISA, and the definition of propaganda derived from it, to bear on iconography. Conveying meaning is one of the great purposes of art in general and Catholic art in particular. Meaning constitutes an apparently neutral way of characterizing a message.[166] By contrast, a message is directed, and as such, it needs a receiver. Iconographic studies often obscure a goal of interpretation: the effect of the interpreted message, for this is where interpellation occurs.

Where the goal of interpellation is concerned, there is no substantial difference between written and visual representations. Andrea Pozzo's fresco cycles and the Chapel of

St. Ignatius act analogously to texts. But the images do so through their own set of cues. They can inscribe the viewer by virtue of their mimetic naturalism: we recognize in the painting something akin to ourselves. At the base of this recognition is the function of exemplarity, that we should imitate the saints whose images we look upon.

The rules against the representation of someone as saintlike prior to canonization point to other cues on which our recognition of images depends. They suggest that images found in certain places (such as an altar or over a tomb) or even images that are printed possessed a truth-value that was widely understood.[167] Even if overt signs of saintliness (diadems, halos) were avoided, the presence of an image at a tomb or a print issued by the Society, full of official-looking inscriptions and permissions, signified approbation. And that approbation could, it came to be feared, effortlessly form subjects.

In Panofsky's famous grid of iconographic meaning a man hailing another on the street was his example of primary or "natural subject," which we need nothing more than practical experience to interpret.[168] Panofsky described this recognition as pre-iconographic because our culture teaches us that a man lifting his hat is a sign of recognition first, greeting and respect for the person greeted. What I have been trying to get at here, in part, is what happens when we recognize that person in an image. Namely, that embedded in the act of recognition is our inscription of ourselves as believers.

5

DIFFUSION

Diffusion is a key element in propaganda. As a directed form of communication, propaganda constitutively looks to its reception. Where the visual arts—architecture in particular—are concerned, diffusion can be approached in two ways. We can view a building in its representative function and evaluate its success by the work it does on the spectator. This is enormously difficult to measure. How would a Jesuit church increase one's spiritual ardor? How does a building form a subject? And how can we tell?[1] First we must establish that architecture was seen as capable of doing this work, that it could contribute to subject formation.

What we can do with more certainty is to track diffusion of the work itself. Works of art have reception histories in the course of their imitation by other artists: in terms of propaganda that amounts to saying they produce results. There are two distinct strands of that reception to be discussed here. First, there is the diffusion of Jesuit architecture within the Society, a practice that contributed to the formation of Jesuit identity. The use of forms (not only architectural) by the institution for this purpose must be established as well. The second and more difficult strand is the reception of Jesuit architecture outside the Society. This is the real challenge in thinking about propaganda since the inventive reuse of past models is inextricable from early modern artistic practice. The question then becomes, is the Jesuit affiliation of a design meaningful at the moment it is imitated? To take an example, when the Gesù produces progeny, are the spin-offs Jesuit? Italian? Catholic? Vignolan? Here I argue that the identity of the design and who diffuses it does matter, even if non-Jesuit artists may not always be "consciously" imitating works, because the imitated works are *Jesuit* in origin.

The nineteenth-century concept of the Jesuit Style is the most forceful testimony of the successful diffusion of Jesuit architecture. Diffusion was one of the constitutive elements of the debunked Jesuit Style.[2] Even in the recent reframing of Jesuit architectural imperialism in a more positive light, most notably by Richard Bösel, Jesuit models and their progeny stand at the center of the story of the Jesuit architectural enterprise.[3] In spite of all of the revision of the diffusion question, little has been said about why the Jesuits may have wanted their buildings to resemble each other. Nor has the diffusion of Jesuit designs in non-Jesuit settings been interpreted once the nineteenth-century argument that the Jesuits imposed their style was laid aside. The mechanisms and meanings of diffusion are the principal subject of this chapter.

ARCHITECTURE AND THE WORK OF SUBJECT FORMATION

Jesuit architecture was, outside of the live presence of Jesuits themselves, the most visible mark of the diffusion of the Society and of Catholicism worldwide in the early modern period. While their buildings—twelve hundred churches in particular[4]—were practical and necessary for their ministry, as many have observed before they also served a representative function. Both Jesuits and the people living in the cities to which their missions traveled were well aware that a building signaled a presence, a call to believer and nonbeliever alike. It was not just the church bell calling people to mass; the stone facade cutting a profile into village or cityscape reminded one that the Jesuits were there. Just as we avert our eyes from evil to keep it from us, simply seeing can move one to enter, perhaps to become a subject as well.

Both in the far-flung missions in Asia and Latin America and in the heart of confessionally divided Europe, architecture did much work for the Jesuits. There is some evidence of how. When they built a modestly scaled church in the "European" style in Beijing, one father remarked: "This building impressed the Chinese far more than we had anticipated, and *many came to see it; by doing so they began to know* our Holy Law."[5] Compare this to the public discussion and viewing of the Chapel of St. Ignatius in Rome in the 1690s, during the construction of which there was much talk around town, and curiosity drew people to view the altar.[6] Curiosity, incitement to knowledge, aroused the hearer and the viewer. Such arousal, as a step toward knowing, was an expectation of public building articulated early on by Leon Battista Alberti:

> There is no doubt that a temple that delights the mind wonderfully, captivates it with grace and admiration, will greatly encourage piety. To the ancients a people seemed to be truly pious when the temples of the gods were crowded. This is why I would wish the temple so beautiful that nothing more decorous could ever be devised; I would deck it out in every part so that anyone who entered it would start with awe for his admiration at all the noble things, and could scarcely restrain himself from exclaiming that what he saw was a place undoubtedly worthy of God.[7]

Admiration works metonymically, passing from the building built *for* God *to* God, producing devotion.

Are we to conclude that the viewing of or meditation on architecture—what we might consider an aesthetic act—is akin to or *is* a devotional act? In Venice in 1726, Luigi Fernando Marsili, commander of the pope's army and a cultivated critic of architecture, spent "an entire morning" carefully examining the facade and interior of the recently completed church of the Gesuiti.[8] Although he disliked the church intensely, Marsili engaged with two polite Jesuits in an extended critique of the building, no doubt spending more time in the church than had he come to attend mass. While the Chinese who came to see the novel Western-style building in Beijing would have asked different questions than Marsili, in both cases the architectural "event" drew people into the church. Alberti summed up the ideal effect of a well-designed building: "who saw it would imagine that he could never be satiated by the view, but looking at it again and again in admiration, would glance back once more as he departed."[9] It may not be too far-fetched to liken what happens to the spectator in a magnificent building to falling in love. Whether captured by a kind of love or engaged by discourse, the engaged viewer had taken a crucial step in subject formation.

The encounter with non-Western architectures is of interest here insofar as it compelled European Jesuits to define their identity in architecture (in addition to language, body, and belief). The radically different materials and forms they found necessitated careful decisions about how much to adapt to local building practices. The Jesuits were cognizant that these decisions amounted to establishing their own identity, visually. The realization that architecture was essential to the success of the missions led the Jesuit Alessandro Valignano to include a chapter on architecture in his handbook for the conduct of the Jesuit missions in Japan (1581). Because of the tenuousness of the Jesuit presence in Japan, they abandoned much of their "modo nostro" to comply with Japanese custom. Valignano advised that Jesuit buildings be built by Japanese architects in local materials and style, with spaces necessary for Japanese ceremonials. But where churches were concerned Valignano was more cautious: "in the construction of churches it would be improper to imitate them, since theirs are synagogues of Satan and ours are churches of God."[10] Accordingly, the main choir and high altar were not to extend, as in Japanese temples, along the short side but along the long side. And yet Valignano also lists several Japanese features that should be included.[11] So while the Jesuit churches in Japan were hybrid forms, there were critical aspects of those buildings that allowed the Jesuit *then* to view them as European and hence Catholic in their essence. By taking a selective view of the building's components, a European (and hence a Catholic) identity could be carved out. The selectiveness of the view in providing a meaningful identity for a building is reminiscent of a Medieval notion of resemblance, which Richard Krautheimer argued was based more on the symbolic than the visual qualities of the prototype.[12] What continues to be true is that, when necessary, a building need only resemble another in part for it to produce a meaningful association, to support an identification.

In cultures where the Jesuits were the only European presence it was sometimes less important to build in a Jesuit way than in a European—and hence in a Catholic—way. But the point here is that such distinctions were articulated at the moment of the encounter of one culture with another. Because establishing a visible presence in a non-Christian place amounted to establishing an identity, much can be learned from the issues raised on those occasions. These cross-cultural encounters, coupled with the enormous wave of building that accompanied the worldwide evangelization of non-European lands, resulted in a heightened awareness of architecture's representative function. Architecture's visibility propelled it into a new status in this period.

ARCHITECTURE AS THEOLOGY: THE NEW RITE

It has been argued that the Counter-Reformation popes placed unprecedented emphasis on making the faith visible. Sixtus V's (1585–90) revival of religious processions, for example, filled Rome's streets with crowds of the devout. Visibility was also an aim of Sixtus's building projects, especially the columns and obelisks erected at the crossroads and at the end of major street axes, creating markers between one basilica and the next visible from the other end of the city.[13] One important index of the desire to render the faith visible is the new prominence of *representations* of sacred architecture.[14] In addition to engraved images, Sixtus V's architectural projects appeared in fresco cycles in the Villa Montalto (destroyed), the Lateran Palace, and the Vatican Library, as well as in engraved portraits of the pope.[15]

In this association with his buildings Sixtus V took his cue from Gregory XIII (1572–85), whose corpus of building projects was dominated by new Jesuit foundations. The Jesuits set the stage for Sixtus's frescoes of his architectural projects in their visual panegyric to Gregory XIII's support of their colleges in the decorations of the Aula Magna, the principal public room of the Collegio Romano. The paintings (which are no longer preserved), completed in 1584, showed Gregory XIII enthroned, surrounded by cardinals, blessing distinguished students of the college. What interests us here are the "very beautiful images of buildings," the colleges "built by the zealous pope in the various parts of the world for the propaganda of Religion, six on the right and six on the left." On the opposite wall, larger than the rest, appeared the very Roman college built by Gregory and five more Jesuit colleges in various parts of the world.[16] The representations of these buildings served various representative agendas; family, papal, Jesuit, and Catholic ties and identities were all implicit in the paintings in the college setting. But the point I want to make about these pictures of buildings is this: in the moment a building is represent*ed*, its function *as representation* can be discerned. This function pertains not only to the painted or engraved scene, but cannot help but rebound back onto the buildings themselves.

It is likely that a later engraving of Gregory surrounded by images of his colleges recapitulates elements of the Collegio Romano scheme (fig. 80).[17] Moreover, the college decorations appear to have stimulated a new portrait type subsequently exploited intensely

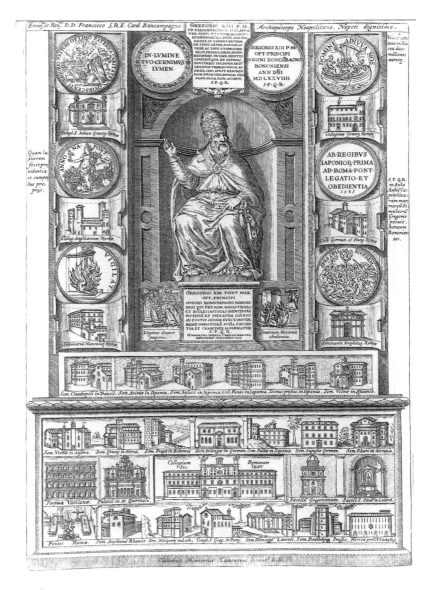

FIG. 80

Gregory XIII and colleges, in Alfonso Chacon, *Vitae et res gestae pontificum Romanorum et S.R.E. cardinalium . . .* (Rome, 1630), vol. 2.

by Gregory's successor, Sixtus V: the pope framed by images of his deeds, most prominent among which are the building projects.[18] In these engravings the small framed pictures of buildings are the equivalent for the patron of the good works and miracles that surrounded saints' portraits in prints of the same period (see fig. 29).

What do these buildings represent? Do they reiterate the territorial claims made by the fourteenth-century city views in Siena's Palazzo Pubblico, or the castles in the *Très*

Anonymous, *Gregory XIII visiting construction of the Collegio Romano*, 1650s (?).

Riches Heures (1412–15) of the Duc de Berry?[19] The cityscape continued to express dominion into the early modern period.[20] The Jesuits themselves represented their own colleges in their courtyards and the rooms of their houses, especially in ephemeral decorations. Such images made visible the extent of their activity, a visualization akin to those of the feudal territorial holdings that had been represented by the Benedictines in the form of inscriptions on the bronze doors of the monastery at Montecassino.[21] But these were not feudal holdings. A change has taken place between the late Medieval representations of the city (which represented a *place* with a population of subjects) and the Jesuit colleges (which represent buildings). Precisely what architecture *could mean* at this moment in the Counter-Reformation must be explored.

Two seventeenth-century paintings that originally hung in the Collegio Romano shed some light. The first seems familiar but is actually a new type: *Gregory XIII visiting construction of the Collegio Romano* shows the pope presented a plan by the architect (fig. 81).[22] The presentation to the patron of the plan by the architect has a telling genealogy. The model for such a scene was the author presenting a manuscript to a patron, an offering in exchange for the patron's favor. That type was, in turn, it has been argued, based on a Medieval type: the patron presenting a model of a building to Christ or the Virgin, a votive offering with an expectation of favor attached to it.[23] In both cases the image was organized by the person on his knees. The meaning shifts when it is not the donor (patron, author) but the receiver who is organizing the image.

FIG. 82

Giorgio Vasari, *Paul III directing Painting, Sculpture, and Architecture in the rebuilding of Rome,* 1556. Sala dei Cento Giorni, Palazzo della Cancelleria, Rome.

The architect presenting a plan to a patron was a subject that Vasari seems to have developed first in two variants, reappearing in papal iconography around the turn of the seventeenth century.[24] In 1546, in the Sala dei Cento Giorni, he represented Paul III dressed in the liturgical garb of an Old Testament priest directing Painting, Sculpture, and Architecture in the rebuilding of St. Peter's (fig. 82). This image draws on diverse pictorial traditions: Solomon building the temple (often represented as a visit to a construction site, like Gregory XIII at the Collegio Romano); and the Franciscan imagery of the renewal of the church, whose decrepitude is represented as a crumbling structure.[25] But in the earlier traditions, it is *a building,* and hence *building* that is intended, rather than architecture per se. In Vasari's image, the pope is a new Solomon; *architecture* symbolizes the moral renewal of the church by means of the physical renewal of Rome following the Sack of 1527.[26] In using the allegorical figure of Architecture, Vasari signals that it is the art of design, "architecture," rather than "building" that is now at the base of the renewal of Rome. This was not a shift in pictorial convention but an indication that a new discursive form, architecture, had become usable by the papacy. Architecture became available to the ruling class precisely because there was now a recognized architectural discourse.

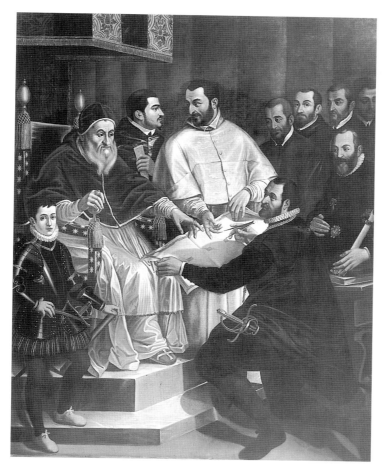

FIG. 83
Pietro Facchetti, *Domenico Fontana presenting the plans of the Sistine Library to Sixtus V*, 1585–90. Biblioteca Vaticana, Vatican City.

Sixtus V must have been aware of Vasari's image of Paul III when he had himself painted by Pietro Facchetti at the entrance to his new library in the Vatican being presented with the plan for the library by his architect Domenico Fontana (fig. 83). Here allegorical imagery is replaced by contemporary reality. With Sixtus and Fontana represented as themselves, no typological parallel to Solomon is implied. Rather, as Alessandro Zuccari has shown, the image was situated as a typological parallel with the nearby scene, *Moses giving the Book of the Law to the Levites to be deposited in the Tabernacle*. In such a context, Sixtus (who is positioned analogously to Moses in the nearby fresco) builds the library as a tabernacle of true wisdom; he is the new Moses conserving and perpetuating wisdom.[27] The architect, then, is cast in the role of the Levites, the priests, who will administer the faith in perpetuity. Architect is priest; architecture as liturgy.

FIG. 84

Sixtus V, in Ioanne Pinadello, *Invicti Quinarii Numeri Series Quae Summatim a Superioribus Pontificibus et Maxime A Sixto Quinto,* Rome, 1589.

Although cast as Moses in the Vatican Library, Sixtus V also represented *himself* as "architect." While the image of God as architect stretches back to St. Augustine, the image of pope as architect was distinctly Sistine: embedded in the type is the idea that patronage is actually the creative authorship behind the Golden Age of a renewed Rome.[28] In one panegyric Sixtus was likened to Christ as architect of the Church on earth: "the om-

FIG. 85

Anonymous, *Gregory XIII distributing plans for the Jesuit missions*, 1650s (?).

nipotent God made him [Sixtus] architect of such an important building, so much so that the first Architect, the Son of God, gave up his life in building it."[29] One of the prints showing Sixtus and his good works—that is, his building projects—bears the inscription "SIXTO QUINTO PONT. MAX. AUCTORI" (fig. 84). Sixtus here is author, that is to say, architect. The image of the pope-as-architect (and Rome, the earthly paradise as building site) made Architecture equivalent to the Church.[30]

Between Paul III and Sixtus V architecture has gone from *symbolizing* the regeneration of the church to *being* the Church. If at the first coming God was made manifest in Christ as a man, then in this second coming, God appears as architecture. This is the transubstantiative moment: architecture no longer stands as a symbol for the (real) church. Rather architecture now *makes real* the symbol (the Church). The church = the Church.

Jesuit architecture provided a slightly different spin on the theme. A pendant to the painting of *Gregory XIII visiting construction of the Collegio Romano* created an imaginary narrative out of Gregory XIII's largesse to the Jesuits and their colleges (fig. 85). Seated under a baldachin, with St. Peter's in the distance on the left, Gregory XIII hands out architectural plans to representatives from Japan, Poland, and other parts of the world. This painting and its pendant position the pope as the fulcrum of these projects. But the Jesuits kneeling behind the pope are the real engine here. For they provide the plans that are received with gratitude, studied, and deciphered by the foreign emissaries. The plans make visible the gift of Catholicism to the world, one all the more striking with the Jesuits as silent partners providing *plans* rather than *missionaries* to move men's hearts. If architecture stands here for Catholicism, the Jesuits are the priests and the theologians of architecture.

It is significant that plans rather than elevations are being distributed. The paintings in the Aula Magna of the Collegio Romano likely represented the facades of the buildings, as in the engraving of Gregory XIII (fig. 80). The offering of ground plans, a comprehensive guide to the *functioning* of the colleges, reflects real practice. For the Jesuits required that only plans, not elevations, be sent from their various outposts to Rome for approval.[31] The emphasis on the arrangement of space (plan) with an eye to function rather than form (elevation) is at the core of the Jesuit notion of a "modo nostro" of building.[32] Hence it is significant that the emissaries receive not the image of their new place as the vertical cut into the cityscape but plans for new spaces with new functions: *these are plans for a change of heart.* In these images, then, a particular understanding of "architecture" is put forth. The territorial or proprietary significance of late Medieval representations of buildings has shifted. What these representations, collectively, suggest is that it is now "architecture" rather than "a building" that is signified. "Architecture" had already been accorded a meaning as such in fifteenth-century representations of antique-style buildings next to crumbling buildings of the "old" order. The modest image of Gregory distributing plans to the Jesuit missions marks, I believe, an important variant. For it tells a story *about* the diffusion of Catholicism, a diffusion for which Jesuit *architecture* has come to stand. Insofar as Catholicism could be understood *as architecture,* and that architecture became a performative, almost a liturgical act, we can speak of the diffusion of architecture as a form of propaganda.

This reading of architecture is reinforced by another anonymous painting that hangs in the anteroom of the sacristy of the Gesù (see fig. 15). It represents the two Farnese cardinals as patrons of the Gesù and the Casa Professa, posing with the models and plans of the buildings inside the nave of the church. Not only is the view of the church interior radical for its time, but with the plans sitting in the place of a prayer book on a prie-dieu and the patrons sitting between the plans and the work as executed, the portrait suggests that it was the devout patronage of the Farnese that brought the building into being. Although architects have disappeared, architecture has not. Patronage is posited here as authorship.

Art historians have been keenly interested in images of architects for what they tell us about the elevation of the status of the artist in the early modern period. The images I have discussed here were not the invention of architects seeking to raise their status. Rather, the elevation of the architect's status was the precondition for the establishment of a discourse of architecture available to popes and other members of the ruling class.[33] In their depiction of the rulers receiving and disseminating design, these images provide evidence that the debates that began in the Renaissance about architecture and its practice produced a discourse.[34] The Catholic Church was not the only potentate to avail itself of the architectural discourse. But of course I am interested in what the Roman Church did with architecture, and the images under discussion here suggest that architecture served it as a new, a performative form of theology. As the priests out in the field, the Jesuits were responsible for performing and diffusing the architectural rite.

COPIES AND IMITATIONS, OR MORE JESUIT FORMS?

There is what appears to be a contradiction in Jesuit culture between an old-fashioned corporate approach to reproducing the same building over and over and a progressive approach to architecture that values design beyond identity production. It is important for us to understand how the Jesuits mediated both the traditional, symbolic practice of iteration and a modern approach to architecture as a self-consciously inventive process.

Early in its architectural history, during the generalate of Eduardo Mercurian (1573–80), the Society flirted with standardizing design. It is believed that a drawing attributed to the Jesuit architect Giovanni De Rosis showing six variants on a longitudinal church was circulated at this time (fig. 86). The drawing has been linked to Mercurian's order to the Jesuit painter and architect Giuseppe Valeriano to write a treatise on architecture (accompanied by drawings) as well as to a circular sent to the father provincial of Spain in 1580.[35] The latter announced the arrival of "piani-tipo comuni" (plans of common types, that is, building types), which, together with written instructions, were to serve as guides to the "form that we judge our buildings should commonly have." While variants and improvements were to be embraced, Mercurian expressed the desirability of "a certain uniformity in the Society in this aspect."[36] Valeriano's treatise is lost; the Modena drawing is of uncertain attribution. In spite of the uncertainty surrounding both, it is clear that in the 1570s the Jesuits viewed standardized guidelines and plans as highly desirable.

While the monastic tradition of replicating the original foundation would have been familiar to the Jesuits, any architect working in the sixteenth century would have been aware of the debates in the middle decades of the sixteenth century over the extent to which architectural practice should be based on rules, the "uso comune," or architectural license (invention).[37] The debates were stimulated by the appearance of illustrated architectural treatises that posed the question as to how moderns should use Vitruvius and the orders: should antique architecture be precisely imitated, never straying from the antique vocabulary (as the Ciceronians argued in the area of literary composition; *imitatio*)? Or should the orders or "the rules" be a flexible system, to be adapted as necessary *(aemulatio)*?[38]

With the publication of Sebastiano Serlio's *Cinque Regole,* a "metodo facile e breve" became available—what Mario Carpo refers to as the architectural equivalent of "citazionismo cinquecentesco" in literature. With its reassurance that the examples could be employed by any "mediocre" architect, Serlio's treatise was widely used by often poorly trained architects or rank amateurs pressed into service for building on the missions (Jesuit and others). The treatise's offer of easily recombined ready-made parts elicited anxiety among the elite that architecture would become a slavish practice of copying. Serlio's text, it has

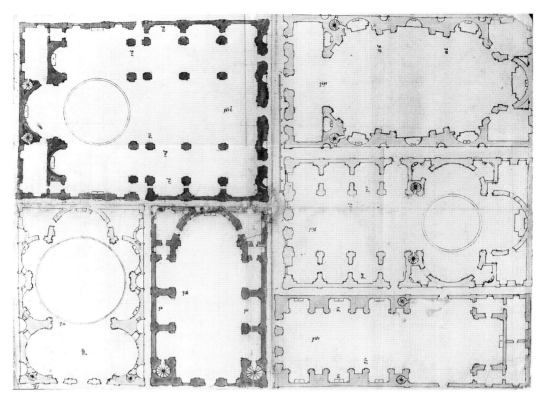

FIG. 86

Giovanni De Rosis (?), *Plans for Jesuit churches,* ca. 1580.

been argued, forced an explicit distinction between architecture, a sophisticated practice based on knowledge of theory, and a less informed practice, recombinatory, the production of ready-mades.[39] The fear of design falling into the hands of the incompetent reveals the extent to which the informed literate ruling class had appropriated design for themselves. It is an index of the ideological use to which "architecture" (as opposed to building) was being put. Were Giovanni De Rosis's plan types a symptom of the problem or a way to avoid it?

Precisely at the height of the debates in architectural circles, around 1560, the Jesuits began construction of their first new buildings in earnest with the Gesù and numerous other churches in Italy and elsewhere. It is striking that one of the most important interlocutors against Serlio was Guillaume Philandrier, a French commentator on Vitruvius, whose argument in favor of an elitist practice of creative imitation was directed to the Farnese court.[40] For it was Alessandro Farnese who insisted on hiring his own architect, Jacopo da Vignola, to build the Gesù at a time when an excellent Jesuit architect (Giovanni Tristano) was available for the job. Farnese has often been viewed as having dominated the Jesuits in his choice of architect and in his insistence on certain features of the design. But is his engagement by the Jesuits not rather a sign that the Jesuit building program was part of an ideological matrix of which architecture was rapidly becoming an explicit part?

The debate over how to use the architectural treatise and Vitruvius in particular is known to have been a source of discussion in the Jesuit milieu later, in the 1590s, under the generalate of Claudio Aquaviva. About this moment, the chapter on architecture in the Jesuit Antonio Possevino's *Bibliotheca Selectae,* a universal Catholic encyclopedia published in 1593, is a precious document. The *Bibliotheca* is a compendium of Catholic "sapienza," a map of knowledge appropriate for a Catholic elite (students and missionaries). Hence it is highly symptomatic of the status of architecture that Possevino devoted a chapter to it. He consulted Valeriano and Bartolomeo Ammannati, who concurred on the unusability of Vitruvius's text as a basis for modern practice. Architecture is better based on reason and on examples that can be seen with the eyes than on Vitruvius's mixed-up text.[41] Echoing Alberti, Possevino argues that architectural theory requires not forms but principles, and the latter are invention, erudition, observation, and use, all expressed exclusively through design. This is a position that resonates with Jesuit rhetoric.[42] Echoing Valeriano's complaints to the general of the disastrous results of incompetent design, Possevino stressed that the Jesuits should always hire competent architects, not hacks who might fall into the misuse of treatises (like Serlio's). Is it any wonder, then, that the use of Giovanni De Rosis's drawings for standardized Jesuit churches was discontinued after Mercurian's death?[43]

While the Jesuits seem to have rejected a rule-bound architectural practice, models, or exemplars, were nonetheless enormously important. This introduces another sense of the term *imitatio,* also fervently debated in the early modern period.[44] Most architectural theorists agreed on the critical importance of exemplars—antique and modern—for the correct practice of imitation, that is to say, the close study of good models on which the architect's invention is based.[45] Imitation was synonymous with invention until the nineteenth century, when it became, conversely, synonymous with copying; at the same time, individuality replaced universality as an artistic goal.[46] Because the practice of imitation was the basis for the development of personal *style,* it stood at the very core of an incipient early modern notion of the aesthetic. And because the origins of the aesthetic are so crucial to our art historical narrative, the virtue of resemblance in imitation is often obscured.

Recently architectural historians have begun to see resemblance to exemplars in Renaissance architecture as a virtue rather than as a failure of individual creativity. With reception study more generally taking hold in the discipline, revisionist accounts of the intertextuality of Renaissance architecture that stress the connections to—rather than the departures from—illustrious models are now being written.[47] What is increasingly being investigated, though evidence is usually lacking, are motives, the ideological core of imitation.[48]

FIG. 87
Jacopo da Vignola and Giacomo della Porta, Il Gesù, begun 1569, Rome.

The challenge here is to sort out the meaning of iteration in a society that has both developed a specialized discourse around architecture and does not always explicitly acknowledge its motives. An institution such as the Society of Jesus is likely to furnish us with answers, for it is in a corporation (which must write down its rules rather than rely on nature to provide them) that identity is always being produced or reiterated.

The church that exemplifies the imitation and diffusion of Jesuit forms more than any other was the Mother Church of the Society, the Roman Gesù (fig. 87; cf. fig. 88). The often-repeated notion that all Jesuit churches are versions of the Gesù is an important al-

FIG. 88
Matteo Castello, Church of Sts. Peter and Paul, begun 1597, Cracow.

beit impressionistic concept born in the nineteenth century. Vociferous objections to this statement have been made often, in part because the way it was originally imagined, Jesuit architecture had the quality of a repressive imposition. The Jesuits neither organized nor anticipated the reception of the Gesù in the pernicious and aggressive manner that many later imagined them doing. But they would not have been embarrassed by the success of their Mother Church: on the contrary, they produced it.

While the nineteenth-century critics of the Jesuit Style exaggerated the impact of the Gesù on the Baroque, Bösel has shown without a shadow of a doubt that those who deny any self-conscious referencing are also mistaken.[49] In a survey of approximately one hundred sixty Jesuit churches in Italy alone Bösel identified thirty that are derivative of the Mother Church.[50] He is inclined to say there are "only" thirty in the service of debunking the seemingly intractable claim that all Jesuit churches are copies of the Gesù. With that generalization dispelled, I am inclined to find this number astonishingly high, the sign of a very intense engagement with important exemplars within the Society itself that were noted as such.

In looking at a few examples of this Jesuit use of models, it is important to distinguish between works that have been linked to models by art historians (like the Church of Sts. Peter and Paul in Cracow, strikingly similar to the Roman Gesù; fig. 88)[51] and those we know for certain from documents to have been based on a specific model. It is probable that many of the works for whose citations we have no written confirmation were quite self-conscious and articulated at the time. I will focus here on the documented cases, for they prove that such citational practice was in the architectural culture of the Society.

We need not look far from the Gesù itself to find the Jesuits wishing to emulate their Mother Church. In 1626, as they prepared to build a new church only three blocks away, they had something just like the Gesù in mind. Eventually designed by the Jesuit father Orazio Grassi, the Church of St. Ignatius, paid for by the Ludovisi family, was opened up to a competition in 1626 (or 1628) in which Stefano Maderno, Borromini, and Domenichino participated.[52] The reference to the Gesù as the model appears in Giovanni Pietro Bellori's *vita* of Domenichino. While the latter, Bellori says, was busy making plans ("fece più inventioni"), "some [Jesuit] fathers went to see him at his house and told him not to tire himself [in making designs], because they wanted to follow the form of their Church of the Gesù, as the first, the most beautiful, which had served as an example, and as a model for the other Churches."[53] Bösel can now show, through the genesis of various plans for the actual church, that this was more than some fathers acting on their own desires.[54] But for my purpose, the recognizability of the prototype in the final work is less important than the expression of *desire* to imitate the Gesù.

The Jesuits did not limit themselves to Roman models. Rather, buildings in important centers (like Milan for northern Italy, or Vienna for Austria and Bohemia) often stimulated imitations in the surrounding region.[55] Since plans circulated widely, diffusion often occurred across regional centers. For instance, for the design of the new church in Noto (Sicily) the Jesuits proposed as models the Society's churches in Cremona, Malta, and Milan.[56] The Church of St. Ignatius in Fano was to be based on the church in Pistoia; on the plan for the Pavia church, the architect wrote "chiesa simile et uguale à quella di Torino."[57]

In their discourse of the example the Jesuits were entirely in step with both the architectural and the literary culture of iteration and of exemplarity that became so important in the Renaissance.[58] It is a discourse that arose from excavation, an attempt to carve a modern identity out of the exploration of the remains of antiquity. And while actual copies in the modern sense of the term became more possible and likely with the graphic reproductions now at architects' disposal,[59] invention was key to imitation, mitigating outright copying at the moment it became truly possible.

The Jesuits were in step with their times here too. For example, they posited the relationship of their new church in Fidenza as an imitation of the Jesuit church of S. Fedele in Milan in the following way: "imitating that great design a second work was formed, which is not a copy of the first, or, in being so it can aspire to the glory of the original."[60] Cognizant of the growing distinction in the figurative arts between originals and lesser copies and the concomitant emphasis on originality that comes of the practice of imitation, the comment shows how a discussion that came about in connoisseurial circles[61] was seeping into architecture as well. Hence, lest the new church in Fidenza be termed a *mere* copy, the commentator terms the new church an "imitation." But it also pays homage to the original, to which this building, if it were a copy, would stand in homage.

A passage about the Jesuit church of S. Lucia in Bologna is even more to the point: "know that our church of Bologna is the whole Gesù corrected."[62] This astonishing remark, commented on previously by Bösel, encapsulates two issues that are reconciled in the diffusion of Jesuit architecture. Within the Society, on the one hand, the Gesù has paradigmatic value; it is a building with which the Jesuits identify, and imitating it produces affiliation. On the other hand, as a design, its defects (in need of revision) as well as its historicity (bound to be superseded) are recognized. Hence the Jesuits were at once highly self-conscious about the use of their own churches as models and entirely in step with their times in wanting the model visible, but not at the expense of new invention.[63]

A further example could be construed as a cautionary statement, the anti-case, that shows that the Jesuits *prevented* their architects from citing certain models. The "bad" example is the Collegio Romano, paid for by Pope Gregory XIII. More sumptuous than the Jesuits had wanted, they found it contrary to holy poverty, a principle to which they held their houses (not their churches). When the Jesuit Collegio Massimo in Naples was being designed (1586), the general warned them not to model the new building on the Collegio Romano, which was not a good example.[64] Or consider the case of the Jesuit church in Antwerp, whose design was rejected by Rome because it was too similar to the Gesù.[65]

Not only were there bad examples, but one Jesuit general once said that there need not be *any* examples. General Aquaviva wrote to the fathers in Verona: "Explain to the most reverend fathers that it is not necessary that the models of our churches all be done in the same way; according to the convenience and circumstances that arise, things can be done in one manner or in another, whatever turns out best."[66] Even when the Jesuits are distinguishing between good and bad models, or liberating their architects from examples altogether, the impulse to refer to Roman (or other Jesuit) buildings was strong. In other words, even when rejecting an example or examples in principle, they demonstrate their investment in the structure of exemplarity.

About the function of exemplarity, Alexander Gelley recently posed this question: "Is the example merely one—a singular, a fruit of circumstance—or the One—a paradigm, a paragon? The tactic of exemplarity would seem to be to mingle the singular with the normative, to mark an instance as fated."[67] This describes well the status of the Gesù: a fated example.

JESUIT FORMS, JESUIT IDENTITY

Having established the existence of an iterative desire in the Jesuit architectural culture, it remains to be seen *why* the Jesuits wanted their churches (or houses) to resemble each other. The answer was self-apparent in the nineteenth century when a mechanized view of the Jesuits producing automatons instead of men, and mechanical architecture instead of works of individual genius, went unquestioned. There are two interrelated questions that need be posed with regard to architecture. What is the role of form in producing a Jesuit identity?

But a more basic question needs to be addressed first. Is form-making an activity that can either make visible or produce identity?[68] Here the Jesuit experience of teaching art to converts on the missions is revealing. From correspondence between the missions and Rome it appears tacit that in a multicultural context, *making something* is a revealing act, one that had the potential to make one's belief system—the invisible—visible. Training the recent convert or the unconverted to make European-style images, the Jesuits hoped that making something in a European style could mean that the subject has assumed the identity of the producer of the prototype: that the subject has become Christian, Catholic. This notion was expressed both positively and negatively. In 1588 in Goa, church authorities forbade non-Christian (Hindu) artists from sculpting or painting Christian religious imagery for fear of doctrinal contamination.[69] By contrast, it was implicit in the Jesuit strategy in Japan and on the Guaraní missions, where artistic training of the non-Europeans was central, that making Christian art could change (or at least reveal) souls. One gauge for this was how a Christian image was copied. But the Jesuits seemed to have been plagued by the difficulty of knowing at what point the "slavish" (the colonial meaning of the term becomes clear) adherence to the copy (mere mimicry) became internalized (authentic conversion) and resulted in imitation. One Jesuit was unconvinced of the latter possibility with the Guaraní:

> They are absolutely incapable of inventing or creating anything by means of their own imagination or thought. Even the simplest work imaginable the father has to be there guiding them; he has to give them above all a model and example. If they have one, then he can be sure that they will imitate the work exactly. They are indescribably talented as imitators.[70]

Without the evidence of human creativity, of the operation of *ingegno* that Alberti saw as evidence of man's ability to progress spiritually,[71] could the mission succeed? Spectacular results of artistic training on the Japanese mission encouraged the Jesuits that virtuoso copying evidenced a change in heart. In spite of persisting doubts, their faith in this possibility is evidenced by the organization in Japan of a "Seminary of Painters" (later called an Academy) where assiduous and talented Japanese apprentices lived "in the manner of a seminary." In their apprenticeship with the Jesuits they received training likened to a discipleship, and some Japanese Christians went on to other countries to spread the image there as well.[72] Apparently there was no fear of doctrinal contamination from these artists' work.

In spite of the uniqueness of the Japanese seminary, its implications are profound. For it shows the extent to which the Jesuits thought that artistic forms were invested with one's system of belief. In Europe, feats of imitation were not usually taken as signs of belief. The kind of skill the Japanese students displayed was read by the Jesuits as a sign that they had been inwardly reformed because the work issued from the hand. Bypassing the avoidance of the hand by art theorists in Europe (who were troubled by the manual because of its negative implications for the artist's status),[73] in this context the Jesuits drew on other associations of the hand; as the intelligence of the body and as our oath-taking limb, the hand will not betray one's inner beliefs.[74] Hence to the question, was it believed in the early modern period that art or architecture had the possibility to form Christian subjects? the answer must be yes. While this conclusion has been drawn from circumstances surrounding *making* art, the issue here is ultimately about the status of form. And this has ramifications for forms diffused within the Society as well as without.

Did the Jesuits see forms as important, even capable of producing *their identity?* The rules for Jesuit dress, formulated in the *Constitutions,* offer some clues. Ignatius was radically relativist in his position on dress. Drawing on his own experience, he adopted a flexible attitude, refusing to dictate a Jesuit uniform. Jesuit priests should wear the costume of honest priests of their locale, varying according to local custom. This flexibility has become a hallmark of Jesuit adaptability in general. But in one critical section of the *Constitutions* clothing, external form, is recognized as capable of fostering "Jesuitness." The passage comes in the section about nurturing a sense of Jesuit purpose, namely, "Helps toward uniting the distant members with their head and among themselves," or "Aids toward the union of hearts." Here it is noted that while the "chief bond to cement the union of the members amongst themselves and with their superior is, on both sides, the love of God the father, a great help can be found towards this in uniformity, both interior uniformity . . . and *exterior uniformity* in respect to clothing," ritual, and so on.[75]

Architecture is not on this list of "helpful" forms. But it is abundantly clear from the practices that developed in the later part of the sixteenth century that it could have been. While it would be going too far to call the Jesuit relation to form Platonic, there is something Platonic in their conception of both their own forms and their architectural forms. When Plato wrote his *Republic* he often reverted to visual analogies in order to explain transcendent ideas, even though he thought them inferior, mere shadows. Like Plato, the Jesuits viewed forms as handmaidens in the effort to know that which cannot be grasped. Both for the subject entering into the built space of the church and those actually engaged in making them, the architectural forms generated within the Society become a way of knowing. The documents that I have cited above suggest that the Jesuits treated their architecture as very much akin to a soul, to be formed, or reformed, a mirror image of a prime form. Jesuit architecture, both the external forms and the references to models, was yet another instance of a deeply engrained mimetic procedure that lay at the heart of religious life.[76]

The repetition of architectural forms engendered traditions and rendered institutional history visible. As such, the process of iteration that served to shape a Jesuit identity helps us to understand why Jesuit architecture had the diffusion that it did. Jesuit forms served both the Jesuit sense of identity and purpose and the shaping of Catholic subjects.

MEANS OF DIFFUSION: ARCHITECTURE IN EARLY MODERN PRINTS

In turning to the reception of Jesuit architecture within and outside of the Society, the mechanics of diffusion are crucial. While architectural design circulated before mechanical reproduction, the book and the engraved plate created the possibility for a shared culture of design far beyond what drawings and other means of transmission already permitted.[77] Two aspects of the mechanics need to be considered. The first concerns the relatively straightforward question of how Jesuits circulated design among themselves. The second, more complex question concerns the authority with which design circulated outside the Society. Under what auspices did Jesuit architecture circulate? To what extent is that authority responsible for the success of the diffusion and the work's subsequent reception?

In the Jesuit milieu drawings, prints (produced especially for patrons), and books (architectural treatises) all played a role in establishing a shared culture of design. Drawings were archived in Rome where they could be referred to by the Jesuit building *revisori,* but they also circulated. A recently discovered cache of drawings by the Jesuit architect Henri Laloyau (Brussels ca.1646–Rome 1723), including a mini-archive of plans of Jesuit churches, helps to explain the ease with which Jesuits drew on plans in distant places.[78]

Beyond drawings, architecture and design circulated under three major aegis in early modern prints.[79] Design circulated under the names of architects in the illustrated treatise, the progeny of Andrea Palladio's *Quattro Libri.* In seventeenth-century Italy relatively few architects managed to publish their own monographs,[80] and publications on single buildings often remained in manuscript, although the first quarter of the eighteenth century saw the publication of several important works.[81] By the end of the sixteenth century it would have been easier to find reproductions of newly completed works published in the name of the patron,[82] an outgrowth of the pamphleteering and engravings of ephemeral architecture.

Where you were most likely to find the works of the major architects reproduced were in the series of engravings of city architecture, the market for which expanded suddenly in mid-seventeenth-century Rome.[83] What is important is the peculiar status of these prints: they were often dedicated to popes, cardinals, and nobles with prominent coats of arms, and yet were speculative, sold on the open market. In buying such a print, the public participated in the preservation of the power structure. This participation encompassed patrons who used the prints to emulate the churches and palaces of their peers as well as artists, whose process of artistic imitation, I argue, essentially amounted to the same thing.

The diversity of the audiences to which these prints were directed is indicated by Giovanni Giacomo De Rossi in the *proemio* to his compendia of sixteenth- and seventeenth-century church and altar designs, the *Disegni di vari Altari e Cappelle*. He intended the work, he wrote, for the "erudition of the *Ingegni,* as exemplary of Art, and for the Glory of this Queen of the World, my Fatherland."[84] The prints truly served multiple interests, first of all a growing public of dilettantes, the erudite who entered the church first of all *to know.* For this group the dedications on the prints were as crucial as the identity of the architect in the diffusion of the designs. For when the engravings reached their destination, it was often the patron who had the collection of prints of art collections and palaces of his peers; it was often he who specified to the artist which models he wanted his own commission to imitate.[85] In citing the works as exemplars, De Rossi acknowledges the architectural cycle of example-imitation-invention that the prints facilitated, this aimed at artists. And finally, in citing the glory of Rome, De Rossi makes the city the subject because of her architecture. In making Rome and her architecture available as a subject (to be imitated or reproduced by courts and nobles, in all media), the print trade supported architecture's part in reinforcing a power structure.

A GOOD EXAMPLE:
THE DIFFUSION OF THE CHAPEL OF ST. IGNATIUS

Reproductions of the Chapel of St. Ignatius issued forth from all possible channels of early modern print distribution. The chapel was reproduced in an engraving paid for and circulated by the Jesuits, in an architect's monograph (Andrea Pozzo's treatise on perspective), and in a suite of prints published by a Parisian print seller on the open market. It is tempting to see the chapel as having been *made* to be reproduced, for even before Andrea Pozzo had finalized his design for the chapel in 1695 the Jesuits contracted for an imperial-size engraving (fig. 89).[86] Vincenzo Mariotti based his plate on Pozzo's drawings, altering it as plans developed so as to satisfy the desire for accuracy. In 1697, in the middle of construction, the Jesuits wanted to get the engraving out. Their General Congregation met in Rome that year, and with dozens of Jesuits coming into the city from abroad they seized the opportunity to send the chapel's design "with the fathers of the General Congregation to all the houses of the Company."[87] Costlier miniatures of the chapel painted on parchment were also produced at this time, no doubt for people of high rank. Reproductive images were not all made equal.[88]

IMAGO SACELLI QUOD S. IGNATIO DE LOYOLA.
Conditori Societatis Iesu erectum est —
in Templo Domus Professæ Romanæ eiusdem Societatis,
in quo Sacra eius ossa venerantur.
An. M.DC.XCVII.

FIG. 89
Vincenzo Mariotti after Andrea Pozzo, *The Chapel of St. Ignatius*, 1697.

We know that the Jesuits systematically distributed Mariotti's engraving to all Jesuit houses. At least twenty-five hundred copies (and perhaps double that number) of a detailed description of the chapel printed as a pamphlet at the same time may indicate the scale of circulation of the engraving (although an engraved plate would not hold up to such a large edition).[89] The print was thus treated like other core Jesuit documents—the *Constitutions*, the *Rules*, the *Ratio Studiorium*—printed works distributed systematically because necessary to the Jesuit life. The Jesuits circulated the engraving under their authority just as they mounted their own printing press in order to have their own means to print textbooks and the primary documents of Jesuit life.[90]

While Mariotti's engraving declares the *Jesuit* origin of both the image and the chapel in its inscription, the accompanying pamphlet makes a slightly different claim:

> On the occasion that many people with singular affection for the glorious Patriarch St. Ignatius of Loyola, have asked with humble pleading that a design of the new chapel newly erected in the Church of the Gesù in Rome honoring said saint, be printed; it was esteemed well to accompany the print with a succinct description of all of its parts, and especially the marbles, precious stones and metals that comprise and enrich it; and in this way to satisfy the shared satisfaction of those devoted to him.[91]

In 1705 the Jesuits revised and reissued the pamphlet. Like the first pamphlet, the new one was issued to satisfy public demand:

> To satisfy the impatient desire of the many people with affection for the Glorious Patriarch St. Ignatius, who waited for a simple explanation of the Chapel newly opened in his honor, and not seeing one they instantly asked for it, the printer decided to bring to light the following, having added to that [pamphlet] printed previously in 1697, only what was missing.[92]

While the engraving asserts the Jesuit source of the project, the pamphlet shifts that authority to the popular cult of the saint. Insofar as the Jesuits were trying to increase Ignatius's cult with the renovation of the chapel, the pamphlet makes it seem as if the chapel has already done its work: it has produced subjects because they demand *to know* the chapel.

What is significant about Mariotti's engraving is that it was commissioned, paid for, and distributed by Jesuits to Jesuits. In this context it is striking that in both the print and the pamphlet, Pozzo's authorship of the chapel is practically suppressed. In Mariotti's engraving his name is barely visible, embedded in the patterned marbles. More astonishing yet, his name appears nowhere in the printed pamphlets. In distributing the print, the Jesuits, whose patronage of the chapel is in the inscription, asserted the chapel's authority as the site of Ignatius's relics, producing Jesuit affiliation first of all to its own members, through it. Prints and books produced or distributed to one audience do not, of course, exclude their use by another, such as artists. I merely wish to underscore the specific circumstances that saw the production of the print and the nature of its immediate recipients.

By contrast, the second set of engravings of Pozzo's new project appeared in a treatise that circulated under Pozzo's name: volume 2 of his *Perspectiva pictorum et architectorum* (1700). This treatise, an instructional manual on perspective, became an international publishing phenomenon. With initial editions in Italian and Latin, it was soon translated into English, French, German, Spanish, Flemish, modern Greek, and Chinese.[93] Pozzo himself seems to have been an effective promoter of the book. For instance, he presented the first volume as a gift to the director of the French Academy in Rome (then La Teulière). In one of his regular news reports about the arts in Rome, the latter informed his counterpart in Paris about the volume and promptly received a request for two copies.[94] As a direct consequence of the availability of the volumes through translation, the artist's works—especially his illusionistic ceilings and altars—were widely imitated well into the eighteenth century all over the world. Particularly striking is the reception of the treatise in Central Europe, specifically in Poland.[95]

Pozzo's treatise had several audiences, principal among them Jesuit mathematicians and architects. Because the volumes contained so many reproductions of Jesuit works, new as well as older projects, it sustained the afterlife of buildings such as Pellegrino Pellegrini's Milanese church of S. Fedele, widely imitated for two hundred years.[96] Most of the second volume was dedicated to Pozzo's own projects (built and unbuilt) for the Society's Roman churches, explicitly reproduced for the purposes of imitation and copying. Pozzo wrote for artists, including advice about building from his designs.[97] It is striking that throughout the text he addresses readers directly, frequently talking about how to make use of ("servirsi di") his plans. In one case Pozzo remarks that a certain design could not be used, so "anyone can use it, as you like."[98] Compare this to Palladio, who introduces his own projects as those of his patrons and describes them without making explicit recommendations about their use.[99] And compare Pozzo's eagerness to encourage the reproducibility of the projects to Borromini, who burned many drawings before taking his life in order that his work not be co-opted by his rivals.[100]

Unlike Mariotti, whose rendering of the Ignatian chapel generates an atmosphere of the space, Pozzo provides a plan and elevation (fig. 90) and a separate perspective (fig. 91). He is almost apologetic about the inclusion of the latter, which he justifies as an embellishment of the treatise.[101] It is one of the few projects so extensively illustrated.

About the third group of seven engravings after Ignatius's chapel, published by a Parisian printmaking concern, little is known (figs. 92, 93).[102] This suite of engravings was part of a series of at least fifteen plates.[103] Unlike Mariotti's and Pozzo's engravings, which give the overall shape of the project, the Parisian suite reproduces the sculptural components: the silver statue (fig. 92) and narrative scenes, including the large stucco reliefs above the cornice executed during the 1672–85 campaign of work on the church.

Since we know nothing of the genesis of the publication of the French series, we must attend carefully to the inscriptions. Captions in French and Latin suggest that an inter-

FIG. 90
Andrea Pozzo, *Elevation and plan of Chapel of St. Ignatius,* in *Perspectiva pictorum et architectorum,* vol. 2 (Augsburg, 1706), fig. 61.

national and an educated audience was anticipated. Even though the subject of the suite is the Roman chapel, only the inscription on the opening image (fig. 92) makes reference to it; the rest are presented with their titles alone.[104] With no mention of either the artist or the medium, the images emphasize Ignatius's life rather than the works of art they reproduce. Since they bank entirely on Ignatius's cult value, it is all the more significant that the series was undertaken speculatively. What this suggests is that there was a market: this is a different way of saying that the production of the series presumes the saint's cult.

All of these engravings, disseminated from different points, had the effect of making Pozzo's chapel an authoritative work. As Joseph Raz has pointed out in his work on authority, an original is not automatically an *authoritative* work. To move between the two statuses (original and authoritative), an *authority* usually intervenes, to declare a work

ALTARE·DI S.IGNATIO NOVAMENTE ERETTO NELLA CHIESA DEL GIESV DI ROMA
Architettura del Padre Andrea Pozzi

Girolimo Frezza Sculp.

FIG. 91
Andrea Pozzo, *Perspective of Chapel of St. Ignatius*, in *Perspectiva pictorum et architectorum*, vol. 2 (Rome, 1700), fig. 60.

FIG. 92
Unsigned, after Pierre Legros,
Statue of St. Ignatius, ca.
1706–18.

authoritative.[105] That is precisely the work that the engravings of Ignatius's chapel were doing. But they were capable of generating slightly different types of authority for the chapel. Whereas Mariotti's engraving unambiguously circulated under the Society's aegis, the authority behind Pozzo's book is more complex. It circulated, like all publications by Jesuit authors, with the Society's approval. And although the Jesuits acted as distributors of the book, it was commercially sold and did not circulate—as Mariotti's engraving did—at the Society's expense.[106] Rather, the authority of the book lies as much in Pozzo's identity as an architect-author as in the institutional affiliation of the project and its author. Books needed authors and the architectural treatise was bound to obscure one part of what Filarete described as the equilibrium between architect and patron, mother and father, which actually produced a building.[107] In Pozzo's case, the tension in which he hovered, in a state of creative obedience during the design, is audible in the treatise.

FIG. 93
Nicolas-Henry Tardieu,
after Renato Frémin,
Miracle of the oil, ca.
1706–18.

Divi Ignatij tumulus multis   *Tombeau de St Ignace illustré*
nobilitatus miraculis.   *par une infinité de miracles.*

On the one hand, he vaunts the originality of the scheme ("I tried that [the design] not appear taken from anyone"). But, he says, this design had its detractors among those that had to choose one among many. This one, having been "mixed in amongst the others[,] . . . was chosen by a famous architect of these times." In his own publication Pozzo conveyed the selection of his design as almost an accident.

In spite of Pozzo's modesty, both the public process of choosing his design as the most meritorious and the treatise increased Pozzo's reputation, to the benefit of the Jesuits. What is more, Ignatius's cult profited: proceeds from the sale of the *Perspectiva* went toward construction of the chapel.[108] Pozzo's publication thus served the interests of the cult twice over: profits helped to pay for construction, and reproductions spread the fame of the architect and the chapel worldwide.

To the news that a French publisher was reproducing the chapel's imagery, the Jesuits would undoubtedly have expressed pleasure. For is it not an indication of the chapel's success that its imagery entered into the market?

If an engraving circulated under one authority it was also capable of generating another without any effort whatsoever. The apparent freedom of the early modern print enterprise is belied by its regulation by the Crown in Paris and its close relations to the papacy (and noble families) in Rome. Striking in this regard are two episodes that show how deeply the commercial printmakers were tied to the power structure. French engravers were closely controlled by Louis XIV. Although engravers were admitted alongside painters and sculptors to the Academy (in 1665), it was with the mandate to reproduce portraits and the king's pictures. Two years later Parisian engravers were prohibited from engraving or selling representations of royal houses and châteaus without authorization from the king.[109] In Rome in 1732, Cardinal Corsini, nephew of Clement XII, blocked the sale of the stock of the De Rossi printing concern (which dominated the market in views of Rome) to a foreign concern. So invested was the papacy in the representation of the city and of itself—De Rossi's inventories are also full of portraits of the ecclesiastical hierarchy—that the Camera Apostolica purchased the De Rossi plates six years later.[110] The papal decree justified the purchase of the engravings for their capacity to "promote the magnificence and splendor of Rome in foreign nations; and as well the advancement of youth who study the liberal arts."[111] There could hardly be a clearer statement of how the free trade of images and the arts themselves supported the Church, the Crown, the Society of Jesus. It is important not to draw too large a distinction between the print sent out by the Jesuits and the suite sold by the French publishers in Paris.

My point about the reproductions of Ignatius's chapel is that the chapel circulated under a variety of authorities and that this increased the possibilities that the images would fall into the hands of, to use De Rossi's list, the patrons (the *eruditi*), artists, and, to expand De Rossi's categories, the devout. The prints could produce devotion directly, or they could stimulate imitations of the chapel, this another route toward the larger goal.

COPIES AND IMITATIONS OF THE CHAPEL OF ST. IGNATIUS

While the Gesù provided an example of a Jesuit building imitated *within* the Society, Jesuit architecture was diffused widely in *non-Jesuit* churches as well. This is by far the more common scenario, and more difficult to interpret: where propaganda is concerned, it is in this type of reception that we can see results. Jesuit architecture imitated by Jesuits proves a predictable outcome of diffusion. But Jesuit architecture imitated in non-Jesuit settings is a measure of the success of propaganda.

The Chapel of St. Ignatius, with its copies and imitations in Jesuit and in non-Jesuit contexts, provides an expedient though complex example. A multimedia ensemble combining painting, sculpture, and architecture, a *bel composto*,[112] the chapel had a wide reception in the eighteenth century, especially in Central and Eastern Europe, but also as far as Goa. Two conditions supported the wide reception of Pozzo's work in Central and Eastern Europe. In addition to his treatise, pupils of Pozzo trained by him in Vienna before his death in 1712 contributed to the diffusion of his style in that region.

Most of the chapel's progeny were not Jesuit projects, and this is the main issue that requires explanation. Has the message gone astray, been co-opted, or so transformed that it perverts the intention of the agent? Or are these uses of Jesuit designs outside the Jesuit milieu evidence precisely of the success of the Jesuit message? These questions will be taken up through an account of the reception of the Ignatian altar primarily in Silesia and Poland.[113] The examples are organized, as far as it is possible, through their relations to each other, noting further layers of citation at each site.

We begin with an example in southeastern Poland, a parish church owned by Jana Klemensa Branickiego, member of the Polish ruling class, with an appetite for architectural books on which he relied for his building projects.[114] The church is located outside of Cracow in Tyczn, the capital town of Branickiego's complex of property in Small Poland. Between 1725 and 1745 the patron transformed an aisleless Gothic sanctuary into a Latin cross church with six new altars, including two side altars and the high altar based on designs from Pozzo's treatise.[115] Just who was responsible for the long renovation remains uncertain, although it seems likely that Jan Henryk Klemm was the architect for the second wave of construction, which included the altars.[116]

The two marbleized side altars nearest to the apse are closely modeled on the Chapel of St. Ignatius. On the left side is the Chapel of the Crucifixion and on the right, that dedicated to the Polish Jesuit St. Stanislas Kostka (fig. 94), founded by the Kostka family at the beginning of the seventeenth century.[117] In both altars the convex four-column aedicula with a broken pediment is akin to the Ignatian aedicula, although the entablature is made up of a more complex and repetitive group of moldings. The niche, one of the most distinctive features of the Ignatian altar, is also retained, as are the rather unusual bases crowned by volutes flanking the altar, now astride with single figures. They are framed by a similar type of articulation of the wall with decorative frames, though here there are no marble reliefs. This altar, like most examples, is a pastiche. From Pozzo's *Chapel of St. Luigi Gonzaga* (fig. 95) Klemm derived a second, flat segmental pediment that crowns the aedicula, and perhaps the idea for the relief of Stanislas Kostka.

It has been reasonably surmised that Pozzo's designs were used here and elsewhere in Poland because they fulfilled the patron's desire for up-to-date Italian designs, supporting an aspiration to be cosmopolitan and Catholic. In evaluating the use of Jesuit designs, we must look closely at what it meant to be Catholic in early modern Poland. To be visibly Catholic was increasingly important to the Polish *szlachta* (roughly translated, "gentry"), in what amounted to a feudal system. For although upheld by the Roman Church as the bulwark of Christianity, keeping heretics and infidels at bay from the rest of

Jan Henryk Klemm (attributed), Chapel of St. Stanislas Kostka, 1725–45. Parish
church, Tyczn.

Western Europe, Poland could hardly be called Catholic in the early modern period. The
Diet of Warsaw (1573) made Judaism, Catholicism, Lutheranism, Calvinism, and Orthodox
Christianity legal. As a result, Poland attracted Europe's religious cast-offs, becoming its
most heterogeneous republic. It is no wonder that the arts in Poland have been judged
rather impoverished by the standards of Italy and other European countries that had stabler populations and religious identities and hence a stabler cultural identity.[118]

Figura 26.

SACELLVM B. ALOYSIO GONZAGÆ. SOC IESV ERECTVM IN TEMPLO COLLEGIJ ROMANI EIVSDEM SOC ANNO 1700.

FIG. 95
Chapel of St. Luigi Gonzaga, in Andrea Pozzo, *Perspectiva pictorum et architectorum,* vol. 2 (Rome, 1700), fig. 26.

Poland was an elective monarchy ruled ostensibly by a king but in actuality by the highly united *szlachta.* These magnates, like Branickiego, kept the authority of both Rome and the king in check.[119] What's more, the clergy lost its juridical power in Poland in the sixteenth century (when it was permitted to judge heresy but became powerless to inflict civil or criminal penalties) and there was no possibility for a national religion, although the magnates were allowed to impose a religion in their territory. Nonetheless, at times the magnates invited specific and diverse religious communities not consonant with their own beliefs to settle on their lands because they brought skills important to economic well-being. Some even built houses of worship to give proof of their tolerance and to encourage these communities to set down roots. What this suggests is that there is the possibility in Poland (and this is also true in Silesia) of a type of ecumenical patronage.[120] We cannot *assume* that patronage amounts to an expression of personal identification.

Yet this potential instability of meaning must be balanced against what Janusz Tazbir refers to as the "Polonization of Catholicism" in the seventeenth century, the consolidation of a Polish identity against the political pressure of Orthodox Russia to the east and Lutheran territories to the west (and Sweden to the north). It was during the seventeenth century that Catholicism was increasingly identified as the native religion and Protestantism the foreign, the "newcomer."[121] While the roots of this essentially anti-German sentiment were laid in the Middle Ages, with the influx of German political refugees during the Thirty Years' War Polish identity organized itself increasingly according to confession, which was, in turn, linked to social status. Catholicism became the unofficial religion of most of the ruling class.[122] Architecture, discourse of the ruling class, became an important form of expressing a pure form of Catholicness. With its Jesuit, Roman, and Catholic pedigree, it is little wonder that Pozzo's treatise had the success in early-eighteenth-century Poland that it did. Tyczn, with its patron known for his use of architectural treatises, can be understood in the context of the consolidation of the Catholic identity of the *szlachta*.

The second example concerns the high altar of a church with a complex history of relations to Italian models. This work raises a further issue, that of the significance of the affiliation of an architectural model when used by another Catholic religious order. The Oratorian Church of the Filippini is located outside Gostyń, a town equidistant to Ląd and Poznan, in Silesia.[123] The patron of the church, Adam Florian Konarzewski (1640–76), brought the Oratorians to Gostyń in 1667 to replace a monastic order that previously occupied a church on the site. An amateur architect, the patron Konarzewski made a plan for a new church based on the Jesuit church of Sts. Peter and Paul in Cracow. It is often asserted that the latter was in turn based on the Roman Gesù.[124]

In spite of Konarzewski's death in 1676, work began under the direction of the Italian Andrea Catenazzi in whose hands the patron's widow, Sofia Opalińska (1643–1700), left the project when she departed on a pilgrimage to Italy. In Venice she was so struck by Baldassare Longhena's church of S. Maria della Salute that she commissioned from him a version of that work for Gostyń. The Jesuit-Roman-Cracowian plan was abandoned. Designed more than forty years after its Venetian prototype, the Gostyń church has been described as a variant replica (rather than a mechanical copy) of the Salute.[125]

While the plan of the Gostyń church produces recognition in the spectator of its Venetian prototype, there are significant departures from the Salute, most notably the design of the high altar, where another prototype would be taken up (fig. 96). On the commission of Teofila Konarzewska (widow of Sofia's third husband), the Austro-Silesian artists Ignazio Provisore and Johann Albrecht Siegwitz built the high altar between 1723 and

FIG. 96

Ignazio Provisore and Johann Siegwitz, High altar, 1723–26. Church of the Filippini, Gostyń.

1726. Their contract (1723) specified that the artists were to imitate the design of the high altar of the Jesuit church of St. Mattia in Wrocław (1722–24).[126]

The high altar of the Jesuit church in Wrocław (fig. 97) on which the Gostyń altar was to be based marks the reentrance of an important Jesuit prototype. The Wrocław altar was designed by a pupil and assistant of Pozzo, the Jesuit coadjutor Christoph Tausch (Innsbruck 1673–Nysa 1731).[127] Typical of the Central European adaptations of Pozzo's de-

FIG. 97
Christoph Tausch, High altar, 1722–24. St. Mattia, Wrocław.

signs, this altar synthesized several designs in the second volume of his treatise: the Chapel of St. Ignatius (the convex plan, multifigured allegorical groupings); and two designs for the Chapel of St. Luigi Gonzaga (the high crowning element; fig. 95; and the rounded entablature over the column in an alternative plan; fig. 98). Tausch's Wrocław altar bears the traces of other works by Pozzo as he had reinterpreted them in preceding works. So, for instance, the broad convex frontispiece and the longer proportions of the columns re-

FIG. 98
Chapel of St. Luigi Gonzaga, in Andrea Pozzo, *Perspectiva pictorum et architectorum*, vol. 2 (Rome, 1700), fig. 65.

call as much Pozzo's Chapel of St. Ignatius as Tausch's high altar in Trenčín, whose most direct source, in turn, was Pozzo's high altar of the Universitätskirche in Vienna. Thus the source specified in the contract came with its own complex history of citations to which the new work would, in part, return directly.

Since Ignazio Provisore is known to have collaborated with Tausch as a *marmista*, the specification in the Gostyń contract of Tausch's recent work as the model is not surprising.[128] Yet Provisore and Siegwitz seem to have gone back to Pozzo's models directly, since two elements of the Gostyń altar are closer to the Ignatian chapel:[129] the Trinity above the pediment (in bas-relief instead of in the round) and the niche, which is articulated with bas-relief patterns while maintaining the illusion that the image floats in the clouds. Jettisoning the allegorical groups that appeared between the columns at the Wrocław altar, in Gostyń statues of St. Ignatius (right) and St. Philip Neri (left) appear as if recalling the dual citations of altars in the Roman mother churches of the two (rival) orders.

We do not know what motivated the patrons in Gostyń to imitate the Jesuit church first and the Venetian church second. Is it significant that an Oratorian church, which replaced that of another order, was to be based on a Jesuit church itself based on the Mother Church? Given the powerful evidence that it mattered *within* the Jesuit order, it is difficult to imagine that it did not matter—somehow—*outside* the Society. But we must rely on rare documented examples to sort out the possible meanings of citation of designs by one religious order, by another. Here, Sofia Opalińska's unusual appeal to Longhena for a second version of S. Maria della Salute is reminiscent of a better documented case: Alessandro Sperelli, bishop of Gubbio, who managed (through a well-placed intermediary) to wrest a plan of the Trinitarian church of S. Carlino from the intractable and anticopying Borromini himself.[130] The plan was to be put to use for a church of the Minims in Gubbio, S. Maria del Prato (begun 1662), which was to be what Joseph Connors ambivalently termed a copy of S. Carlino.[131] Connors suggests that in Gubbio it was the patron's political ties to Rome that motivated the copy of a Roman church, just as the numerous copies of Bernini's *Baldachin* that appeared in Umbria after joining the papal states expressed dependency on its new master. What interests me here is that there seems to have been no problem in the use for the Minim church in Gubbio of a plan of a Trinitarian church. We know that the Trinitarians actively showed the church to visitors from all over Europe and could easily have spawned its wide reception had Borromini only been willing to make a plan that could be engraved. From the perspective of the Trinitarians, the adoption of the plan of their church would have been a mark of their success. For the secrets of design, of architecture, had become useful to a class of patrons who kept their eye on the commissions of their peers.

While we have little evidence in Gostyń of motives, the example of Gubbio suggests that this sort of architectural imitation was likely to have been motivated. This applies to places (like Tyczn) that are customarily explained as a question of taste (usually Italian), a personal rather than a political designation. Although the use of specific models may have been tied to their institutional identities, other factors such as location and architectural prestige were just as crucial and loaded. Where the religious orders were concerned, this was a win-win situation. Churches paid for by prominent patrons easily stimulated the benefactors' peers, in addition to providing the order with a recognizable and imitable plan for its own foundations.

In the same region, near Poznan, a radical addition of an octagonal nave to the Cistercian church of Sts. Mary and Nicholas at Ląd bears a strong resemblance to the Ora-

FIG. 99
Pompeo Ferrari, Chapel of the Crucifixion, after 1730. Sts. Mary and Nicholas, Ląd.

torian church in Gostyń.[132] This is no coincidence, for the octagonal space was designed by Pompeo Ferrari (ca. 1670–1736), the Roman architect who arrived in Poland in 1696 and who completed the cupola of the Gostyń octagon beginning in 1728, following the death of his former master, Giovanni Catenacci.[133] While Ferrari has been attributed with little of the design of that project, in his other projects in Poland he produced variants on recognizable projects by Rome's most advanced architects, either from firsthand knowledge or from later publications.[134] At Ląd, Ferrari designed several altars, including the right transept Chapel of the Crucifixion (fig. 99), which returns us to Pozzo's prototypes.[135] Erected after 1730, the altar also has a strong resemblance to the high altar in Gostyń: the number of columns (the disposition altered so that the work generates a single organized movement rather than being tied to the surrounding walls), the forms of the bases, the flat gilded decoration of the niche, the oval relief and angels arranged in the second story rising above the columns. While the Ląd altar has no pediment, the restoration of the deepened niche, one of the identifying features of the Ignatian altar, links it to the latter. And look at how Pozzo's volutes for his allegorical groups have been reinterpreted as the entastic swelling of the angels' bases. With the outer columns now freestanding rather than encased in the apse wall (as at Gostyń) and a kind of complexity of the wall surface flanking the columns recalling Pozzo's elevation of the Ignatian chapel, Ferrari has, it seems, strengthened the resemblance to Pozzo's designs (figs. 91, 96).

　　If the Gostyń altar, based on the Wrocław altar, provided the basis for the Chapel of the Crucifixion at Ląd, the latter, in turn, was the model for another chapel: the Chapel of the Crucifixion (fig. 100) located on the terminal wall of the left side aisle of the cathedral in Chelmza, north of Torun. The design is securely dated to 1741 when Giovanni Battista Cocchi's plan was approved by the patron.[136] Work was complete by 1744. The earlier altar at Ląd is undeniably being followed here: the disposition of the figures in the niche, the angels posed on now columnar bases just beyond the second pair of columns. And yet Cocchi too has brought the chapel closer to Pozzo's prototype: he has restored the sense of the aedicula as a singular convex structure by simplifying the pediment and the bases, and he restored reliefs (though not historiated) to the base of the structure. Here as elsewhere the design draws from the "original" (Pozzo's) and its recent interpretations.

　　The patron of the Chelmza chapel was the local bishop from 1739 to 1746, Andrea Stanislao Kostka Zaluski (1695–1768). Although named for a Jesuit, he was far from sympathetic to the Society.[137] Zaluski founded the first public library in Poland, which opened in Warsaw in 1747. His brother wanted him to give it to the Jesuits, but Zaluski opposed the narrow-minded Jesuit educational system and the Jesuits' excessive power.[138] Is this a case of an unwitting use of a Jesuit plan by a patron who was anti-Jesuit? Or was the source not legible, with the Ląd altar as the visible mediator of the source? Or did it not matter?

　　In the first four works discussed here (Tyczn, Gostyń, Ląd, Chelmza) the form of the Ignatius chapel underwent significant alterations, but in the next, Pozzo's altars were faithfully followed. The entire interior of a small traditional wooden parish church in Welna, in the vicinity of Torun, is painted with *quadratura* paintings and stage set–like altars (1727–31) derivative of Pozzo's treatise.[139] The artist, Adam Swach, a Franciscan from Poznan, had worked previously in the Cistercian church at Ląd where Pompeo Ferrari did his Pozzoesque altar. Swach's project, in one of the best preserved examples of wooden

FIG. 100
Giovanni Battista Cocchi, Chapel of the Crucifixion, 1741–44. Cathedral, Chelmza.

architecture in the region, was an object lesson in how to work from Pozzo's treatise. Not only the high and two side altars but the *quadratura* painting enlivening the flat wooden ceiling are all based on Pozzo's treatise. For the altars Swach cut flat sheets of plywood to the shape of aediculas, following Pozzo's illustration of a like project for the high altar of the Jesuit Church of the Missionaries at Mondoví (Piedmont).[140]

FIG. 101
Adam Swach, Chapel of St. Lawrence, 1727–31. Parish church, Wełna.

In the right transept Chapel of St. Lawrence (fig. 101), Swach imitated quite precisely Pozzo's Chapel of St. Ignatius. Although simplified and with a different program, this is the closest imitation of Pozzo's architecture yet: the artist has represented the lapis lazuli columns (painting them blue) and capitals faithfully, the pediment and trabeation, the unusual base on which the saint is posed, the deep niche (into which the cutout of Lawrence casts a shadow), and the reliefs on the bases of the columns. With a window to the left of the altar throwing light on the statue of St. Lawrence, Swach also mimicked the effect of Pozzo's hidden light source. Both his use of illumination and his imitation of the distinctive blue lapis lazuli columns in Rome suggest that he had firsthand information about the Roman altar as built. Of course, adjustments for the new program were also made.[141]

In this rural church[142] did it matter to the Franciscan painter that the architect and monuments whose designs he followed so closely were Jesuit? Is his use of Pozzo's book a conscious (or unconscious) expression of alliance with international Catholicism? And if Pozzo's designs were used because they were the only or even the best source material available, how are we to understand this Franciscan's enthusiastic use of it? To begin to answer these questions we must keep in mind that printing was a privilege in this period: expensive and exclusive, requiring approval by authorities. Pozzo published his treatise because he had a powerful institution seeing to it that Jesuit designs were out in the world. It was no accident that Pozzo's designs fell into Swach's hands. But Swach *chose* to hold Pozzo's Jesuit designs in his hands rather than something else, rather than nothing at all. In other words, even if Swach himself would have said that he used Pozzo's designs because they were good, or because they represented the latest architecture, this amounts to the architect's participation in a discourse of cosmopolitanism and innovation driven by new designs published by groups like the Jesuits. The very existence of Pozzo's treatise is of the utmost significance. Books needed authors and readers. In publishing the treatise the Jesuits could not but have anticipated its reception.

One further example, in Germany, brings us to the point about the imitation of Ignatius's chapel in non-Jesuit contexts. The cathedral in Fulda was designed in the most up-to-date Italianate style in 1704 by Johann Dientzenhofer who had been recently in Rome.[143] The church is riddled with citations, but the transept altars, dedicated to St. Benedict (left; fig. 102) and St. Julian (right), are particularly striking citations of Pozzo's Chapel of St. Ignatius. Although the light pastel color scheme breathes an entirely different air from the saturated antique marbles employed in Rome, some components of the chapel were adopted wholesale. The allegorical groups are *identical,* and the base of the aedicula is taken up by narratives from the life of St. Benedict, also an order founder. The niche, though detailed differently, also has a statue raised on a pedestal with a stained glass window throwing a halo around Benedict's head. This detail could only have been made by an architect who knew the work firsthand, for the hidden window in Ignatius's niche (see fig. 65) was not publicized.

What are we to make of the adoption here of the forms and some of the content of Ignatius's chapel for St. Benedict? In this and other cases (and there are more), it is unclear to what extent if any the Ignatian and Jesuit identity of the cult site motivated citation of it. Are we to understand that Benedict and the Benedictines are like Ignatius and the Jesuits? In one important respect Benedict, also an order founder, *was* like Ignatius. How else can we explain the adoption of Ignatius's virtues for Benedict? Is it possible to entirely separate the resemblance of the saint from the resemblance of the chapel? For citation, visually, or described verbally, brings Benedict and Ignatius together in our minds and, should we utter the comparison, in our mouths.

FIG. 102
Johann Dientzenhofer, Chapel of St. Benedict, 1704–12. Cathedral, Fulda.

By contrast to the Fulda and Wełna examples, in two geographically distant chapels—
both dedicated to St. Ignatius—devotion to Ignatius and affiliation to Jesuit Rome clearly
drove citation of the Roman design. The first is the spectacular gilded wood high altar
of the Jesuit Church of the Bom Jesus in Goa (fig. 103), the major center of Portuguese
trade and missionary activity in India in the early modern period.[144] The aedicula has
been flattened and the columns varied in form, but it is the only example I know in

FIG. 103
Unknown Indian or European architect, High altar, begun 1699 (?). Church of the Bom Jesus, Goa.

which the cultic core of the Roman prototype was reproduced: the statue of the saint gazing up to the Trinity and the IHS produced as a result of the vision have been grasped as a narrative ensemble. While virtually nothing is known about its construction (thought begun as early as 1699),[145] the chapel was based on Mariotti's engraving (see fig. 89). This is evident from the pose of St. Ignatius, which differs from the statue as actually executed, as shown in Pozzo's definitive engraving of the altar (see fig. 91).[146] The chapel of Ignatius in Goa is located next to the tomb of the great missionary St. Francis Xavier that was renovated by Florentine sculptors on the commission of Florentine Grand Duke Cosimo III around the time that the Ignatian chapel was being designed.[147] In adopting the Roman design of Ignatius's reliquary chapel for an altar located next to Xavier's tomb, the two saints, close companions in life, were, in a sense, architecturally reunited. This is the clearest case in the reception of the Ignatian altar of a copy motivated by cultic desire.

The Roman Chapel of St. Ignatius also received prompt homage in the eponymous chapel in the Jesuit Church of SS. Stanislaus and Wenceslas in Swidnica (Silesia; fig. 104). The renovation of this chapel (begun 1699–1700) was part of a long-term renovation of a Gothic church carried out by the Jesuit architect Johann Riedel.[148] While the aedicula has been made low and wide to accommodate the Gothic structure, other elements of the Roman chapel are copied with precision. The distinctive allegorical groups (fig. 105) are slightly simplified and benign versions of the Roman groupings (see fig. 70), and while the miracle reliefs have been replaced with different scenes, their number and placement are imitated as well.[149] The image currently on the altar (the Madonna of Czestochowa) is modern, but there is a canvas representing St. Ignatius before the Trinity below the altar that can be raised with a crank to cover the niche, as in Rome.[150] It is likely that Riedel had Mariotti's engraving and the printed pamphlet in hand when designing the Swidnica chapel.

As was the case with the Jesuit imitations of the Gesù, these two last imitations of the Chapel of St. Ignatius for new chapels of St. Ignatius satisfied an affiliatory desire. The imitation of the Roman chapel in a chapel of the same dedication in a Jesuit church recalled the site of the relics in a distant place. All of the examples in Silesia and Poland (and the example of Fulda) are, by contrast, located in parish churches or in those of other religious orders. In one case the artist was himself a Franciscan and in another the patron was anti-Jesuit. In all cases the dedication of the original Ignatius altar was changed to other saints or the Crucifixion (including, in one case, a different Jesuit), making it quite clear that these works were not built *for* Ignatius. None were cultically motivated.

Unlike the imitations of the Gesù or other Jesuit churches discussed above, Pozzo's designs were often used without conscious and explicit regard to their specific institutional point of origin. The designs circulated freely, readily used by a Franciscan, readily taken up for a Cistercian or a Benedictine church. The reproductions represented excellent architecture and did not automatically proclaim their institutional origins. So,

FIG. 104
Johann Riedel, Chapel of St. Ignatius, begun 1699–1700. SS. Stanislaus and Wenceslas, Swidnica.

FIG. 105
After Jean-Baptiste Théodon, *Religion triumphing over paganism*, begun 1699–1700. SS. Stanislaus and Wenceslas, Swidnica.

then, is there no meaning to the use of a Jesuit's book of Jesuit architectural projects in Poland? Were the imitators indifferent to—or did they use Pozzo's works in spite of—their Jesuit identity?

When a Franciscan like Adam Swach, the Franciscan painter in Wełna, held Pozzo's treatise in his hand, an identificatory process was taking place. Indeed, Swach may very well have learned perspective from the step-by-step instructions in the first volume of Pozzo's treatise. Instructing students to draw to the only true point (which is God), Pozzo made the process of learning perspective explicitly one of Catholic subject formation.[151] Hence the artistic process of imitation, by which an artist found himself, was bound up in a Jesuit system. In late-sixteenth-century Poland an attempt was made to remove from Catholic churches all works of art not made by Catholic hands. It is unlikely that Jews were painting Catholic altarpieces. It is more likely that the ban pertained to Eastern Orthodox or Lutheran artists. Although not carried out, the impulse behind the ban is instructive, another instance in which Catholics affirmed that the identity of the maker matters.

We often describe adherence to an original in devotional terms: he followed the model religiously, he made a faithful copy. These linguistic conventions echo the mimetic structures that have been discussed in the last two chapters of this study. For the greater glory of God, Jesuit missionaries assumed the clothing, the external forms of the Chinese, of the Japanese, peoples for whom they expressed deep admiration. But we cannot take on the forms of those we despise. I believe the same holds for architecture.

Imitation is a not an ideology-blind practice, and to make this point clear, it is perhaps best to return to the example with which this study began: Nazi architecture. The eclipse of an identifiably Nazi architecture in the postwar period provides us with the negative example against which to measure the ideology of imitation. It is self-evident that after the war, architects could not have conceived of a representative German architecture[152] in Albert Speer's style.

At various points I have suggested that works of art can carry aesthetic and/or political authority. But I do not mean for the aesthetic to stand for a resistance to or a draining of the political authority of the work. An aesthetically motivated citation is not, as Richard Krautheimer postulated, an emptying of the *meaning* of the work,[153] a depoliticized alternative to religious authority. For architecture had become in the Renaissance a deeply ideological, discursive structure in the hands of the ruling class. In such a situation, there is no such thing as a mere aesthetic use of a model. Or more to the point, in the moment that such a scenario can be imagined, architecture has served its role as propaganda well. For at that moment, Catholicism, specifically, Jesuit Catholicism, is deeply embedded in the culture; it is not resisted.

There can be no such thing as a purely aesthetic borrowing. Or rather, that one can even conceive of such a thing suggests that the authority which stands behind the chapel and its reproductions is unquestioned, or at least not pressingly problematic.[154] For all of its political instability, Poland was really becoming Catholic. And judging by the use of Pozzo's designs, that Catholic stamp looked very Jesuit. That Pozzo's treatise should circulate and be used freely by patrons, artists, and Catholic religious orders that were often rivals of the Jesuits suggests that the institution that stood behind that work was, so to speak, in the water.

POSTSCRIPT FROM BERLIN

Anyone who thinks this building is a Nazi building is on the wrong track. It is an example of the conservative modern style of architecture.

HANS KOLLHOFF, ARCHITECT OF THE NEW FOREIGN MINISTRY OF BERLIN (2000), AN ADDITION TO THE REICHSBANK (1933–39)

I have always objected when people say, "Oh these [Nazi] buildings are merely neoclassical buildings. They are harmless, innocent stones that one can deal with today." They remain bloodily entangled and one must see them in their entirety or do injustice to history.

WINFRIED NERDINGER, DIRECTOR, MUNICH ARCHITECTURE MUSEUM (1995)

In the introduction to this study I noted that Jesuit architecture had been neutralized with time—both with the receding of the political heat on the Society and the emergence of more threatening ideologies and their architectures. To illustrate the kind of affect that can surround the art historical use of propaganda, I invoked National Socialist architecture because it still proves very troubling. For propaganda to be a productive category of analysis, we need not ourselves experience the kind of threat that imbued Jesuit architecture with its ominous overtones in the nineteenth century. However, in order that the essence of propaganda be recognized in art history, we must maintain the kind of pressure that is present when there is something at stake.

Throughout the last three chapters I have argued that what was at stake in Jesuit propaganda was the formation of subjects. While my formulation of this core aspect of the Jesuit mission may differ somewhat in terminology, this is a well-recognized fact. My aim has been to show how art and architecture contributed to this activity: in the disciplining of its own members, in the inscription and interpellation of the viewer, and in the diffusion of Jesuit imagery. I wished to foreground the concrete accomplishment of subject formation that can result from the more conventionally explored aspects of Baroque art, expression, and meaning. For the Catholic Church of the early modern period, subject formation was an urgent project. And because the Society began as an energetic young institution with an international mandate, it was well positioned to contribute to the larger goal of the Catholic Church. The Jesuit use of art and architecture as tools for this project was given a name in the nineteenth century, when resistance to the Society's influence produced the concept of the Jesuit Style. That term, I argue, was a critical precursor to the application of the term "propaganda" to the Baroque in the twentieth century.

Here I have made no judgments as to whether either the means or the stakes of Jesuit propaganda were good or bad. I have emphasized directedness as the crucial aspect of propagandistic art, that which distinguishes it from the goal (however delusional) of disinterestedness. If anything, I have endeavored here to shed a more positive light on interestedness without displacing disinterestedness, which is a critical possibility, one that we need. To some, the withholding of judgment may seem an abandonment of an essential aspect of propaganda, crucial to much of the historical experience of it. My hesitancy here is one indication of the difficulty of recapturing that which is no longer truly threatening (in spite of my own efforts at reconstruction). But more important, the judgment of art as propaganda has stood in the way of understanding its mechanisms. And, even more important, I also believe—and here I follow Ellul—that propaganda corresponds more broadly to human urges, both to reach an audience and, from the audience's perspective, to have the choices before us reduced, made understandable. When one considers the increasingly complex confessional choices that faced early modern men and women, propaganda is eminently understandable as a historical phenomenon.

Propaganda has been used responsibly and, lest we forget, utterly irresponsibly. I have argued throughout this study that while the term has a range of inflections, from neutral to incriminating, the most inflammatory use remains crucial. For a variety of reasons, National Socialist art and architecture (rather than Soviet or Chinese examples, comparatively isolated, geographically and linguistically) continue to set the limits for the term. In bringing this discussion of propaganda to a close, a brief look at current evaluations of National Socialist art and architectural propaganda is productive. For as Germany's confrontation with its Nazi past moves into a more confident phase, the art and architecture of that period are being actively revisited. Indeed, recent debates in Germany provide us with some measure of where we stand now with the term "propaganda."

I remarked in the introduction to this study that it was unlikely that Nazi architecture would be neutralized in the foreseeable future. Well before I wrote those lines vociferous debate was taking place over precisely this question: could and should Nazi architecture (and art) be neutralized?[1] These questions are still being raised following the decision (in 1991) to move the government back to Berlin from its postwar headquarters in Bonn. With the need for dozens of government buildings to house ministries and foreign embassies pressing, some of the lands and buildings of the 1930s needed to be put to use. But the buildings that remained standing after the war are among the most potent memories of the Nazis themselves. Just as the Nazis made modernist architecture the *cause* rather than the *symbols* of the social and cultural ills of Weimar Germany,[2] today their buildings seem to bypass the symbolic, often taken as direct embodiments of Nazism.

In a country where the sale of Nazi symbols, books, or artifacts is illegal, buildings pose a special problem. If the same criteria were to be followed for architecture as for every other such propagandistic production of the Third Reich, architecture too would be illegal. But Nazi architecture is not illegal, and so it has a very peculiar status as the only form of Nazi propaganda that is not. Hence the notion that National Socialist buildings (some of the most notorious) be reused for specifically governmental purposes raised fears that the German government of the end of the twentieth century would be confused with the buildings' former occupants. Over the objections of preservationists who viewed the buildings as historical artifacts of the first order, many wished for a tabula rasa. But since razing the past was an unaffordable luxury, they had to confront the possibility that the reuse of Nazi buildings be perceived as *motivated*.

Throughout the postwar period the German government reshaped the vocabulary of state architecture.[3] It distanced itself from the classical forms used by Hitler, aligning architecturally with international modernism. For the Parliament in Bonn, it made a friendlier eagle and avoided colors strongly associated with National Socialism. Above all it eschewed monumentality, avoiding verticality, choosing forms that hugged the landscape. Figurative art and often-used materials were also taboo. Glass was preferred to stone and accompanied by an iconography of transparency and openness, the material of democracy.[4]

What emerges from the postwar effort to define an architecture of democracy is that not only the stripped-down classicism favored by Hitler, but *any* representative architecture had become problematic. Because the activity of governing itself had become such a source of shame, the forms that represented that function also bore that shame. Insofar as a state architecture existed in postwar Germany, it pointed to the existence of government. One gets the sense that the German government would have preferred to lie low on the ground than to raise itself up off the ground, vertically. The architecture that resulted from this quagmire attempted to be not only the antithesis of totalitarian architecture, but also the antithesis of architectural propaganda.

During the rebuilding of Berlin, various strategies were adopted to contend with the continued embarrassment over architecture. One approach to ward off nationalist discourse has been to populate competition juries with non-German architects and to award some of the most sensitive commissions to non-German architects (like the renovation of the Reichstag by Norman Foster). Interior furnishings by international modernist architects are often mentioned in publicity on the buildings, in stark contrast to the Germanness of the fittings of Hitler's buildings. One example is telling. In his early designs for the massive government structures aligned along the Spreebogen, to unite former East and West Berlin, Axel Schultes proposed a civic forum. The space was to be a break on a long corridor, the monumentality of which made some uncomfortable. His idea was that there be a public place of assembly, an area where Germans can "heal themselves of the malady of being German." The implication is that architecture itself (because representative) is a burden to the Germans, and hence relief is a space *without* architecture. This iconography of the void suggests the extent to which the identification of architecture itself with Nazism is one important legacy of that period. Indeed, during the competition for the Spreebogen plan, foreign jurors found the German preoccupation with historical sensitivities "superfluous and outmoded," a French juror going so far as to find the Germans afraid of architecture itself.[5]

In the meantime, a new generation of German architects has pleaded to be released from its elders' shackles, to some, an offensive view. According to Torsten Krüger (one young architect interviewed by Michael Wise), to his teacher a row of more than three columns evoked the sound of marching. Krüger told Wise that support for his team's design for the new Chancellery (which featured a colonnade) was sabotaged by a parliamentarian who circulated a photocopy juxtaposing their plan to Albert Speer's. He expressed the wish of his generation to be free of the comparison to National Socialist architecture, for his generation has "another biography."[6]

Although discussions do not revolve around the buildings as propaganda (the term has been tellingly absent from the discussions), in the efforts to retain these relics of past propagandas the German government is reiterating that the German nation defines itself against its National Socialist past. In other words, though unnamed as such, National Socialist architectural propaganda is being kept alive in order to form subjects: not Nazi subjects, but penitential subjects who must bow not before the altar of art, but of historical propaganda, lest they be shaped by a more live form. These National Socialist buildings, preserved and responded to, are monuments *against* propaganda. They bear the message that propaganda remains a possibility in the present and the future.

In the context of such a highly crafted structure of reading, one can see the attractiveness of disinterestedness, of allowing viewers to take the buildings as they are. Indeed, a new generation aspires to liberate this architecture, to allow it to live as art. One official suggested that museums or schools be the living teachers about the past in order that buildings be set free.[7] While the discussions focus on whether or not stones bear guilt for what happened within the walls, or whether architectural style is an expression of National Socialism that can be permitted to still speak, what I think is really going on here is a confrontation with Nazi architectural *propaganda,* forms that have two lives.

In the effort to recuperate Berlin with its National Socialist relics, the split between art and ideology that has always characterized—and vexed—the notion of art serving as propaganda is renewed. In spite of the self-conscious discussion (rather than dismissal) of Nazi art/propaganda, the art/propaganda polarity continues to play itself out in exhibitions of the Nazi period today. The installations of two recent exhibitions of German art thematize the problem. In the massive centenary exhibition, *Das XX. Jahrhundert: Ein Jahrhundert Kunst in Deutschland,* Nazi art was displayed against a circus-like backdrop of regime propaganda and theatrically installed in a Nazi *Gesamtkunstwerk*.[8] The installation of this work (which presented Nazi art in an analogous way to the mocking installation of modernist art in the famous *Entartete Kunst* exhibition of 1937) contrasted starkly with surrounding exhibition rooms in which works preceding and following the Nazi period were hung on white walls. By contrast, the curators of *Taking Positions,* on figurative sculpture of the 1930s, pushed the Nazi discourse literally to the margins of the exhibition, in an attempt to "see these works as works of art."[9] In arguing for art, against the dominant reading of the works as propaganda, the authors continue to see these readings as distinct and unrelated possibilities. This split and the efforts to negotiate it do not mark the death of propaganda but reiterate the crucial characteristic of art historical discourse about propaganda. In Berlin the effort is to keep one eye open: to see the object as such and to see beyond it to its ideological emplotment (a glance at the past with an eye to the future). Art that is organized as propaganda has to be viewed in this complex, multilayered way, for it is its essence.

The study of Jesuit art and architecture has been organized around the same polarities and its resulting tensions since the nineteenth century. The polarity between art and ideology that resides at the center of the historiography is not historically anachronistic. There was an aesthetic discourse in the early modern period: when the Jesuits produced images before the canonization of their founder, they were aware of the authority accorded to images, and their ability to shape subjects as a result; when they elected their own architect to design the Chapel of St. Ignatius, they were aware of the public discourse about architecture and the value of great architecture for the success of their project; the designs of their buildings that circulated bore their larger designs, to shape Catholic subjects before the end of time.

Nor is the polarity between art and ideology fatal. In this study, I have foregrounded the key elements of Jesuit art and architecture from the specific perspective of propaganda analysis: the propagandist, message, and diffusion. If the art historical view finds common ground with the analysis of propaganda, there is a better chance that we will be able to productively hold on to both aspects, not only of Jesuit art, but of any art that is produced under pressure to form subjects. Propaganda is an important category because it challenges us to keep in focus two distinct lenses that appear to interfere with one another.

ACKNOWLEDGMENTS

This book began to take shape in Berlin in 1993, when a Deutscher Akademischer Austauschdienst postdoctoral fellowship permitted me to cast my net beyond Rome, where I had done the majority of my research up until that point. Subsequent research was supported by the Woodrow Wilson Foundation East European Studies Program; a travel grant from the International Research and Exchanges Board permitted me to take a second trip to Poland; generous fellowships from the Metropolitan Museum of Art and the Canadian Centre for Architecture (CCA) made further research possible. My thanks to two chairs of the Department of Fine Art of the University of Toronto, Margaret Miller and Marc Gotlieb, and associate deans of the humanities at the University of Toronto at Mississauga, Catherine Rubincam and Michael Lettieri, for supporting crucial leaves from teaching to complete the project. The text was completed in Berlin in 2001 in a villa with the kind of fraught past that first stimulated this project. My thanks to its director, Gary Smith, and to the American Academy in Berlin for providing the stimulating setting in which this chapter on propaganda has been brought to a close.

I am indebted to numerous friends and scholars for incisive comments and for help in solving specific problems along the way. Their appearance in a list in no way diminishes the singular help each one offered at various moments: Fabio Barry, Geoffrey Batchen, Maarten Delbeke, Gabi Dolf-Bonnekamper, Steven Eisenmann, David Freedberg, Anthony Grafton, Cynthia Halpern, Thomas DaCosta Kaufmann, Joseph Koerner, Jane Kramer, Michael Koortbojian, Jerzy Kowalczyk, Michael J. Lewis, Jennifer Montagu, Alex Nagel, Werner Oechslin, Eric Rentschler, Philip Sohm, and Michael Stone-Richards.

Special thanks to colleagues and friends who read and commented on the manuscript in part or in its entirety as it evolved: Daniel Boyarin, Vincent Crapanzano, W. J. T. Mitchell, and especially John Beldon Scott, Andrew Payne, and Joseph Imorde. Alina Payne's and Jeffrey Hamburger's comments, continual stream of references, and good advice were much appreciated. My thanks to two angelic research assistants, Lise Hosein, who whipped the apparatus into shape, and Alexandra Gerstein, of the CCA, for making the search for the origin of the Jesuit Style a shared adventure. Finally, thanks to my editor at the University of California Press, Deborah Kirshman, for her commitment to this project, and to Sue Heinemann for ushering the manuscript so gracefully into print.

Throughout the years in which this project took on form, I have been blessed (and humored) by close friends and family. My heartfelt thanks to my parents, Anita von Bachellé Levy and Walter Kahn Levy, for cheering all along the way; to Thomas Y. Levin for opening a new path at the very beginning; to Julie Bargmann, Christina Corsiglia, Lucy James, and David J. Levin, for their sustaining friendship. In the kitchen of the Olga Korper Gallery, "the Queen" and Claire Christie were more giving of time, friendship, and humor than seems humanly possible; on jogs through my West End Toronto neighborhood, Michelle Sale learned more about Jesuit art than any non–art historian has ever had the patience to hear. With Jill Caskey, I experienced the good fortune and richness of being on the same path of discovery at the same time with a very dear friend. A special word of thanks to Steven F. Ostrow for his abiding friendship within and without Baroque Rome and for his careful and thoughtful reading and commentary on the entire manuscript.

Samuel Stein and Emily Bakemeier know better than anyone else why I wrote this book and not another. This book is dedicated to them in gratitude for their continuous presence of heart and for their commitment to the project of understanding.

NOTES

INTRODUCTION

1. Hitler used this phrase in a speech delivered at the German Architecture and Crafts Exhibit, Munich, 22 January 1938. Robert R. Taylor, *The Word in Stone: The Role of Architecture in National Socialist Ideology* (Berkeley: University of California Press, 1974), 30 n.62. For Nazi views of architecture as propaganda, see ibid., 81–86, as well as Tim Benton, "Speaking without Adjectives: Architecture in the Service of Totalitarianism," in *Art and Power: Europe under the Dictators, 1930–1945*, ed. Dawn Ades, Tim Benton, David Elliott, and Ian Boyd White (London: Thames and Hudson, 1995), 36–42; Barbara Miller Lane, "Nazi Architecture," chap. 8 in *Architecture and Politics in Germany, 1918–1945* (Cambridge, Mass.: Harvard University Press, 1985); Karl Arndt, "Architektur und Politik," in Albert Speer, *Architektur: Arbeiten 1933–1943,* with foreword by Albert Speer and essays by Karl Arndt, Georg Friedrich Koch, and Lars Olof Larsson (Berlin and Vienna: Ullstein and Propyläen, 1978), 113–35; Angela Schönberger, "Die Neue Reichskanzlei in Berlin von Albert Speer," in *Die Dekoration der Gewalt: Kunst und Medien im Faschismus,* ed. Berthold Hinz et al. (Giessen: Anabas, 1979), 163–72.

2. The best sources for Hitler's preferences in architecture are Albert Speer, *Inside the Third Reich: Memoirs,* trans. Richard Winston and Clara Winston (New York: Macmillan, 1970); Taylor, *The Word in Stone,* 19 ff.; Albert Speer, *Architecture 1932–1942,* with essays by Albert Speer, Leon Krier, and Lars Olof Larsson (Brussels: Archives d'Architecture Moderne, 1985).

3. The first contradiction lies in Hitler's simultaneous admiration for the "mysterious gloom" of Catholic churches (presumably Gothic), "which made men more ready to submit to

the renunciation of self," and his preference for brightly lit, nonmystical spaces. See Norman H. Baynes, ed. and trans., *The Speeches of Adolf Hitler, April 1922–August 1939: An English Translation of Representative Passages*, 2 vols. (London: Oxford University Press, 1942), 1:599; and Taylor, *The Word in Stone*, 33. Second, already in Vienna, Hitler was known for his hatred of the Jesuits (and the "Reds"). Ian Kershaw, *Hitler, 1889–1936: Hubris* (London: Allen Lane, 1998), 58, 64.

4. For Nazi attitudes toward foreign styles versus innate Germanness, see Taylor, *The Word in Stone*, 78 ff.; Lane, *Architecture and Politics in Germany*, esp. 162–67.

5. "This structure, the greatest assembly hall in the world ever conceived up to that time, consisted of one vast hall that could hold between one hundred fifty and one hundred eighty thousand persons standing. In spite of Hitler's negative attitude toward Himmler's and Rosenberg's mystical notions, the hall was essentially a place of worship. The idea was that over the course of centuries, by tradition and venerability, it would acquire an importance similar to that St. Peter's in Rome has for Catholic Christendom." The Great Hall would contain "sixteen times the volume of St. Peter's." Speer, *Inside the Third Reich*, 152–53. Hitler declared the center of Berlin would "be built on such a scale that St. Peter's and its Square will seem like toys in comparison!" Adolf Hitler, *Hitler's Secret Conversations, 1941–1944*, introd. Hugh Trevor-Roper (New York: New American Library, 1961), 81.

6. Alfred Rosenberg, one of the architects of Nazi ideology, wrote in *Der Mythus des 20. Jahrhunderts* (Munich: Hoheneichen, 1930), 374–75, that the Baroque, a "'Jesuit Style,'" amounted to "an almost purely sensual mixture of a powerful will to decorate and a complete artistic degeneration." Cited in Taylor, *The Word in Stone*, 99. Although as opposed to organized religion as Rosenberg, Hitler tended to be "more reticent" in expressing his antireligious views in public. Robert Cecil, *The Myth of the Master Race: Alfred Rosenberg and Nazi Ideology* (London: B. T. Batsford, 1972).

7. See Erwin Panofsky, "The History of Art," in *The Cultural Migration: The European Scholar in America*, introd. W. Rex Crawford (Philadelphia: University of Pennsylvania Press, 1953), 82–111; Kevin Parker, "Art History and Exile: Richard Krautheimer and Erwin Panofsky," in *Exiles and Emigrés: The Flight of European Artists from Hitler*, ed. Stephanie Barron and Sabine Eckmann (Los Angeles: Los Angeles County Museum of Art; New York: Harry N. Abrams, 1997), 317–25.

8. Erwin Panofsky, "What Is Baroque?" in *Three Essays on Style*, ed. Irving Lavin (Cambridge, Mass.: MIT Press, 1995), 88.

9. Taylor described the study of Nazi architecture in 1974 in these terms: "Very little serious work has been done on the relationship between the National Socialist government and the arts. Art historians, when they deal with this problem, usually express only moral disapproval, which, justifiable though it may be, does not aid in understanding the phenomenon." Taylor, *The Word in Stone*, x. Since Taylor, a rich and less unproductively judgmental literature on the subject has developed, especially in Germany. Some important contributions include Berthold Hinz et al., eds., *Die Dekoration der Gewalt*; Aa.vv., *Inszenierung der Macht: Ästhetische Faszination im Faschismus* (Berlin: NGKB and Nischen, 1987); Brandon Taylor and Wilfried van der Will, eds., *The Nazification of Art: Art, Design, Music, Architecture and Film in the Third Reich* (Winchester: Winchester Press, 1990),

especially the outline of the phases of debate; Walter Grasskamp, "The De-Nazification of Nazi Art: Arno Breker and Albert Speer Today," ibid., 231–48; Penelope Curtis, ed., *Taking Positions: Figurative Sculpture and the Third Reich* (Leeds: Henry Moore Institute, 2001), esp. Ursel Berger, "'Modern Sculpture' versus 'The Decoration of Power': On the Perception of German Sculpture of the Twenties and Thirties after 1945," 60–75.

10. Some of the studies that have been stimulating to this author include Susan Sontag, "Fascinating Fascism," in *A Susan Sontag Reader,* introd. Elizabeth Hardwick (New York: Vintage Books, 1983), 305–25; Eric Rentschler, *The Ministry of Illusion: Nazi Cinema and Its Afterlife* (Cambridge, Mass.: Harvard University Press, 1996); Susan Suleiman, *Authoritarian Fictions: The Ideological Novel as a Literary Genre* (Princeton: Princeton University Press, 1983); Aa.vv., *Inszenierung der Macht.* See also the publication on the public debates of the latter, controversial exhibition, Aa.vv., *Erbeutete Sinne: Nachträge zur Berliner Ausstellung "Inszenierung der Macht: Ästhetische Faszination im Faschismus"* (Berlin: NBGK and Nischen, 1988).

11. The genealogy of Italian Baroque studies in U.S. Ph.D. programs is discussed in Tod Marder, "Renaissance and Baroque Architectural History in the United States," in *The Architectural Historian in America: A Symposium in Celebration of the Fiftieth Anniversary of the Founding of the Society of Architectural Historians,* ed. Elisabeth Blair MacDougall (Washington, D.C.: National Gallery of Art, 1990), 161–74. For a little-known rant against Marxist orthodoxy by one of the early North American Baroquists, see John R. Martin, "Marxism and the History of Art," *College Art Journal* 11 (1951): 3–9.

12. For Wittkower's assessment and defense of the positivistic direction of Italian Baroque studies in the early 1960s, see Rudolf Wittkower, "Il barocco in Italia," in *Manierismo, barocco, rococò: Concetti e termini; Convegno Internazionale, Roma 21–24 aprile 1960* (Rome: Accademia Nazionale dei Lincei, 1962), 320.

13. Francis Haskell, *Patrons and Painters: A Study in the Relations between Italian Art and Society in the Age of the Baroque,* 2d rev. ed. (New Haven: Yale University Press, 1980). A notable exception is the recent study by Karen-edis Barzman, *The Florentine Academy and the Early Modern State: The Discipline of Disegno* (New York: Cambridge University Press, 2000).

14. See, for example, Elizabeth Cropper, ed., *The Diplomacy of Art: Artistic Creation and Politics in Seicento Italy,* Villa Spellman Colloquia, 7 (Milan: Nuova Alfa, 2000); Anthony Colantuono, *Guido Reni's Abduction of Helen: The Politics and Rhetoric of Painting in Seventeenth-Century Europe* (New York: Cambridge University Press, 1997).

15. Studies organized around institutions (papacy, religious orders, academies, noble families, etc.) are at the core of Baroque studies and are too numerous to enumerate. The following studies are notable for the density of research on the institutions and their practices: John Beldon Scott, *Images of Nepotism: The Painted Ceilings of Palazzo Barberini* (Princeton: Princeton University Press, 1991); Tod Marder, *Bernini's Scala Regia at the Vatican Palace* (New York: Cambridge University Press, 1997); Louise Rice, *The Altars and Altarpieces of New St. Peter's: Outfitting the Basilica, 1621–1666* (New York: Cambridge University Press, 1997).

16. Rudolf Wittkower, *Art and Architecture in Italy, 1600–1750* [1958], 6th ed., rev. Joseph Connors and Jennifer Montagu (New Haven: Yale University Press, 1999), 3 vols.

There is an introduction to the new edition, a revised bibliography, but the text was left intact.

17. Wittkower, *Art and Architecture in Italy*, 1:4.

18. Things have not changed substantially since Wittkower wrote the lines quoted below. In their assessment of Baroque studies since Wittkower, the editors note: "Propaganda has seemed a positive quality to a generation that enjoys explicating complex ideologies." Ibid., 1:xiii.

19. David Freedberg, *The Power of Images: Studies in the History and Theory of Response* (Chicago: University of Chicago Press, 1989).

20. "No doubt other such topics might have merited attention; above all I am conscious of the absence here of an approach to the problem of figurated propaganda and of arousal to political action." Freedberg, *The Power of Images*, xxiv.

21. I am in sympathy here with T. J. Clark's definition of propaganda: "Propaganda is a representation of events and problems, simplified in such a way that the meaning of the events, and the solution to the problems, seems immediately present in the representation itself; and perceivable in a flash, in a manner that brooks no argument. The representation serves the interests of those who ordered it. It invites its viewers and readers to take sides, or better, it assumes that there is only one side for viewers and readers (as opposed to enemies and cretins) to take. It tries to tune out or drown out contrary understandings. It says the facts—the ethical facts, the facts of allegiance and human sympathy—speak for themselves." T. J. Clark, *Farewell to an Idea: Episodes from a History of Modernism* (New Haven: Yale University Press, 1999), 292.

22. For earlier, "naive" Marxist conceptions of art as a transparent bearer of ideology, and more complex later formulations that take into account the specificity of the aesthetic conditions of production, "ideology as art," or "art as ideological form," see Janet Wolff, *The Social Production of Art* (London: Macmillan, 1981), 49 ff.; Terry Eagleton, *Marxism and Literary Criticism* (Berkeley: University of California Press, 1976), esp. 20–36 ("Form and Content").

23. Hans Belting, *The Germans and Their Art: A Troublesome Relationship*, trans. Scott Kleager (New Haven: Yale University Press, 1998), esp. 34–35, 81ff.

24. Edgar Wind argued that Wölfflin's formalism helped along the regrettable process (first pointed to by Hegel) by which art lost its ability to trouble us in *Art and Anarchy* (London: Faber and Faber, 1963), 21–23. One of the specific benefits of this is the appreciation of the "peculiar quality" of the Baroque, for example, one of the formerly despised "arts of decline." For iconology's ideological blindness, see Keith Moxey, "The Politics of Iconology," in *Iconography at the Crossroads*, ed. Brendan Cassidy (Princeton: Index of Christian Art and Princeton University, 1993), 27–31.

25. Theodore K. Rabb, "Play, not Politics: Who Really Understood the Symbolism of Renaissance Art?" *Times Literary Supplement*, 10 November 1995, 18.

26. Most notably the excellent volume on political imagery, Allan Ellenius, ed., *Iconography, Propaganda, and Legitimation* (Oxford: Clarendon Press; New York: Oxford University Press, 1998). An exception is James A. Leith, *The Idea of Art as Propaganda in France, 1750–1799: A Study in the History of Ideas* (Toronto: University of Toronto Press, 1965).

In this study propaganda arts from antiquity through the French Revolution are placed against the alternative view of the autonomy of art. Propaganda is synonymous here with a social or political role for art (at a moment when the Rococo hedonism, or *l'art pour l'art,* was viewed as pernicious).

27. For an argument that the early modern period is the beginning of mass culture, see José Antonio Maravall, *Culture of the Baroque: Analysis of a Historical Structure,* trans. Terry Cochran (Minneapolis: University of Minnesota Press, 1986).

28. For a discussion of the problem in modern literature, see Suleiman, *Authoritarian Fictions.*

29. This question was taken up in a similar spirit in Linda Nochlin and Henry A. Millon, introduction to *Art and Architecture in the Service of Politics* (Cambridge, Mass.: MIT Press, 1978), ix; see also the brief treatment in Toby Clark, *Art and Propaganda in the Twentieth Century: The Political Image in the Age of Mass Culture* (New York: Harry N. Abrams, 1994). Clark's study differs from mine in considering exclusively political images.

30. See the discussion of the polarities of the categories art vs. propaganda in film studies in Linda Schulte-Sasse, *Entertaining the Third Reich: Illusions of Wholeness in Nazi Cinema* (Durham: Duke University Press, 1998), 36 ff.; for a discussion of the issues with regard to fiction, see Suleiman, *Authoritarian Fictions,* introduction.

31. Hellmut Lehmann-Haupt, *Art under a Dictatorship* (New York: Oxford University Press, 1954), 123.

32. Jacques Ellul, *Propaganda: The Formation of Men's Attitudes,* trans. Konrad Kellen and Jean Lerner (New York: Alfred Knopf, 1965), 6.

CHAPTER 1. THE "JESUIT STYLE"

Part of this chapter was first presented as "Art History's Baroque: The Jesuit Contribution" at the conference "The Jesuits: Culture, Sciences, and the Arts 1540–1773," Boston College, 1997. The acts of that conference have appeared as John O'Malley et al., eds., *The Jesuits: Culture, Sciences, and the Arts, 1540–1773* (Toronto: University of Toronto Press, 1999), with an essay by Gauvin Alexander Bailey ("'Le style jésuite n'existe pas': Jesuit Corporate Culture and the Visual Arts," 38–89), which was not presented at the conference and reprises some of the material presented by me there.

1. Carlo Galassi Paluzzi, *Storia segreta dello stile dei gesuiti* (Rome: Francesco Mondini, 1951). The conspiratorial tone of the title recalls two famous texts: the widely read vehemently anti-Jesuit seventeenth-century tract, the *Monita secreta,* and René Fülöp-Miller's popular history of the Society, *The Power and Secret of the Jesuits,* trans. F. S. Flint and D. S. Tait (New York: Viking Press, 1930). The first, written by a Polish ex-Jesuit (1614), purportedly exposed the Society's internal instructions, including a panoply of highly manipulative techniques for insinuating the Society's members, to dubious ends. Widely translated and reprinted into the twentieth century, the *Monita* played a key role in establishing the Jesuit conspiracy theory at which Fülöp-Miller cast one of the heretofore most impartial looks. See Sabina Pavone, *Le astuzie dei gesuiti: Le false 'Istruzioni segrete' della Compagnia di Gesú e la polemica antigesuita nei secoli XVII e XVIII* (Rome: Salerno Editrice, 2000).

2. Galassi Paluzzi, *Storia segreta*, esp. 8–9, 16–17.

3. Rudolf Wittkower and Irma Jaffe, eds., *Baroque Art: The Jesuit Contribution* (New York: Fordham University Press, 1972).

4. At the time the Jesuits devised the fourth vow many thought it superfluous, since all Christians implicitly pledged loyalty to the pope. But when Paul III approved the Society's rule, the vow was retained because it sent out an important message. Dauril Alden, *The Making of an Enterprise: The Society of Jesus in Portugal, Its Empire, and Beyond, 1540–1750* (Stanford: Stanford University Press, 1996), 13.

5. See Alden, *The Making of an Enterprise,* 17, table I. For the catalogs of the Society's houses and members, the first of which was printed in 1574, with several following at approximately ten-year intervals, see Edmond Lamalle, S.J., "Les Catalogues des provinces et des domiciles de la Compagnie de Jesus," *AHSI* 13 (1944): 77–101. See also the broadsheet enumerating the growth of the Society in Thomas M. Lucas, ed., *Saint, Site and Sacred Strategy: Ignatius, Rome and Jesuit Urbanism* (Vatican City: Biblioteca Apostolica Vaticana, 1990), 140.

6. Thomas M. Lucas, *Landmarking: City, Church & Jesuit Urban Strategy* (Chicago: Loyola University Press, 1997).

7. For a recent assessment of the genesis and impact on the early Society of the colleges, see John W. O'Malley, *The First Jesuits* (Cambridge, Mass.: Harvard University Press, 1993), chap. 6, "The Schools," 200–242.

8. "By the mid-seventeenth century, the Society enjoyed exclusive control of higher education in Italy, Poland, and Portugal and administered more academies than any other entity in Spain, France, the Spanish Netherlands, or the Catholic controlled regions of the Germanies and Hungary." Alden, *The Making of an Enterprise,* 19.

9. "This . . . [as well as the recent scandalous accusation of the Papal Post Master against the Jesuits and the Casa S. Marta] contributes to undoing our work for the greater service of God our Lord." Lucas, *Landmarking,* 149.

10. The discussion of French anti-Jesuitism that follows is drawn from Geoffrey Cubitt, *The Jesuit Myth: Conspiracy Theory and Politics in Nineteenth-Century France* (Oxford: Clarendon Press, 1993). A parallel study, which emphasizes anti-Jesuitism in literature, is Michel Leroy, *Le mythe jésuite: De Béranger à Michelet* (Paris: Presses Universitaires de France, 1992).

11. *Le Juif errant* appeared in the anticlerical *Le Constitutionnel, en feuilleton.* For editions and responses to it, see Augustin de Backer and Carlos Sommervogel, *Bibliothèque de la Compagnie de Jésus,* 12 vols. (Brussels: O. Schepens, 1890–1932), 11: no. 2029–42; Anne Hélène Hoog, "L'ami du peuple ou 'Le Juif errant' d'Eugène Sue," in *Le Juif errant: Un témoin du temps* (Paris: Musée d'art et d'histoire du Judaisme, 2001), 109–25.

12. On anti-Jesuit themes in the nineteenth-century novel, see Leroy, *Le mythe jésuite,* part 3; Joseph N. Moody, *The Church as Enemy: Anticlericalism in Nineteenth-Century French Literature* (Washington, D.C.: Corpus Books, 1968), esp. 40, 46, 49.

13. Jules Michelet and Edgar Quinet, *Des Jésuites,* 3d ed. (Paris: Hachette, 1843). All citations from this work that follow are drawn from idem, *The Jesuits,* trans. C. Cocks, 3d English ed. (London: Longman, Brown, Green and Longmans, 1846). For editions, translations, and responses to the lectures, see de Backer and Sommervogel, *Bibliothèque,* 11: no. 2003–13.

14. Leroy, *Le mythe jésuite*, 21.

15. Michelet and Quinet, *The Jesuits*, 5.

16. Cubitt, *The Jesuit Myth*, 137.

17. Michelet and Quinet, *The Jesuits*, 96.

18. Count Alexis de Saint-Priest, *History of the Fall of the Jesuits in the Eighteenth Century* [1844], trans. from the French (London: Murray, 1845), 139–41.

19. Owen Chadwick, *The Secularization of the European Mind in the Nineteenth Century* (Cambridge: Cambridge University Press, 1975), esp. chap. 5, "The Rise of Anticlericalism."

20. *Encyclopedia Brittanica*, 9th ed., 13 (1885): 656, s.v. "Jesuits."

21. Cubitt, *The Jesuit Myth*, 39.

22. One of the best indices of the Jesuit-Rome axis is the lengthy treatment in Vincenzo Gioberti, "Ossequio dei gesuiti verso Roma," in *Il gesuita moderno* (1846–47); reprint, ed. M. F. Sciacca, 6 vols. (Milan: Fratelli Bocca, 1940–42), vol. 4.

23. Theodor Griesinger, *The Jesuits: A Complete History of Their Open and Secret Proceedings from the Foundation of the Order to the Present Time* [1866], trans. A. J. Scott, 3d ed. (London: W. H. Allen, 1892), 740.

24. Griesinger, *The Jesuits*, 812.

25. For orientation to the vast corpus of anti-Jesuit literature, see the extensive though somewhat rambling account in Alexandre Brou, *Les Jésuites de la légende*, 2 vols. (Paris: Victor Retaux, 1907); László Polgár, S.J., *Bibliographie sur l'histoire de la Compagnie de Jésus, 1901–1980* (Rome: Institutum Historicum Societatis Iesu, 1981), 1: pt. 7, "Écrits polemiqués," 529–56.

26. Cubitt, *The Jesuit Myth*, 16.

27. Pierre Larousse, *Grand Dictionnaire Universel du XIXe siècle français*, 9 (1873): 958, s.v. "Jesuite."

28. See, for example, "The Confessional as the Key to the Money-Chest," in Griesinger, *The Jesuits*, bk. IV.

29. Cubitt, *The Jesuit Myth*, 281–84.

30. Michelet and Quinet, *The Jesuits*, 86.

31. Cubitt, *The Jesuit Myth*, 39.

32. Ibid., esp. 44–56.

33. Ibid., esp. chaps. 5, 6, on Jesuit imagery. On Enlightenment images of light and darkness and their anticlerical orientation, see Rolf Reichardt, "Light against Darkness: The Visual Representations of a Central Enlightenment Concept," *Representations* 61 (1998): 95–148.

34. Cubitt (*The Jesuit Myth*, 226) used this analogy to compare affiliation with the Jesuits to the ambivalent protection provided by the mafia lord.

35. Sylvia Lavin, "Re-Reading the Encyclopedia: Architectural Theory and the Formation of the Public in Late-Eighteenth-Century France," *Journal of the Society of Architectural Historians* 53 (1994): 185.

36. See A. D. Potts, "Political Attitudes and the Rise of Historicism in Art Theory," *Art History* 1 (1978): 193–94.

37. The self-conscious development of new building types in relation to social institutions is discussed in Anthony Vidler, *The Writing of the Walls: Architectural Theory in the Late*

Enlightenment (New York: Princeton Architectural Press, 1987). For the political proclivities of the late-eighteenth-century theorists and their impact on the rise of architectural theory, see Potts, "Political Attitudes."

38. S. Lavin, "Re-Reading the Encyclopedia," 184–92. For Quatremère's conservative position that institutions of the arts could provide some top-down stability amid the political upheaval of the day, see Potts, "Political Attitudes," 201–2.

39. This is a reduction of the more complex argument made in Sylvia Lavin, *Quatremère de Quincy and the Invention of a Modern Language of Architecture* (Cambridge, Mass.: MIT Press, 1992). For the notion of *ut architectura poesis,* see 114 ff.

40. Victor Hugo, *Notre-Dame of Paris* (1831; trans. John Sturrock, Middlesex: Penguin, 1978), 189–90.

41. For Hugo's political conversion in 1830 (away from his Catholic and Royalist position of the 1820s) as he began writing *Notre-Dame,* see the translator's introduction in Hugo, *Notre-Dame of Paris,* 20.

42. See S. Lavin, *Quatremère de Quincy,* 184–85. Although Quatremère opposed the use of the arts for propagandistic purposes (149), his rhetorically based notion of architecture as a language (see esp. 144) and his conviction that architecture/signs "must not be used to say nothing" (185) point in that direction.

43. Quatremère de Quincy, cited in ibid., 154.

44. Ibid., 188.

45. On the publishing history of these volumes, see Vidler, *The Writing of the Walls,* 220 n.22; S. Lavin, "Re-Reading the Encyclopedia," 186 ff. For the meaning and importance of "character" from Aristotle to Lebrun and in architectural theory at the turn of the nineteenth century, see S. Lavin, *Quatremère de Quincy,* 137 ff.

46. The relation of the moral quality of "character" to style is inferred in a later publication: "Sans aucun doute, c'est de la litterature que l'emploi moral du mot style aura passé dans le langue théoriques des beaux arts." A. C. Quatremère de Quincy, *Dictionnaire historique d'architecture: Comprenant . . . les notions historiques, descriptives, archaeologiques, biographiques, théoriques, didactiques et pratiques . . .* (Paris: Adrien le Clere, 1832), 2:501.

47. A. C. Quatremère de Quincy, *Architecture,* 3 vols. (Paris and Liège: Panckoucke and Plomteux, 1788–1825), 3:412.

48. S. Lavin, "Re-Reading the Encyclopedia," 189; idem, *Quatremère de Quincy,* 131 ff.

49. Quatremère de Quincy, *Architecture,* 1:283.

50. Ibid., 1:210.

51. See Hans Tintelnot, "Zur Gewinnung unserer Barockbegriffe," in *Die Kunstformen des Barockzeitalters,* ed. Rudolf Stamm (Munich: Leo Lehnen, 1956), 13–91; and Werner Oechslin, "'Barock': Zu den negativen Kriterien der Begriffsbestimmung in klassizistischer und späterer Zeit," in *Europäische Barock-Rezeption,* ed. Klaus Garber, Wolfenbütteler Arbeiten zur Barockforschung, vol. 20 (Wiesbaden: Otto Harrassowitz, 1991), 2:1225–45.

52. For example, in the running debate over the "causes of perfection of antique sculpture" (the title of a competition in 1805) Eméric-David, a political moderate, argued for the role played by institutions (over natural conditions) in fostering great art, although he did not consider any religious corporations, or the papacy as an institution. Religion,

like climate, was a condition for the production of Greek art. Eméric-David, *Recherches sur l'Art Statuaire* (1805), cited in Potts, "Political Attitudes," 202–3.

53. Potts, "Political Attitudes," 195.

54. J. G. Forster, "Die Kunst und das Zeitalter" (1791), cited in ibid., 198.

55. The connection between institutions of reform and historiography is stressed in Vidler, *The Writing of the Walls.*

56. The print is signed "Gemine fecit" on the spine of a book on the left side, above the column. An engraver by this name is unknown. But the name is so similar to François Génin, a prominent anti-Jesuit author of the period, that I suspect it refers to him. Indeed, so many of the themes intoned by Génin in his major anti-Jesuit work, *Les Jésuites et l'Université* (Paris: Paulin, 1844), conform to the views expressed in the print that I suspect he had something to do with the work. See Leroy, *Le mythe jésuite,* 80–81.

57. For orientation to the vast literature on the Gothic revival, see David Watkin, *The Rise of Architectural History* (London: Architectural Press, 1980), chaps. 1 and 3, and *The Dictionary of Art* (London: Macmillan, 1996), 13:198–206, s.v. "Gothic Revival" (Georg Germann); for Germany, see the excellent study by Michael J. Lewis, *The Politics of the German Gothic Revival: August Reichensperger* (New York: Architectural History Foundation; Cambridge, Mass.: MIT Press, 1993); for England, see Kenneth Clark, *The Gothic Revival: An Essay in the History of Taste,* 3d ed. (London: John Murray, 1962).

58. The nationalist interests of an art history that repelled foreign influences were recently stressed in Hans Belting, *The Germans and Their Art,* esp. the introduction to the English edition and chap. 2.

59. The definitions of the modern styles in Thomas Richards, *The Dictionary of Architecture,* 8 vols. (London: Thomas Richards, 1848–92), one of the most comprehensive architectural publications of the mid-nineteenth century, is symptomatic of the fluidity of period designations for modern architecture. In the entry under "Italian Architecture," divided into four periods, the most recent is "Modern, Neo-classic, including the Risorgimento (Cinque-cento) and its development into the Italian Style." "Risorgimento" is defined as "Renaissance, or revival" (as begun in the 1300s), culminating in the pure "stile cinque-cento," which lasts until 1550, when "it sank into the debased style of the Renaissance properly so called, and at last yielded to the bizarre, the barocco, and the rococo at the end of the seventeenth century." Ibid., 4:55, 57.

60. In James Elmes, *A General and Bibliographical Dictionary of the Fine Arts* . . . (London: Thomas Tegg, 1826), some Italian schools of painting are designated by geographic region, but otherwise there is little interest in designating period styles. In Wilhelm G. Bleichrodt, *Architektonische Lexikon, oder Allgemeine Real-Encyclopädie der gesammten architektonischen und dahin einschlagenden Hilfswissenschaften* . . . , 3 vols. (Ilmenau: B. F. Voigt, 1830–31), the term "Barock" is used but in its eighteenth-century definition as the bizarre rather than as a period style (1:96). Gothic is championed here, although style is still designated less in historical terms than in terms of character (1:176).

61. "Modern" is the most common rubric for post-Medieval architecture in the first half of the nineteenth century. Léonce Reynaud, *Traité d'architecture: Contenant des notions generales sur les principes de la construction et sur l'histoire de l'art,* 2 vols. (Paris: Carilian-Goeury et V. Dalmont, 1850–58), vol. 2, terms architecture after St. Peter's "modern"; Antoine

Guillaume Bernard Schayes, *Histoire de l'architecture en Belgique* (Brussels: A. Jamar, 1848), vol. 4, in which modern architecture encompasses the post-Gothic style introduced in Belgium in the seventeenth century.

62. For example, Thomas Rickman, *An attempt to discriminate the styles of architecture in England, from the Conquest to the Reformation . . .* , 4th rev. ed. (London: Longman, Rees, Orme, Green and Longman, 1835), in which post-Medieval architecture is termed "Italian"; Léon Vaudoyer, "Études d'architecture en France, ou notions relatives à l'age et au style. . . . Des Eglises au dix-septième siècle," *Magasin Pittoresque* 14 (1846): 105–7, in which post-Gothic churches are called "Italian" and, significantly, Jesuit churches are singled out as having their own style within that category.

63. In a guidebook to continental churches the ecclesiologist Benjamin Webb used both "modern" and "Renaissance" in reference to what are now considered Baroque buildings. He writes that "pseudo-classical or revived-classical have been occasionally synonymous with Renaissance. Cinque-cento means a peculiar form of Renaissance." Benjamin Webb, *Sketches of Continental Ecclesiology, or, Church Notes in Belgium, Germany, and Italy* (London: Joseph Masters, 1848), xvi.

64. Thomas Hope, *An Historical Essay on Architecture, Illustrated from Drawings Made in Italy and Germany,* 3d ed., 2 vols. (London: J. Murray, 1840), 2:45–46. For the spread of Italian Cinque-Cento style to the rest of Europe (an unnamed style whose "proper name" "should be the inane or frippery style"), see chap. 48.

65. "Until after the year 1770 this French word [Baroque] signified anything of an irregular figure or form; but in 1832 it had attained to such common use as a term of criticism both in French and English as to be described by Quatremère de Quincy as the culmination, or if the term may be allowed, abuse of the bizarre. . . . The word Baroque involves the idea of anything unintentionally absurd, while the term rococo appears to express a work of architecture in which every license has been intentionally exceeded." Richards, *The Dictionary of Architecture,* 1:26. See Tintelnot, "Zur Gewinnung unserer Barockbegriffe," for further sources.

66. A generation of architectural histories drawing on Schnaase's (1834) and Kugler's (1842) new comprehensive histories of art used the Baroque as a period term, although confusion remained. So, for instance, in 1857 Rosengarten would designate the Baroque "Der Barockstyl der Renaissance (Rococostyl)." A. Rosengarten, *Die Architektonischen Stylarten . . .* (Braunschweig: Friedrich Vieweg und Sohn, 1857), 326. In the 4th edition of Wilhelm Lübke, *Geschichte der Architektur* (1870), the Baroque is subsumed under the Italian Renaissance. Tintelnot, "Zur Gewinnung unserer Barockbegriffe," 32.

67. Burkhardt's authorship of the entry was noted by Werner Kaegi, *Jacob Burckhardt: Eine Biographie* (Basel: Schwabe, 1947–82), 2:528–29. Burckhardt's engagement with Jesuit issues will be explored by this author in a future study on the historiography of the Jesuit Style.

68. Brockhaus was the leading German encyclopedia in the first half of the nineteenth century, widely circulated (editions of 30,000), translated, adapted, and plagiarized. New editions were rapidly produced and included up-to-date information. Robert Collison, *Encyclopaedias: Their History throughout the Ages . . .* , 2d ed. (New York and London: Hafner Publishing, 1966), chap. 6; Alain Rey, *Encyclopèdies et dictionnaires* (Paris:

Presses Universitaires de France, 1982), 107–12. On the ideological biases of nineteenth-century encyclopedias, see *Encyclopaedia Brittanica,* 15th ed., 18 (1998): 376, s.v. "Encyclopaedias and Dictionaries."

69. "Jesuitenstil nennt man in der Baukunst und Decoration diejenige Behandlungsweise der Formen, welche den Jesuitenkirchen und Jesuitenanstalten seit der Mitte des 17. Jahrh. vorzüglich eigen war. Die Jesuiten meinten es mit der Architektur so wenig ernst, wie mit irgend einer andern Seite des geistigen Völkerlebens; nur imponiren wollten sie mit ihr. Zunächst bis gegen die Mitte des 17. Jahrh. hielten die deutschen Jesuiten mit affectirter Ehrbarkeit fest am gothischen, ja selbst am byzantin. Stil, wie ihre Kirchen zu Koblenz, Bonn und Köln beweisen. Das Innere ihrer Gebäude aus damaliger Zeit ist mit heiterer Pracht ausgestattet, voll Vergoldung und Schnitzwerk; besonders sind die Altäre ihrer Kirchen kolossale, großentheils vergoldete Zusammensetzungen von Blumen, Wolken, Engeln, Heiligen und Architektur, mit oft drei meist sehr schlechten Gemälden übereinander. Seit der Mitte des 17. Jahrh. treten sie so ziemlich an die Spitze der kirchlichen Baukunst, und der ausgeartete ital. Stil wurde nun ihr rechtes Eigenthum. Damals auf der Höhe ihrer Macht, bauten sie ihre größten Kirchen und zwar meist mit grosser Solidität und Pracht. Sehr kostbare Stoffe, Jaspis, Porphyr, Lapis Lazuli u.s.w. wurden zumal in Italien, zur Decoration gewählt; Decken, Gewölbe, Pilaster u.s.w. mit den reichsten Caskettirungen, Laubwerk und Festons überladen. Ärmlich blieb aber die phantasielose Composition des Ganzen, so reich und wunderlich man auch Thürme und Kuppeln verschnörkelte. Der große Pomp ihres Kirchenstils bei innerer Armseligkeit riß die ganze katholische Kirchenbaukunst ihrer Zeit mit sich fort, die nach dem Vorgange der Jesuiten dem rohen Effect Alles, auch das Letzte opferte. Gegenwärtig steht der Jesuitenstil etwa auf dem Standpunkt der Classicität vom Ende des vorigen Jahrhunderts. Auch in dieser einfachern Form verschmähen die Jesuiten den Effect nicht, zu welchem Behufe sie z.B. weismarmorne Capitäle auf schwarze Pilaster setzen, wie sie denn auch geheimnißvolle Lichteffecte durch Gardinen hervorzubringen suchen. Hier und da, z.B. in der neuen Kirche zu Schwyz, nähern sie sich sogar dem münchener Stile. Doch ihre Zeit ist vorüber; die Kunst läst sich nicht mehr von ihnen bevormunden." *Allgemeine deutsche Real-Encyklopedie für die gebildeten Stände. Conversations-Lexikon,* 10th ed., 8 (1845): 657–58, s.v. "Jesuitenstil."

70. Alina A. Payne, *The Architectural Treatise in the Renaissance: Architectural Invention, Ornament, and Literary Culture* (New York: Cambridge University Press, 1999).

71. My account of this is not entirely dissimilar from Galassi Paluzzi's. Where we differ is in my emphasis on the character of the Jesuit as providing the foundation of the Jesuit Style, whereas Galassi Paluzzi avoids the vexed question of character, pointing to (without mapping out) political and social anti-Jesuitism, as if politics had no place in the serious matter of designating art historical styles. See Galassi Paluzzi, *Storia segreta,* esp. 20–21.

72. Barry Bergdoll, *Léon Vaudoyer: Historicism in the Age of Industry* (New York: Architectural History Foundation; Cambridge, Mass.: MIT Press, 1994), esp. chap. 4.

73. About the Jesuit church in Paris, St. Paul–St. Louis, Vaudoyer writes: "Le style de l'architecture de cette église est celui que les jésuites importèrent dans tous les pays de l'Europe où ils formèrent des établissements de leur ordre. Cette style ne brille ni par la sim-

plicité ne par la correction, mais il est empreint d'une grande richesse, et ne laisse pas que de produire un certain effet." Léon Vaudoyer, "Études d'architecture en France," 107.

74. Jules Gailhabaud, ed., *Monuments anciens et modernes, collection formant une histoire de l'architecture des différents peuples a toutes les epoques*, 4 vols. (Paris: F. Didot, 1846–50). For Vaudoyer's contributions, which have not been identified, see Bergdoll, *Léon Vaudoyer*, 167. Given Vaudoyer's article on Jesuit churches, it is conceivable that he contributed the sections of Gailhabaud under discussion here.

75. The passage is in the English edition of Jules Gailhabaud, *Ancient and Modern Architecture; consisting of views, plan, elevations, sections, and details of the most remarkable edifices in the world . . .*, trans. F. Arundale and T. L. Donaldson (London: F. Didot, 1846–49), 3 (1849): s.v. "St. Paul and St. Louis." The same holds true in the assessment, heavily influenced by Quatremère de Quincy, of the late-seventeenth-century altars designed by Pozzo for the Church of St. Ignatius in Rome: "Deux riches et somptueux autels, tous les caractères de l'architecture jésuitique: c'est un assemblage incohérent de colonnes torses, de frontons coupés, de figures et d'ornements divers; un tout, enfin, qui n'a aucun analogue, et qu'on ne trouve qu'à cette époque de la décadence de l'art." *Monuments anciens et modernes*, 4, *Période moderne*, s.v. "Église de St. Ignace."

76. Gailhabaud, *Ancient and Modern Architecture*, 3: s.v. "Église de St. Gervasius et St. Protasius."

77. The Gesù is an "espèce de style, qu'on pourrait appeler celui de Vignole, mais auquel on a donné la qualification de jésuitique." Gailhabaud, *Monuments anciens et modernes*, 4: s.v. "Église de Jésus." Emphasis mine.

78. See Bergdoll, *Léon Vaudoyer*, 115.

79. Antoine Guillaume Bernard Schayes, the author of the first architectural history of Belgium, writes, in a far more positive vein, of Jesuit churches in Belgium, which he groups together under the rubric "modern." While he does not name the Jesuit Style, he nonetheless says that most Jesuit churches are "distinguished by their size and the luxuriousness of their decoration, [and which] *occupy a principal place in the history of the architecture of this era,* and those [Jesuit churches] in Belgium can figure on the highest rung of those monumental buildings." The author remarks that had the book not been begun as a chronological sequence of buildings, he would have wanted to discuss the Jesuit churches as a group. Schayes, *Histoire de l'architecture in Belgique*, esp. 4:155–237. Emphasis mine.

80. "Jesuitenstil, der ausgeartete Renaissancestil, den die Jesuiten seit dem 17. Jahrh. in ihren Kirchenbauten befolgten, und der sich durch Ueberladung in der Dekoration der Decken, Gewölbe, Pilaster mit Laubwerk, Festons, Kassettirungen u., überhaupt durch Effekthascherei und leeren Prunk bei phantasieloser Komposition des Ganzen charakterisirt [sic]. *Er fällt unter den Begriff des Barockstils.*" (Changes to the entry from the previous edition are italicized.) *Meyers Konversations-Lexikon*, 3d ed., 9 (1876): 540, s.v. "Jesuitenstil."

81. "Jesuitenstil, der ausgeartete Barockstil, den die Jesuiten seit dem 17. Jahrh. auf Grund der Bestrebungen von Borromini und Pozzo in ihren Kirchenbauten befolgten, und der sich durch Emanzipation der Form von der Konstruktion, durch regellose Überladung in der Dekoration, durch Effekthascherei in der Komposition des Ganzen charakterisiert,

womit eine die Sinne berauschende Wirkung zur Erreichung der Ordenzwecke beabsichtigt war." *Meyers Konversations-Lexikon*, 5th ed., 9 (1895): 558, s.v. "Jesuitenstil."

82. Hippolyte Taine, *Voyage en Italie* (1866; reprint, Paris: Julliard, 1965), 1:249. Galassi Paluzzi (*Storia segreta*, 13–14) also cites this and other passages, attributing Taine with more of a role in the birth of the Jesuit Style than is warranted. Galassi Paluzzi blames Taine for having collapsed what would later emerge as two distinct phases of Jesuit building (the first, more austere, the second, more sumptuous), helping to spread an erroneous characterization of all Jesuit churches as sumptous "banquet halls" (i.e., secular places of distraction, not worship). Although his essays were widely read, Taine was not prescient but a synthesizer of opinions already in play for twenty years.

83. See Eugène Sue, *Le Juif errant;* Edgar Quinet's lecture on the Spiritual Exercises, in Michelet and Quinet, *The Jesuits*, esp. 83–86.

84. Hugo, *Notre-Dame of Paris*, 129.

85. Bergdoll, *Léon Vaudoyer*, 109 ff.

86. See chapter 5.

87. The "conquest of minds and spirits" is borrowed from Galassi Paluzzi, *Storia segreta*, 9.

88. Quinet criticizes the Spiritual Exercises as yet another example of how the Jesuits created automatons deprived of their capacity to think. Michelet and Quinet, *The Jesuits*, 85.

89. "Great error has been committed by some of the recent historians of modern art, who have not hesitated to apply the title 'Jesuit Style' to representations of decoration that are really in the style Louis XV; but the 'Jes. Style' might be illustrated by decoration in a better as well as in a worse stage of the art as practiced 1575–1775." *The Dictionary of Architecture*, 1853–92, 4, s.v. "Jesuit Buildings."

90. In his *Der Cicerone: Eine Anleitung zum Genuss der Kunstwerke Italiens* (1855), Jacob Burckhardt used the Baroque as a period designation but without characterizing it to the extent that other authors had done for the Jesuit Style. See Hans Tintelnot, "Zur Gewinnung unserer Barockbegriffe"; Werner Oechslin, "'Barock': Zu den negativen Kriterien."

91. Galassi Paluzzi also notes this (along with the fact that the Jesuit Style was identified with Mannerism, the Rococo, and the Counter-Reformation). But since his position is essentially that the Jesuit Style did not exist, the period style takes priority, and the idea that the Jesuits might have been responsible for the period as a whole becomes something of a laughing matter. Galassi Paluzzi, *Storia segreta*, 7.

92. Baroque had been used, hesitantly, in reference to early modern architecture between 1841 and 1887 and was preceded by a wave of building in the neo-Baroque style across Europe beginning in the 1860s. See Tintelnot, "Zur Gewinnung unserer Barockbegriffe."

93. Cornelius Gurlitt, *Geschichte des Barockstiles, des Rococo, und des Klassicismus*, vol. 3, *Geschichte des Barockstiles und des Rococo in Deutschland* (Stuttgart: Von Ebner and Seubert, 1889), 15.

94. Heinrich Wölfflin, *Renaissance and Baroque* [1888], trans. Kathrin Simon (Ithaca: Cornell University Press, 1966). Unlike Gurlitt's weightier tomes, Wölfflin's saw numerous editions (during his lifetime in 1906, 1908, 1925, 1926; posthumous reprintings in 1961, 1965, 1968, 1986) and was widely translated (into French, English, and Spanish).

95. *Renaissance and Baroque* has had a symptomatic change in reception over time. In his introduction to the first English translation of the book Peter Murray states: "[O]ne of

the reasons for producing an English translation of *Renaissance and Baroque* three-quarters of a century after its original appearance is because it contains a larger proportion of acute visual analysis and a smaller proportion of generalisation than the later works." Peter Murray, introduction to Wölfflin, *Renaissance and Baroque*, 4. By contrast, all of the reviewers of the book when it first came out saw its main contribution in its philosophical framework. Joan Goldhammer Hart, "Heinrich Wölfflin: An Intellectual Biography" (Ph.D. diss., University of California, Berkeley, 1980), 194–96.

96. Michael Ann Holly, "Wölfflin and the Imagining of the Baroque," in *Europäische Barock-Rezeption*, ed. Klaus Garber, Wolfenbütteler Arbeiten zur Barockforschung, vol. 20 (Wiesbaden: Otto Harrassowitz, 1991), 2:1258.

97. Wölfflin, *Renaissance and Baroque*, 76.

98. Warnke cites analogous passages in Gurlitt's *Geschichte des Barockstiles, des Rococo, und des Klassizismus*, relating them to his views, encouraged by his association with Julius Langbehn (author of *Rembrandt als Erzieher*, 1890), of a conservative ideology of individualism distinct from the liberal view of the individual. See Martin Warnke, "Die Entstehung des Barockbegriffs in der Kunstgeschichte," in Garber, ed., *Europäische Barock-Rezeption*, 2:1215–16, esp. n.23. On the growing discontent in Germany with the impact of urbanism and the forces of industrialization on the individual as measured by the wild success of Langbehn's foray into art history, see Fritz Stern, *The Politics of Cultural Despair: A Study in the Rise of the Germanic Ideology* (Berkeley: University of California Press, 1961), chap. 2.

99. Wölfflin, *Renaissance and Baroque*, 86.

100. The Jesuits "kindled" the new religious fervor, which had been prepared long before and was already detectable in the work of, for example, Raphael. Wölfflin, *Renaissance and Baroque*, 86–87.

101. See especially the chapter "Massiveness" for repeated reference to the Baroque facade as "imprisoning" those elements that had, by contrast, been endowed with independence in Renaissance architecture. Ibid., 50, 52, 57. For an excellent analysis of Wölfflin's views on the interdependence of painting, sculpture, and architecture, see Eric Garberson, "Historiography of the Gesamtkunstwerk," in *Struggle for Synthesis: The Total Work of Art in the Seventeenth and Eighteenth Centuries*, ed. Luís de Moura Sobral and David W. Booth (Lisbon: Instituto Português do Património Arquitectónico, 1999), 1:62–63.

102. Warnke, "Die Entstehung des Barockbegriffs," in Garber, ed., *Europäische Barock-Rezeption*, 2:1218–19. See also Garberson, "Historiography of the Gesamtkunstwerk," 62, 70, n.22, 35.

103. I am struck by the consonance of Wölfflin's view of Renaissance architecture with his thinking about his resignation from the university. He wrote in his diary in May 1923: "The decisive consideration for resigning is: no longer to have to represent a department, but instead just to do what one wants; to become personal; to become young; to become beautiful, etc." Cited in Martin Warnke, "On Heinrich Wölfflin," trans. David Levin, *Representations* 27 (1989): 182–83.

104. *Encyclopedia Brittanica*, vol. 3 of the supplement to the 13th ed. (1922): 235–36, s.v. "Propaganda."

105. "Der religiöse Propagandagedanke, auf den fortab sich alle Energien Roms konzentrieren, wurde tief in den Boden der geistigen und künstlerischen Ideenwelt der italienischen Renaissance hineingesenkt. Diese selber ward dadurch allerdings in eine veränderte Richtung geleitet, blieb aber in ihrem innersten Kern durchaus die alte. Der nationale italienische Gedanke, nicht imstande sich in einem einheitlichen, unabhängigen Staatswesen politisch zu vollenden, ward nun zu einem religiöse-politischen Werbemittel über Italiens Grenzen hinaus, ward durch seinen eminent künstlerischen Gehalt zu einer wesentlichen Grundlage des gemeinsamen europäischen Empfindens der ganzen Folgezeit." Hermann Voss, *Die Malerei des Barock in Rom* (Berlin: Propylaen-Verlag, 1924).

106. I agree with David Watkin (*The Rise of Architectural History*, 29) that Emile Mâle was influenced by Weisbach in his turn to the Counter-Reformation in his *L'art religieux après le Concile de Trente: Ètude sur l'iconographie de la fin du XVIe siècle, du XVIIe, du XVIIIe siècle* (Paris: Armand Colin, 1932).

107. "Der Jesuitismus hat Kräfte entfesselt, die auf lange hinaus in der Bewegung fortwirkten." Werner Weisbach, *Der Barock als Kunst der Gegenreformation* (Berlin: Paul Cassirer, 1921), 12.

108. Ibid., esp. chap. 1.

109. "It is the same in architecture as with ancient languages, which became richer as they lost their energy and beauty, as is easily proved for Greek and Latin; as architects saw they could neither surpass nor even equal their predecessors in beauty, they tried to supply it by richness and profusion." Winckelmann cited in Vidler, *The Writing of the Walls*, 133.

110. Weisbach, *Der Barock als Kunst der Gegenreformation*, 204–6.

111. Nikolaus Pevsner, "The Counter-Reformation and Mannerism" [1925], in *From Mannerism to Romanticism*, vol. 1 of *Studies in Art, Architecture and Design* (London: Thames and Hudson, 1968), 11–33.

112. Louis Serbat, *L'Architecture gothique des Jésuites au XVIIe siècle* (Caen: Henri Delesques, 1903); Joseph Braun, *Die Belgische Jesuitenkirchen: Ein Beitrag zur Geschichte des Kampfes zwischen Gotik und Renaissance* (Freiburg im Breisgau: Herdersche, 1907); idem, *Die Kirchenbauten der deutschen Jesuiten: Ein Beitrag zur Kultur- und Kunstgeschichte des 16., 17., und 18. Jahrhunderts* (Freiburg im Breisgau: Herdersche, 1910); idem, *Spaniens alte Jesuitenkirchen: Ein Beitrag zur Geschichte der nachmittelalterlichen kirchlichen Architektur in Spanien* (Freiburg im Breisgau: Herdersche, 1913).

113. The entry in the 7th edition of *Meyers Lexikon*, 6 (1927): 330, s.v. "Jesuitenstil," noted that the concept was incorrect: "Jesuitenstil, landläufige Bezeichnung des ausgearteten, durch leeren Prunk gekennzeichneten Barockstils. Der Name führt irre; denn die Jesuiten haben in allen Stilarten und oft sehr einfach gebaut." The definition is similarly revised in the 15th ed. of *Der Grosse Brockhaus*, 9 (1931): 414, s.v. "Jesuitenstil": "Jesuitenstil, Bezeichnung des überladenen, ins Prunkvoll-Leere entarteten Barockstils in der Baukunst, den die Jesuiten gepflegt und verbreitet haben sollen. Doch trifft das nicht zu, denn die Jesuitenkirchen sind meist streng und einfach gebaut, und die reichen Schmuckformen des Innern sind in dieser Zeit (17. und 18. Jahrh.) allgemein üblich. Die Jesuiten sind fast stets den gerade die Zeit beherrschenden künstlerischen

Strömungen gefolgt und haben vor allem in Deutschland meist an die heimische Bauüberlieferung angeknüpft. Es it wohl hauptsächlich das Verdienst der Jesuiten, den Barockstil in die Kolonien Spaniens und Portugals (Südamerika) eingeführt zu haben."

114. For the internationalist dimension of the Jesuit Style from the 1840s to the 1940s, see Evonne Levy, "The Internationalist Jesuit Style, Evil Twin to National Styles," in *Spirit, Style, Story: Essays Honoring John W. Padberg, S.J.*, ed. Thomas M. Lucas, S.J. (Chicago: Loyola University Press, 2003), 181–202.

CHAPTER 2. RHETORIC VERSUS PROPAGANDA

1. Reference to continuity in the use of language to influence events and others as a "persistent human trait" is made in Ted Smith, introduction to *Propaganda: A Pluralistic Perspective*, ed. idem (New York: Praeger, 1989), 1.

2. For the "discovery" by Renaissance historians of rhetoric as a "culture" (rather than a discipline), see Randolph Starn, "Pleasure in the Visual Arts," in *Meaning in the Visual Arts: Views from the Outside: A Centennial Commemoration of Erwin Panofsky (1892–1968)*, ed. Irving Lavin (Princeton: Institute for Advanced Study, 1995), 154–56.

3. Erwin Panofsky, *Perspective as Symbolic Form* [1927], trans. Christopher S. Wood (New York: Zone Books, 1991). For Panofsky's debt to Cassirer's *Philosophy of Symbolic Forms* (1923), see Silvia Ferretti, *Cassirer, Panofsky and Warburg: Symbol, Art, and History*, trans. Richard Pierce (New Haven: Yale University Press, 1989), 202–3.

4. There is a brief reasoned account in the introduction to Clark, *Art and Propaganda in the Twentieth Century*; see also the perspicacious remarks, with an eye to propaganda in Russian painting, post-1917, in Clark, *Farewell to an Idea*, 291–94.

5. See, for example, Brian Vickers, *In Defence of Rhetoric* (Oxford: Clarendon Press, 1988), esp. chap. 1.

6. I have relied for what follows primarily on the following general histories of rhetoric. George A. Kennedy, *Classical Rhetoric and Its Christian and Secular Tradition from Ancient to Modern Times*, 2d rev. ed. (Chapel Hill: University of North Carolina Press, 1999); Renato Barilli, *Rhetoric*, trans. Giuliana Menozzi (Minneapolis: University of Minnesota Press, 1989); and Vickers, *In Defence of Rhetoric*. For a brief, comprehensive orientation to fairly recent literature, see Winifred Bryan Horner, ed., *The Present State of Scholarship in Historical and Contemporary Rhetoric* (Columbia: University of Missouri Press, 1983); and the longer articles in Marc Fumaroli, ed., *Histoire de la rhétorique dans l'Europe moderne: 1450–1950* (Paris: Presses Universitaires de France, 1999).

7. Kennedy, *Classical Rhetoric*, 21.

8. Ibid., 45.

9. Gorgias, *On the Nonexistent, or On Nature*, as discussed in ibid., 36.

10. Vickers, *In Defence of Rhetoric*, 84.

11. Vickers argues that Plato's text (and the opening of the debate between rhetoric and philosophy) must be understood as a highly personal view based on Plato's perception of the decline of Athenian democracy in part brought about by the pandering to the desires of the Athenians by the empty sophists. Ibid., chap. 2. Nietzsche read Plato's

condemnation of rhetoric as envy of the power of the Athenian rhetoricians, and therefore expression of his own hidden "will to power." Samuel Ijsseling, *Rhetoric and Philosophy in Conflict: An Historical Survey* (The Hague: Martinus Nijhoff, 1976), 9, 107–8.

12. Vickers, *In Defence of Rhetoric*, 128 ff.

13. Epedeictic rhetoric would be emphasized by Quintillian, and in Medieval and Renaissance treatises. Ibid., 54. For the critique of epedeictic as more about exemplification than bringing men to action (and an opposing view of epedeictic as the educational genre of rhetoric), see Chaim Perelman, "The New Rhetoric," in *The Prospect of Rhetoric; Report of the National Development Project, Sponsored by Speech Communication Association,* ed. Lloyd F. Bitzer and Edwin Black (Englewood Cliffs, N.J.: Prentice-Hall, 1971), 116.

14. Vickers, *In Defence of Rhetoric*, 19–20.

15. Jane Sutton, "The Death of Rhetoric and Its Rebirth in Philosophy," *Rhetorica* 4 (1986): 203–26. "Primary" and "secondary" are terms of George Kennedy, which, as Sutton points out (215–16), reiterate the critique of rhetoric as persuasion.

16. Kennedy, *Classical Rhetoric*, 5, as discussed in Sutton, "The Death of Rhetoric," 220.

17. Plato, *Phaedras* 271 a–b; see Vickers, *In Defence of Rhetoric*, 17–18.

18. "In a survey of the history of ancient Greece, one immediately perceives a number of prominent figures who fulfilled an important role in politics on account of their rhetorical skill. One also notices certain important people who taught this skill. Finally one sees those who, although truly talented and knowledgeable, turned away from public life and politics which were looked upon with contempt. The greatest of these was Socrates who, according to the witnesses of his day, excelled all other Greeks through his keenness of mind, lucidity of thought and his ability to introduce subtle distinctions, thereby revealing his magnificent erudition and sheer eloquence. . . . He separated (the external and material word of the rhetorician) and the internal word of the heart of the real meaning. This distinction is quite absurd, useless and objectionable since it implies that some people would teach us to know and others would teach us to speak." Cicero, *De Oratore,* III 16, 59–61.

19. Vickers, *In Defence of Rhetoric*, 35, 74.

20. Ibid., 75–80.

21. Ibid., 64.

22. Jerrold E. Seigel, *Rhetoric and Philosophy in Renaissance Humanism: The Union of Eloquence and Wisdom, Petrarch to Valla* (Princeton: Princeton University Press, 1968).

23. Frederick J. McGinness, *Right Thinking and Sacred Oratory in Counter-Reformation Rome* (Princeton: Princeton University Press, 1995).

24. The personal identification of orator with his message is a specific application of Aristotle as developed by Cicero and Quintillian. Ibid., 22–23, 41.

25. Ibid., 35–36.

26. Ibid., esp. chap. 2.

27. See the magisterial study by Marc Fumaroli, *L'Age de l'Eloquence: Rhétorique et "res literaria" de la Renaissance au seuil de l'époque classique* (Geneva: Librairie Droz, 1980).

28. Ibid., 20–21.

29. Ibid., 418–23.

30. Ibid., 5.

31. Marc Fumaroli, "Baroque et classicisme: *L'Imago Primi Saeculi Societatis Jesu* (1640) et ses adversaires," in *L'École du silence: Le sentiment des images au XVIIe siècle* (Paris: Flammarion, 1998), 446–49, 473–76.

32. I have drawn for what follows on Hayden White, "The Suppression of Rhetoric in the Nineteenth Century," in *Rhetoric Canon*, ed. Brenda Deen Schildgen (Detroit: Wayne State University Press, 1997), 21–31.

33. Ibid., 27–28.

34. Eugene Sue, *The Wandering Jew* (London: Routledge and Sons, n.d.), 115.

35. White, "The Suppression of Rhetoric," 26–27.

36. See note 39 (on rhetoric and the arts) below.

37. Giulio Carlo Argan, "La 'rettorica' e l'arte barocca," in *Retorica e barocco: Atti del III Congresso Internazionale di Studi Umanistici*, ed. Enrico Castelli (Rome: Fratelli Bocca, 1955), 11. Reprinted in Giulio Carlo Argan, *Immagine e persuasione: Saggi sul barocco*, ed. Bruno Contardi (Milan: Feltrinelli, 1986), 19–29.

38. Elizabeth Cropper and Charles Dempsey, "The State of Research in Italian Painting of the Seventeenth Century," *Art Bulletin* 69 (1987): 506, noted that seventeenth-century art is usually considered rhetorical, although little had yet been done to substantiate the claim. There is now a substantial literature on the subject. See, for example, Wittkower, *Art and Architecture in Italy,* 138–40; Irving Lavin, "Bernini and Antiquity—The Baroque Paradox: A Poetical View," in *Antikenrezeption im Hochbarock,* ed. Herbert Beck and Sabine Schulze (Berlin: Gebr. Mann, 1989), 9–10; various essays in Christine Göttler et al., eds., *Diletto e Maraviglia: Ausdruck und Wirkung in der Kunst von der Renaissance bis zum Barock* (Emsdetten: Edition Imorde, 1998).

39. Rensselaer W. Lee, *Ut pictura poesis: Humanistic Theory of Painting* (1943; reprint, New York: W. W. Norton, 1967); Michael Baxandall, *Giotto and the Orators: Humanist Observers of Painting in Italy and the Discovery of Pictorial Composition, 1350–1450* (Oxford: Clarendon Press, 1971); Gerard LeCoat, *The Rhetoric of the Arts, 1550–1650* (Bern and Frankfurt: Herbert Lang, 1975); David Summers, *Michelangelo and the Language of Art* (Princeton: Princeton University Press, 1981); Carl Goldstein, "Rhetoric and Art History in the Italian Renaissance and Baroque," *Art Bulletin* 73 (1991): 641–52 (with previous bibliography, but to be read with caution). For a summary of rhetorical theory and the visual arts with an emphasis on Alberti, see "Rhetoric and the Sister Arts," in Vickers, *In Defence of Rhetoric,* 340–60. On the role of language in shaping architectural theory, see Christine Smith, *Architecture in the Culture of Early Humanism: Ethics, Aesthetics, and Eloquence, 1400–1470* (New York: Oxford University Press, 1992), esp. pt. 3; Georgia Clarke and Paul Crossley, eds., *Architecture and Language: Constructing Identity in European Architecture, c. 1000–c. 1650* (Cambridge: Cambridge University Press, 2000). On architecture as rhetorical persuasion, see especially Caroline van Eck, "Architecture, Language, and Rhetoric in Alberti's *De Re Aedificatoria,*" in Clarke and Crossley, eds., *Architecture and Language,* 72–81; Karl Noehles, "Rhetorik, Architekturallegorie und Baukunst an der Wende vom Manierismus zum Barock in Rom," in *Die Sprache der Zeichen und Bilder: Rhetorik und nonverbale Kommunikation in der frühen Neuzeit,* ed. Volker Kapp (Marburg: Hitzeroth, 1990), 190–227; Friedrich Polleross, "Architecture and Rhetoric in the Work of Johann Bernhard Fischer von Erlach," in *Infinite Boundaries:*

Order, Disorder, and Reorder in Early Modern German Culture, ed. Max Reinhardt (Kirksville, Mo.: Sixteenth Century Journal Publishers, 1998), 121–46.

40. For example, David Summers, *Michelangelo and the Language of Art*; for decorum and other rhetorical themes in sixteenth-century architectural discourse, see Payne, *The Architectural Treatise in the Renaissance*.

41. Jacqueline Lichtenstein, *La couleur éloquente: Rhétorique et peinture à l'âge classique* (Paris: Flammarion, 1989).

42. Gabriele Paleotti, *Discorso intorno alle immagini sacre e profane* [1582], in *Trattati d'arte del cinquecento fra manierismo e controriforma*, ed. Paola Barocchi (Bari: G. Laterza, 1961), 2:117–509. For a summary of the treatise, see Giuseppe Scavizzi, *The Controversy on Images from Calvin to Baronius* (New York: Peter Lang, 1992), 131–40.

43. The three aims are discussed in a series of chapters in Book I: "Della dilettazione che apportano le imagini christiane" (chap. XXII); "Che le imagini cristiane servono grandemente per ammaestrare il popolo al ben vivere" (chap. XXIII); "Che le imagini cristiane servono molto a movere gli affetti delle persone" (chap. XXV).

44. Paleotti, *Discorso intorno alle immagini sacre e profane*, in Barocchi, ed. *Trattati d'arte del cinquecento*, 2:214; he footnotes Cicero, *De Inventione* I, 5 [sic] 6.

45. Paleotti, *Discorso intorno alle immagini sacre e profane*, in Barocchi, ed. *Trattati d'arte del cinquecento*, 2:215.

46. McGinness, *Right Thinking and Sacred Oratory*, 53ff.

47. "It is primarily through the word that pursuing and defending a political policy, forcing certain political decisions upon the people, occur within democracy—the ideal polity for the ancient Greeks. So that 'rhetorikè techné' and 'aretè politiké' were also identical." Ijsseling, *Rhetoric and Philosophy in Conflict*, 12.

48. On the new emphasis on the passions, see LeCoat, *The Rhetoric of the Arts*, 21–22; Jennifer Montagu, *The Expression of the Passions: The Origin and Influence of Charles Le Brun's "Conference sur l'expression generale et particulière"* (London: Yale University Press, 1994), esp. 50 ff.; for Guercino's change in style as a function of a new adherence to rhetorical principles, see Sybille Ebert-Schifferer, "'Ma c'hanno da fare I precetti dell'oratore con quelli della pittura?' Reflections of Guercino's Narrative Structure," in *Guercino: Master Painter of the Baroque*, ed. Denis Mahon (Washington, D.C.: National Gallery of Art, 1992), 75–110.

49. Le Brun intended to publish both the lecture and the accompanying illustrations but did not. After his death, many of the drawings appeared in several editions. Montagu, *The Expression of the Passions*, pt. 2 and App. 2, 6.

50. Indicative of this is the recent volume of conference proceedings, Sible de Blaauw et al., eds., *Docere, delectare movere: Affetti, devozione e retorica nel linguaggio artistico del primo barocco romano* (Rome: Edizioni de Luca, 1998), the introduction to which passes over what is obvious by now.

51. Argan, "La 'rettorica' e l'arte barocca," 20.

52. Ibid.

53. Two years prior to the appearance of Argan's essay, Arnold Hauser published his *Sozialgeschichte der Kunst und Literatur* (Munich: C. H. Beck, 1953), an important work that has had surprisingly little resonance in the study of the Italian Baroque. The same

year Meyer Schapiro underscored the importance of institutions in broad explanations of artistic style: "It is when these ways of thinking and feeling or world views have been formulated as the outlook of a religion or dominant institution or class of which the myths and values are illustrated or symbolized in the work of art that the general intellectual content seems a more promising field for explanation of style." Meyer Schapiro, "Style" [1953], in *Theory and Philosophy of Art: Style, Artist, and Society: Selected Papers* (New York: George Braziller, 1994), esp. 85, 99–100. Argan and Hauser are taken up by Maravall, *Culture of the Baroque*, who argues for the Baroque as a mass culture employing artistic media as a technique to propagandistic ends.

54. Argan, "La 'rettorica' e l'arte barocca," 22.

55. Ibid., 13.

56. See Argan's remarks on the influence (and limitations) of Croce's *Storia dell'età barocca* (1929) on art historians of his generation in his preface to *Immagine e persuasione*, vii, and "La 'rettorica' e l'arte barocca," 24. On Croce's position on rhetoric, see the brief account in Barilli, *Rhetoric*, 100–101; and Vickers, *In Defence of Rhetoric*, 204–9.

57. Wittkower cited Argan's essay and included a section on rhetoric in his *Art and Architecture in Italy*, 2:3, the first edition of which was published in 1958.

58. In a lecture on the state of Italian Baroque studies delivered in 1960, Wittkower argued that those who had sought a pan-European explanation for the Baroque saw it as the product of the Counter-Reformation, or of the Jesuits, or an expression of absolutism. All of these solutions had been discarded as unsatisfying or incorrect. "But recently a unifying theory has appeared by Argan, in his important essay 'La rettorica e l'arte barocca.' According to Argan, the fundamental difference between the Baroque and the other historical periods is the method of persuasion of neo-Aristotelian rhetoric—a technique of communication characteristic of the Baroque and one which Baroque art and all the other forms of Baroque life have in common. In other words, Argan has substituted the old cause-effect with a structural affinity among various forms of expression of the age" (translation mine). Wittkower, "Il barocco in Italia," 324.

That same year Wittkower organized the conference in New York, resulting in the volume *Baroque Art: The Jesuit Contribution*. The title indicates the main thrust of the argument, namely, that the Jesuits were supportive patrons of the Baroque, not inventors of it via the Jesuit Style.

59. Giulio Carlo Argan, "Rettorica e architettura" [1964], in *Immagine e persuasione*, 25.

60. Ibid., 26.

61. For what follows I have relied primarily on the excellent study, Jape Van Ginneken, *Crowds, Psychology, and Politics, 1871–1899* (Cambridge: Cambridge University Press, 1992).

62. Ibid., 5, 37.

63. Ibid., 145.

64. Ibid., 148.

65. Ibid., 171. Analogously, revolutionary celebrations replaced religious liturgy, with journalism providing daily reinforcement of the new emotional ties to nation. Hagen Schulze, "The Revolution of the European Order and the Rise of German Nationalism," in *Nation-Building in Central Europe*, ed. idem (Leamington Spa and Hamburg, N.Y.: Berg, 1987), 10.

66. Van Ginneken, *Crowds, Psychology, and Politics*, 148.

67. I have not found any direct evidence that Wölfflin read the mass psychologists' work, but he need not have actually read the scientific literature to have been familiar with the issues that reached the popular press. See Goldhammer Hart, "Heinrich Wölfflin," 214–24, for Wölfflin's brief stay in Paris after completing *Renaissance and Baroque* and his encounter with Taine's philosophy of art.

68. For a brief introduction to the organization, preceded by a commission of the same name formed after Trent by Gregory XIII, see Peter Guilday, "The Sacred Congregation De Propaganda Fide (1622–1922)," *Catholic Historical Review* 6 (1921): 478–94 (with previous bibliography).

69. Wolfgang Schieder and Christof Dipper, "Propaganda," in *Geschichtliche Grundbegriffe: Historisches Lexikon zur politisch-sozialen Sprache in Deutschland,* ed. Otto Brunner, Werner Conze, and Reinhart Koselleck (Stuttgart: Klett-Cotta, 1984), 5:69.

70. Ibid.

71. Ibid., 78.

72. Ibid., 71.

73. Ibid., 72–74.

74. Ibid., 82, 87.

75. Ibid., 87, 91.

76. *Nouveau Larousse Illustré* 7 (1904): 50, s.v. "Propagande."

77. Hans Speier, "Morale and Propaganda," in *Propaganda in War and Crisis: Materials for American Policy,* ed. Daniel Lerner (New York: George W. Stewart Publisher, 1951), 4–6.

78. Garth S. Jowett and Victoria O'Donnell, *Propaganda and Persuasion,* 2d ed. (Newbury Park, Calif.: Sage, 1986), 172.

79. Ibid., 165–66; Robert Jackall and Janice M. Hirota, "America's First Propaganda Ministry: The Committee on Public Information during the Great War," in *Propaganda,* ed. Robert Jackall (New York: New York University Press, 1995), 158.

80. For a sober estimation of the British reassessment of propaganda in the immediate aftermath of the war, see the new entry on propaganda in the *Encyclopedia Britannica,* supplement to the 13th ed., 3 (1922): 235–36, s.v. "Propaganda." On the debates in the United States through the 1950s, see J. Michael Sproule, *Propaganda and Democracy: The American Experience of Media and Mass Persuasion* (New York: Cambridge University Press, 1997).

81. An extremely influential early account of how authorities shaped the news in favor of their policies is to be found in Walter Lippmann, *The Phantom Public, a Sequel to "Public Opinion"* (New York: Macmillan, 1927). On Lippmann, see Sproule, *Propaganda and Democracy,* 92–97.

82. Edward L. Bernays, *Propaganda* (New York: Liveright, 1936), 20. For an analogous position held by a newspaper executive, see Ivy Lee, *Publicity; Some of the Things It Is and Is Not . . .* (New York: Industries Publishing Company, 1925).

83. Erika G. King, "Exposing the 'Age of Lies': The Propaganda Menace as Portrayed in American Magazines in the Aftermath of World War I," *Journal of American Culture* 12 (1989): 35–40.

84. J. Michael Sproule, "Social Response to Twentieth-Century Propaganda," in Smith, ed., *Propaganda,* 10.

85. Leonard W. Doob, *Propaganda: Its Psychology and Technique* (New York: H. Holt and Company, 1935), 4.

86. Lippmann, *The Phantom Public.*

87. Alfred McClung Lee, *How to Understand Propaganda* (New York and Toronto: Rinehart and Company, 1952), 23.

88. Sproule in Smith, ed., *Propaganda.*

89. Oscar Wetherhold Riegel, *Mobilizing for Chaos: The Story of the New Propaganda* (New Haven: Yale University Press, 1934).

90. Sproule in Smith, ed., *Propaganda*, 15; Sproule, *Propaganda and Democracy*, 193–208.

91. Hans Speier, introduction to *The Truth in Hell and Other Essays on Politics and Culture, 1935–1987* (New York: Oxford University Press, 1989), 15. For the view of propaganda analysis itself as standing in the way of intervention, see Sproule, *Propaganda and Democracy*, 178–93.

92. See the alarm voiced in 1937 that only 63 percent of social studies teachers regarded training students "to recognize and guard against propaganda by special interests" as one of their teaching objectives. Roy A. Price, "Teaching Students in Social-Studies Classes to Guard against Propaganda," in *Education against Propaganda: Developing Skill in the Use of the Sources of Information about Public Affairs*, ed. Elmer Ellis (Philadelphia: National Council for Social Studies, 1937), 127–33.

93. Violet Edwards, *Group Leader's Guide to Propaganda Analysis: Revised Edition of Experimental Study Materials for Use in Junior and Senior High Schools in College and University Classes and in Adult Study Groups* (New York: Institute for Propaganda Analysis, 1938), 9, 11, 22.

94. See Edwards, *Group Leader's Guide to Propaganda Analysis*, 21; for a brief overview of the IPA, see Jowett and O'Donnell, *Propaganda and Persuasion*, 182–84, and the extended treatment by Sproule, *Propaganda and Democracy*, chap. 5. The Institute's best-known text, "How to Detect Propaganda" [1937], is reprinted in Jackall, ed., *Propaganda*, 217–24.

95. Schieder and Dipper, "Propaganda," 106.

96. *Meyers Lexikon*, 7th ed., 9 (1928): 1319, s.v. "Propaganda."

97. "Propaganda [von lat. propagāre 'verbreiten'] *w*, im Werbungswesen eine Tätigkeit jeder Art, die auf breiteste Kreise zu wirken sucht. (——→Werbung) **P. der Tat**, ——→Anarchismus. **Propagandistisch**, werbungsgemäß; angreifend." *Der Große Brockhaus*, 15th ed., 15 (1933): 160, s.v. "Propaganda."

98. Ralf Georg Reuth, *Goebbels*, trans. Krishna Winston (San Diego: Harcourt Brace, 1993), 173 and 396 n.11.

99. Doob, *Propaganda*, 3.

100. Ibid., 75–76.

101. Leonard Doob, *Public Opinion and Propaganda* (New York: H. Holt and Company, 1948), 240.

102. Speier argued that psychological warfare was a misnomer for the Cold War because the distinction between war and peace was becoming blurred and traditional warfare was no less psychological than noncombative forms of propaganda. Hans Speier, "Psychological Warfare Reconsidered," in Lerner, ed., *Propaganda*, 463–66. Lasswell argued that psychological warfare (a traditional technique) included propaganda and was the

mark of economy of means in warfare. Harold D. Lasswell, "Political and Psychological Warfare," in ibid., 261–66.

103. Lerner, ed., *Propaganda*, xii.

104. Ralph K. White, "The New Resistance to International Propaganda," *Public Opinion Quarterly* 16 (1952–53): 539–51.

105. Ellul, *Propaganda*.

106. Jacques Ellul, *The Technological Society*, trans. John Wilkinson (New York: Alfred A. Knopf, 1964).

107. Although numerous authors voiced this opinion earlier, Ellul provided a more profound argument. See Bernays, *Propaganda*, 12–13; Edward William Hummel and Keith Huntress, *The Analysis of Propaganda* (New York: Dryden Press, 1949), 3; Alfred McClung Lee, *How to Understand Propaganda*, 6.

108. Ellul, *Propaganda*, xiv–xv.

109. Ibid., 5.

110. Ibid., 20.

111. See Barzman, *The Florentine Academy*.

112. Following the publication of Ellul's book propaganda disappeared from school curricula in the United States and scholarly work on the subject declined. Ted J. Smith, introduction to Smith, ed., *Propaganda*, 2.

113. Ibid.

114. Karen Michels, "Transfer and Transformation: The German Period in American Art History," in Barron and Eckmann, eds., *Exiles and Emigrés*, 306.

115. Walter Friedlaender, *Caravaggio Studies* (Princeton: Princeton University Press, 1955), 122.

116. Paul Zanker, *The Power of Images in the Age of Augustus*, trans. Alan Shapiro (Ann Arbor: University of Michigan Press, 1988), 3.

117. Idem., *Augustus und die Macht der Bilder* (Munich: C. H. Beck, 1987), 159, cited in Andrew Wallace-Hadrill, "Rome's Cultural Revolution, review of *The Power of Images in the Age of Augustus*, by Paul Zanker," *Journal of Roman Studies* 79 (1989): 157–64. I am grateful to Michael Koortbojian for bringing this review to my attention.

118. Zanker, *The Power of Images*, 154, as pointed out by Wallace-Hadrill, "Rome's Cultural Revolution," 158.

119. On the isolation of Nazi art in German art history, in contrast to other disciplines, see Paul B. Jaskot, "Art and Politics in National Socialist Germany," review of *Auschwitz, 1270 to the Present*, by Deborah Dwork and Robert Jan Van Pelt, *Oxford Art Journal* 22 (1999): 176–84.

120. Jane DeRose Evans, *The Art of Persuasion: Political Propaganda from Aeneas to Brutus* (Ann Arbor: University of Michigan Press, 1992), 1, and n.1.

121. Carl C. Christensen, *Princes and Propaganda: Electoral Saxon Art of the Reformation* (Kirksville, Mo.: Sixteenth Century Journal Publishers, 1992), 2.

122. One scholar has argued that art that served as propaganda during and following the French Revolution was set against art. But in that case, a moral and socially useful art (propaganda) was positioned against the immoral and socially useless art of the ancien régime. Leith, *The Idea of Art as Propaganda*, 3–26, 143 ff.

123. John Bender and David E. Wellbery, "Rhetoricality: On the Modernist Return of Rhetoric," in idem, eds., *The Ends of Rhetoric: History, Theory, Practice* (Stanford: Stanford University Press, 1990), 13–15.

124. George L. Dillon, "Rhetoric," in *The Johns Hopkins Guide to Literary Theory and Criticism,* ed. Michael Groden and Martin Kreiswirth (Baltimore: Johns Hopkins University Press, 1994), 615–17. For the reconciliation of literature and rhetoric by English and French authors, see also Fumaroli, *L'Age de l'Eloquence,* 9–16.

125. Nietzsche lectured on rhetoric in 1872–74 at the University of Basel. Some of those notes were published in 1912 (and translated into French in 1971), but half were not published until the recent edition of Nietzsche's writings on rhetoric. Sander L. Gilman, Carole Blair, and David J. Parent, eds. and trans., *Friedrich Nietzsche on Rhetoric and Language* (New York: Oxford University Press, 1989), ix–xxi.

126. Ian Angus, "Learning to Stop: A Critique of General Rhetoric," in *The Critical Turn: Rhetoric and Philosophy in Postmodern Discourse,* ed. Ian Angus and Lenore Langsdorf (Carbondale and Edwardsville: Southern Illinois University Press, 1993), 178–79.

127. On philosophy and rhetoric, see especially Ijsseling, *Rhetoric and Philosophy;* on philosophy's absorption of rhetoric at its "death," see Sutton, "The Death of Rhetoric," 203–26.

128. Dilip Parameshwar Gaonkar, "Rhetoric and Its Double: Reflections on the Rhetorical Turn in the Human Sciences," in *The Rhetorical Turn: Invention and Persuasion in the Conduct of Inquiry,* ed. Herbert W. Simons (Chicago: University of Chicago Press, 1990), 341–66.

129. Bender and Wellbery, "Rhetoricality," 5.

130. Ibid., 38–39.

131. Jacques Derrida, "Plato's Pharmacy," in *Dissemination,* trans. Barbara Johnson (Chicago: University of Chicago Press, 1981), 61–171.

132. Christopher Norris, *Derrida* (Cambridge, Mass.: Harvard University Press, 1987), 42.

133. Ellul, *Propaganda,* xi.

134. Along these lines Fumaroli argues that Ernst-Robert Curtius's recuperation (in *Die Europaisches Literatur und mittelalterisches Latin* [Bonn, 1947]) of rhetoric as a vital principle of humanist culture could only have been produced after the experience of a far more barbarous form of propaganda under the Nazis. Fumaroli, *L'Age de l'Eloquence,* 11.

135. Ellul, *Propaganda,* 251.

136. For an emplotment of rhetoric's habitual fall into sophistical literary persuasion and reacquisition of logos as a tragic drama, see Sutton, "The Death of Rhetoric."

137. I am abusing a dream that Freud recounted for entirely different purposes in *The Interpretation of Dreams,* as discussed (and similarly abused) in Martin Jay, *Downcast Eyes: The Denigration of Vision in Twentieth-Century French Thought* (Berkeley: University of California Press, 1993), 329 ff.

CHAPTER 3. THE PROPAGANDIST

The second epigraph is from the necrologia of Lorenzo Tristano, quoted in Pietro Pirri, *Giovanni Tristano e i primordi della architettura gesuitica* (Rome: Institutum Historicum Societatis Iesu, 1955), doc. XLV, 258.

1.　Benedetto Croce, *Il Seicento e il settecento*, vol. 2 of *La letteratura italiana* (Bari: Editori Laterza, 1957), 3, 20–21. Croce here restates views advanced in two important articles: "Controriforma," *La Critica* 22 (1924): 321–33; "Il concetto del barocco," *La Critica* 23 (1925): 129–43. The phrase "il 'secentismo' o 'barocchismo' non è altro che il 'gesuitismo nell'arte'" is actually a citation of L. Settimbrini, *Lezioni di Letteratura italiana*, 1875.

2.　Stefano della Torre and Richard Schofield, *Pellegrino Tibaldi architetto e il S. Fedele di Milano: Invenzione e costruzione di una chiesa esemplare* (Como: Nodo Libri, 1994).

3.　Rudolf Wittkower, "Problems of the Theme," in Wittkower and Jaffe, eds., *Baroque Art*, 12.

4.　Exceptions include Richard Bösel, who undertook research on the Italian Jesuit buildings precisely because they offered a historical corpus of a cohesive organization. See his *Jesuitenarchitektur in Italien (1540–1773). Teil I. Die Baudenkmäler der römischen und der neapolitanischen Ordensprovinz*, 2 vols. (Vienna: Österreichischen Akademie der Wissenschaft, 1986). Some synthetic remarks are made in an important article: idem, "Tipologie e tradizioni architettoniche nell'edilizia della Compagnia di Gesù," in *L'architettura della Compagnia di Gesù in Italia XVI–XVIII secolo: Atti del Convegno, Milano, Centro Culturale S. Fedele, 24–27 Ottobre 1990*, ed. Luciano Patetta and Stefano della Torre (Milan: Marietti, 1992), 13.

5.　Diego Angeli, "I gesuiti e la loro influenza nell'arte," *Nuova Antologia di Lettere, Scienze ed Arti* 138 (1908): 208.

6.　Luciano Patetta, "Le chiese della Compagnia di Gesù come tipe: Complessità e sviluppo," in *Storia e tipologia: Cinque saggi sull'architettura del passato* (Milan: Clup, 1989), 163.

7.　Michelangelo's famous freedom to determine the program of the Sistine Chapel ceiling program was unusual. To cite one contrary example, Maria de' Medici made a stringent contract with Rubens for the Luxembourg Palace cycle. Winner writes that concerning the political content, the queen restricted Rubens's freedom. Matthias Winner, "The Orb as the Symbol of the State in the Pictorial Cycle by Rubens Depicting the Life of Maria de' Medici," in Ellenius, ed., *Iconography, Propaganda, and Legitimation*, 63–86.

8.　Vincenzo Scamozzi, *L'idea dell'architettura universale* (Venice, 1615), 17. Scamozzi "seems to have been the first to see or at least to fomulate the political ambivalence of the architect." Hanno-Walter Kruft, *Storia delle teorie architettoniche: Da Vitruvio al settecento* (Rome and Bari: Editori Laterza, 1988), 116.

9.　In postwar Italy, Cesare Brandi, Giulio Carlo Argan, and Lionello Venturi debated whether Italian art should express a national or international identity, and whether through abstraction or figuration. By the end of the 1950s several critics abandoned their earlier belief in the moral possibility for art, and of collective expression, embracing the individual as the focus of artistic creation. See the excellent article by Marcia E. Vetrocq, "National Style and the Agenda for Abstract Painting in Post-War Italy," *Art History* 12 (1989): 448–71. For a sustained rant against the obscuring of the individual in architectural histories from Pugin to Pevsner, see David Watkin, *Morality and Architecture: The Development of a Theme in Architectural History and Theory from the Gothic Revival to the Modern Movement* (Oxford: Clarendon Press, 1977).

10.　See, above all, Pirri, *Giovanni Tristano*, and idem, *Giuseppe Valeriano S.I. architetto e pittore (1542–1596)*, (Rome: Institutum Historicum Societatis Iesu, 1970). Much material on Jesuit architects has been amassed in Gauvin Alexander Bailey, *Art on the Jesuit Missions in Asia and Latin America, 1542–1773* (Toronto: University of Toronto Press, 1999), which treats primarily remote missions, where the choice of Jesuit or non-Jesuit architect had more to do with available skill and labor than external patrons and their architectural desires.

11. Francis Haskell (*Patrons and Painters,* 64–66) came out strongly for the Jesuits' powerlessness before their princely patrons (and their anxiety about it) because of their lack of resources. Later he made reference to the dependence of "docile artists" on their Jesuit patrons. Francis Haskell, "The Role of Patrons: Baroque Style Changes," in Wittkower and Jaffe, eds., *Baroque Art,* 52. The desire for the vault is the patron's, but the idea for it is attributed to Vignola in Clare Robertson, *Il Gran Cardinale: Alessandro Farnese, Patron of the Arts* (New Haven: Yale University Press, 1992), 189. The issue of Jesuit concern with aesthetics over practical aspects of the design is given further treatment in idem, "Two Farnese Cardinals and the Question of Jesuit Taste," in O'Malley et al., eds., *The Jesuits,* 134–47.

12. Robertson, *Il Gran Cardinale,* 144.

13. Manfredo Tafuri, "J. Barozzi da Vignola e la crisi del manierismo a Roma," *Bollettino del Centro Internazionale di studi di architettura Andrea Palladio* 9 (1967): 394.

14. See Wolff, *The Social Production of Art.*

15. Although individual style has been less theorized than regional and period styles (see, for example, the essays from a variety of disciplinary perspectives in Berel Lang, ed., *The Concept of Style,* rev. ed. [Ithaca: Cornell University Press, 1987]), it remains a cornerstone of the discipline. In summarizing the state of Italian Baroque studies in 1962, Wittkower wrote: "The monograph has always been and will always be one of the primary requirements of our discipline. There is perhaps no better way to consolidate the subtle relationship between the artist/creator and his creation, to affront the evaluation of individual works, of the circumstances in which they were commissioned, of that complex game of give and take which links the artist to his surroundings." Wittkower, "Il barocco in Italia," 320–21.

16. Schapiro, "Style," in *Theory and Philosophy of Art,* 65. For further reflections on the individual and formalism, see T. J. Clark and Charles Reeve, "An Art History without Endings: A Conversation with T. J. Clark," *Documents* 18 (2000): 15 ff.

17. New studies of prominent Quattrocento artist-monks reconsider the role of the religious vocation in artistic production. See William Hood, *Fra Angelico at San Marco* (London: BCA; New Haven: Yale University Press, 1993); Meghan Holmes, *Fra Filippo Lippi: The Carmelite Painter* (New Haven: Yale University Press, 1999).

18. See chapter 1, note 112, for Joseph Braun's studies of Jesuit architecture. This view is echoed by Pirri, *Giovanni Tristano,* 160–62, and Sandro Benedetti, *Fuori dal classicismo: Sintetismo, tipologia, ragione nell'architettura del Cinquecento* (Roma: Multigrafica, 1984).

19. The argument was substantiated first and best by Braun, followed by François de Dainville, "La légende du style jésuite," *Études* 287 (1955): 14–15, in an article reviewing Galassi Paluzzi's *Storia segreta* and Pierre Moissy's *Les Eglises des Jésuites de l'Assistance de France* that argued for the French character of Jesuit churches in France over their "Jesuit" character. Drawing from documents that speak of architecture as conforming

to "nostra consuetudine" or "il modo che usa la compagnia," Ackerman argued that the Jesuit Style exists but in so general a sense that it does not affect the significant forms of architecture. James Ackerman, "The Gesù in the Light of Contemporary Church Design," in Wittkower and Jaffe, eds., *Baroque Art,* 26–27. For Claire Roberston (in O'Malley et al., eds., *The Jesuits,* 14) the Jesuit modus nostrus is not "a specific architectural style" but a "mode of operating and an attitude to a degree of austerity in many of their churches. The priorities were speed and economy of building." See also similar views expressed in various essays in Patetta and della Torre, eds., *L'architettura della Compagnia di Gesù in Italia.*

20. I am in sympathy with some of the observations of Angela Marino, "L'idea di tradizione e il concetto di modernità nell'architettura della Compagnia di Gesù," in Patetta and della Torre, eds., *L'architettura della Compagnia di Gesù in Italia,* 53–56. Marino argues for the "modo nostro" as an organization of Jesuit architecture, likening it to Jesuit education, which she characterizes as rational and technical rather than ideological. Here we differ; I would argue that even when content is not dictated, technique itself is the ideological substance of both activities.

21. For Bösel's publications, see chapter 5, note 3.

22. Sandro Benedetti (*Fuori dal classicismo,* 68–70) reached the same conclusion but pointed to typology as key to a Jesuit architecture. Giosi Amirante, "La pianta centrale nelle chiese della provincia napoletana," in Patetta and della Torre, eds., *L'architettura della Compagnia di Gesù in Italia,* 125–30, concurs.

23. For instance, General Aquaviva wrote to the p. Malevolti, provincial of Bologna, about the vexed planning for the church in Mantua: "Et *perché noi non pretendiamo altro che il maggior servitio di Dio et far cosa che riesca,* et perché anco V.R. istessa con il sito in mano et disegno mostri a chi bisognerà che non si poteva altrimenti, desidero che si faccia quest'ultima diligenza, secondo l'incluso foglio . . ." Letter, 25 April 1592, quoted in Pietro Pirri and Pietro Di Rosa, "Il P. Giovanni de Rosis (1538–1610) e lo sviluppo dell'edilizia gesuitica," *Archivum Historicum Societatis Iesu* 44 (1975): 99, doc. 8 (emphasis mine).

24. Although the Benedictine order (which produced the plan of St. Gall) did not require conformity to an ideal plan, the rule itself inspired the development of a layout that engendered a "standardized approach" (see *Dictionary of Art,* s.v. "Monastery"). A "mendicant type" of architecture has been widely recognized, although it seems that none of the orders took active measures to centralize design. The evidence for building legislation is as follows. In 1134 the Cistercian order passed rules regarding the poverty of its buildings but did not exert centralized control over design. In 1260 the Franciscans issued similar statutes for their churches but did not require approval for plans. Wolfgang Braunfels, *Monasteries of Western Europe: The Architecture of the Orders* (Princeton: Princeton University Press, 1972), doc. XI, 243, doc. XIV, 246. The Dominicans legislated humility in their architecture (1220), limited scale and the use of stone ribs (1228), and prohibited painted or sculpted decoration (1252). The rules on scale were loosened in 1298 as congregations grew. See *Dictionary of Art,* s.v. "Dominican Order." For a brief survey of the building practices of the Counter-Reformation orders, see Richard Bösel, "Typus und Tradition in der Baukultur gegenreformatorischer Orden," *Römische historische Mitteilungen* 31 (1989): 240–42.

25. Lucas, *Landmarking.*

26. Mario Scaduto, "La corrispondenza dei primi gesuiti e le poste italiane," *AHSI* 19 (1950): 237–53.

27. Acta in Congregationis Generalis I, 1558, Decretum 34, "De ratione aedificiorum." Excerpted in Isabella Balestreri, "L'architettura negli scritti della Compagnia di Gesù," in Luciano Patetta et al., eds., *L'architettura della Compagnia di Gesù in Italia XVI–XVIII sec. Catalogo della mostra* (Brescia: Grafo, 1990), 20–21.

28. Canones secundae Congregationis, canon 9 in the Institutum S.I., 2:531, cited in Jean Vallery-Radot and Edmond Lamalle, *Le recueil de plans d'édifices de la Compagnie di Jésus conservé a la Bibliothèque Nationale de Paris* (Rome: Institutum Historicum Societatis Iesu, 1960), 6 n.2.

29. ARSI, Epp. Comm. B, fol. 52, cited in Vallery-Radot and Lamalle, *Le recueil de plans d'édifices de la Compagnie di Jésus*, 6*. Several times in the seventeenth century the generals renewed their order that two sets of drawings be sent to Rome: one to be returned to the building site with the approval and alterations recorded and one to be preserved in the Roman archive. See ibid., 14*–15*.

30. On the role of the consiliarius aedilicius, see Pirri, *Giovanni Tristano,* 40–44; Pirri and Di Rosa, "Il P. Giovanni de Rosis," 20–23.

31. Giuseppe Valeriano, "Informatione delle fabriche. Contra nostros aedificatores," quoted in full in Pirri, *Giuseppe Valeriano,* doc. XVII, 2, 387–92 and 219–23. Valeriano had already made many of these observations in his report of 1579 on the progress of projects in Spain. Pirri, *Giuseppe Valeriano,* doc. II, A, 238–46.

32. Letter from Rome to the rector of Loreto, 26 September 1561, excerpted in Pirri, *Giovanni Tristano,* 162.

33. "Mà perche à ben condurre una tal opera, vi si richiede, non solo particolare attentione, e sollecitudine; mà anco un riflesso di prudenza, per non sbagliare nelle Cose essentiali; potendo seguire in progresso errori irreparabili; ò quando si potessero riparare, ciò non si eseguirebbe, salvo con eccessivo dispendio, e forse tale, che verrebbe ad incagliare l'impresa, in vece di ridurla al suo Compimento; perciò prima di dare il sudetto principio, resta spediente di esaminare seriamente il tutto, col parere anco de più esperti, per potere indi operare con sicurezza." "Memoria circa laborem suscipiendam," 29 December 1694, Archivum Romanum Societatis Iesu (hereafter ARSI), Rom 140, fols. 113r–v. Full transcription in Evonne Levy, "A Canonical Work of an Uncanonical Era: Re-Reading the Chapel of St. Ignatius in the Gesù of Rome (1695–1699)" (Ph.D. diss., Princeton University, 1993), 428–33.

34. Valeriano, "Informatione delle fabriche," in Pirri, *Giuseppe Valeriano,* 389, 391.

35. Ibid., 390, 391–92.

36. The dual meaning of the term in Italian is known from at least the fourteenth century. *Dizionario etimologico italiano* (Florence: G. Barbèra Editore/Università degli Studi, 1968), s.v. "edificare." But it derives from a metaphor of Paul's (building a temple in the soul), reworked by hagiographers. Cynthia Hahn, *Portrayed on the Heart: Narrative Effect in Pictorial Lives of Saints from the Tenth through the Thirteenth Century* (Berkeley: University of California Press, 2001), 34–35. For Michelangelo's (and Vasari's) play with edification around the construction of the dome of St. Peter's, see Paul Barolsky, *Michelan-*

gelo's Nose: A Myth and Its Maker (University Park: Pennsylvania State University Press, 1990), 49–51.

37. Letter from Ignatius of Loyola to Alphonso Roman, cited in Lucas, *Landmarking*, 152.

38. On the preference for Jesuit architects and their formation, see Benedetti, *Fuori dal classicismo*, esp. 72; Ugo Baldini, "La formazione degli architetti gesuiti (secoli XVI–XVII)," chap. 3 in *Saggi sulla cultura della Compagnia di Gesù (secoli XVI–XVIII)* (Padua: Cleup, 2000).

39. Giuseppe Valeriano (L'Aquila 1542–Naples 1596), who entered the order at thirty-two years of age, trained as a painter with a minor follower of Raphael, Pompeo Cesura. According to Bellori's *postille* to Baglione's *Le vite de' pittori, scultori et architetti* [1642], Valeriano was an autodidact in architecture. Pirri, *Giuseppe Valeriano*, doc. XVIII, no. 4, n.2.

40. The first study to posit the formative impact of a Jesuit spirituality on the figurative arts (specifically Bernini) was Walther Weibel, *Jesuitismus und Barockskulptur in Rom* (Strassburg: J.H. E. Heitz, 1909). More recently, see Heinrich Pfeiffer, S.J., "Pozzo e la spiritualità della Compagnia di Gesù," in *Andrea Pozzo*, ed. Alberta Battisti (Milan: Luni Editore, 1996), 13–17.

41. For the legislation of obedience at the Accademia del Disegno in Florence and the challenge to traditional accounts of the Accademia as expression of the possibility of self-determination, see Barzman, *The Florentine Academy*, 39–42.

42. A. Lynn Martin, *The Jesuit Mind: The Mentality of an Elite in Early Modern France* (Ithaca: Cornell University Press, 1988), 30. See also Joseph de Guibert, *The Jesuits: Their Spiritual Doctrine and Practice; A Historical Study*, ed. George E. Ganss, S.J., trans. William J. Young (Chicago: Institute of Jesuit Sources, 1964), 90–93.

43. George E. Ganss, S.J., ed. and trans., *The Constitutions of the Society of Jesus by Saint Ignatius of Loyola* (St. Louis: Institute of Jesuit Sources, 1970), no. 547, 248–49.

44. Michelet pounded on Jesuit obedience in a lecture of 1843: "If we could believe that a faculty long time *swaddled* could ever become active, it would be sufficient to place side by side with this wheedling expression the much franker word which they [the Jesuits] have been so bold as to write in their regulations, which indicates pretty strongly the kind of obedience they require, and what man will be in their hands; –*a stick, a corpse!*" Michelet and Quinet, *Des Jésuites*, 28–29. See also comments throughout Quinet's lectures, esp. 94–95. On nineteenth-century views of Jesuit obedience, see Cubitt, *The Jesuit Myth*, 281.

45. Ignatius of Loyola, "Letter to the Members of the Society in Portugal on Perfect Obedience," in W. W. Meissner, S.J., *Ignatius of Loyola: The Psychology of a Saint* (New Haven: Yale University Press, 1992), Appendix B, 409.

46. Ibid., Appendix B, 413.

47. Letter from general Thyrsio Gonzalez to rector Ardelio della Bella, 23 November 1699, cited in Bösel, *Jesuitenarchitektur in Italien*, 1: doc. 13, 57.

48. In a report to the curia in Rome Valeriano railed against the overly ambitious and incompetent design work ("arte malentendida") of p. Bartolomeo Bustamante (1501–70), in charge of several major building projects (Granada, Sigueros, Sevilla). Pirri, *Giuseppe Valeriano*, 29–32; see also Valeriano's report (1579) on his tour of construction in Andalusia and the shorter version in his "Informatione delle fabriche," in ibid., doc. II, 6, 238–47, and doc. XVII, 2, 389–90.

49. Letter from general Gian Paolo Oliva to the provincial of Naples, 5 May 1681, cited in Bösel, *Jesuitenarchitektur in Italien,* 1: doc. 13, 360; see also 1: 358 and n.18.

50. Letter from general Franz Retz to vice rector Giuseppe Vanuzzi, 7 September 1739, cited in ibid., 1: doc. 10, 28.

51. Letter from general Michelangelo Tamburini to rector Salvatore Pastina, 27 September 1717, cited in ibid., 1: doc. 14, 496.

52. Letter from general Gian Paolo Oliva to rector Giacinto Toppi, 5 June 1667, cited in ibid., 1: doc. 6, 513.

53. Letter from p. Gilles François de Gottignies, 16 December 1668, cited in Vallery-Radot and Lamalle, *Le recueil de plans d'édifices de la Compagnie di Jésus,* no. 60, 18.

54. The inscription on the plan is cited in ibid., no. 117, 34. See also Adriano Ghisetti Giavarina, "Tre insediamenti della Compagnia in Abruzzo," in Patetta and della Torre, eds., *L'architettura della Compagnia di Gesù in Italia,* 102–3.

55. Letter from p. François de Gottignies, 25 March 1679, cited in Vallery-Radot and Lamalle, *Le recueil de plans d'édifices de la Compagnie di Jésus,* no. 276, 74.

56. For other examples, see Bösel, "Tipologie e tradizioni," 16–18.

57. Fr. Carlo Mauro Bonacina, "Diligenze fatte per l'elezzione del Disegno p la nuova cappella del N.S.P. Ignazio dà farsi in questa Chiesa del Giesù di Roma," ARSI, Rom 140, fols. 46r–66r. Full transcription in Levy, "A Canonical Work of an Uncanonical Era," 526–47.

58. Fr. Carlo Mauro Bonacina, "Ristretto dell'avvenuto nella fabrica della Cappella del nostro santo padre Ignatio nella Chiesa della Casa Professa della Compagnia di GIESÙ di Roma con l'aggiunta d'un Istruzzione per chi volesse fare un opera S^(im)ile," ARSI, Rom 140, fols. 3r–41v. Full transcription in Levy, "A Canonical Work of an Uncanonical Era," 494–525.

59. "il P. Generale il dì 25. Di Luglio del 1695. Ne dichiarò Soprintendente il Pr'e Pier Francesco Orta, Proc.re Gen'le, con cui se l'avesse ad'intendere il Fr. Bonacina. Con ciò mise in salvo la sostanza della già presa risoluzione, e solo le cambiò l'apparenza; poiche in tal guisa il titolo era del P. Orta, mà il maneggio del Bonacina." It should be kept in mind that this is Bonacina's view. "Ristretto," fol. 12v.

60. "Che non sia di corto intendimento, mà sia accorto ed avveduto, di natura un po' bilioso, mà che si sappia moderare, altrimenti sarà ingannato, e fuggito, come intrattabile, e se sarà troppo flemmatico, non la finirà mai." "Metodo, che potrebbe osservarsi da chi volesse fabbricare una simil' Opera," in "Ristretto," fol. 34r–41v. This section is transcribed in Vittorio De Feo, *Andrea Pozzo: Architettura e illusione* (Rome: Officina Edizioni, 1988), 103.

61. "scudi 2. Conti alli copisti, che hanno fatto due copie dell'Istoria eseguita, p li pareri, p l'elezzione del Disegno &." ARSI, Chiesa del Gesù 2056, fol. 8.

62. "Diligenze," fol. 62r.

63. The Chapel of St. Ignatius documents, preserved in ARSI, have been studied and given different inflection by the following authors. The richest account of the intrigue surrounding the proceedings is Pio Pecchiai, *Il Gesù di Roma* (Rome: Società Grafica Romana, 1952), chap. 6. The first art historical account, with a focus on design development, is Bernhard Kerber, *Andrea Pozzo* (Berlin: Walter de Gruyter, 1971), chap. 7. Both Pecchiai and Kerber quote from documents but did not publish more than fragments of the archival corpus. Some significant documents related to construction appear with-

out significant commentary in De Feo, *Andrea Pozzo: Architettura e illusione.* The archival material was first given comprehensive treatment and the documents transcribed in extenso in this author's dissertation, "A Canonical Work of an Uncanonical Era." The latter, revised and including full transcriptions of the documentation of the chapel, including those cited below, is to be published by the Jesuit Institutum Historicum. Since then, two Italian scholars have run through some of the documents again in fragmentary form: Roberta Dal Mas, "L'altare di sant'Ignazio nel Gesù di Roma: Cronache del progetto," in *Andrea Pozzo,* ed. Vittorio De Feo and Vittorio Martinelli (Milan: Electa, 1996), 144–55 (this publication is distinguished by the author's precise plans of the chapel); Maurizio Gargano, "L'altare di sant'Ignazio nel Gesù di Roma: Committenza e cantiere," in ibid., 156–67. Given the excellence of Pecchiai's and Kerber's accounts, the contributions of the latter publications are modest.

64. For a thorough account of the fragmentary evidence of the early tombs of Ignatius with previous literature, see Levy, "A Canonical Work of an Uncanonical Era," chap. 1.

65. The discussion of Oliva's master plan that follows is treated extensively in Evonne Levy, "The Institutional Memory of the Roman Gesù: Plans for Renovation of the 1670s by Carlo Fontana, Pietro da Cortona and Luca Berrettini," *Römisches Jahrbuch der Bibliotheca Hertziana* 33 (1999/2000): 373–426.

66. The documents on the revival of the plan were first published in Pietro Tacchi Venturi, "Di una mutazione architettonica ideata nel 1692 per la tribuna del Gesù in Roma," *Atti del Primo Congresso Nazionale di Studi Romani* 1 (1929): 641–60. See Levy, "The Institutional Memory of the Roman Gesù," for further discussion.

67. For the documents concerning the cessation of rights, see De Feo, *Andrea Pozzo: Architettura e illusione,* 79–82.

68. "In questo giorno il fratello Andrea Pozzo della n'ra Comp.a hà presentato al M.to R.do P. N'ro Tyrso Gonzalez Generale, un Disegno fatto per d.a Cappella, supplicando sua Paternità di farlo esaminare per emendarlo, e migliorarlo dove fosse di bisogno." "Diligenze," fol. 46r.

69. "Diligenze," fols. 46r–v. Pecchiai, *Il Gesù,* 153.

70. The design can be pieced together from Pozzo's note accompanying his submission (ARSI, FG 494, fol. 43), comments on it by numerous Jesuits and non-Jesuits reported in the "Diligenze" (fols. 46v–50r), the letters submitted by p. Filippo Bonanni (ARSI, Rom 140, fol. 146), p. Guglielmo Hagheman (ARSI, Rom 140, fol. 145r), p. Antonio Baldigiani (ARSI, Rom 140, fols. 148r–150v) as well as the summary of all of the remarks (ARSI, Rom 140, fol. 144), and the report on the latter in the "Diligenze" (fol. 50).

71. "Diligenze," fol. 48r.

72. "Nota d'alcuni Corpi Santi, e reliquie insigni, che del continuo stanno sopra gli Altari." ARSI, Rom 140, fols. 72r–73v.

73. Bonacina reports the consultation with signor abbate Piazza in the "Diligenze," fol. 49v, and with the papal master of ceremonies signor Fanti in the "Ristretto," fols. 10v–11r.

74. "Osservazioni fatte per ordine de PP. Superiori sul Disegno per altro nobile del fr. Pozzo, di alcuni inconvenienti . . . ," in the "Diligenze," fols. 49v–50v.

75. In a note dated 26 January 1695 Bonanni wrote: "Il disegno è fatto con degradatione prospetica, onde non si può formare pieno giuditio delle parti, proportioni, e misure di

tutto l'ornato, e può accadere che molte cose poste in veduta degradata nel disegno non disdicano, dove che nel reale potranno riuscire sproportionati fra di loro, e di brutta apparenza: stimo per tanto che prima di porsi in modello reale, sene debba fare un disegno geometrico con le proportioni corrispondenti alle reali fitere [?]." ARSI, Rom 140, fol. 146. Bonacina summarizes this recommendation as follows: "Che essendo fatto con degradatione prospetica si può m.to errare nel giudicarlo, e che stimarebbe bene se ne formasse un modello." "Diligenze," fol. 51r.

76. ARSI, Rom 140, fol. 148, and Bonacina's summary of his remarks in the "Diligenze," fol. 51r.

77. "Diligenze," fol. 51v.

78. "Diligenze," fol. 52r.

79. "Ristretto," fol. 9v.

80. "Diligenze," fol. 52r.

81. "Diligenze," fols. 52r–v.

82. "si sarebbero impiegati, perche fosse assistita di proposito dall'Architetto l'opera." "Diligenze," fol. 52v.

83. ARSI Rom 140, fols. 154r–155r. Letter quoted in part in Pecchiai, *Il Gesù*, 159–60.

84. "Si taccia doltre con questi Personaggi degni d'ogni riguardo il giudicio di nri Vechi Assist. Consulti e periti. Ricevuto l'ord.e espostomi da VP.tà di far vedere da P[ad]ri di casa primarij li disegni e portasi li stessi disegni d mia . . . [?] tre classi de Pre Assistenti di Pri Consultori di casa e da frelli di qualche peritia di tal materia (tutte come pre osservasi ad alon [?]) ed corsero alla universale approvazione di tal disegno dato per il migliore dalle Personaggi li P[ad]ri i Frelli non furono nè Mri nè partiali del disegn.re e con rivitudine [?] soma i con desid.i della yta [?] del S.o Pre e di VP.ta." ARSI, Rom 140, fol. 152.

85. "Hò voluto udire a p:e il parere d'altri Periti e se[g]narò il giuditio loro circa li disegni proposti e particolar.e di quello del nro domestico disegnatore e si come hanno preferito l'eletto da Personaggi, così hanno manifestati li difetti graviss.i dell'altro." ARSI, Rom 140, fol. 152.

86. "Il p.o punto della poca intelligenza e contrario alla fama publica in Roma di tali personaggi, di quali la maggior parte, nè sanno per dire modesta.ti al pari di primi professori di Roma e tal fama non corre." ARSI, Rom 140, fol. 152.

87. "Si è mostrato al P. Giulio Balbi Assistente d'Italia, disse piacergli il Disegno, mà, che il suo parere l'appoggiava à quello degli Architetti, e della Professione." "Diligenze," fol. 48r.

88. "Il P. Francesco Guarino Segretario dopo havere veduto il Disegno disse, che il dare giudizio s.a L'Architettura non era di sua professione, mà che in ordine alla quantità de bronzi era di parere, che si tenesse la mira alquanto bassa per non competere con S. Pietro. . . ." "Diligenze," fol. 47v.

89. "Diligenze," fol. 47r.

90. "Diligenze," fol. 49r.

91. "Il S.e Cav.re Fontana, alla presenza delli sud.ti trè cioè SS.ri Lavazza, Marcello, e Tedeschi, e delli ffr. Ruffini, e Cappone visitò due volte tutti Li Disegni, cioè Li 3. del sig.re Cipriani, quello del S.r Origone, e varij del fr. Pozzo, e poi portatosi avanti l'ultimo modello si fermò lungam.te à considerarlo, e disse: *questo è quello si deve fare, Li PP. non si partano dà questo, accorda ottimam.te. col resto del Cappellone, è ben proportionato* &. con m.te

altre Lodi. Si pregò à dire il suo sentimento, se c'era, che levare, aggiungere, ò mutare, non desiderandosi altro, che il bene dell'opera, accio possa riuscire d'ogni perfezzione, rispose. *Li due pilastri sotto le due statue laterali fanno accuto troppo gagliardo in fuori li vorrei più in drittura, del resto stiano contenti li P'ri di questo, e non cerchino altro,* e l'andò di nuovo riconoscendo per partes, e confermò, che quello meritava dà mettersi in esecutione, aggiungendo: *se il P. Pozzi fosse all'Indie bisognarebbe mandarlo à chiamare, e quando non havesse fatto altro, che quella Cupola maravigliosa di S. Ignatio bastarebbe, p non haver dubbio delle sue opere.* Finito questo Discorso allora se gli nominarono gl' Autori de Disegni ad uno p uno, *dicendo questi trè sono del S.r Cipriani, questo d'un tal S.r Origone, qsti altri del P. Pozzo:* mentre si stava discorrendo ritornò à Casa N.P., e à sua P.tà confermò quello che haveva qui sopra detto, e poi hà dato anche il suo parere in scritto del tenore seguente cioè." "Diligenze," fol. 55r.

92. "Il Fr. Pozzo, fatto già venir in Roma ancor egli dalla Provincia di Milano, religioso non men d'arte, che di virtù singolare, mà umilissimo, e non curante di comparire, che non sapea spacciar le sue cose, nè criticate le difendea, in qualche stima di buon Pittore, mà non in credito di grande Architetto." "Ristretto," fols. 9v–10r.

93. "A di 12. d.o Il S.r Gio. Antonio de Rossi confermò il suo parere e disse che quando i PP. si fossero sodisfatti nel fare visitare il Disegno, il fr. Pozzo dovea poi essere l'Architetto, non solo p essere della Comp.a, e di gusto del P. Gnale, mà come meritevole, e capace." "Diligenze," fol. 54r.

94. Undated note [before 31 May 1695] from Andrea Pozzo to Carlo Mauro Bonacina, transcribed in Pecchiai, *Il Gesù di Roma,* 160–61.

95. Note from Andrea Pozzo to Luigi Restori. ARSI, Rom 140, fol. 169. Quoted in Pecchiai, *Il Gesù di Roma,* 161–62.

96. Note from Carlo Mauro Bonacina to Andrea Pozzo, 31 May 1695. ARSI, Rom 140, fol. 164r.

97. Ignatius of Loyola, Letter to the members of the Society in Portugal on perfect obedience, in Meissner, *Ignatius of Loyola,* Appendix B, 410.

98. After collecting letters from architects and Jesuits electing Pozzo's design, the general held a "Consulta Generale" with the secretary and the assistants of France, Italy, Germany, and Portugal. Together they decided to proceed with Pozzo's design on *carta turchina,* subject to the changes recommended to the drawing and the terra-cotta model, 2 June 1695, "Diligenze," fol. 62r.

99. "Precisando nel mio parere stimo che essendosi Nro Padre sufficient.te trastenuto il far considerare li Disegni debba omni na:te fermarsi il quello del F. Pozzo con la sola approva:ne del Caval: Fontana, il quale potendo essere l'unico che potesse far cosa Bona per questa Cappella; Impegnare sopra tal Disegno per mezzo d'Una sua sì decorosa approvatione sarà sempre assistente per Una felice condotta di essa Cappella. Come seguì col Baciccia proposto et approvato dal Caval. Bernini al P. Oliva, il quale senza far considerar Disegni ad altri sotto la pura Direzzione et Approva:ne del Caval. Bernini fece operar il Baciccia tutto.

Questo è un vantaggio mirabile ch'hà questo Disegno che non havrà veruno altro d'Autori di credito, il quale non vorrà operare sotto la Direttione del Fontana ne pure di Nro Padre, che non sarà più Padrone di esso, una volta che gl'li havrà approvato." "Parere del P. [Filippo] Guarnieri sopra li Disegni Della Cappella di S. Ignatio," n.d., ARSI, Rom 140, fol. 171.

100. An undated list of "Punti da consultare col Sig Caval.e Fontana" must date to around this time. It includes eight points, including a visit to the model to determine stone choices as well as practical points of procedure for erecting scaffolding, moving tombs, and proceeding with construction. ARSI, Rom 140, fols. 183r–v.

101. A note written by Bonacina dated 15 September 1695 explains that Fontana was being solicited by "questi Padrazi" who wanted to have him change, that is to say, to impede the project. ARSI, Rom 140, fol. 175r.

102. "Caris. Fllo Sospendiamo l'andar dal Fontana, tiramo avanti il modello, e finiamolo per non metter in maggior impegno e poi lo lascieremo dire. Se Nostro Pre vorrà che io dipenda da un tal Architetto non sincero che sotto pretesto di dar pareri vol ficcarsi dentro per compagno et anco escludermi affatto, e meglio che ad esso dia tutta l'incombenza, e me buttino nel mare che subito ossava si gran tempesta. Che havete fin hora patito e sarete per patire. Parlatene vi prego al Pre Gen.le et informatelo di quanto passa, et esponete la mia renuntia che volentieri l'offerischo nelle mani della volontà di Dio di S. Ignatio e de Superiori. Non mando dunque il Bilietto al Fontana ne io hoggi mi posso muovere perche e cresciuto il mio male del piede. A Dio Pozzo." Note from Pozzo to Bonacina, n.d. ARSI, Rom 140, fol. 217. Previously published by Robert Enggass, "The Altar-Rail for St. Ignatius's Chapel in the Gesù di Roma," *Art Bulletin* 116 (1974): 189.

103. "Ristretto," fols. 11r–v. Quoted in Pecchiai, *Il Gesù di Roma*, 152.

104. "Ristretto," fol. 12v.

105. ARSI, Rom 140, fol. 229, records the names of visitors to the model and their comments. A summary of observations on the model, mostly comments not found in the previous documents, is in ARSI, Rom 140, fols. 225r–226v.

106. "Ristretto," fols. 20v–21r.

107. See the description of the competition in the "Ristretto," fols. 21r–22r.

108. "Andovi egli una Domenica mattina col Fr. Pozzo el Cardinale gli dichiarò la pena, che sentiva per le cattive nuove, che correan per Roma d'un' opera di tanta spesa, e di tanto impegno, sì mal maneggiata, e con sì poca speranza di riuscimento pari all'espettazione, che se ne avea; e ciò in una Città, ove vengono ad imparare i primi virtuosi del Mondo, ed ove si [?] vogliono criticate eziando le opere più perfette." "Ristretto," fol. 17r.

109. "Ristretto," fol. 18v.

110. "Ristretto," fol. 13r.

111. P. Filippo Bonanni (ARSI, Rom 140, fol. 156r); p. Giovanni Francesco Durazzi (ARSI, Rom 140, fol. 157); p. Francesco Eschinardi (ARSI, Rom 140, fol. 161r); p. Francesco Antonio Febei (ARSI, Rom 140, fol. 162); p. Antonio Baldigiani (ARSI, Rom 140, fol. 167); p. Filippo Guarnieri (ARSI, Rom 140, fol. 171); and lay architects Matthia de'Rossi (ARSI, Rom 140, fol. 181v), Carlo Fontana (ARSI, Rom 140, fol. 173r), and Giovanni Antonio de'Rossi (ARSI, Rom 140, fol. 179r) who, uniquely, left no further recommendations in writing.

112. "N.P. sentito qsto parere disse, che si formasse un modello di creta sopra detto disegno emendando, levando, accrescendo, ò mutando secondo ciò si giudicava meglio, e qsto, à fine li potesse fare poi il Disegno purgato dà sottoscriversi e passare al modello di legno p dare l'ultima mano à qsta Idea." "Diligenze," fol. 53v.

113. "Sugo, ò sia ristretto di tutti li pareri dati da Periti si d'esterni, come nostri sopra l'ul-

timo modello, che possa servire p fare con sodisfatt.e il modello grande di Legno." "Dili-genze," fols. 6or–6ir.

114. ARSI, Rom 140, fol. 229.

115. Tod Marder, *Bernini: The Art of Architecture* (New York: Abbeville Press, 1998), 138.

116. For a rare analysis of the structure of text and image in the posters, see Andreas Fleischer and Frank Kämpfer, "The Political Poster in the Third Reich," in Taylor and van der Will, eds., *The Nazification of Art,* 183–203. They note that it would be possible to distinguish between hands in Nazi posters, but they themselves did not think it important to do so.

117. Marla Stone, *The Patron State: Culture and Politics in Fascist Italy* (Princeton: Princeton University Press, 1998).

118. Note the difference between Pozzo, who renounced the project, and Borromini, who was relieved of the Oratorio project and later chafed at the obedience expected of him by the Oratorians: "Prego dunq[ue] chi leggerà queste mie dicerie à riflettere, che ho havuto à servire una Cong[regatio]ne di animi così rimessi che nell'ornare mi hanno tenuto le mani, e consequentem[en]te mi è convenuto in più luoghi obedire più al voler loro che all'arte. . . ." "Alli benigni lettori," in *Opus Architectonicum,* by Francesco Borromini, ed. Joseph Connors (Milan: Il Polifilo, 1998), 2r.

119. In explaining the emergence in quattrocento Florence of "a large number" (six) of painters who were also members of religious orders, Meghan Holmes speculates that the orders embarked on a "media spectacle" about monasticism; aware of the new prestige attached to painting by highly skilled artists, they used the talents of their artists for the purposes of power brokering. Holmes, *Fra Filippo Lippi,* 93–97.

120. Argan describes the rise of a system of criticism as a function of the new autonomous art market, middlemen, and the public exerting an influence on art. Giulio Argan, *The Baroque Age* (New York: Rizzoli, 1989), originally published as the first part of *Europe of the Capitols, 1600–1700* (Geneva: Skira, 1964), 20.

121. Paul Fréart de Chantelou, *Diary of the Cavaliere Bernini's Visit to France,* ed. and introd. Anthony Blunt, trans. Margery Corbett, annot. George C. Bauer (Princeton: Princeton University Press, 1985), 116.

122. Hundreds of notices of artistic projects culled from *avvisi* were published in the journal *Roma* from the 1920s through the 1940s. For an overview, see Cesare D'Onofrio, "Gli 'avvisi' di Roma dal 1554 al 1605 conservati in biblioteche ed archivi romane," *Studi Romani* 10 (1962): 529–48.

123. And Urban VIII's insistence on hearing "the judgment and opinion of various persons concerning the great work [before giving the artist his reward]." Filippo Baldinucci, *The Life of Bernini* [1682], trans. Catherine Enggass, with foreword by Robert Enggass (University Park: Pennsylvania State University Press, 1966), 17.

CHAPTER 4. MESSAGE

1. Louis Althusser, "Ideology and Ideological State Apparatuses (Notes towards an Investigation)," in *Lenin and Philosophy and Other Essays,* trans. Ben Brewster (London: New Left Books, 1971), 144–45.

2. Jane P. Tompkins, "The Reader in History: The Changing Shape of Literary Response," in *Reader Response Criticism: From Formalism to Post-Structuralism,* ed. idem (Baltimore: Johns Hopkins University Press, 1980), 203. An art historical study that weds iconography and reception is Hahn, *Portrayed on the Heart.*

3. Roman Jakobsen's model of communication graphically places the message between addresser and addressee. Two literary approaches to the exchange are relevant here: speech-act theory, drawing upon the rhetorical tradition, sees literature not as series of structures and meanings, but as a "set of acts and practices." A materialist approach will see this activity as an ideological one, with consequences for the spectator (i.e., J. L. Austin's notion of "perlocution," or the effect we want to have on someone in saying something). See Douglas Robinson, "Speech Acts," in *The Johns Hopkins Guide to Literary Theory and Criticism,* ed. Michael Groden and Martin Kreiswirth (Baltimore: Johns Hopkins University Press, 1994), 684.

4. W. J. T. Mitchell, "Iconology, Ideology, and Cultural Encounter: Panofsky, Althusser, and the Scene of Recognition," in *Reframing the Renaissance: Visual Culture in Europe and Latin America,* ed. Claire Farago (New Haven: Yale University Press, 1995), 292–300.

5. Erwin Panofsky, "Iconography and Iconology: An Introduction to the Study of Renaissance Art," in *Meaning and the Visual Arts* (Garden City, N.Y.: Doubleday Anchor, 1955), 26–54.

6. Panofsky's iconography is, admittedly, an extreme case. Semiotics is less impervious to the social in stressing that meaning is produced in the interaction between producer and interpretant. Stephen Bann, "Meaning/Interpretation," in *Critical Terms for Art History,* ed. Robert S. Nelson and Richard Shiff (Chicago: University of Chicago Press, 1996), 87–100. For the place of the interpretant in Peirce's semiotics and its absence in de Saussure's, see Alex Potts, "Sign," in ibid., 17–30.

7. "The inculcation of traditional value attitudes is generally called education, while the term propaganda is reserved for the spreading of subversive, debatable or merely novel attitudes." Harold Lasswell, "Propaganda" [1934], in Jackall, ed., *Propaganda,* 13.

8. Ellul, *Propaganda,* 25–32.

9. See the pamphlet intended for East German party propagandists that introduced Soviet propaganda ideas, "Die Aufgaben der Parteipropaganda," *Sozialistische Bildungshefte* 5 (1950), trans. Randall L. Bytwerk and available on the "German Propaganda Archive" Web site www.calvin.edu/academic/cas/gpa/sedprop.htm.

10. For example, Alfred McClung Lee doubted the distinction between propaganda and education, between propaganda and science, citing the pressures on both. The premise of his book, however, is that a liberal arts education equips one to "resist the facile pitch." Lee, *How to Understand Propaganda,* 8–9. Leonard Doob was aware that his vague definition of the propagandist as one who influences another (and is negatively regarded) is made problematic by the positive regard held for teachers, who likewise aim to influence the individual: "The educator has prestige in our society because it is presumed that he teaches what people want and need to be taught, in order to be socialized according to our standards. If he mixes radicalism with arithmetic or exposés with civics, he is branded a propagandist by the majority of people in the U.S. If he mixes imperialism with geography or capitalism with economics, he is likewise angrily labeled a propagandist cer-

tainly not by the majority but by the radical-minded minority. Pick your science or the values you consider important in society, and then you can decide what education is." Ultimately he distinguishes education from propaganda as a matter of the perceived (positive or negative) value of the opinions/behavior the educator/propagandist is attempting to affect. Leonard W. Doob, *Public Opinion and Propaganda*, 231, 240. Domenach argues that propaganda is like education in attempting to influence fundamental attitudes but differs in its purpose, to convince and to subjugate. Jean-Marie Domenach, *La propagande politique*, 8th ed., Que sais-je? no. 448 (Paris: Presses Universitaires de France, 1979), 8.

11. See, for example, Anthony Pratkanis and Elliot Aronson, *Age of Propaganda: The Everyday Use and Abuse of Persuasion* (New York: W. H. Freeman and Company, 1991), 215–18. Yet the illusion of the neutrality of education still remains; it has resurfaced in the view of advertising posing a threat to educational materials. Remarkable in this respect was the recent concern about a mathematics textbook liberally sprinkled with brand-name consumer products. In justifying the use of Oreo cookies over a less recognizable brand, one company spokesperson remarked that "Oreo is an American Icon." Constance L. Hays, "Math Book Salted with Brand Names Raises New Alarm," *New York Times*, 21 March 1999, sec. I, 1, 22. Another symptomatic example is the labeling of American late-night comedy interview shows as political propaganda. It seems that anyone with a point of view or an alliance with a mass audience is prone to be called a propagandist. Needless to say, I disagree with this definition. See Marshall Sella, "The Stiff Guy vs. the Dumb Guy," *New York Times Magazine*, 24 September 2000, 74.

12. Althusser, "Ideology," 144–45.

13. A third form, "gray propaganda," uses information of uncertain accuracy and may or may not identify its source. Jowett and O'Donnell, *Propaganda and Persuasion*, 8–13.

14. In the wake of World War I the definition was contested. For example, Ivy Lee, an American newspaper publisher, disputed a distinction made by President Coolidge (in a speech to the American Association of Newspaper Editors) between the propagandists' presentation of only "part of the facts" resulting in distortions and "education and real information" that present a "candid survey of all the facts." Since all presentations of events are selective, propaganda's "essential evil" was its "failure to disclose the source of the information." Ivy Lee, *The Problem of International Propaganda: A New Technique Necessary in Developing Understanding Between Nations . . .* , Occasional Papers, no. 3 (New York, 1934).

15. See, for example, a recent revisionist study of Nazi propaganda: "A second basic misconception is the entirely erroneous conviction that propaganda consists only of lies and falsehood. In fact it operates with many different kinds of truth—the outright lie, the half truth, the truth out of context." David Welch, *The Third Reich: Politics and Propaganda* (New York: Routledge, 1993), 5.

16. The Roosevelt administration distinguished its public relations from Goebbels's by its basis in fact. In reality, there were opposing views of propaganda within the administration, some more intent on molding public opinion and raising morale than in maintaining transparency. Richard W. Steele, *Propaganda in an Open Society: The Roosevelt Administration and the Media, 1933–1941* (Westport, Conn.: Greenwood Press, 1985), esp. 81–84, 90–92. See also chapter 2 above, 57–64.

17. Ellul, *Propaganda,* 84–87. Others have also stressed the emotional appeal of propaganda. "Through combinations of words, personalities, music, drama, pageantry, and other symbols, the propagandist attempts to make impressions upon masses of people. These impressions are sometimes vivid. They are frequently charged with emotion. They may be wholly or partly 'true,' confusing, or 'false.' When such impressions are transmitted in our society in a detailed and accurate manner rather than in the shorthand of the propagandist, few bother to listen. Such reports are too 'academic.' They bore and fail to impress. In moments given to decision, vividness and emotion quite often override commonsense demands for accurate facts and for an opportunity to question and to discuss." Lee, *How to Understand Propaganda,* 2–3. See also Institute for Propaganda Analysis, "How to Detect Propaganda," in Jackall, ed., *Propaganda,* 217–24, first published in the journal of the Institute for Propaganda Analysis, *Propaganda Analysis* 1 (1937).

18. Ellul, *Propaganda,* 84–87.

19. See the stimulating, but not overly, exhibition catalog: Bartomeu Marí, Jos ten Berge, and Georg Simmel, *Stimuli: Too much noise, too much movement* (Rotterdam: Witte de With Center for Contemporary Art, 1999).

20. See chapter 2, 54–55.

21. Siegfried Kracauer, "Propaganda and the Nazi War Film," in *From Caligari to Hitler: A Psychological History of the German Film* (Princeton: Princeton University Press, 1947), 278. Kracauer acknowledges the propaganda analysts Ernst Kris and Hans Speier in the preface (274).

22. Schapiro helped Kracauer escape Nazi Europe to the United States in 1941. Mark M. Anderson, "Siegfried Kracauer and Meyer Schapiro: A Friendship," *New German Critique* 54 (1991): 19–29. On Kracauer's desperate attempts to leave Europe, see Thomas Y. Levin, introduction to *Mass Ornament,* by Siegfried Kracauer, trans. Thomas Y. Levin (Cambridge, Mass.: Harvard University Press, 1995), 1–2.

23. Letter from Meyer Schapiro to Siegfried Kracauer, 12 August 1942, in Anderson, "Siegfried Kracauer," 25–26.

24. Siegfried Kracauer, "The Mass Ornament," in *Mass Ornament,* 75–86. See the remarks on the essay by Thomas Y. Levin in the introduction, 17–18.

25. Letter from Meyer Schapiro to Siegfried Kracauer, 12 August 1942, in Anderson, "Siegfried Kracauer," 25–26.

26. Leah Bendavid-Val, *Propaganda and Dreams: Photographing the 1930s in the USSR and the US* (Zurich and New York: Edition Stemmle, 1999).

27. Ibid., 38–39.

28. Debates heated up around Michelangelo's *Last Judgment.* See Alexander Nagel, *Michelangelo and the Reform of Art* (New York: Cambridge University Press, 2000), esp. chap. 7.

29. See the excellent study by Pamela M. Jones, *Federico Borromeo and the Ambrosiana: Art Patronage and Reform in Seventeenth-Century Milan* (New York: Cambridge University Press, 1993).

30. See chapter 2, 49–50, on Paleotti and the reform of images.

31. Ellul served as a pastor and was on the national council of the Reformed Church of France for twenty-one years. See Jacques Ellul, *Perspectives on Our Age: Jacques Ellul Speaks on His Life and Work,* ed. William H. Vanderburg, trans. Joachim Neugroschel (Toronto:

Canadian Broadcasting Corporation, 1981); and idem, *In Season Out of Season: An Introduction to the Thought of Jacques Ellul,* based on interviews with the author by Madeleine Garrigou-Lagrange, trans. Lani K. Niles (San Francisco: Harper and Row, 1982), esp. 84–116. I am grateful to John Brown for bringing these sources to my attention.

32. Jacques Ellul, *Histoire de la propagande,* Que sais-je? no. 1271 (Paris: Presses Universitaires de France, 1967), 34–41, 57–61; idem, *Propaganda,* 228–32.

33. See, for example, Mark U. Edwards, Jr., *Printing, Propaganda and Martin Luther* (Berkeley: University of California Press, 1994); Robert W. Scribner, *For the Sake of the Simple Folk: Popular Propaganda for the German Reformation,* 2d ed. (Oxford: Oxford University Press, 1994), esp. the introduction; and idem, "Reformatische Bildpropaganda," in *Historische Bildkunder: Probleme—Wege—Beispiele,* ed. Brigitte Tolkemitt and Rainer Wohlfeil, Zeitschrift für Historische Forschung, vol. 12 (Berlin: Duncker and Humbolt, 1991), 83–106.

34. See, for example, the quasi-scholarly studies, Oliver Thomson, *Mass Persuasion in History: An Historical Analysis of the Development of Propaganda Techniques* (Edinburgh: Paul Harris Publishing, 1977); Gorham Munson, *Twelve Decisive Battles of the Mind: The Story of Propaganda during the Christian Era, with Abridged Versions of Texts Which Have Shaped History* (New York: Greystone Press, 1942).

35. Keith Moxey, *The Practice of Theory: Poststructuralism, Cultural Politics and Art History* (Ithaca: Cornell University Press, 1994), 44–45.

36. Althusser, "Ideology," 152.

37. Althusser broke with the Church after World War II. See Yann Moulier Boutang, *La formation du mythe (1918–1956),* vol. 1 of *Louis Althusser: Une biographie* (Paris: Bernard Grasset, 1992), esp. chap. 7.

38. Althusser, "Ideology," 167.

39. For Althusser's dependence on Lacan's theory of the mirror stage for his notion that the subject is brought into being by his encounter with the symbolic, see Moxey, *The Practice of Theory,* 45–46.

40. There is a large bibliography on this essay. See, for example, Gregory Elliott, "Althusser," in *A Dictionary of Cultural and Critical Theory,* ed. Michael Payne et al. (Cambridge, Mass.: Blackwell Reference, 1996), 23–26; the special issue of *Yale French Studies* on Althusser, 88 (1995), esp. the essays by Thomas Pepper, "Kneel and You Will Believe," and Warren Montag, "'The Soul Is the Prison of the Body': Althusser and Foucault, 1970–75"; and Rosalind Krauss, "Welcome to the Cultural Revolution," *October* 77 (1996): 84–85.

41. W. J. T. Mitchell, *Iconology: Image, Text, Ideology* (Chicago: University of Chicago Press, 1986), 170 n.23. On this complex theme, whose major formulation is in the work of Augustine, see John Edward Sullivan, *The Image of God: The Doctrine of St. Augustine and Its Influence* (Dubuque, Iowa: Priory Press, 1963).

42. For the account of mimesis that follows I draw on Karl Morrison, *The Mimetic Tradition of Reform in the West* (Princeton: Princeton University Press, 1982). See also Gunter Gebauer and Christoph Wulf, *Mimesis: Culture, Art, Society,* trans. Don Reneau (Berkeley: University of California Press, 1992).

43. Morrison, *The Mimetic Tradition,* 54.

44. For Augustine imitation, an augmentative process, was the culmination of a string of

previous processes: knowing God begets loving God, and from loving follows imitation. The role of love as a force that binds asymmetries echoes Plato's notion that love is the attraction of dissimilar things to each other. Ibid., 58.

45. On the necessity of considering both reader and author in defining the roman à thèse, see Suleiman, *Authoritarian Fictions*, 9–10.

46. Suleiman defines the roman à thèse similarly, not in terms of its specific content but as "a type of novel that manifests the intention of being read in a particular way." Ibid., 25.

47. "The end of this Society is to devote itself with God's grace not only to the salvation and perfection of the members' own souls, but also with that same grace to labor strenuously in giving aid toward the salvation and perfection of the souls of their fellowmen." Ganss, trans. and ed., *The Constitutions of the Society of Jesus*, [3]–2, 77–78.

48. Marjorie Reeves, *Joachim of Fiore and the Prophetic Future* (London: S.P.C.K., 1976), 116–24. The link between the Jesuits and Joachimite prophecy was made in the 1590s and was repeated throughout the seventeenth century.

49. See the compelling account of the early historiography of Ignatius in François Durand, "La première historiographie ignatienne," in *Ignacio de Loyola y su tiempo: Congreso Internacional de Historia (9–13 Setiembre 1991)*, ed. Juan Plazaola (Bilbao: Ediciones Mensajero, 1992), 23–35.

50. For the peculiar status of this account, and why autobiography is a misnomer for it, see Louis Marin, "Le 'Récit,' Réflexion sur un testament," in *Les Jésuites à l'âge baroque, 1540–1640*, ed. Luce Giard and Louis de Vaucelles (Paris: Jérome Millon, 1996), 63–76. The text, which is variably referred to as "Chronicon" and "autobiography," will be referred to here as the 'Récit.'

51. General Francis Borgia first asked Ribadeynera to write a biography of Ignatius in 1567, and the first of several he would write over the course of the next four decades was a private Jesuit publication. The Jesuits ordered only five hundred copies of the original Latin text from their Neapolitan printer in 1572 and only circulated the book internally. Later the *vita* enjoyed a wide circulation, first in a Spanish translation (1578; published 1583) and then an improved Latin version (1586). In 1601 Ribadeynera wrote a second and shorter biography of Ignatius as an addendum to the *Flos Sanctorum* that featured Ignatius's miracles. This shorter text, crucial for the canonization, would be the most reprinted *vita*. See Durand, "La premiere historiographie Ignatienne." All citations of Ribadeynera (whose name is variably spelled) are to an early Italian translation based on Ribadeynera's Spanish version, Pedro de Ribadeynera, *Vita del P. Ignatio Loiola fondatore della Religione della Compagnia di Giesù* (Venice: Gioliti, 1587). The 'Récit' circulated in manuscript form, as had several earlier accounts of Ignatius's life. All of these were suppressed once Ribadeynera's longer and more comprehensive *vita* came out.

52. For an account of the conversion based on the 'Récit' alone, see André Ravier, *Ignatius of Loyola and the Founding of the Society of Jesus*, trans. Joan Maura and Carson Daly (San Francisco: Ignatius Press, 1987), 406–29.

53. Ignatius of Loyola, *Il racconto del Pellegrino: Autobiografia di Sant'Ignazio di Loyola*, ed. Roberto Calasso (Milan: Adelphi, 1966), 22–23.

54. Ribadeynera, *Vita del P. Ignatio Loiola*, 8. See the interesting discussion of Ignatius's spir-

itual conversion in his 'Récit' in Marjorie O'Rourke Boyle, *Loyola's Acts: The Rhetoric of the Self* (Berkeley: University of California Press, 1997), esp. 36 ff.

55. Ribadeynera, *Vita del P. Ignatio Loiola,* 9.

56. Imitation is as old as hagiography itself. See Thomas J. Heffernan, *Sacred Biography: Saints and Their Biographers in the Middle Ages* (New York: Oxford University Press, 1988), esp. chaps. 1, 5. For what Ignatius drew from saints and doctors of the Church, see Hugo Rahner, *The Spirituality of St. Ignatius Loyola: An Account of Its Historical Development,* trans. Francis John Smith (Westminster, Md.: Newman Press, 1953).

57. On the relief of the burden of proof attained by writing as a brother to his brothers, see David J. Collins, "Life after Death: A Rhetorical Analysis of Pedro de Ribadeineira's *Vida del padre Ignazio de Loyola, Fundador de la Compañia de Jesus*" (licentiate thesis in Sacred Theology, Weston Jesuit School of Theology, Cambridge, 1998), 110–11. Collins notes that a second prologue addressed to the "christiano lector" in the second Spanish edition of the *vida* now appeared before the address to the Jesuit brothers in the first edition.

58. Ribadeynera, *Vita del P. Ignatio Loiola,* 86.

59. Ibid., 89.

60. Ignatius of Loyola, *Il racconto del Pellegrino,* 24.

61. This point was made cursorily in Rafael Lapresa, "La 'Vida de San Ignazio' del P. Ribadeneyra," *Revista de filología española* 21 (1934): 29–50.

62. Ribadeynera, *Vita del P. Ignatio Loiola,* Book V, chap. XIII, "De' miracoli, che Iddio operò col mezo suo," 656–84. I arrived at some of the same conclusions regarding Ribadeynera's rhetorical strategy as David Collins ("Life after Death"). We disagree on the motive for Ribadeynera's revisionist treatment of miracles. Working from the rhetorical and historiographic tradition, Collins views the shift as an indication of a humanist outlook whereas I view the new strictures around canonization proceedings and the very apparent lack of miracles as having compelled the shift. See n.102.

63. Pedro de Ribadeynera, *Flos Sanctorum: O Libro delle Vite de' Santi . . . ,* 2 vols. (Milan: G. B. Bidelli, 1618–21), 2:27. The first edition appeared in 1601.

64. Ribadeynera, *Vita del P. Ignatio Loiola,* 412–15.

65. Ibid., 411. My reading of the Society's history as integral to Ignatius's hagiography, not extraneous to it, differs from that of Jodi Bilinkoff, "The Many 'Lives' of Pedro de Ribadeynera," *Renaissance Quarterly* 52 (1999): 180–96.

66. Ribadeynera, *Vita del P. Ignatio Loiola,* 321.

67. Ignatius of Loyola, *Il racconto del Pellegrino,* 13. Emphasis mine. St. Benedict's *vita* was viewed similarly, as analogous to the Benedictine way of life, as laid out in the *Rule*. See John B. Wickstrom, "Gregory the Great's 'Life of St. Benedict' and the Illustrations of Abbot Desiderius," *Studies in Iconography* 19 (1998): 31–73.

68. P. Jerome Nadal, prologue [ca. 1567] to the 'Récit.' Ignatius of Loyola, *Il racconto del Pellegrino,* 5–7.

69. Marin, "Le 'Récit.'"

70. A large painting commissioned by Ribadeynera out of devotion to Ignatius was also represented. See Ursula König-Nordhoff, *Ignatius von Loyola: Studien zur Entwicklung einer neuen Heiligen-Ikonographie im Rahmen einer Kanonisationskampagne um 1600* (Berlin: G. Mann, 1982), 43.

71. Ribadeynera was so pleased with the portrait that he had sixteen copies made. Ibid., 46, 57–59, and fig. 55. See also fig. 56 for a larger version, tentatively attributed to Coello, with an inscription and Ignatius looking toward the heavens. I refer to this image below.

72. See ibid., 60–62, 261–70. They were soon supplanted by the longer series of noncontinuous narratives attributed to Rubens and distributed at the time of the canonization.

73. The inscription reads: "He u quã sordet terra cu[m] caelu[m] aspicio?" ("How dirty the earth looks when you look at the heavens"). Ibid., 58. My thanks to Cecilia Hurley and Fabio Barry for the translation. According to Mâle, this phrase was inscribed on the sill of the window in Ignatius's rooms. Emile Mâle, *L'art religieux après le Concile de Trente*, 152–53.

74. Dedication to Cardinal Gaspare Quiroga, Ribadeynera, *Vita del P. Ignatio Loiola*.

75. In the *Flos Sanctorum* (2:28) Ribadeynera wrote: "And because Ignatius is not yet a canonized saint, nor is he put forth *(proposta)* to be invoked and revered as are the others of whom we have described [here], it has been necessary to refer to some more particular things and miracles than in the lives of the other saints that could have been omitted if it had been certain that . . . he were to be made saint, to manifest his virtue as an example for us, so that he is made known to those who do not know him, and who could take devotion to his saintly person."

76. Jean-Michel Sallmann, "Il santo e le rappresentazioni della santità: problemi di metodo," *Quaderni storici* 41 (1979): 586. For a general introduction to Counter-Reformation sanctity, see Peter Burke, "How to Be a Counter-Reformation Saint," in *The Historical Anthropology of Early Modern Italy: Essays on Perception and Communication* (Cambridge: Cambridge University Press, 1987), 48–62. For the Oratorian Antonio Gallonio's research in the 1590s and early 1600s for the Congregation of Rites on the treatment of the noncanonized and its relation to his biography of Filippo Neri (published 1600), see the excellent study by Simon Ditchfield, *Liturgy, Sanctity and History in Tridentine Italy: Pietro Maria Campi and the Preservation of the Particular* (Cambridge: Cambridge University Press, 1995), esp. 49–50.

77. The tombs of both Ignatius and Philip Neri were closely monitored in the years before their canonization. König-Nordhoff, *Ignatius von Loyola*, 40–41, 129–30; for Clement VIII's prohibition, see 32–33, 156 n.219. For further examples dating to the 1620s in Naples, see Sallmann, "Il santo e le rappresentazioni della santità," 587.

78. Dispatch from nuncio of Spain from Valladolid to Cardinal Pietro Aldobrandini, 2 August 1602, in Ignace de Récalde, *Les Jésuites sous Aquaviva* (Paris: Libraire Moderne, 1927), 24–25.

79. Letter from Cardinal Pietro Aldobrandini to nuncio Domenico Ginnaso, 8 October 1602, in ibid., 26–27.

80. Letter from nuncio Domenico Ginnasio (Madrid) to Cardinal Pietro Aldobrandini (Rome), 26 November 1602, in ibid., 25.

81. This campaign is the subject of the most extensive study of Counter-Reformation iconography of a single figure undertaken to date. König-Nordhoff, *Ignatius von Loyola*.

82. See, for example, the title page from the edition of the *Spiritual Exercises* (Lyon, ca. 1600), in ibid., fig. 136.

83. While papal control over book printing dated back to 1487, and there is evidence that

printmakers sought papal privileges in the sixteenth century, the earliest evidence of control specifically over engravings is an edict of 1591 that included images in a list of printed materials for which papal privilege was required before publication. Engravings were subsequently singled out in 1597 and 1599. The privileges served both economic interests (copyright for artisans, taxes for Papal States) and maintenance of orthodoxy. For prints and privileges during the reigns of Clement VIII and subsequent popes, with some hasty conclusions, see Eckhard Leuschner, "The Papal Printing Privilege," *Print Quarterly* 15 (1998): 359–70. For Diana Mantovana's privilege of 1575 and the 1591 edict issued by the maestro del Sacro Palazzo, see Evelyn Lincoln, *The Invention of the Italian Renaissance Printmaker* (New Haven: Yale University Press, 2000), 123–24, 152, and 182 n.19.

84. The order is passed on to the father provincial of the Roman province by general Aquaviva in a letter of 6 June 1601: "Se bene NS ha ordinato che per l'avenire non si stampino più immagini del N.B.P. Ignatio con miracoli senza suo ordini per giusti rispetti che hanno mosso la sua S.ma mente, come anche ha ordinato il medesimo in altre, e da noi conviene più d'ogni altro senza replica ubidire come veri figli d'ubidienza. . . . Nondimeno vuole S. B.ne che l'imagini già impresse con i miracoli del N.B.P. Ignatio si possano vendere publicamente per tutto come s'è fatto in Roma di suo consenso, più non se n'imprimano senza suo ordine." The letter is transcribed in König-Nordhoff, *Ignatius von Loyola,* 189 n.806.

85. The engraving, which served as a model for several subsequent works, is discussed at length in ibid., esp. 101–9. A second state, in the Bibliothèque nationale, Paris, with the inscription of "Beatus" changed to "Sanctus" was published by Alfredo Petrucci, "Milesiana," *Studi Romani* 4 (1956): 578–80. See also Reinhold Baumstark, ed., *Rom in Bayern: Kunst und Spiritualität der ersten Jesuiten* (Munich: Hirmer Verlag, 1997), 326–28. A newly discovered pendant by Camillo Cungi, of Francis Xavier, whose canonization the Jesuits also sought, is in Leuschner, "The Papal Printing Privilege," 359 and fig. 178.

86. Pierre Delooz, "Towards a Sociological Study of Canonized Sainthood in the Catholic Church," in *Saints and Their Cults: Studies in Religious Sociology, Folklore and History,* ed. R. Hertz (Cambridge: Cambridge University Press, 1983), 208.

87. Sallmann, "Il santo," 587.

88. The Counter-Reformation papacy's juridical requirement of spontaneous cult has been interpreted as a product of the increasingly political nature of the sanctification process, which had a much higher rate of success when powerful lobbyists, often a religious order, put their weight behind their candidate. Delooz, "Towards a Sociological Study of Canonized Sainthood," 199–200.

89. Sallmann, "Il santo," 588–89.

90. König-Nordhoff, *Ignatius von Loyola.*

91. For a thorough discussion of the plans for renovation of the Gesù in the 1670s, see Levy, "The Institutional Memory of the Roman Gesù."

92. At least since the general congregation of 1645–46, the Jesuits had discussed a more dignified housing for Ignatius's relics. Discussions continued in the 1650s, when a significant donation from Peru was designated for the project and when Casimir of Poland left an enormous sum in his will for the construction of the chapel. Both came

to naught. See the documents and brief history of these desires in Pecchiai, *Il Gesù di Roma*, 139–42, 352–55.

93. For a full transcription and further discussion of plans for renovation in the 1670s, see Levy, "The Institutional Memory of the Roman Gesù."

94. For the fate of the plans of the 1670s, see chapter 3 above, 88–91; and the extended treatment in Levy, "The Institutional Memory of the Roman Gesù."

95. For an overview of Jesuit church decoration in Rome through the seventeenth century, see esp. Evonne Levy, "'A Noble Medley and Concert of Materials and Artifice': Jesuit Church Interiors in Rome, 1567–1700," in Lucas, ed., *Saint, Site, and Sacred Strategy*, 46–61.

96. Because the major projects are by Pozzo they have been treated as a group of projects by the artist, although very little attention has been paid to iconography, with the exception of the vault of the Church of St. Ignatius.

97. In 1602 general Aquaviva ordered that the rooms not be demolished, and in 1605 the first mass was celebrated in one of the rooms, now a chapel. For the history and description of the space, see Pietro Tacchi Venturi, *La casa di S. Ignazio di Loiola in Roma* (Rome: Casa Editrice 'Roma,' ca. 1924). The dates are from the diary of Jesuit Antonio Presutti for which see idem, "Il fratel Antonio Presutti e i suoi 'ricordi' sopra i festeggiamenti nelle chiese e case della Compagnia di Gesù per la canonizzazione di Ignazio di Loiola e Francesco Saverio," in *La canonizzazione dei santi Ignazio di Loyola, fondatore della Compagnia di Gesù e Francesco Saverio, apostolo dell'oriente* (Rome: Grafia, 1922), 88 n.1.

98. The restoration of the Ignatian rooms undertaken in 1990 under the direction of Thomas Lucas is described in his "Le camere di sant'Ignazio a Roma," *La Civiltà Cattolica* 3, nos. 3387–88 (1991): 280–86.

99. The dating of these works, executed in tempera on plaster, to 1661–63, is based on a letter of 24 December 1661 written by the artist that first attests to his presence at the Gesù (and Casa Professa), where he continued to work with one interruption until 1663 when he moved to the novitiate. Francesco Alberto Salvagnini, *I pittori Borgognoni Cortese (Courtois) e la loro casa in Piazza di Spagna* (Rome: Fratelli Palombo, 1937), 109. For a list of the corridor scenes, see Kerber, *Andrea Pozzo*, 50–53.

100. "Alcune Considerationi da ponderarsi bene, e molto maturatamente intorno al fare, ò non fare l'Ingresso delle Cappelle di S. Ignatio nel Corridore," Archivum Romanum Societatis Iesu, Rom 144, fols. 303r–306v. The document was first cited in Tacchi Venturi, *La casa di S. Ignazio de Loiola*, 32–35, where it was dated to Noyelle's generalate. Kerber (*Andrea Pozzo*, 51 n.47) found confirmation for the dating to Noyelles's generalate in Francesco Saverio Baldinucci, *Vite di artisti dei secoli XVII–XVIII: Prima edizione integrale del Codice Palatino 565*, ed. Anna Matteoli (Rome: De Luca, 1975), 323. For a full transcription, see Levy, "A Canonical Work of an Uncanonical Era," doc. 76.

101. During the 1990 restoration of the corridor frescoes, a test was made on the walls surrounding the window bays at the top of the stairs (now outside the wall erected at the time Pozzo worked on the corridor), suggesting that Borgogone's cycle extended further into the corridor. See Thomas Lucas, S.J., "La Galleria del Pozzo nella Casa Professa a Rome," in Battisti, ed., *Andrea Pozzo*, 141 n.5. See also in the same volume Mau-

rizio De Luca, "Gli affreschi della Galleria del Gesù a Roma," esp. 150–52, with excellent illustrations of the corridor during and after restoration. The cycle is also discussed, with a focus on the perspectival construction, in Daniela Gallavotti Cavallero, "Gli esordi pittorici a Roma: il corridoio del Gesù e la cappella della Vigna," in De Feo and Martinelli, eds., *Andrea Pozzo,* 42–53.

102. See De Luca, "Gli affreschi della Galleria del Gesù," in Battisti, ed., *Andrea Pozzo,* 150, for traces of candle wax that suggest the presence of an altar against the wall.

103. Andrea del Sarto's *Virgin of the Harpies* is similarly described by Stephen J. Campbell, "'Fare una Cosa Morta Parer Viva': Michelangelo, Rosso, and the (Un)Divinity of Art," *Art Bulletin* 84 (2002): 606.

104. This image of the urn is too small to be certain whether Pozzo intended to represent it as it is, with a bronze relief, or with a transparent front. For a closer evaluation of the evidence, see Levy, "A Canonical Work of an Uncanonical Era," 69.

105. Kerber (*Andrea Pozzo,* 53) misidentified the scene as an encounter with Francis Borgia.

106. David J. Collins, "Life after Death," 85–100.

107. Bartoli's *vita* went through numerous translations and reprints through the nineteenth century. See De Backer and Sommervogel, *Bibliothèque,* 2:968–69. For an introduction to the Ignatian historiography after Ribadeynera, see Jos E. Vercruysee, "L'historiographie ignatienne aux XVI–XVIII siècles," in Plazaola, ed., *Ignacio de Loyola y su tiempo,* 37–53.

108. Daniello Bartoli, *Della Vita e dell'Istituto di S. Ignatio, fondatore della Compagnia di Gesu* [1650], 2d expanded ed. (Rome: Nella Stamperia d'Ignatio de'Lazari, 1659), 1. He completed volumes on Asia (1653), Japan (1660), China (1663), England (1667), and Italy (1673).

109. "Che se bene mentre egli visse . . . supplicò a Dio, che per suo mezzo non operasse miracoli, onde altri l'havesse in credito, e veneratione di Santo, e il P. Ribadeneira nelle prime vite, che di lui pubblicò, scrisse, che Iddio l'havea condotto per via piu di virtù interne, che d'esterne maraviglie: pure il vero si è (e se ne avvide, e corresse di poi anco il Ribadeneira) che S. Ignatio vivendo operò non pochi, e non ordinari miracoli." Bartoli, *Della Vita e dell'Istituto di S. Ignatio,* 373.

110. Ignacio Iparraguirre, "Historiografia ignaciana: La figura de S. Ignacio a través de los siglos," in *Obras completas de San Ignazio de Loyola,* ed. Ignacio Iparraguirre (Madrid: Biblioteca de Autores Cristianos, 1952), 2:17–18.

111. Numerous miracles were also included in the series of *Ignatius's* life engraved after designs by Rubens around the canonization. See König-Nordhoff, *St. Ignatius von Loyola,* 120–21.

112. Mâle, *L'art religieux après le Concile de Trente,* 186–88. The recent argument (following Mâle) that miracle scenes declined at the end of the seventeenth century needs refinement. See Zirka Zaremba Filipczak, "'A Time Fertile in Miracles': Miraculous Events in and through Art," in *The Age of the Marvellous,* ed. Joy Kenseth (Hanover, N.H.: Hood Museum, Dartmouth College, 1991), 192–211.

113. Vigilio Nolarci, *Compendio della vita di S. Ignatio di Loiola raccolto con fedeltà, e con brevità da quanto n'hanno provatamente stampato in un secolo gravi autori* (Venice: Combi e la Nou, 1680). Nolarci is a pseudonym for Luis Carnoli (1618–93). See Vercruysse,

"L'historiographie ignatienne," in Plazaola, ed., *Ignacio de Loyola y su tiempo*, 48, for other works derivative of Bartoli. The entry on Ignatius in the *Acta Sanctorum* 7 (1731), which reprints the 'Rècit' and Ribadeynera's *vita*, also emphasizes the miracles, with evidence gathered from different parts of the world. Baudouin de Gaiffer, "Une collaboration fraternelle: La dissertation sur S. Ignace par les pères Jean et Ignace Pinius dan les 'Acta Sanctorum,'" *Archivum Historicum Societatis Iesu* 25 (1956): 183.

114. Alonso de Andrade, *Veneracion de las Santas Imagenes: Origen, y milagros de la de San Ignacio de Munebrega, fundador de la Compañia de Iesus* (Madrid: Ioseph Fernandez de Buendia, 1669).

115. Ibid., 225.

116. The building, now owned by the Antoniani, is referred to as the Vigna Antoniana. It appears to have been purchased by the Jesuits in 1555 and used for the recreation of students and repose for the sick. See Antonio Coccia, "Nota storica sulla Vigna Antoniana dei frati minori conventuali in Roma (1555–1972)," *Miscellanea francescana* 73 (1973): 171–90. It is referred to by Pascoli as the chapel at the Villa Balbina, "che stata era prima stanza, ritiro, e sollievo dell'indisposizioni di S. Ignazio." Lione Pascoli, *Vite de' pittori, scultori, ed architetti moderni* (1730–36; reprint, edited by C. Ricci, 2 vols., Rome: E. Calzone, 1933), 1:253. Ignatius officiated in a chapel on the ground floor, later destroyed. He slept in the room above the chapel, converted into a chapel at the time of his beatification and later decorated by Pozzo.

117. On the apse fresco mostly completed 1685–88, and altered between 1697 and 1701, see Bernhard Kerber, "Zur Chorgestaltung von S. Ignazio in Rom," *Pantheon* 23 (1965): 84–89.

118. See above all Peter Wilberg-Vignau, *Andrea Pozzos Deckenfresko in S. Ignazio* (Munich: Uni-Druck, 1970); and Hermann Schadt, "Andrea Pozzos Langhausfresko in S. Ignazio, Rom: Zur Thementradition der barocken Heiligenglorie," *Das Munster* 24 (1971): 153–60.

119. Pozzo's description of the fresco was included in later printings of the first volume of his treatise, *Perspectiva pictorum et architectorum*, first published in 1693, when the fresco was still incomplete. The text appears opposite fig. 101 in vol. 1 of the 1717 edition published in Rome. It was republished in a rare pamphlet, Enrico Filiziani, *Sul significato delle pitture esistenti nella volta della chiesa di S. Ignazio in Roma* (Rome: "Vera Roma," 1910).

120. For the belated approval process of Ignatius's mass (approved 1673, first printed in 1675), see Thomas Lucas in Lucas, ed., *Saint, Site, and Sacred Strategy*, 182.

121. Wilberg-Vignau, *Andrea Pozzos Deckenfresko*, 21–22.

122. Wilberg-Vignau pointed out that the mirror inscribed with the name of Christ is an attribute of Ignatius in the *Imago primi saeculi*, Antwerp, 1640. Ibid., 22.

123. Wilberg-Vignau argued that the frontispiece to Bartoli's life of Ignatius provided a visual source for the idea, also used in sermons and other sources. Ibid., 21–22 n.32, 40–41.

124. This interchangeability was also noted in late Medieval northern painting. See Patrick Reuterswärd, "What Color Is Divine Light?" in *The Visible and Invisible in Art: Essays in the History of Art* (Vienna: IRSA, 1991), 148.

125. Gabriel María Verd, "De Iñigo a Ignacio: El cambio de nombre en San Ignacio de Loyola," *Archivum Historicum Societatis Iesu* 60 (1991): 113–60, with previous bibliography. The author here revises his conclusions in an earlier article on the theme, "El 'Iñigo' de San Ignazio de Loyola," *Archivum Historicum Societatis Iesu* 45 (1976): 95–128.

126. "Se dize, que dudandose quando bautizaban a San Ignazio, como le llamarian, el mismo niño se puso nombre: con el qual se significa el oficio qua aria de hazer en la Iglesia." J. E. Nieremberg, *Honor del gran Patriarca San Ignazio de Loyola, Fundador de la Compañia de Iesus* (Madrid, 1645), 4, cited in Verd, "De Iñigo a Ignacio," 124 n.70.

127. "Ignatio, ò sia in sua materna lingua Ignigo [*sic*], che vuol dir tutto fuoco . . ." Filippo Picinelli, "Il Mongibello. Nevoso ed infuocato. Applauso settimo alle glorie del Patriarca S. Ignatio di Loiola. Detto in Pistoia l'anno 1647 quando fù posta la prima pietra del Tempio a lui dedicato," in *Applausi festivi nelle solennità d'alcuni santi* (Milan: Dionisio Gariboldi, 1650), 339–40.

128. The sacristy paintings, by Jesuit Pierre de Lattre, date to 1647–49. See Carlo Galassi Paluzzi, "La decorazione della sacrestia di S. Ignazio e il loro vero autore," *Roma* 4 (1926): 542–46. For further archival evidence for their dating, see Levy, "A Canonical Work of an Uncanonical Era," 244–45.

129. "Une montage qui jette des flâmes. . . . Pour le zele de Saint-Ignace"; "Le P. Bovio pour exprimer les Missions Apostoliques entreprise par Saint Ignace . . . a peint un canon qui envoye des boulets, avec ces mots. IGNE PROCUL MITTENTE. C'est le feu qui les fait aller"; "Un fer rouge du feu qui imprime sa figure sur du bois . . . Luccarini l'applique à S. Ignace, qui estant tout penetré de l'amour de Dieu, imprimoit ce même amour dans le coeur des autres." P. C. F. Menestrier, *La Philosophie des Images: Composée d'un ample Recueil de Devises, & du Jugement de tous les Ouvrages qui ont êtê faits sur cette Matiere,* 2 vols. (Paris: Robert J. B. De La Caille, 1682), 2: no. 24, 46; no. 25, 86; no. 11, 94.

130. Filippo Picinelli, *Il Mondo Simbolico . . . ,* 2d ed. (Venice: Presso Paolo Baglioni, 1678), 407, first noted in Wilberg-Vignau, *Andrea Pozzos Deckenfresko,* 40 n.32.

131. "Un miroir concave qui assemble les rayons pour brûler. Cogit ut cremet. Il les assemble, & les met tout en feu. Le pere Bovio a fait cette Devise pour les Compagnons que S. Ignace assembla, pour en faire des hommes Apostoliques"; "Le Pere Engelgrave applique à Saint Ignace une Devise du miroir ardent, qui reçoit les rayons du soleil avec ce vers de Virgile. Solis in ardescit radiis, longeque refulget. Tout ardent du soleil, il répand ses lumieres. Pour un homme rempli de l'esprit de Dieu, qu'il communique aux autres." Menestrier, *La Philosophie des Images,* 2: no. 10, 166, and no. 34, 231. Bovio also used the mirror as an emblem of Ignatius's purity. Carolo Bovio, *Ignatius Insignium, Epigrammatum et Elogiorum Centuriis Expressus* (Rome, 1655), 250–52.

132. Athanasius Kircher, *Ars Magna lucis et umbrae, in decem libros digesta . . . ,* 2d ed. (Amsterdam: Joannem Janssonium à Waesberge, 1671), 912.

133. In an unsigned document (1688) an argument for the pictorial decoration of the church was put forth. Against those who were against the project, the anonymous author wrote: "La bianchezza non è la speciale vaghezza delle Chiese." Document transcribed in Wilberg-Vignau, *Andrea Pozzos Deckenfresko,* 33 n.5.

134. The documentation for the chapel was treated most comprehensively in Pecchiai, *Il*

Gesù di Roma, 139–203; 259–65; and Kerber, *Andrea Pozzo.* Virtually all of the chapel's sculptural components (contracts, payments, and style) were treated in Robert Enggass, *Early Eighteenth-Century Sculpture in Rome: An Illustrated Catalogue Raisonné,* 2 vols. (University Park: Pennsylvania State University Press, 1975), with comprehensive previous bibliography. Two new surveys, primarily photographic, of seventeenth-century sculpture in Rome add little to previous accounts. Andrea Bacchi, *Scultura del '600 a Roma* (Milan: Longanesi, 1996); Oreste Ferrari and Serenita Papaldo, *Le sculture del Seicento a Roma* (Rome: Ugo Bozzi, 1999), 95–102 (to be used with caution). The discussion that follows is drawn from this author's dissertation, "A Canonical Work of an Uncanonical Era," to which I refer readers for a bibliography on artists and works in the chapel and further elaborations on the iconography of the chapel. The dissertation, the first sustained iconographic study of the chapel, is to be published by the Jesuit Historical Institute as *The Chapel of St. Ignatius: A Study Based on Documents in the Jesuit Archive in Rome,* including a large corpus of documents relating to the design, imagery, and debates around both. See also Levy, "'A Noble Medley,'" and entries related to Ignatian sites in Lucas, ed., *Saint, Site and Sacred Strategy.* Here bibliographic citations are limited to selected recent publications and material directly relevant to the arguments at hand.

135. The stucco scenes are, left to right, *St. Ignatius liberating a man possessed* (a scene repeated in the bronze reliefs below), *St. Ignatius's vision of the Virgin, St. Ignatius aided by the Virgin in the composition of the Spiritual Exercises,* and *A flame appears over the head of St. Ignatius while saying mass.* For documents attributing the reliefs to Leonardo Reti, see Levy, "A Canonical Work of an Uncanonical Era," 320, 542.

136. This is true of the large lunette-shaped canvas of this subject (anonymous and undated, probably from the first half of the seventeenth century) hanging in the ante-sacristy of the Gesù in Rome. See König-Nordhoff, *Ignatius von Loyola,* fig. 1 and figs. 21–29 for representations of Ignatius's canonization.

137. The three parts of the taper—wax, wick, and flame—signified the three substances—corporal, spiritual, and divine—contained in Christ. The presentation of the taper indicates that the saints followed Christ and were given the gift of "the light of eternal life." Luca Antonio Chracas, *Breve, et erudita Spiegazione di tutte le cose Misteriose, che nella solenne Celebrità, e Funzione della Canonizazione de' Santi si sogliono offerire al Sommo Pontefice . . .* (Rome, 1712).

138. For the documents on the urn and Pietro da Cortona's work on the altar surround at the same time, see Jennifer Montagu, *Alessandro Algardi,* 2 vols. (London and New Haven: Yale University Press, 1985), 1:24–26; 2:387–89; and Levy, "A Canonical Work of an Uncanonical Era," 65–78.

139. From left to right: Renato Fremin's *St. Ignatius extinguishing a fire,* Angelo De'Rossi's *St. Ignatius liberating a possessed man,* Pietro Reiff's *St. Ignatius healing a nun,* Lorenzo Merlini's *St. Peter appearing to St. Ignatius,* Francesco Nuvolone's *St. Philip Neri recognizes St. Ignatius's radiance,* Renato Fremin's *Healings by the oil hanging before St. Ignatius's tomb,* and Pierre Stephan Monnot's *St. Ignatius freeing prisoners.* For a discussion of the style of the reliefs as a group, see Robert Enggass, *Early Eigtheenth-Century Sculpture in Rome,* 1:46–47.

140. Pozzo provided designs for Fremin's *St. Ignatius extinguishing a fire,* Angelo De'Rossi's

St. Ignatius liberating a possessed man, Reiff's *St. Ignatius healing a nun,* Fremin's *Healings by the oil hanging before St. Ignatius's tomb,* and Monnot's *St. Ignatius freeing prisoners.* Although the bozzetti are lost, most agree that the sculptors were given some freedom in developing Pozzo's designs. The relationship between corridor frescoes and the reliefs was established by Bernhard Kerber, "Designs for Sculpture by Andrea Pozzo," *Art Bulletin* 47 (1965): 499–502. See further discussion in Robert Enggass, "Un problème du baroque romain tardif. Projets de sculptures par des artistes non sculpteurs," *Revue de l'art* 31 (1976): 21 ff.

141. So it is described in a pamphlet published by the Jesuits in 1697 and 1705. In Merlini's autobiography, the subject is noted, more accurately, as follows: "Li 12 Novembre del 1695 feci un'Apoca con il Reverendissimo Padre Generale de' Gesuiti, di fare un Bassorilievo di Bronzo . . . che contiene la conversione di S. Ignazio, che stando in Letto ferito in una Gamba da una Palla di Cannone ricevuta nell'Assedio di Pamplona con un Libro in Mano leggendo le Vite de' Santi, li comparve S. Pietro portato da una gloria di Angioli." Autobiography of Lorenzo Merlini, cited in Enggass, *Early Eighteenth-Century Sculpture in Rome,* 1:121.

142. The episode appeared in the Rubens/Barbè *Vita Beati P. Ignatii,* Rome, 1609/1622 (König-Nordhoff, *Ignatius von Loyola,* fig. 479), and later copies of that pictorial *vita* (Augsburg, 1616; ibid., fig. 508; see also fig. 527).

143. The painting, ascribed to Maratti in an inventory of 1800, is part of a group of works that ended up in the Pinacoteca Vaticana following the suppression of the Society. The attribution was questioned by Gianni Papi (in Aa.vv., *La regola e la fama: San Filippo Neri e l'arte* [Milan: Electa, 1995], cat. 124, 567–68), who dated the work to the 1640s. Federica Papi (in *Athanasius Kircher: Il Museo del Mondo,* ed. Eugenio del Sardo [Rome: De Luca, 2001], 311–12) retains the attribution to Maratti and likewise looks to a date around 1640.

144. The relationship between Neri and Loyola is a problem for Oratorian and Jesuit historians. The most detailed considerations of the issues are found in a study by the Jesuit Hugo Rahner, "Ignatius of Loyola and Philip Neri," in *Ignatius of Loyola: His Personality and Spiritual Heritage, 1556–1956: Studies on the 400th Anniversary of His Death,* ed. F. Wulf (Saint Louis: Institute of Jesuit Sources, 1977), 45–68; and by the historians of the Oratorian Congregation, Louis Ponnelle and Louis Bordet, *Saint Philippe Néri et la société romaine de son temps, 1515–1595* (Paris: Bloud and Gay, 1929), 53–55. Rahner (45) dates their encounter to 1538–39 and Ponnelle and Bordet (53) more generally to the period 1537–47.

145. Ponnelle and Bordet (*Saint Philippe Néri,* 54) believe this was the case, whereas Rahner ("Ignatius of Loyola and Philip Neri," 49) casts doubt on it. The documents in support are discussed in Giovanni Incisa della Rocchetta and Nello Vian, eds., *Il primo processo per San Filippo Neri nel codice Vaticano Latino 3798 e in altri esemplari dell'archivio dell'Oratorio di Roma,* 4 vols. (Vatican City: Biblioteca Apostolica Vaticana, 1957–63), 1:180 n.494.

146. The witness was Olivier Mannaerts, a student of Ignatius's who had met Neri. Rahner, "Ignatius of Loyola and Philip Neri," 68.

147. Antonio Gallonio, secretary and nurse to Neri at his death, testified that "cognosceva il padre [Neri] li huomini santi sul viso, onde soleva dire che'l P. Ignatio di santa memo-

ria haveva la faccia che li risplendeva." Incisa della Rocchetta and Vian, eds., *Il primo processo per San Filippo Neri*, 1:179 and n.492.

148. The engraving, inscribed "Vede risplendere la faccia di S. Carlo, e di S. Ignatio. Vit. Volg. lib.3. cap.2. no.12," is in the VITA DI S. FILIPPO NERI FIORENTINO. FONDATORE DELLA CONGREG.NE DELL'ORATORIO DI ROMA . . . J. STELLA INVENTOR. CHRISTIANUS SAS SCULP., of which there is an exemplar in the Biblioteca Vallicelliana, Rome, O. 14, pl. 14. Luca Ciamberlano contracted in 1610 and 1612 for engravings of Neri and Borromeo. See O. Melasecchi in Aa.vv., *La regola e la fama*, cat. 38, 484–85.

149. For a summary of the evidence, see Ponnelle and Bordet, *Saint Philippe Néri*, 55–56 n.2.

150. Polemical tracts devoted to this issue appeared in the eighteenth century, stimulated by the Jesuit account of the relationship in the *Acta Sanctorum* entry on Ignatius, which appeared in 1731. Oratorian Carlo Barbieri, *Giunta alla difesa de' scrittori della vita di S. Filippo Neri o sia confutazione di ciò, che Altri asseriscono, avere S. Filippo domandato a S. Ignazio l'ingresso nella Compagnia di Gesù, ed averne avuta la ripulsa* (Bologna, 1742); and idem, *Appendice alla confutazione della pretesa domanda di S. Filippo Neri a Sant'Ignazio per l'ingresso nella Compagnia di Gesù* (Bologna, 1742). A second edition of the latter came out in 1752. According to Ponnelle and Bordet, *Saint Philippe Néri* (55–56 n.2), Barbieri's second edition was written in response to p. Francesco Antonio Zaccaria's praise—in his *Storia letteraria d'Italia*—of the Jesuit confutation of the Oratorian version in the *Acta Sanctorum* and in later biographies. See also de Gaiffier, "Une collaboration fraternelle," 187–89.

151. Agostino Cusani testified (28 January 1596): "Et, in questo particolare del magisterio de guidare le anime alla sua salute, egli era eminentissimo, poiché ha salvate tante centinara de anime, et parte levandole dalla mala strada, restando nel secolo, et parte in diverse religioni, come Cappucini, di S. Domenico, Gesuiti et Theatini. Onde egli soleva dire, che'l p. Ignatio, fundatore della Compagnia del Giesù, diceva, che era come la campana, perché egli chiamava li altri alla religione, et non volse entrare nella Compagnia, nella qual era pregato ad intrarvi dal predetto p. Ignatio. Nel che si é veduta la gran providentia de Iddio, la qual designava di servirse di questo suo servo a fundare un'altra congregatione" (Incisa della Rocchetta and Vian, eds., *Il primo processo per San Filippo Neri*, 2:38). Marco Antonio Maffa testified (13 May 1596): "Nasceva, da tutto questo, che molti si facevano religiosi in religioni molto riformate, quali uscivano da questa schola. Et soleva il p. Ignatio, che fu homo di tanta santità et fondatore della preclarissimo Compagnia del Giesù, dire a detto padre: 'voi sete come la campana, che chiama li altri alla chiesa, et ella non vi va,' volendo inferire, che mandava molti alla Compagnia et egli non vi entrava, come haverebbe voluto detto p. Ignatio" (ibid., 2:85). Marco Antonio Vitelleschi, bother of the Society's general, Muzio Vitelleschi, testified: "Et lui istesso [Neri] mi ha detto, che il beato Ignatio desiderava, che egli si facesso [*sic*] gesuito, e che lui lo desiderava, particularmente, per andar alle Indie, ma che era stato avisato, che non era volontà di Dio, e che lui sarebbe stato la campana per il beato Ignatio, per condurre genti alla sua Compagnia" (ibid., 4:67). See the similar testimonies of Fabrizio Massimo (ibid., 2:338) and Germanico Fedeli (ibid., 3:261).

152. Neri was finally ordained in 1551, five years before Ignatius's death.

153. For changes made to the statue see Levy, "A Canonical Work," 329–33. For the nine-teenth-century statue, see See Carmen Lorenzetti, "Uno stuccatore bolognese a Roma: Luigi Acquisti," *Accademia Clementina. Atti e memorie*, n.s., 28–29 (1991): 153–54.

154. See Joseph Braun, *Die Reliquiare des christlichen Kultes und ihre Entwicklung* (Freiburg im Breisgau: Herdersche, 1940), 92–95.

155. "S'inganna di gran tratto chi stima l'argento vivo di natura freddo; Egli è freddo alla mano, che lo tocca; ma è caldo in terzo grado. Che ciò sia vero, ed abbrucia, e perfora, ed incide: tutti effetti, che da vigoroso caldo vengono operati. Habbiasi pur dunque il motto; FLAGRAT, ET ALGET, dice il mio Carducci, e sarà una bella immagine, di Sant'Ig-natio Loiola, attualmente cercato entro un gelato stagno, che tutto al di fuori, era di ri-gore sorpreso, & al di dentro dalle fiamme della carità predominato." Picinelli, *Il Mondo Simbolico*), 447. The other was St. Bernard.

   Picinelli used a similar image in a sermon (1647), in which he compared Ignatius to Mount Etna (il Mongibello), assailed by the snows without and burning with fire within. Picinelli, "Il Mongibello. Nevoso ed infuocato," in *Applausi festivi*, 323–72.

156. The plan for the light source is mentioned in recommendations to Pozzo for changes to his model: "10. Vestire la testa del nicchio con Rame dorato, bucatò, acciò possa rice-vere il lume da procurarsi verso strada." "Diligenze," fol. 6ov. A long set of instruc-tions for the maintenance of the chapel is more specific about the mirrors: "Quando si tiene scoperta la nicchia una giornata prima di alzare il quadro se gli dà una spolve-rata senza scale, stando nella med.ma nicchia con pennaggi longhi, e piccioli: Qualche volta si procuri di levar la polvere dalli specchi, che posano sul finestrolo dietro la statua, perche quando il sole batte nel Palazzo Altieri p via di riflesso fa brilare le gioie, che sono nella cuppola della stessa nicchia." "Governo della nuova Cappella del Nro S.P. Ignazio nella Chiesa del Giesù di Roma," in ARSI, Rom 140, fol. 103r.

157. In this space, now the Chapel of the Crucifixion, a Crucifix hangs on the back of the door that previously provided access to the chapel from the street. The emblems are not mentioned by Pecchiai, who noted that Francesco Guarnieri worked in the vestibule. Pecchiai, *Il Gesù di Roma*, 259.

158. An overlooked observation first made by Mâle, *L'art religieux après le Concile de Trente*, 156, who underscored the importance of the scene in Jesuit iconography.

159. This is the substance of the contradictory accounts that record the event. See Ravier, *Ignatius of Loyola and the Founding*, 424–25.

160. Much ink has been spilled over the attribution of this and a pendant canvas of St. Fran-cis Xavier (attributed since Titi to Van Dyck) and their identification with the paintings that hung in the transept chapels of the Gesù at the time of the canonization. The first modern study to connect the Vatican canvases with the works seen by Titi was Redig de Campos, "Intorno a due quadri d'altare del Van Dyck per il Gesù di Roma ritrovati in Vaticano," *Bollettino d'arte* 30 (1936–37): 150–65. For a detailed analysis of paintings of the saints in the early Gesù, see König-Nordhoff, *Ignatius von Loyola*, 76–96; and Levy, "A Canonical Work of an Uncanonical Era," 55–65, for more recent bibliography. For the attribution of the works to Seghers, see Arnout Balis, "Van Dyck: Some Prob-lems of Attribution," in *Van Dyck 350*, ed. Susan J. Barnes and Arthur Wheelock, Jr., Studies in the History of Art, 46 (Washington, D.C.: National Gallery of Art, 1994),

180–81. The painting is not mentioned in the most recent study on the artist, Dorothea Bieneck, *Gerard Seghers 1591–1651: Leben und Werk des Antwerpener Historienmalers* (Lingen: Luca, 1992).

161. The first Christian king of the realm of the Congo (the northern part of Angola) was baptized in 1491, well before the Jesuit arrival in 1548. As the Jesuits were not responsible for the conversion (and in fact their difficult mission in the region was abandoned in 1669), this figure is to be understood as a representative conversion. See Teobaldo Filesi, *San Salvador: Cronache dei Re del Congo* (Bologna: E.M.I., 1974); and Levy, "A Canonical Work of an Uncanonical Era," 303.

162. The inscription has been traced to the sixteenth-century Jesuit missionary Alessandro Valignano's history of the Jesuit mission in Asia that circulated in manuscript form until its publication at the turn of this century. CAMES is the Latinized version of the Japanese word for spirit, or, the Shinto gods. FOTOQUÈS is from the Japanese word for Buddha. AMIDA refers to the amidism sect of Buddhism and XACA is the Portuguese translation of the Chinese branch of the family of Buddha. Pasquale D'Elia, "CAMES FOTOQUÈS AMIDA ET XACA: Kurze Bemerkung zu einer römischen Barock-Inschrift," *Römische Quartalschrift für Christliche Alterstumkunde und Kirchengeschichte* 56 (1961): 78–80.

163. For the payments to the sculptors who modeled the various figures and sections and the eight lamps at the interstices of this eight-section balustrade, see Enggass, "The Altar-Rail for St. Ignatius's Chapel." The model of the balustrade was made by Francesco Maglia and that for the gate by Pietro Papaleo. Pecchiai and Kerber attributed the design to Pozzo while Enggass attributed it to Fontana. I disagree with Enggass's attribution of the altar rail to Carlo Fontana, for reasons that will be argued more fully in Levy, *The Chapel of St. Ignatius*.

164. "Obedientiam proprium Societati Characterem Facit Ignatius. Teneriores cum ex arte flores inteximus, eorum facili A FLEXU FORMA quaeuis effingitur. Ordinis sui Socios in omne Maiorem imperium & nutum non aliter Ignatius pro indito Iesu nomine volvit esse flexibiles." Bovio, *Ignatius Insignium*, 208.

165. In Greek mythology, Neptune's dolphins persuaded Amphitrite to marry him. Vincenzo Cartari, *Le vere e nove imagini de gli dei delli antichi* (Padua: Pietro Paolo Tozzi, 1615), 534–35.

166. For a call to recognize the politicized stance of the apolitical in iconographic studies see Moxey, "The Politics of Iconology," in Cassidy, ed., *Iconography at the Crossroads*, 27–31.

167. For the use of images of miracles and historical events as documentary proof in Venice, especially in the late Middle Ages, see Patricia Fortini Brown, "Painting and History in Renaissance Venice," *Art History* 7 (1984): 263–93.

168. Panofsky, "Iconography and Iconology," 40–41.

CHAPTER 5. DIFFUSION

1. On the difficulties of gauging conversion, see the stimulating account of three Chinese converted by the Jesuits in Willard J. Peterson, "Why Did They Become Christians?

Yang T'ing-yüng, Li Chih-tsao, and Hsü Kuang-ch'i," in *East Meets West: The Jesuits in China, 1582–1773,* ed. Charles E. Ronan and Bonnie B. C. Oh (Chicago: Loyola University Press, 1988), 129–52; Jacques Gernet, *Chine et Christianisme: Action et reaction* (Paris: Gallimard, 1982), 46–47.

2. See chapter 1, 33–34.

3. Sandro Benedetti ("Tipologia ragionevolezza e pauperismo nel 'modo nostro' dell'architettura gesuitica," in *Fuori dal classicismo,* 83), Luciano Patetta ("Le chiese della Compagnia di Gesù" in *Storia e tipologia*), and Richard Bösel all argue that the coherence of Jesuit architecture is the result of an approach to building via typologies, thus underscoring the essential unity of Jesuit architecture without recourse to style. Of these authors, Bösel has made the most sustained inquiry into the Jesuit use of models and my thinking on the subject is indebted to his sustained archival research and commentary. In addition to Bösel's publications already cited ("Typus und Tradition" and *Jesuitenarchitektur in Italien, 1540–1773*), see "Die Nachfolgebauten von S. Fedele in Mailand," *Wiener Jahrbuch für Kunstgeschichte* 37 (1984): 67–87; idem, "La chiesa di S. Lucia: L'invenzione spaziale nel contesto dell'architettura gesuitica," in *Dall'Isola alla città: I Gesuiti a Bologna,* ed. Gian Paolo Brizzi and Anna Maria Matteucci (Bologna: Nuova Alfa, 1988), 19–30; idem, "La chiesa dei Gesuiti a Venezia: Un'ipotesi di interpretazione tipologica," in *I Gesuiti e Venezia: Momenti e problemi di Storia Veneziana della Compagnia di Gesù,* ed. Mario Zanardi (Venice: Giunta Regionale del Veneto, 1994), 690–703; idem, "Grundsatzfragen und Fallstudien zur Jesuitischen Bautypologie," in *Die Jesuiten in Wien: Zur Kunst- und Kulturgeschichte der Oesterreichischen Ordensprovinz der Gesellschaft Jesu im 17. und 18. Jahrhunderts,* ed. Werner Telesko and Herbert Karner (Vienna: Oesterreichische Akademie der Wissenschaften, forthcoming).

4. Patetta, "Le chiese della Compagnia di Gesù," 161.

5. The description is Sebastiano de Ursis's, the father who supervised construction. Pietro Tacchi Venturi, ed., *Opere storiche del P. Matteo Ricci* (Macerata, 1911–13), 1:613 n.2, as quoted in Bailey, *Art on the Jesuit Missions,* 94. Emphasis mine.

6. See chapter 3.

7. Leon Battista Alberti, *On the Art of Building in Ten Books,* trans. Joseph Rykwert, Neil Leach, and Robert Tavernor (Cambridge, Mass.: MIT Press, 1988), Book 7, chap. 3, 194. See the discussion of this passage in Van Eck, "Architecture, Language and Rhetoric," in Clarke and Crossley, eds., *Architecture and Language,* 79–81.

8. The episode was recounted by Marsili in a letter written to the general Michelangelo Tamburini in 1726. Bösel, "La chiesa di S. Lucia," 697.

9. Alberti, *On the Art of Building,* Book 9, chap. 9, 314. See Van Eck, "Architecture, Language and Rhetoric," in Clarke and Crossley, eds., *Architecture and Language,* 80–81, for a discussion of this passage as the solution to the absence of the rhetorical *res* in architectural theory.

10. Alessandro Valignano, *Il Ceremoniale per i missionari del Giappone,* quoted in Bailey, *Art on the Jesuit Missions,* 64. The *Advertimentos* are discussed at length in Josef Franz Schütte, S.J., *Valignano's Mission Principles for Japan,* trans. John J. Coyne (St. Louis: Institute of Jesuit Sources, 1983), 2:158–90.

11. For instance, the churches were to have *zashiki* (reception rooms for high-ranking visi-

tors) separated by sliding doors, an open space in front of the church, and a place to clean one's feet, following Japanese custom. Schütte, *Valignano's Mission Principles*, 2:189.

12. Richard Krautheimer, "Introduction to an 'Iconography of Medieval Architecture,'" *Journal of the Warburg and Courtauld Institutes* 5 (1942): 1–33. For further discussion of the form-content problem posed by Krautheimer, with specific regard to early modern architecture, see Evonne Levy, "Locating the *bel composto:* Copies and Imitations in the Late Baroque," in Sobral and Booth, eds., *Struggle for Synthesis*, 1:73–84.

13. Helge Gamrath, *Roma Sancta Renovata: Studi sull'urbanistica di Roma nella seconda metà del sec. XVI con particolare riferimento al pontificato di Sisto V (1585–1590)* (Rome: Bretschneider, 1987), esp. 165–66.

14. There is a large bibliography on Sixtus V's fresco cycles. To my knowledge, Charles Burroughs first pointed to the importance of these (and the engraved maps of Sistine Rome) *as representations*. Charles Burroughs, "Absolutism and the Rhetoric of Topography: Streets in the Rome of Sixtus V," in *Streets: Critical Perspectives on Public Space,* ed. Zeynep Celik, Diane Favro, and Richard Ingersoll (Berkeley: University of California Press, 1994), 189–202.

15. The complex components of Sixtus's projects are identified in Maria Luisa Madonna, ed., *Roma di Sisto V: Le arti e la cultura* (Rome: De Luca, 1993). For a reconstruction of the architectural views in the frieze of the Sala Sistina of the demolished Villa Montalto, see tav. XVII–XXIII; on the architectural works as "opere di Sisto V" in the Salone Sistino of the Biblioteca Vaticana, see Angela Böck, in idem., 77–90, esp. 82 (for Rome as synonymous with papacy and Church). For Sixtus's buildings as good works, see Corinne Mandel, *Sixtus V and the Lateran Palace* (Rome: Istituto Poligrafico e Zecca dello Stato, 1994).

16. Matteo Neroni and Paul Brill executed the architectural paintings. The description is from the *Annuae Litterae 1584,* transcribed in Pirri, *Giuseppe Valeriano,* 69–70.

17. The engraving, commissioned by canon Claude Menestrier in 1630, shows Pietro Paolo Olivieri's statue of Gregory XIII, commissioned by three conservatori for the Sala dei Tribunali of the Senator's Palace on the Capitoline in 1577 (moved to the Aracoeli in 1876). The engraving appeared in Alfonso Chacon, *Vitae et res gestae pontificum Romanorum et S.R.E. cardinalium . . .* (Rome, 1630), vol. 2. Of three popes (Sixtus V, Paul V, Gregory XIII) whose medals are represented, Gregory is the only one to whom a supplementary engraving of the buildings is dedicated. On the dating of the engraving and the circumstances of its publication, see Jürgen Krüger, "Das ursprüngliche Grabmal Gregors XIII. in St. Peter zu Rom," *Korrespondenzblatt Collegium Germanicum Hungaricum* 95 (1986): 52 n.39.

    The surrounding fields of decoration in the engraving do not pertain to the Campidoglio mise-en-scène of the statue (see Filippo de Rossi, *Ritratto di Roma Moderna* [1645; anastatic reprint, Rome: Logart Press, 1989], 404, where the pictorial decorations of that room are described) but rather elaborate on the Roman College decorations.

18. At least three engravings of this format, two with bust-length portraits, one a half-length portrait showing the pope blessing, were made to commemorate Sixtus V in 1589. For the portrait in Ioanne Pinadello, *Invicti Quinarii Numeri Series Quae Summatim a Superioribus Pontificibus et Maxime A Sixto Quinto . . .* (Rome: F. Zannettum, 1589), and the anonymous engraving published by Nicolas van Aelst, also in 1589, see Corinne Man-

del, "Golden Age and the Good Works of Sixtus V: Classical and Christian Typology in the Art of a Counter-Reformation Pope," *Storia dell'Arte* 62 (1988): figs. 13–14. For the half-length version, also published by Giuseppe Pinadello in 1589, see Eamon Duffy, *Saints and Sinners: A History of the Popes* (New Haven: Yale University Press, 1997), 171.

19. On architecture in late Medieval paintings as territorial possession, see Carlo Bertelli, "A Tale of Two Cities: Siena and Venice," in *The Renaissance from Brunelleschi to Michelangelo: The Representation of Architecture*, ed. Henry A. Millon and Vittorio Magnano Lampugnani (New York: Rizzoli, 1997), 373–97; Max Seidel, "'Castrum pingatur in palatio': Richerche storiche e iconografiche sui castelli dipinti nel palazzo Pubblico di Siena," *Prospettiva* 28 (1982): 17–41.

20. A good example is the so-called sala del dominio Fiorentino in the Medici Palace (Rome, ca. 1587), for which, see Philippe Morel in Madonna, ed., *Roma di Sisto V*, 324–26. On the rise of the related city view in the fifteenth and sixteenth centuries, particularly its use at court, see Richard L. Kagan, "Phillip II and the Art of Cityscape," in *Art and History: Images and Their Meaning*, ed. Robert I. Rotberg and Theodore K. Rabb (Cambridge: Cambridge University Press, 1988), 115–35.

21. See Herbert Bloch, *Monte Cassino in the Middle Ages*, 3 vols. (Cambridge, Mass.: Harvard University Press, 1986), 1:esp. 492–94.

22. The paintings, now at the Università Gregoriana, were first mentioned in Riccardo G. Villoslada, S.J., *Storia del Collegio Romano dal suo inizio (1551) alla soppressione della Compagnia di Gesù* (Rome: Universitatis Gregorianae, 1954), 153–54. For a proposed dating to the 1650s, based on new documents, see Evonne Levy in Lucas, ed., *Saint, Site, and Sacred Strategy*, cat. 95, 161–63.

23. Roger Chartier, "Princely Patronage and the Economy of Dedication," in *Forms and Meanings: Texts, Performances, and Audiences from Codex to Computer* (Philadelphia: University of Pennsylvania Press, 1995), 29. For examples of both types, see *Les Fastes du gothique: Le siècle de Charles V* (Paris: Éditions de la Réunion des musées nationaux, 1981), no. 53 (for a sculpture of Jean Tissendier, donor of the chapelle de Rieux in Toulouse) and nos. 257, 258, 285 (for illuminations of authors and their patrons).

24. Cosimo I seems to have been first represented with his architects in Vasari's *Cosimo de' Medici and His Architects* (Sala di Cosimo I, Palazzo Vecchio, Florence). Kirwin pointed out the novelty of the image and cited the author presenting manuscript to patron as precedent. The argument is well supported by Vasari's variants on the theme for Lorenzo the Magnificent (surrounded by scholars) and Cosimo il Vecchio (with artists and scholars) in nearby rooms. Chandler Kirwin, "Vasari's Tondo of 'Cosimo with his architects, engineers and sculptors' in the Palazzo Vecchio," *Mitteilungen der Kunsthistorisches Institut in Florenz* 15 (1971): 105–22.

The presentation type (architect before the patron) is developed further in images of Michelangelo standing before his patrons, the subject that dominates the Galleria of the Casa Buonarotti (1615–22, Florence). Ugo Procacci, *La Casa Buonarotti a Firenze* (Milan: Electa, 1967), 10–13, 173–75, figs. 8–18; Adriaan Willem Vliegenthart, *De Galleria Buonarotti Michelangelo en Michelangelo il Giovane* (Rotterdam: Bronder-Offset, 1969), 119–22; 142–47; Millon and Lampugnani, eds., *The Renaissance from Brunelleschi to Michelangelo*, cat. 234, 399.

A third type is the patron with his building, an extension to portraiture of the donation portrait. See Francesco Salviati (attributed), *Portrait of Giovanni and Paolo Rucellai* (private collection), with S. Maria Novella in the background (illustrated in Millon and Lampugnani, eds., *The Renaissance from Brunelleschi to Michelangelo*, 18) and *Cardinals Alessandro and Odoardo Farnese* inside the nave of the Roman Gesù (fig. 15).

25. Sixtus V's renovation of the Lateran Palace was literally compared (in an inscription in the Salone dei Papi, Lateran Palace) to Francis supporting the building on his shoulders. Mandel reads Sixtus's architectural works in general as a fulfillment of this Franciscan image, on the one hand, and the Catholic expression of imperium, on the other. Mandel, *Sixtus V and the Lateran Palace*, 25, 94, 110.

26. See the subtle analysis by Monica Grasso in Luciana Cassanelli and Sergio Russi, eds., *Oltre Raffaello: Aspetti della cultura figurativa del cinquecento Romano* (Rome: Multigrafica, 1984), 133–34.

27. Alessandro Zuccari, *I pittori di Sisto V* (Rome: Fratelli Palombi, 1992), 61.

28. Mandel, "Golden Age and the Good Works of Sixtus V." Heavy emphasis was placed on the renewal of sacred building in sacred oratory during the reigns of Sixtus V and Gregory XIII. McGinness, *Right Thinking and Sacred Oratory*, chap. 7, "From Vices to Virtues, Punishment to Glory: Rome, *Civitas Sancta*." For the idea of patron as author, who brings the work into being, see Chartier, "Princely Patronage and the Economy of Dedication," 42.

29. Catervo Foglietta, letter dated 10 May 1587, transcribed in Mandel, "Golden Age and the Good Works of Sixtus V," 50 n.101.

30. The Christianization of Rome is literally represented as an architectural event in the frontispiece to Cesare Rasponi, *De Basilica et Patriarchio Lateranensi, De basilica et patriarchio Lateranensi libri quattuor: ad Alexandrum VII, pont. max* (Rome: Typis I. de Lazzeris, 1656). The Michelangelesque architect and compliment to Innocent X cum Constantine are noted in Joseph Connors, introduction to *Opus Architectonicum*, by Borromini, xlvi.

31. This was the case until the 1660s when General Oliva required elevations. See Vallery-Radot and Lamalle, *Le recueil de plans d'édifices de la Compagnie di Jésus*, 15*. The significance of the shift was emphasized by Francis Haskell, "The Role of Patrons: Baroque Style Changes," in Wittkower and Jaffe, eds., *Baroque Art*, 59–60.

32. See the discussion of the "modo nostro" as "rational organization" rather than a priori forms in Benedetti, "Tipologia ragionevolezza e pauperismo," in *Fuori dal Classicismo*, 90.

33. For the contribution of the new Accademia del Disegno (founded 1563) to the availability of art as a discourse see Barzman, *The Florentine Academy*.

34. The precondition for such a development was the humanist description of architecture according to antique rhetorical models, for which see Smith, *Architecture in the Culture of Early Humanism*, part 3, esp. 136–38.

35. Patetta, "Le chiese della Compagnia di Gesù," 171.

36. Mercurian's letter, "Istruzioni per l'uso degli edifici della nostra Compagnia che si inviano in Spagna," is transcribed in Balestreri, "L'architettura negli scritti della Compagnia di Gesù," in Patetta et al., eds., *L'architettura della Compagnia di Gesù*, 24.

37. For the debate over common use and license stimulated by Michelangelo's inventiveness, see Payne, *The Architectural Treatise in the Renaissance*, 15–23.

38. On this issue, see Mario Carpo, *L'architettura dell'età della stampa: Oralità, scrittura, libro stampato e riproduzione meccanica dell'immagine nella storia delle teorie architettoniche* (Milan: Jaca Book, 1998), chap. 4, "Il disegno d'architettura all'epoca della sua riproducibilità meccanica"; Payne, *The Architectural Treatise in the Renaissance;* and Clarke and Crossley, eds., *Architecture and Language.*

39. Mario Carpo, *Metodo ed ordini nella teoria architettonica dei primi moderni: Alberti, Raffaello, Serlio e Camillo* (Geneva: Drosz, 1993), chap. 1, "Regole, esempi e parti."

40. Carpo, *L'architettura dell'età della stampa*, 78–79, 103.

41. Antonio Possevino, *Bibliotheca selecta de ratione studiorum [. . .] recognita novissime ab eodem, et aucta* (1593), as discussed in Carpo, *L'architettura dell'età della stampa*, 122–23. On Possevino's *Bibliotheca*, see Luigi Balsamo, "Venezia e l'attività editoriale di Antonio Possevino," in Zanardi, ed., *I Gesuiti e Venezia*, 629–60; Alessandro Gambuti, "Il Gesuita Antonio Possevino, o del come 'costruire e fondare' vantaggiosamente edifici per 'uomini religiosi,'" in *Altari controriformati in Toscana: Architettura e arredi*, ed. Carlo Cresti (Florence: A. Pontecorboli, 1997), 133–41; Werner Oechslin, "*Architectura est scientia aedificandi:* Reflections on the Scope of Architectural and Architectural-Theoretical Literature," in *The Triumph of the Baroque: Architecture in Europe, 1600–1750*, ed. Henry A. Millon (New York: Rizzoli, 1999), 213–14; Balestreri, "L'architettura negli scritti della Compagnia," in Patetta et al., eds., *L'architettura della Compagnia di Gesù*, 19–20.

42. Carpo, *L'architettura dell'età della stampa*, 124. On Jesuit attitudes toward imitation in the debates over rhetoric, see Fumaroli, *L'Age de l'Eloquence*, esp. 673–82.

43. After Mercurian's death general Aquaviva (1581–1615) returned to the more flexible model. Cristiana Coscarella, "La tipologia della chiesa gesuitica," in Patetta et al., eds., *L'architettura della Compagnia di Gesù*, 12–13.

44. On the theory of imitation and architecture, see Payne, *The Architectural Treatise in the Renaissance*, and a condensed version in idem, "Architects and Academies: Architectural Theories of Imitatio and the Literacy Debates on Language and Style," in Clarke and Crossley, eds., *Architecture and Language*, 118–33.

45. The early modern sense of the exemplar marks a shift from the Medieval *exemplum*, which meant both faithful copy and original. Robert W. Scheller, *Exemplum: Model-Book Drawings and the Practice of Artistic Transmission in the Middle Ages (ca. 900–ca. 1450)* (Amsterdam: Amsterdam University Press, 1995), esp. 9–17.

46. Richard Schiff, "The Original, the Imitation, the Copy, and the Spontaneous Classic," *Yale French Studies* 66 (1984): 28.

47. See the perceptive remarks on the high value placed on individuality in Marvin Trachtenberg, "On Brunelleschi's Old Sacristy as Model for Early Renaissance Church Architecture," in *L'Église dans l'architecture de la Renaissance: Actes du colloque tenu à Tours du 28 au 31 mai 1990*, ed. Jean Guillaume (Paris: Picard, 1995), 9–39; Cammy Brothers, "Architecture, Texts, and Imitation in Late-Fifteenth- and Early-Sixteenth-Century Rome," in Crossley and Clarke, eds., *Architecture and Language*, 82–101. See the ex-

emplary study of the mechanics of prototypes and their progeny in Switzerland, Werner Oechslin, ed., *Die Vorarlberger Barockbaumeister* (Einsiedeln and Zürich: Benziger, 1973).

48. For arguments that architectural styles were deployed to assert political allegiances or to establish identity more broadly, see the essays by Yves Pauwels, Peter Draper, Caroline Bruzelius, Christy Anderson, and Deborah Howard in Crossley and Clarke, eds., *Architecture and Language.*

49. Bösel's often-cited complaint that previous scholars viewed "every Jesuit church" as "a little Gesù" is not referenced. For arguments against the Gesù as preeminent model, see Galassi Paluzzi, *Storia segreta dello stile;* Pierre Moisy, *Les Églises des Jésuites de l'ancienne Assistance de France* (Rome: Institutum Historicum Societatis Iesu, 1958), 362 ff.; for a brief historiography and arguments against the preeminence of the Gesù (both as longitudinal plan and the facade), see Patetta, "Le chiese della Compagnia di Gesù," 165–68. Bailey has mocked the purported influence of the Gesù in "Le style jésuite n'existe pas," 45, and *Art on the Jesuit Missions,* 44, 110–11. He reconsiders his position in "'Just like the Gesù': Sebastiano Serlio, Giacomo Vignola, and Jesuit Architecture in South America," *Archivum Historicum Societatis Iesu* 70 (2001): 233–65.

50. Bösel, "La chiesa di S. Lucia," 30. The facades of the Jesuit churches in Cracow, Ferrara, Lecce, Frascati, Dubrovnik, Vienna, Besançon, Avignon, Montpellier, and the novitiate in Paris are based on the Gesù. Patetta, "Le chiese della Compagnia di Gesù," 168; for imitation of the plan, see ibid., 173–74.

51. There is no documentary evidence that Sts. Peter and Paul was based on the Gesù. For a summary of formal arguments as to whether the Cracow church (originally designed in 1596 by Giovanni De Rosis in Rome, later modified by Jan Maria Bernardoni and Matteo Castello) is based on the Gesù or on other Roman churches, see Mariusz Karpowicz, *Matteo Castello Architekt Wczesnego Baroku* (Warsaw: Wydawnictwo Neriton, 1994), 53 ff.

52. For the building history, see Bösel, *Jesuitenarchitektur in Italien,* 1:191–200 (with previous bibliography); and idem, "Grundsatzfragen und Fallstudien zur Jesuitischen Bautypologie."

53. Giovanni Pietro Bellori, *Le Vite de' Pittori, Scultori e Architetti moderni* (1672; reprint, ed. Evelina Borea, Turin: Giulio Einaudi, 1976), 362. See the discussion of the passage in Bösel, *Jesuitenarchitektur in Italien,* 1:192; for its value in attesting to the Jesuit use of architecture in the service of a corporate identity, see idem, "Grundsatzfragen und Fallstudien zur Jesuitischen Bautypologie." Bösel argues that the Jesuits meant by copy a further development of the typology.

54. Richard Bösel in *Borromini e l'universo barocco,* vol. 2, *Catalogo della mostra,* ed. Richard Bösel and Christoph Luitpold Frommel (Milan: Electa, 2000), 91.

55. Thomas DaCosta Kaufmann, "East and West: Jesuit Art and Artists in Central Europe, and Central European Art in the Americas," in O'Malley et al., eds., *The Jesuits,* esp. 285–87 (on the spread of the Vienna church typology in the Austrian province); for an example of a French church (in Grenoble, to be based on the novitiate in Lyon), see Moisy, *Les Églises des Jésuites de l'ancienne Assistance de France,* 362.

56. Bösel, "Typus und Tradition," 248.

57. For the Fano church, see Bösel, *Jesuitenarchitektur in Italien*, 1:71 doc. 4; for Pavia, see idem, "Die Nachfolgebauten," 70 n.12.

58. See Timothy Hampton, *Writing from History: The Rhetoric of Exemplarity in Renaissance Literature* (Ithaca: Cornell University Press, 1990); John D. Lyons, *Exemplum: The Rhetoric of Example in Early Modern France and Italy* (Princeton: Princeton University Press, 1989).

59. See, for example, the worldwide impact of precise reproductions of the Santa Casa di Loreto. Massimo Bulgarelli, "La Santa Casa di Loreto: L'edificio sacro e le sue copie," *Lotus International* 65 (1990): 78–89.

60. "imitando quel gran disegno s'è formato un secondo lavoro, il quale non è copia del primo, o nell'esserlo può pretendere la gloria di originale." Bösel, "Typus und Tradition," 250–51. He points out the importance of the document as proof that strings of typologically related buildings are not historically anachronistic.

61. On the rise of connoisseurship and the implications for the terms "copy" and "original," see Jeffrey M. Muller, "Measures of Authenticy: The Detection of Copies in the Early Literature on Connoisseurship," in *Retaining the Original: Multiple Originals, Copies, and Reproductions,* ed. Kathleen Preciado, Studies in the History of Art, vol. 20 (Washington, D.C.: National Gallery of Art, 1989), 141–49. For extensive documentation of attitudes toward copying, see Richard R. Spear, *The 'Divine' Guido: Religion, Sex, Money and Art in the World of Guido Reni* (New Haven: Yale University Press, 1997), 253–74.

62. "sappi che la predetta nostra (di Bologna) è tutto il Gesù corretto." Bösel, "Typus und Tradition," 251.

63. As Alina Payne has put it in a discussion of the Renaissance treatise-writer's search for his own identity in relation to the architecture of antiquity, "invention and search for rules were two sides of the same coin." Payne, *The Architectural Treatise in the Renaissance,* 32.

64. Letter from Acquaviva to p. Maselli, provincial of Naples, 26 May 1584: ". . . io mi rallegro della buona volontà della Sig. Duchessa [di Maddaloni]; ma che non conviene che il Collegio [di Napoli] si metta a competenza con la fabbrica del Collegio Romano, perché se bene qua ha potuto Sua Santità ordinare quanto l'è piaciuto, negli altri luoghi nondimeno è ragione che noi procuriamo di mantenerci nella mediocrità religiosa." Transcribed in Pirri, *Giuseppe Valeriano,* 289 (doc. VI, 4) and 86–87. See also Benedetti, "Tipologia ragionevolezza e pauperismo," in *Fuori dal classicismo,* 74; and Bösel, "Typus und Tradition," 243.

65. Moisy, *Les Églises des Jésuites de l'ancienne Assistance de France,* 363.

66. "Et intendano le RR. VV. Che non è necessario che i modelli delle nostre chiese siano tutte ad un modo; secondo le commodità et circostanze che occorrono si possono fare o in una maniera o nell'altra, come torna meglio." Quoted in Pirri and Di Rosa, "Il P. Giovanni De Rosis," 41 n.205.

67. The contrast is between a Platonic notion of exemplar *(paradeigma)* as model, the ideal form, the transcendent source from which all objects derive, and Aristotle's examples, from his rhetoric, which are parts that link to other parts (an example of something that always implies the existence of other examples). Alexander Gelley, introduction to *Unruly Examples: On the Rhetoric of Exemplarity,* ed. idem (Stanford: Stanford University Press, 1995), 2.

68. I addressed this question in the previous chapter, where forming and reforming was a crucial process of subject formation, a subject of Jesuit imagery.

69. Bailey, *Art on the Jesuit Missions*, 19 and n.11.

70. Anton Sepp (1655–1733), *Relación de viaje a las misiones jesuíticas*, cited in ibid., 178.

71. The argument is made in Alberti's letter to Brunelleschi, the preface to the Italian edition of *Della pittura* (1436). See Smith, *Architecture in the Culture of Early Humanism*, 19–21.

72. For the Seminary's activities from the 1580s and the Annual Letter of 1601 praising the aptitude of the Japanese students "which causes us great admiration" and their works (indistinguishable from works sent from Rome), see Bailey, *Art on the Jesuit Missions*, 67–72.

73. On the avoidance of the hand in early modern art theoretical definitions of style, see Philip Sohm, "*Maniera* and the Absent Hand: Avoiding the Etymology of Style," *Res* 36 (1999): 101–24; on the hand, see Spear, *The 'Divine' Guido*, 259–65.

74. "From Aristotle came the repeatedly reworked topos that 'the hand is for the body as the intellect is for the soul.' . . . The mechanism of the hand was seen as perfectly designed for *apprehensio*, that is to say 'grasping,' and it is fitting that 'apprehension' in Latin as in English came to assume the dual meaning of taking hold and becoming cognizant of new ideas." Martin Kemp, "The Handy Worke of the Incomprehensible Creator," in Claire Richter Sherman, ed., *Writing on Hands: Memory and Knowledge in Early Modern Europe* (Carlisle, Pa.: Trout Gallery, Dickinson College, 2000), 22.

75. *Constitutions*, Part VIII, Chapter 1, specifically [671]–8. The connection between spiritual uniformity and the uniformity of Jesuit architecture is alluded to in Pirri and Di Rosa, "Il P. Giovanni De Rosis," 39.

76. See chapter 4. Bösel has remarked that architecture became part of the Jesuits' spiritual property, a crucial component of the order's traditions.

77. Mario Carpo, *L'architettura dell'età della stampa;* idem, "The Making of the Typographical Architect," in *Paper Palaces: The Rise of the Renaissance Architectural Treatise*, ed. Vaughan Hart (New Haven: Yale University Press, 1998), 158–70; idem, "How Do You Imitate a Building That You Have Never Seen? Printed Images, Ancient Models, and Handmade Drawings in Renaissance Architectural Theory," *Zeitschrift für Kunstgeschichte* 64 (2001): 223–33.

78. For the drawings, currently on the art market in New York, see Bösel, "Grundsatzfragen und Fallstudien zur Jesuitischen Bautypologie." Bösel is preparing a catalog of the 284 drawings (not all are by Laloyau). A two-volume collection of eighteenth-century drawings after engravings of the work of Pozzo and others is discussed in Oechslin, ed., *Die Voralberger Barockbaumeister*, 62–77.

79. For a general introduction to the culture and protagonists of the Italian print industry, see Paolo Bellini, *Storia dell'incisione Italiana: Il seicento* (Piacenza: Tip.le.co, 1992). For an overview of the major European print establishments and their marketing strategies, see Anton W. A. Boschloo, *The Prints of the Remondinis: An Attempt to Reconstruct an Eighteenth-Century World of Pictures* (Amsterdam: Amsterdam University Press, 1998), 5–9.

80. On the publication history of Francesco Borromini's *Opus Architectonicum*, monographs of two of his buildings, published posthumously in 1720 and 1725, see Joseph Connors, "Sebastiano Giannini: *Opus Architectonicum*," in *In Urbe Architectus: Modelli, Disegni, Misure. La Professione dell'architetto Roma 1680–1750*, ed. Bruno Contardi and Giovanna Curcio (Rome: Museo Nazionale di Castel Sant'Angelo, 1991), 204–10; idem, ed., introduction to Francesco Borromini, *Opus architectonicum*. Bernini never published a treatise, although he supervised engravings of his projects. On Carlo Fontana's printed works, see Hellmut Hager, "Le opere letterarie di Carlo Fontana come autorappresentazione," in Contardi and Curcio, eds., *In Urbe Architectus*, 155–203.

81. On the brief history of the architectural monograph, see Connors in Contardi and Curcio, eds., *In Urbe Architectus*, 205; and idem, ed., introduction to Francesco Borromini, *Opus architectonicum*.

82. On the mutually beneficial relationship between dedicatee and dedicator, see Anna Grelle Iusco, *Indice delle stampe intagliate in rame a bulino e in acqua forte esistenti nella stamperia di Lorenzo Filippo De' Rossi: Contributo alla storia di una stamperia romana* (Rome: Artemide, 1996), 78 n.41; for the endowing of authorship to the patron in book dedications, see Chartier, "Princely Patronage and the Economy of Dedication," 42; for the rhetoric of dedications in thesis prints, see Louise Rice, "Jesuit Thesis Prints and the Festive Academic Defense at the Collegio Romano," in O'Malley et al., eds., *The Jesuits*, 148–69; on pamphlets accompanying prints and their authors, see Maurizio Fagiolo dell'Arco, *La festa barocca* (Rome: Edizioni de Luca, 1997), 38–39.

83. The major series were Giovanni Battista Falda, *Il nuovo teatro delle fabriche, et edificij, in prospettiva di Roma moderna sotto il felice pontificato di N.S. Papa Alessandro VII* (Rome: Giovanni Giacomo De Rossi, 1665); Giovanni Giacomo De Rossi, *Insignium Romae Templorum Prospectus* (Rome: Giovanni Giacomo De Rossi, 1683); Domenico De Rossi, *Studio d'architettura civile . . . ,* 3 vols. (Rome: Domenico De Rossi, 1702–21). See Iusco, *Indice delle stampe*, 34. See Daniela del Pesco, "Le incisioni e la diffusione internazionale dell'immagine della Roma di Alessandro VII," in *Alessandro VII Chigi (1599–1667): Il Papa Senese di Roma Moderna*, ed. Alessandro Angelini et al. (Siena and Florence: Artout/Mascietto & Musolino, 2000), 254–56.

84. "erudizione de' gl'Ingegni, per essempio dell'Arte e per gloria di questa Reggia del Mondo mia Patria." Giovanni Giacomo De Rossi, *Disegni di vari Altari e Cappelle* (Rome: Giovanni Giacomo De Rossi, 1684), cited in Gabriele Morolli, "Un saggio di editoria barocca: I rapporti Ferri—De Rossi—Specchi e la trattatistica architettonica del Seicento romano," in *Gian Lorenzo Bernini e le arti visive*, ed. Marcello Fagiolo (Rome: Istituto della Enciclopedia Italiana, 1987), 213.

85. Helene Trottmann, "La circolazione delle stampe come veicolo culturale nella produzione figurativa del XVII e XVIII secolo," *Arte Lombarda* 98–99 (1991): 15–16, cites documents dating to the late seventeenth and early eighteenth century in which patrons request that an artist follow engraved reproductions in the patrons' collection.

86. For the contract (signed 22 June 1695) and Mariotti's dispute with the Jesuits over emendments see Levy, "A Canonical Work of an Uncanonical Era," docs. 77–79.

87. "Procura Gle//Alle Diverse scudi cento cinquanta p la Stampa, e parte d[e]ll'Imagini d.la

Capp.a d'ordine di N'ro Pre havendo servito p mandare co' PP. d.a Cong.ne Gle à tutte le Case d.a Comp.a." Payment for the engraving, 8 August 1697. ARSI, Chiesa del Gesù 2056, fol. 284.

88. For an example of the ranking of reproductions, see Rita Parma, "Su una raccolta di stampe del fondo Barberini della Biblioteca Vaticana: Appunti storico-iconografici," in *Culto dei santi: Istituzioni e classi sociali in età preindustriale,* ed. Sofia Boesch Gajano and Lucia Sebastiani (L'Aquila and Rome: L. U. Japadre, 1984), 705–11.

89. Payment for the pamphlets was made from a miscellaneous account on 30 May 1697 "p[er] tiratura di n.o 2500 *altre* relationi," suggesting that this was a second round of printing. ARSI, Chiesa del Gesù 2056, fol. 261. Emphasis mine.

90. Ignatius was trying to acquire a printing press just before he died. The first Jesuit publication appeared in 1556. Giuseppe Castellani, "La tipografia del collegio romano," *Archivum Historicum Societatis Iesu* 2 (1933): 11–16.

91. *BREVE DESCRIZIONE DELLA CAPPELLA DI SANT'IGNAZIO LOIOLA Eretta nella Chiesa del GIESÙ di Roma Publicato in Stampa con la seguente Iscrizzione. Imago Sacelli, quod Sancto Ignatio de Loyola Conditori Societatis IESU erectum est in Templo Domus Professæ Romanæ eiusdem Societatis, in quo sacra eius ossa veneramur, Anno MDCXCVII* (Rome, 1697). For a full transcription see Levy, "A Canonical Work of an Uncanonical Era," doc. 8.

92. *BREVE DESCRIZIONE DELLA CAPPELLA DI SANT'IGNAZIO LOJOLA Eretta nuovamente nella Chiesa del GIESÙ di ROMA* (Rome, 1705). For a full transcription, see De Feo, *Andrea Pozzo: Architettura e illusione,* 95–98.

93. For a list of editions, see Kerber, *Andrea Pozzo,* 267–70. On the treatise and its theological-political implications, see Werner Oechslin, "Pozzo e il suo trattato," in Battisti, ed., *Andrea Pozzo,* 189–201.

94. La Teulière to Villacerf, 27 April 1693: "Un Père Jésuitte [*sic*], nommé le P. Pozzo, Peintre de réputation, vient de donner un livre de perspective, in folio, qui continent une centaine de planches gravées en cuivre. Comme l'explication de ces planche est au dos de chaque feuille, l'escriture n'en grossit pas le livre, qui n'est que cent feuilles, sans compter la Dédicace à l'Empereur, la préface et le frontispice, qui occupent chascun une feuille. Je vous donne cet avis conformément aux ordres que vous m'avés donné de vous informer des nouveautés qui regardent les Arts." Anatole de Montaiglon, *Correspondance des Directeurs de l'Académie de France a Rome avec les surintendants des Batiments* (Paris: Charavay Frères, 1888), 1:384.

95. See Jerzy Kowalczyk, "Andrea Pozzo a Późny Barok w Polsce. Cz. I. Traktat i Ołtarze," *Biuletyn Historii Sztuki* 37 (1975): 163–68.

96. See Bösel, "Die Nachfolgebauten"; and della Torre and Schofield, *Pellegrino Tibaldi architetto,* 12–13.

97. The director of the French Academy said Pozzo's book is the only perspective treatise the students need since it is written for artists. See Montaiglon, *Correspondance des Directeurs,* 13:81, 158.

98. After explaining why an alternative for the Chapel of St. Luigi Gonzaga could not be used, Pozzo remarks: "Dirò solo, che per il poco aggetto che hà, mi saria parsa più confacente al luogo, onde sarebbe stata più commoda, e godibile. *Comunque ciò sia, ella si è*

rimasta senza padrone, onde potrà ogn'uno servirsene à suo piacere." Pozzo, *Perspectiva,* 2: fig. 64 (emphasis mine). About his design first used as a *40 Ore* decoration but adapted for a permanent high altar in the Gesù, a project still under discussion, Pozzo wrote, "e perche pare che fosse ricevuto con plauso, hò voluto inserirlo in questo libro, *accio che i posteri possan di esso servirsi e considerarlo fra quegli di altri Authori;* affinche se loro piacesse e coll'approvazione di quei, à quali spetta, lo mandino ad effetto." Pozzo, *Perspectiva,* 2: fig. 71 (emphasis mine). By contrast, he included his "Altare capriccioso" (fig. 75) "sol per mostra," adding that because the bent columns are "cosa insolita" in antique architecture "nessuno vorrà essere il primo à servirsene."

99.   Andrea Palladio, *I Quattro Libri dell'Architettura,* repr. ed. edited by Licisco Magagnato and Paola Marini (Milan: Il Polifilo, 1980), 146 ff.

100.   Paradoxically, Borromini became the best published architect of the Roman Baroque through posthumous publication. See Connors, introduction to Francesco Borromini, *Opus Architectonicum,* esp. xi, lx.

101.   "Per nobilitar questo libro, & accioche spicchi maggiormente questa regola di prospettiva, l'hò fatta entrare obliquamente nel dissegno di questa Capella, da me fatto in Roma, e messo in opera l'anno 1700 ad onore di Santo Ignatio di Loiola." Pozzo, *Perspectiva,* 2: fig. 60.

102.   The Audran, "rue St. Jacques" (inscribed on fig. 92) is probably the shop of Girard Audran (1640–1703), run by his widow until 1718, when sold (providing a *terminus ante quem* for the Ignatian engravings). Three engravers signed plates: Nicolas-Henry Tardieu (Paris 1674–1749); Jean (called Jean-Baptiste) de Poilly (Paris 1669–1728) may have made the drawings on which the engravings were based on his trip to Rome in 1700–1706, providing a tentative *terminus post quem* of 1706 for the series; François de Poilly (1671–1723) signed two prints. The prints can thus be dated to after 1706 and before 1718. See *The Grove Dictionary of Art,* s.v. "Audran," "Tardieu," and "Poilly, de"; and José Lothe, *L'Oeuvre gravé de François et Nicolas de Poilly d'Abbeville graveurs parisiens du XVIIe siècle* (Paris: Commission des Travaux historiques de la Ville de Paris, 1994), 377.

     Two engravings (after Cametti's *Canonization* and Legros's statue of Ignatius) have been published in König-Nordhoff, *Ignatius von Loyola,* fig. 39 and 153, nn.187–88; and Geoffroy de Grandmaison, *Saint Ignace de Loyola: L'art et les Saints* (Paris, 1930), 60. My thanks to Jennifer Montagu for bringing the series to my attention.

103.   The engravings are numbered in the upper left and proceed more or less from the central image of the saint (1: "Statue en argent de St. Ignace enrichie d'Or, et de pierreries telle qu'elle est à Rome dans la chapelle de ce Saint") to the marble reliefs (4: "Le Souverain Pontife approve la Compagnie et donne à St Ignace la Bulle des Papes"), the bronze reliefs (9: "Saint Ignace éteint le feu d'un incendie"; 11: "Tombeau de St. Ignace illustré par une infinite de miracles"; 12: "Saint Ignace guérit les Energumenes") and the stucco reliefs above the cornice (13: "Une langue de feu paroit avec eclat sur la tête de St. Ignace le jour de la Pentecôte"; 15: "St. Ignace éxerce son pouvoir sur la malice des Demons, délivre les possedés et rend la santé aux malades"). If the remaining two stucco reliefs, four bronze reliefs, and the second marble relief made up part of the series, fourteen of fifteen are accounted for.

104.   See note 103.

105. Joseph Raz, *Authority* (Oxford: B. Blackwell, 1990), 2.

106. The director of the French Academy in Rome, La Teulière, who regularly sent reproductive engravings back to Paris, does not mention Mariotti's engraving. By contrast, in January 1697 he sent two copies of an engraving of "an altar" in the Church of St. Ignatius, engraved by Nicholas Dorigny after a painting by Pozzo. The work is probably the 1689 engraving of Pozzo's first plan for the high altar of the church. Pozzo undertook the reproduction himself, Teulière notes, "parce que c'est un particulier qui l'a faite graver à ses despens et qui la vend chez luy." Montaiglon, *Correspondance des Directeurs,* 2:289. On the project and a rare exemplar of the engraving, see Kerber, *Andrea Pozzo,* 62–64 and fig. 46.

107. This point was made by Connors in Contardi and Curcio, eds., *In Urbe Architectus,* 209; and idem, introduction to Francesco Borromini, *Opus Architectonicum,* LXXXVII.

108. For the construction of the Chapel of St. Ignatius, there was a separate rubric in the accounts called the "conti dei libri."

109. Lothe, *L'Oeuvre gravé de François et Nicolas de Poilly d'Abbeville,* 13.

110. This sale began the collection that became the Calcografia Nazionale. Simona Ciofetta, "Lo *Studio d'Architettura Civile* edito da Domenico De Rossi (1702, 1711, 1721)," in Contardi and Curcio, eds., *In Urbe Architectus,* 214; Iusco, *Indice delle stampe,* 23–24.

111. "conferiscono a promuovere la magnificenza, e splendore di Roma appresso le Nazioni Straniere, come pure . . . a coltivare l'esercizio e l'avanzamento della gioventù studiosa." *Foglio sopra la Stamperia di Filippo de Rossi alla Pace* (1738), quoted in Iusco, *Indice delle Stampe,* 61, and in Helene Trottmann, "La circolazione delle stampe," 18 n.29.

112. See the discussion of the extent to which the Ignatian chapel was copied as an ensemble in Evonne Levy, "Locating the *bel composto:* Copies and Imitations in the Late Baroque," in Sobral and Booth, eds., *Struggle for Synthesis,* 1:73–84.

113. See Kerber, *Andrea Pozzo,* 209–16; Kowalczyk, "Andrea Pozzo a Późny Barok w Polsce"; idem, "Andrea Pozzo e il tardo barocco in Polonia," in *Barocco fra Italia e Polonia,* ed. Jan Ślaski (Warsaw: Państwowe Wydawnictwo Naukowe, 1977), 111–29; Pavel Preiss, "Pozzo e il pozzismo in Boemia," in Battisti, ed., *Andrea Pozzo,* 430–39; Jerzy Kowalczyk, "La fortuna di Andrea Pozzo in Polonia. Altari e finte cupole," in ibid., 440–51; idem, "Rola rzymu w Późnobarokowej Architekturze Polskiej," *Rocznik Historii Sztuki* 20 (1994): 215–308. For the reception of Pozzo's work in Switzerland, see Oechslin, ed., *Die Voralberger Barockbaumeister,* esp. 52–53, 63–67.

114. In 1738 Branickiego wrote to his architect, Jan Henryck Klemm, to bring three French books and others because he wished to rebuild his palace. Jerzy Kowalczyk, "Ołtarze w Tyczynie a wzory Pozza," in *Podług nieba i zwyczaju polskiego: Studia z architektury, sztuki i kultury of iarowone Adamowi Milobedzkiemu,* ed. Zbigniew Bania et al. (Warsaw: Państwowe Wydawnictwo Naukowe, 1988), 363.

115. Ibid., 353–65.

116. Klemm began the second phase of work in 1735. The sculptural decoration of the altars, including the relief of Stanislas Kostka, was completed in 1743. Ibid., 354.

117. Ibid., 353.

118. It has been suggested that the openness to Italian architecture in seventeenth-century Poland was in part a product of the lack of enduring native architectural traditions, in-

timately related to Poland's ethnic and religious heterogeneity. Tadeusz Chrzanowski, "A Variety of Religious Architecture in Poland," in *Faith and Identity: Christian Political Experience,* ed. David Loades and Katherine Walsh (London: Basil Blackwell, 1990), 161–71. The problem of the Polishness of Polish art is recently posed in Thomas Da-Costa Kaufmann, "Definition and Self-Definition in Polish Culture and Art," in *Art in Poland, 1572–1764: Land of the Winged Horsemen,* ed. Jan K. Ostrowski et al. (Alexandria: Art Services International, 1999), 15–25. Kaufmann normatizes Poland's cultural heterogeneity by pointing out how much less homogeneous the major artistic centers actually were in the period.

119. For example, in 1565 Polish leaders stopped sending annates to Rome, signaling that they were not beholden to the pope. Throughout the seventeenth century Poland refused to join the Holy League in the fight against the Turks.

120. To cite one example in Silesia, the Protestant Baron Schönaich made a donation of materials to the Jesuit College in Glogow for the construction of their church in the last years of the seventeenth century. Bernhard Patzak, *Die Jesuitenkirche zu Glogau und die Kirche zu Seitsch: Zwei schlesische Barockbaudenkmäler* (Glogow: Hellmann, 1922), 5. Regarding the shared use of churches by both Reformed and non-Reformed groups in principalities of the Bohemian Crown and Upper Silesia in the seventeenth century, see Jan Harasimowicz, "'Was kann nun besser seyn fuer die Freyheit streiten und die Religion.' Konfessionalisierung und ständische Freiheitsbestrebungen im Spiegel der schlesischen Kunst des 16. und 17. Jahrhunderts," in *1648: Krieg und Frieden in Europa,* ed. Klaus Bussmann and Heinz Schilling, vol. 2, *Kunst und Kultur* (text volumes accompanying exhibitions in the Westfällischen Landesmuseum für Kunst und Kulturgeschichte, Münster and Kunsthalle Dominikanerkirche, Osnabrück, published by the Veranstaltungsgesellschaft 350 Jahre Westfällischer Friede, 1998), 297.

121. The words are of Chancellor Jerzy Ossoliński, arguing against a Protestant as a Sejm in 1648: "Your religion [Protestant] is a newcomer which recently came to us from foreign countries, while the Catholic faith was and is mistress in her own house." Conversely, Protestants made the Catholics foreign or more precisely, "Roman." Janusz Tazbir, "The Polonization of Christianity in the Sixteenth and Seventeenth Centuries," in Loades and Walsh, eds., *Faith and Identity,* 117–35.

122. Tazbir notes that there were exceptions. Faith kept Jews, German Protestants, and Dutch Mennonites from entering the ruling class, while this was not the case for Lithuanian Tartars (who were orthodox practitioners of Islam) and the Ukrainian Orthodox (who were Socinian). Ibid., 125–26.

123. See Elena Bassi and Jerzy Kowalczyk, "Longhena in Polonia: La Chiesa dei Filippini di Gostyń," *Arte Veneta* 26 (1972): 250–62; and an expanded study in idem, "Dzieło Baltazara Longheny w Polsce: Kościół Filipinów w Gostyniu," *Kwartalnik Architektury i Urbanistyki* 23 (1978): 3–38.

124. See note 51.

125. Bassi and Kowalczyk, "Dzieło Baltazara Longheny w Polsce," 37. These authors make the important point that even though Longhena himself provided the plans, it is unlikely that he would have made an exact replica of his own work. The patron requested that the Gostyń church take the shape ("forma") and the scale ("norma") of the Vene-

tian prototype (Bassi and Kowalczyk, "Longhena in Polonia," 37). The patron's directive helps to resolve the long-standing debate about the authorship of the church, which has been ascribed to Longhena (who provided the original design) and to Giorgio Catenacci (who carried out the work). Confusion resulted from the Oratorian Grudowicz's designation of Catenacci as "meus architectus." But insofar as the designation appears in a letter addressed to Longhena (14 April 1683) to clarify the latter's design (ibid., 252), it is clear that authorship was elastic.

126. Kowalczyk, "Andrea Pozzo e il tardo barocco," 117.

127. Tausch worked for the Jesuits throughout Central Europe. He was in Silesia following a trip to Rome in 1720. Henryk Dziurla, "Christophorus Tausch, allievo di Andrea Pozzo," in Battisti, ed., *Andrea Pozzo*, 408–29; idem, *Christophorus Tausch uczeń Andrei Pozza* (Wrocław: Wydawnictwo Uniwersytetu Wrocławskiego, 1991).

128. Dziurla in Battista, ed., *Andrea Pozzo*, 409.

129. Kowlaczyk ("Andrea Pozzo e il tardo barocco," 117), while citing the Wrocław altar in the contract, sees this work as symbiosis of Pozzo's Chapel of St. Ignatius and the Chapel of St. Luigi Gonzaga.

130. Joseph Connors, "A Copy of Borromini's S. Carlo alle Quattro Fontane in Gubbio," *Burlington* 137 (1995): 588–99.

131. Borromini wrote on the one surviving plan: "simile a quello di S. Carl[in]o." While Connors deemed the building worthy of serious study, he also doomed it. For it failed as a copy (because of Berninian elements that compromised the purity of the replica) and failed as an original (because a copy). Ibid.

132. The structure was begun by Tomasso Poncino (1651), continued by Giorgio Catenacci (1679) assisted by Giuseppe Bellotti, under whom a Latin cross church with tower was built. Pompeo Ferrari was asked to complete the church in 1728, hence the work follows immediately upon the project at Gostyń. Gil R. Smith, "Pompeo Ferrari: A Disciple of Carlo Fontana in Poland," in *An Architectural Progress in the Renaissance and Baroque: Sojourns in and out of Italy*, ed. Henry A. Millon and Susan Scott Munshower (University Park: Department of Art History, Pennsylvania State University, 1992), 2:768–69.

133. Ferrari's adjustments to the plan mark at least one of the important departures from Longhena's design, with paintings rather than coffers in the cupola vault. See ibid., 767.

134. Ferrari was a pupil at the Roman Accademia di San Luca, where he won first prize in the competitions in 1694 and 1696. His close knowledge of Pozzo's designs came from Pozzo's treatise. See ibid., 770–72.

135. Kowalcyzk, "Andrea Pozzo a Późny Barok w Polsce," 170.

136. On Cocchi, see Eugeniusz Gasiorowski, "Jan Baptysta Cocchi—Architekt Toruński," *Rocznik Muzeum w Toruniu* 8 (1982): 7–26. Cocchi's plan is reproduced on 20, fig. 18.

137. On Zaluski's patronage, see Marianna Banacka, "Działalność biskupa Andrzeja Stanisława Kostki Załuskiego na polu kultury artystycznej" (Ph.D. diss, Instytut Sztuki Polskiej Akademii Nauk, Warsaw, 1994), esp. 58–61. I am grateful to Dr. Banacka for sharing her archival research on the patron with me.

138. The information about Zaluski in this paragraph was communicated to me orally by Marianna Banacka and is based on her reading of Zaluski's correspondence.

139. For timber churches in Poland and examples of painted interiors, see David Buxton, *The Wooden Churches of Eastern Europe: An Introductory Survey* (Cambridge: Cambridge University Press, 1981), chap. 6. For the church in Wełna, see *Katalog Zabytków Sztuki w Polsce* (Warsaw: Instytut Sztuki Polskiej Akademii Nauk, 1974), 5, pt. 20: 20–23; Adam Dubowski, *Zabytkowe Kościoł Wielpolski* (Lublin, Poznan, and Warsaw: Albertinum, 1956), 276–77.

140. On the Mondovì altars in relation to Pozzo's illustrations in the *Perspectiva pictorum et architectorum*, see Giuseppe Dardanello, "La sperimentazione degli effetti visivi in alcuni altari di Andrea Pozzo," in Battisti, ed., *Andrea Pozzo*, 120–31; idem, "Altari piemontesi prima e dopo l'arrivo di Juvarra," in *Filippo Juvarra a Torino: Nuovi progetti per la città*, ed. Giovanni Romano and Andrea Griseri (Turin: Casa di Risparmio di Torino, 1989), 154.

141. Swach turned the IHS held by Monnot's angels in the Ignatian chapel into a martyr's crown; for the Trinity is substituted an image of Anthony of Padua (a Franciscan), and the grisailles imitating the reliefs below the columns in the Ignatian chapel are now an assortment of saints including Ignatius and Francis Xavier alongside non-Jesuit saints.

142. It is described as a succursal church in *Katalog Zabytków Sztuki w Polsce*, 5, pt. 20. I am supposing that the church is a parish church given the small size of the town.

143. Hellmut Hager, "Johann Dientzenhofer's Cathedral in Fulda and the Question of Its Roman Origins," in *Light on the Eternal City: Observations and Discoveries in the Art and Architecture of Rome*, ed. Hellmut Hager and Susan Scott Munshower (University Park: Department of Art History, Pennsylvania State University, 1987), 188–229.

144. The church, built 1594–1605 to the design of the Portuguese Jesuit architect Domingo Fernandes, is modeled on the principal Jesuit church in Portugal, the Espírito Santo in Lisbon. The chapel has been dated to the late seventeenth century based on style, although the connection to the Roman altar has not, to my knowledge, been noted. For an excellent discussion of Jesuit architecture in Portuguese Goa, see David M. Kowal, "Innovation and Assimilation: The Jesuit Contribution to Architectural Development in Portuguese India," in O'Malley et al., eds., *The Jesuits*, 480–504.

145. According to Pereira, the chapel was commissioned to celebrate the proclamation in 1699 of Francis Xavier as Defender of the East by King Pedro II (1683–1706). José Pereira, *Baroque Goa: The Architecture of Portuguese India* (New Delhi: Book and Books, 1995), 84–85.

146. Although the competition for the silver statue concluded in early June 1697, in time for Mariotti to emend his design for the General Congregation meeting, the sculptor, Pierre Legros, made changes as late as June 1698. Bonacina, "Ristretto," fol. 22r–v. On the statue, see Pecchiai, *Il Gesù di Roma*, 180–83; Enggass, *Early Eighteenth-Century Sculpture in Rome*, 1:133–34; Levy, "A Canonical Work of an Uncanonical Era," 332–45.

147. The original casket was made in 1624 by Indian artists and enhanced with more elaborate architectural frame and narrative scenes based on European prints in 1636–37.

Cosimo III (1670–1723) commissioned from Giovanni Battista Foggini a freestanding marble altar supporting the tomb and balustrade, installed by Florentine artists in Goa in 1698. On the silver shrine of the 1630s, see George Schurhammer, "Der Silberschrein des hl. Franz Xaver in Goa. Ein Meisterwerk christlicher indischer Kunst," *Das Münster* 7 (1954): 137–52; P. Rayanna, *St. Francis Xavier and His Shrine*, 3d ed. (Goa: Panjim, 1982), 189–95. For the Florentine additions, see Klaus Lankheit, *Florentinische Barockplastik: Die Kunst am Hofe der letzten Medici* (Munich: F. Bruckmann, 1962), 102–9.

148. Swidnica is located southwest of Wrocław. The fourteenth-century church was used as a Lutheran church from 1561 to 1633, after which it was given to the Jesuits. Jesuit coadjutor Johann Riedel renovated the altars in 1694–1710. Hermann Hoffmann, *Die Katholische Pfarrkirche Schweidnitz Niederschlesien* (Munich: Verlag Dr. Schnell and Dr. Steiner, 1940).

149. The scenes are St. Peter appearing to St. Ignatius (after an engraving by Wierx); St. Ignatius crossing a bridge sees a soul ascending to heaven, a presentiment of Francis Xavier's death; St. Ignatius writing the *Spiritual Exercises* inspired by the Virgin; St. Ignatius's Vision at La Storta; St. Ignatius hears an angelic chorus at the mass; St. Ignatius's Vision of the Virgin and Child; St. Ignatius with pilgrim's hat and staff has a vision before an altar of Christ carrying the cross; St. Ignatius exorcises a possessed man, frees a prisoner, and heals the ill; St. Ignatius emits a divine radiance (after Wierx).

150. I was not able to view the painting when I visited the church. The crank mechanism that is currently on the altar looks suspiciously modern, but there does not seem to have been disruption to the altar, suggesting that the sliding altar was part of the eighteenth-century renovation of the chapel. Even if the painting currently below the altar was designed by Riedel, it is unlikely that he knew about Pozzo's painting covering the silver statue. For this element had not been decided by the time the 1697 pamphlet was printed, and the painting was omitted altogether in the revision of the pamphlet in 1705.

151. "Cominciate dunque i mio Lettore allegramente il vostro lavoro; con risoluzione di tirar sempre tutte le linee delle vostre operazioni al vero punto dell'occhio, che è la gloria Divina." Pozzo, *Perspectiva*, 1: "Al Lettore."

152. For the continuities with the Nazi period in other aspects of architecture and planning, especially the "Heimatschutzstil," see Joachim Petsch, "Zum Problem der Kontinuität nationalsozialistischer Architektur in den fünfziger Jahren am Beispiel der Zeitschrift 'Baumeister,'" in Hinz et al., eds., *Die Dekoration der Gewalt*, 231–42.

153. In Krautheimer's account of the history of architectural meaning, copies based on symbolic values in the Middle Ages were gradually drained of meaning while gaining actual resemblance in modernity. The early modern period was one of transition, when replication of both form and content were possible (in copies). For further critique of his argument and its relation to Walter Benjamin's "Work of Art in the Age of Mechanical Reproducibility," see Levy, "Locating the *bel composto:* Copies and Imitations in the Late Baroque," in Sobral and Booth, eds., *Struggle for Synthesis*, 1:73–84.

154. For the lavish edition of Pozzo's treatise as produced in a moment of political *aperture* to Catholic Europe, see Oechslin, "Pozzo e il suo trattato," in Battisti, ed., *Andrea Pozzo*, 194.

1. For the tendency in the 1970s to aestheticize Nazism, see the foreword to Berthold Hinz et al., eds., *Die Dekoration der Gewalt*, 5.
2. Lane, *Architecture and Politics in Germany*, 148.
3. For what follows I am indebted to Michael Z. Wise, *Capital Dilemma: Germany's Search for a New Architecture of Democracy* (New York: Princeton Architectural Press, 1997). See also Hans Wilderotter, "Politische Architektur in Berlin," in *Das Haus am Werderschen Markt: von der Reichsbank zum Auswärtigen Amt*, ed. Hans Wilderotter (Berlin: Jovis, 2000), 26–48.
4. Hans Kollhoff remarked: "we must distance ourselves from this simplistic level of discussion about the use of materials in architecture, about allegedly democratic glass and authoritarian stone." Hans Wilderotter, "'We have respect for the historical substance,' Interview with Hans Kollhoff," in Wilderotter, ed., *Das Haus am Werderschen Markt*, 273.
5. Wise, *Capital Dilemma*, 61.
6. Wise, *Capital Dilemma*, 68. On the claim made by Walter Karschies, presidential aide responsible for administering the Spree plan, that politicians were more aware of historical sensitivities than were architects, see ibid., 84.
7. "Everyone, whether left or right, wants a beautiful city, apart from a few intellectuals who say that we must continue to suffer from our Nazi-era sins and that these must remain visible. We see that as totally perverse. It is very important for the history of National Socialism to be taught and remembered in museums, concentration camps, memorials, and so on. But it makes no sense to overload the city with these pedagogical things and have every building and empty lot proclaim forever, 'You evil Germans. You made the war and now you must put up with an ugly city.' The city must be beautiful so that people will be happy and they will not repeat these mistakes." Annette Ahme, head of the Society for Historical Berlin, quoted in Wise, *Capital Dilemma*, 114–15.
8. Almut Otto, Lars Blunck, and Anke Plötscher, eds., *Das XX. Jahrhundert: Ein Jahrhundert Kunst in Deutschland* (Berlin: Nationalgalerie, 1999).
9. Curtis, ed., *Taking Positions*.

BIBLIOGRAPHY

Aa.vv. *Inszenierung der Macht: Ästhetische Faszination im Faschismus.* Berlin: NGKB and Nischen, 1987.

———. *Erbeutete Sinne: Nachträge zur Berliner Ausstellung "Inszenierung der Macht: Ästhetische Faszination im Faschismus."* Berlin: NBGK and Nischen, 1988.

———. *La regola e la fama: San Filippo Neri e l'arte.* Milan: Electa, 1995.

Ades, Dawn, et al., eds. *Art and Power: Europe under the Dictators, 1930–1945.* London: Thames and Hudson, 1995.

Alberti, Leon Battista. *On the Art of Building in Ten Books.* Trans. Joseph Rykwert, Neil Leach, and Robert Tavernor. Cambridge, Mass.: MIT Press, 1988.

Alden, Dauril. *The Making of an Enterprise: The Society of Jesus in Portugal, Its Empire, and Beyond, 1540–1750.* Stanford: Stanford University Press, 1996.

Althusser, Louis. "Ideology and Ideological State Apparatuses (Notes towards an Investigation)." In *Lenin and Philosophy and Other Essays,* translated by Ben Brewster, 123–73. London: New Left Books, 1971.

Anderson, Mark M. "Siegfried Kracauer and Meyer Schapiro: A Friendship." *New German Critique* 54 (1991): 19–29.

Andrade, Alonso de. *Veneracion de las Santas Imagenes: Origen, y milagros de la de San Ignacio de Munebrega, fundador de la Compañia de Iesus.* Madrid: Ioseph Fernandez de Buendia, 1669.

Angeli, Diego. "I gesuiti e la loro influenza nell'arte." *Nuova Antologia di Lettere, Scienze ed Arti* 138 (1908): 195–211.

Angelini, Alessandro, et al., eds. *Alessandro VII Chigi (1599–1667): Il Papa Senese di Roma moderna.* Siena and Florence: Artout/Mascietto & Musolino, 2000.

Angus, Ian. "Learning to Stop: A Critique of General Rhetoric." In *The Critical Turn: Rhetoric and Philosophy in Postmodern Discourse,* edited by Ian Angus and Lenore Langsdorf, 175–208. Carbondale and Edwardsville: Southern Illinois University Press, 1993.

Argan, Giulio Carlo. "La 'rettorica' e l'arte barocca." In *Retorica e barocco: Atti del III Congresso Internazionale di Studi Umanistici,* edited by Enrico Castelli, 9–14. Rome: Fratelli Bocca, 1955.

———. *Immagine e persuasione: Saggi sul barocco.* Ed. Bruno Contardi. Milan: Feltrinelli, 1986.

———. *The Baroque Age.* New York: Rizzoli, 1989.

Bacchi, Andrea. *Scultura del '600 a Roma.* Milan: Longanesi, 1996.

Bailey, Gauvin Alexander. *Art on the Jesuit Missions in Asia and Latin America, 1542–1773.* Toronto: University of Toronto Press, 1999.

———. "'Just like the Gesù': Sebastiano Serlio, Giacomo Vignola, and Jesuit Architecture in South America." *Archivum Historicum Societatis Iesu* 70 (2001): 233–65.

Baldini, Ugo. *Saggi sulla cultura della Compagnia di Gesù (secoli XVI–XVIII).* Padua: Cleup, 2000.

Baldinucci, Filippo. *The Life of Bernini.* 1682. Trans. Catherine Enggass, with foreword by Robert Enggass. University Park: Pennsylvania State University Press, 1966.

Baldinucci, Francesco Saverio. *Vite di artisti dei secoli XVII–XVIII: Prima edizione integrale del Codice Palatino 565.* Ed. Anna Matteoli. Rome: De Luca, 1975.

Balis, Arnout. "Van Dyck: Some Problems of Attribution." In *Van Dyck 350,* edited by Susan J. Barnes and Arthur Wheelock, Jr., 177–96. Studies in the History of Art, vol. 46. Washington, D.C.: National Gallery of Art, 1994.

Banacka, Marianna. "Działalność biskupa Andrzeja Stanisława Kostki Załuskiego na polu kultury artystycznej." Ph.D. diss., Instytut Sztuki Polskiej Akademii Nauk, Warsaw, 1994.

Barbieri, Carlo. *Appendice alla confutazione della pretesa domanda di S. Filippo Neri a Sant'Ignazio per l'ingresso nella Compagnia di Gesù.* Bologna, 1742.

———. *Giunta alla difesa de' scrittori della vita di S. Filippo Neri o sia confutazione di ciò, che Altri asseriscono, avere S. Filippo domandato a S. Ignazio l'ingresso nella Compagnia di Gesù, ed averne avuta la ripulsa.* Bologna, 1742.

Barilli, Renato. *Rhetoric.* Trans. Giuliana Menozzi. Minneapolis: University of Minnesota Press, 1989.

Barocchi, Paola, ed. *Trattati d'arte del cinquecento fra manierismo e controriforma.* 3 vols. Bari: G. Laterza, 1960–62.

Barolsky, Paul. *Michelangelo's Nose: A Myth and Its Maker.* University Park: Pennsylvania State University Press, 1990.

Barron, Stephanie, and Sabine Eckmann, eds. *Exiles and Emigrés: The Flight of European Artists from Hitler.* Los Angeles: Los Angeles County Museum of Art; New York: Harry N. Abrams, 1997.

Bartoli, Daniello. *Della Vita e dell'Istituto di S. Ignatio, fondatore della Compagnia di Gesù.* 2d expanded ed. Rome: Nella Stamperia d'Ignatio de' Lazari, 1659.

Barzman, Karen-edis. *The Florentine Academy and the Early Modern State: The Discipline of Disegno.* New York: Cambridge University Press, 2000.

Bassi, Elena, and Jerzy Kowalczyk. "Longhena in Polonia: La chiesa dei Filippini di Gostyń." *Arte Veneta* 26 (1972): 250–62.

————. "Dzieło Baltazara Longheny w Polsce: Kościół Filipinów w Gostyniu." *Kwartalnik Architektury i Urbanistyki* 23 (1978): 3–38.

Battisti, Alberta, ed. *Andrea Pozzo*. Milan: Luni Editore, 1996.

Battisti, Carlo. *Dizionario etimologico italiano di Carlo Battisti e Giovanni Alessio*. Florence: Barbèra Editore/Università degli Studi, 1968.

Baumstark, Reinhold, ed. *Rom in Bayern: Kunst und Spiritualität der ersten Jesuiten*. Munich: Hirmer Verlag, 1997.

Baxandall, Michael. *Giotto and the Orators: Humanist Observers of Painting in Italy and the Discovery of Pictorial Composition, 1350–1450*. Oxford: Clarendon Press, 1971.

Baynes, Norman H., ed. and trans. *The Speeches of Adolf Hitler, April 1922–August 1939: An English Translation of Representative Passages*. 2 vols. London: Oxford University Press, 1942.

Bellini, Paolo. *Storia dell'incisione Italiana: Il seicento*. Piacenza: Tip.le.co, 1992.

Bellori, Giovanni Pietro. *Le Vite de' Pittori, Scultori e Architetti moderni*. 1672. Reprint, edited by Evelina Borea, Turin: Giulio Einaudi, 1976.

Belting, Hans. *The Germans and Their Art: A Troublesome Relationship*. Trans. Scott Kleager. New Haven: Yale University Press, 1998.

Bendavid-Val, Leah. *Propaganda and Dreams: Photographing the 1930s in the USSR and the US*. Zurich and New York: Edition Stemmle, 1999.

Bender, John, and David E. Wellbery. "Rhetoricality: On the Modernist Return of Rhetoric." In *The Ends of Rhetoric: History, Theory, Practice*, edited by John Bender and David E. Wellbery, 3–40. Stanford: Stanford University Press, 1990.

Benedetti, Sandro. *Fuori dal classicismo: Sintetismo, tipologia, ragione nell'architettura del Cinquecento*. Rome: Multigrafica, 1984.

Bergdoll, Barry. *Léon Vaudoyer: Historicism in the Age of Industry*. New York: Architectural History Foundation; Cambridge, Mass.: MIT Press, 1994.

Bernays, Edward L. *Propaganda*. New York: Liveright, 1936.

Bieneck, Dorothea. *Gerard Seghers 1591–1651: Leben und Werk des Antwerpener Historienmalers*. Lingen: Luca, 1992.

Bilinkoff, Jodi. "The Many 'Lives' of Pedro de Ribadeynera." *Renaissance Quarterly* 52 (1999): 180–96.

Bleichrodt, Wilhelm G. *Architektonisches Lexikon, oder Allgemeine Real-Encyclopädie der gesammten architektonischen und dahin einschlagenden Hilfswissenschaften. . . .* 3 vols. Ilmenau: B. F. Voigt, 1830–31.

Bloch, Herbert. *Monte Cassino in the Middle Ages*. 3 vols. Cambridge, Mass.: Harvard University Press, 1986.

Borromini, Francesco. *Opus Architectonicum*. Ed. Joseph Connors. Milan: Il Polifilo, 1998.

Boschloo, Anton W. A. *The Prints of the Remondinis: An Attempt to Reconstruct an Eighteenth-Century World of Pictures*. Amsterdam: Amsterdam University Press, 1998.

Bösel, Richard. "Die Nachfolgebauten von S. Fedele in Mailand." *Wiener Jahrbuch für Kunstgeschichte* 37 (1984): 67–87.

————. *Jesuitenarchitektur in Italien (1540–1773). Teil I. Die Baudenkmäler der römischen und der neapolitanischen Ordensprovinz*. 2 vols. Vienna: Österreichischen Akademie der Wissenschaft, 1986.

————. "La chiesa di S. Lucia: L'invenzione spaziale nel contesto dell'architettura gesuitica."

In *Dall'Isola alla città: I Gesuiti a Bologna,* edited by Gian Paolo Brizzi and Anna Maria Matteucci, 19–30. Bologna: Nuova Alfa, 1988.

———. "Typus und Tradition in der Baukultur gegenreformatorischer Orden." *Römische historische Mitteilungen* 31 (1989): 239–53.

Bösel, Richard, and Christoph Luitpold Frommel, eds. *Borromini e l'universo barocco.* Vol. 2, *Catalogo della mostra.* Milan: Electa, 2000.

Boutang, Yann Moulier. *La formation du mythe (1918–1956).* Vol. 1 of *Louis Althusser: Une biographie.* Paris: Bernard Grasset, 1992.

Bovio, Carolo. *Ignatius Insignium, Epigrammatum et Elogiorum Centuriis Expressus.* Rome, 1655.

Boyle, Marjorie O'Rourke. *Loyola's Acts: The Rhetoric of the Self.* Berkeley: University of Califorrna Press, 1997.

Braun, Joseph. *Die Belgische Jesuitenkirchen: Ein Beitrag zur Geschichte des Kampfes zwischen Gotik und Renaissance.* Frieburg im Breisgau: Herdersche, 1907.

———. *Die Kirchenbauten der deutschen Jesuiten: Ein Beitrag zur Kultur- und Kunstgeschichte des 16., 17., und 18. Jahrhunderts.* Freiburg im Breisgau: Herdersche, 1910.

———. *Spaniens alte Jesuitenkirchen: Ein Beitrag zur Geschichte der nachmittelalterlichen kirchlichen Architektur in Spanien.* Frieburg im Breisgau: Herdersche, 1913.

———. *Die Reliquiare des christlichen Kultes und ihre Entwicklung.* Freiburg im Breisgau: Herdersche, 1940.

Braunfels, Wolfgang. *Monasteries of Western Europe: The Architecture of the Orders.* Princeton: Princeton University Press, 1972.

Brou, Alexandre. *Les Jésuites de la légende.* 2 vols. Paris: Victor Retaux, 1907.

Brown, Patricia Fortini. "Painting and History in Renaissance Venice." *Art History* 7 (1984): 263–93.

Bulgarelli, Massimo. "La Santa Casa di Loreto: L'edificio sacro e le sue copie." *Lotus International* 65 (1990): 78–89.

Burckhardt, Jacob. *Der Cicerone: Eine Anleitung zum Genuss der Kunstwerke Italiens.* Basel, 1855.

Burke, Peter. *The Historical Anthropology of Early Modern Italy: Essays on Perception and Communication.* Cambridge: Cambridge University Press, 1987.

Burroughs, Charles. "Absolutism and the Rhetoric of Topography: Streets in the Rome of Sixtus V." In *Streets: Critical Perspectives on Public Space,* edited by Zeynep Celik, Diane Favro, and Richard Ingersoll, 189–202. Berkeley: University of California Press, 1994.

Bussmann, Klaus, and Heinz Schilling, eds. *1648: Krieg und Frieden in Europa.* 2 vols. Text volumes accompanying the exibitions in the Westfällischen Landesmuseum für Kunst und Kulturgeschichte, Münster and Kunsthalle Dominikanerkirche, Osnabrück, published by the Veranstaltungsgesellschaft 350 Jahre Westfällischer Friede, 1998.

Buxton, David. *The Wooden Churches of Eastern Europe: An Introductory Survey.* Cambridge: Cambridge University Press, 1981.

Bytwerk, Randall L., trans. "Die Aufgaben der Parteipropaganda." *Sozialistische Bildungshefte* 5 (1950). Available on the "German Propaganda Archive" Web site, www.calvin.edu/academic/cas/gpa/sedprop.htm.

Campbell, Stephen J. "'Fare una Cosa Morta Parer Viva': Michelangelo, Rosso, and the (Un)Divinity of Art." *Art Bulletin* 84 (2002): 596–620.

Carpo, Mario. *Metodo ed ordini nella teoria architettonica dei primi moderni: Alberti, Raffaello, Serlio e Camillo*. Geneva: Drosz, 1993.

———. *L'architettura dell'età della stampa: Oralità, scrittura, libro stampato e riproduzione meccanica dell'immagine nella storia delle teorie architettoniche*. Milan: Jaca Book, 1998.

———. "The Making of the Typographical Architect." In *Paper Palaces: The Rise of the Renaissance Architectural Treatise*, edited by Vaughan Hart, 158–70. New Haven: Yale University Press, 1998.

———. "How Do You Imitate a Building That You Have Never Seen? Printed Images, Ancient Models, and Handmade Drawings in Renaissance Architectural Theory." *Zeitschrift für Kunstgeschichte* 64 (2001): 223–33.

Cartari, Vincenzo. *Le vere e nove imagini de gli dei delli antichi*. Padua: Pietro Paolo Tozzi, 1615.

Cassanelli, Luciana, and Sergio Rossi, eds. *Oltre Raffaello: Aspetti della cultura figurativa del cinquecento Romano*. Rome: Multigrafica, 1984.

Cassidy, Brendan, ed. *Iconography at the Crossroads*. Princeton: Index of Christian Art and Princeton University, 1993.

Castellani, Giuseppe. "La tipografia del collegio romano." *Archivum Historicum Societatis Iesu* 2 (1933): 11–16.

Cecil, Robert. *The Myth of the Master Race: Alfred Rosenberg and Nazi Ideology*. London: B. T. Batsford, 1972.

Chadwick, Owen. *The Secularization of the European Mind in the Nineteenth Century*. Cambridge: Cambridge University Press, 1975.

Chantelou, Paul Fréart de. *Diary of the Cavaliere Bernini's Visit to France*. Ed. and introd. Anthony Blunt, trans. Margery Corbett, and annot. George C. Bauer. Princeton: Princeton University Press, 1985.

Chartier, Roger. *Forms and Meanings: Texts, Performances, and Audiences from Codex to Computer*. Philadelphia: University of Pennsylvania Press, 1995.

Chracas, L. A. *Breve, et erudita Spiegazione di tutte le cose Misteriose, che nella solenne Celebrità, e Funzione della Canonizazione de' Santi si sogliono offerire al Sommo Pontefice. . . .* Rome, 1712.

Christensen, Carl C. *Princes and Propaganda: Electoral Saxon Art of the Reformation*. Kirksville, Mo.: Sixteenth Century Journal Publishers, 1992.

Clark, Kenneth. *The Gothic Revival: An Essay in the History of Taste*. 3d ed. London: John Murray, 1962.

Clark, T. J. *Farewell to an Idea: Episodes from a History of Modernism*. New Haven: Yale University Press, 1999.

Clark, T. J., and Charles Reeve. "An Art History without Endings: A Conversation with T.J. Clark." *Documents* 18 (2000): 6–18.

Clark, Toby. *Art and Propaganda in the Twentieth Century: The Political Image in the Age of Mass Culture*. New York: Harry N. Abrams, 1994.

Clarke, Georgia, and Paul Crossley, eds. *Architecture and Language: Constructing Identity in European Architecture c. 1000–c. 1650*. Cambridge: Cambridge University Press, 2000.

Coccia, Antonio. "Nota storica sulla Vigna Antoniana dei frati minori conventuali in Roma (1555–1972)." *Miscellanea francescana* 73 (1973): 171–90.

Colantuono, Anthony. *Guido Reni's Abduction of Helen: The Politics and Rhetoric of Painting in Seventeenth-Century Europe*. New York: Cambridge University Press, 1997.

Collins, David J. "Life after Death: A Rhetorical Analysis of Pedro de Ribadeineira's *Vida del padre Ignazio de Loyola, Fundador de la Compañia de Jesus*." Licentiate thesis in Sacred Theology, Weston Jesuit School of Theology, Cambridge, 1998.

Collison, Robert. *Encyclopaedias: Their History throughout the Ages: A Bibliographical Guide with Extensive Historical Notes to the General Encyclopaedias Issued throughout the World from 350 B.C. to the Present Day*. 2d ed. New York and London: Hafner Publishing, 1966.

Connors, Joseph. "A Copy of Borromini's S. Carlo alle Quattro Fontane in Gubbio." *Burlington* 137 (1995): 588–99.

Contardi, Bruno, and Giovanna Curcio, eds. *In Urbe Architectus: Modelli, Disegni, Misure. La Professione dell'architetto Roma, 1680–1750*. Rome: Museo Nazionale di Castel Sant'Angelo, 1991.

Croce, Benedetto. "Controriforma." *La Critica* 22 (1924): 321–33.

———. "Il concetto del barocco." *La Critica* 23 (1925): 129–43.

———. *Il Seicento e il settecento*. Vol. 2 of *La letteratura italiana*. Bari: Editori Laterza, 1957.

Cropper, Elizabeth, ed. *The Diplomacy of Art: Artistic Creation and Politics in Seicento Italy*. Villa Spellman Colloquia, 7. Milan: Nuova Alfa, 2000.

Cropper, Elizabeth, and Charles Dempsey. "The State of Research in Italian Painting of the Seventeenth Century." *Art Bulletin* 69 (1987): 494–509.

Cubitt, Geoffrey. *The Jesuit Myth: Conspiracy Theory and Politics in Nineteenth-Century France*. Oxford: Clarendon Press, 1993.

Curtis, Penelope, ed. *Taking Positions: Figurative Sculpture and the Third Reich*. Leeds: Henry Moore Institute, 2001.

Dainville, François de. "La légende du style jésuite." *Études* 287 (1955): 3–16.

Dardanello, Giuseppe. "Altari piemontesi prima e dopo l'arrivo di Juvarra." In *Filippo Juvarra a Torino: Nuovi progetti per la città*, edited by Giovanni Romano and Andrea Griseri, 153–221. Turin: Casa di Risparmio di Torino, 1989.

de Backer, Augustin, and Carlos Sommervogel. *Bibliothèque de la Compagnie de Jésus*. 12 vols. Brussels: O. Schepens, 1890–1932.

de Blaauw, Sible, et al., eds. *Docere, delectare, movere: Affetti, devozione e retorica nel linguaggio artistico del primo barocco romano*. Rome: Edizioni de Luca, 1998.

De Campos, Redig. "Intorno a due quadri d'altare del Van Dyck per il Gesù di Roma ritrovati in Vaticano." *Bollettino d'arte* 30 (1936–37): 150–65.

De Feo, Vittorio. *Andrea Pozzo: Architettura e illusione*. Rome: Officina Edizioni, 1988.

De Feo, Vittorio, and Vittorio Martinelli, eds. *Andrea Pozzo*. Milan: Electa, 1996.

D'Elia, Pasquale, S.J. "CAMES FOTOQUÈS AMIDA ET XACA: Kurze Bemerkung zu einer römischen Barock-Inschrift." *Römische Quartalschrift für Christliche Alterstumkunde und Kirchengeschichte* 56 (1961): 78–80.

della Torre, Stefano, and Richard Schofield. *Pellegrino Tibaldi architetto e il S. Fedele di Milano: Invenzione e costruzione di una chiesa esemplare*. Como: Nodo Libri, 1994.

Delooz, Pierre. "Towards a Sociological Study of Canonized Sainthood in the Catholic Church." In *Saints and Their Cults: Studies in Religious Sociology, Folklore and History*, edited by R. Hertz, 189–216. Cambridge: Cambridge University Press, 1983.

del Sardo, Eugenio, ed. *Athanasius Kircher: Il Museo del Mondo.* Rome: De Luca, 2001.

De Rossi, Domenico. *Studio d'architettura civile sopra gli ornamenti di porte e finestre tratti da alcune fabbriche insigni di Roma, con le misure, piante, modini, e profili. . . .* 3 vols. Rome: Domenico De Rossi, 1702–21.

De Rossi, Filippo. *Ritratto di Roma Moderna.* 1645. Anastatic reprint, Rome: Logart Press, 1989.

De Rossi, Gian Giacomo. *Disegni di vari Altari e Cappelle.* Rome: Gian Giacomo De Rossi, 1684.

De Rossi, Giovanni Giacomo. *Insignium Romae Templorum Prospectus.* Rome: Giovanni Giacomo De Rossi, 1683.

Derrida, Jacques. *Dissemination.* Trans. and introd. Barbara Johnson. Chicago: University of Chicago Press, 1981.

Dillon, George L. "Rhetoric." In *The Johns Hopkins Guide to Literary Theory and Criticism,* edited by Michael Groden and Martin Kreiswirth, 615–17. Baltimore: Johns Hopkins University Press, 1994.

Ditchfield, Simon. *Liturgy, Sanctity and History in Tridentine Italy: Pietro Maria Campi and the Preservation of the Particular.* Cambridge: Cambridge University Press, 1995.

Domenach, Jean-Marie. *La propagande politique.* 8th ed. Que sais-je? no. 448. Paris: Presses Universitaires de France, 1979.

D'Onofrio, Cesare. "Gli 'avvisi' di Roma dal 1554 al 1605 conservati in bibioteche ed archivi romane." *Studi Romani* 10 (1962): 529–48.

Doob, Leonard W. *Propaganda: Its Psychology and Technique.* New York: H. Holt and Company, 1935.

———. *Public Opinion and Propaganda.* New York: H. Holt and Company, 1948.

Dubowski, Adam. *Zabytkowe Kościoł Wielpolski.* Lublin, Poznan, and Warsaw: Albertinum, 1956.

Duffy, Eamon. *Saints and Sinners: A History of the Popes.* New Haven: Yale University Press, 1997.

Dziurla, Henryk. *Christophorus Tausch uczeń Andrei Pozza.* Wrocław: Wydawnictwo Uniwersytetu Wrocławskiego, 1991.

Eagleton, Terry. *Marxism and Literary Criticism.* Berkeley: University of California Press, 1976.

Ebert-Schifferer, Sybille. "'Ma c'hanno da fare I precetti dell'oratore con quelli della pittura?' Reflections of Guercino's Narrative Structure." In *Guercino, Master Painter of the Baroque,* edited by Denis Mahon, 75–110. Washington, D.C.: National Gallery of Art, 1992.

Edwards, Mark U., Jr. *Printing, Propaganda and Martin Luther.* Berkeley: University of California Press, 1994.

Edwards, Violet. *Group Leader's Guide to Propaganda Analysis: Revised Edition of Experimental Study Materials for Use in Junior and Senior High Schools, in College and University Classes, and in Adult Study Groups.* New York: Institute for Propaganda Analysis, 1938.

Ellenius, Allan, ed. *Iconography, Propaganda, and Legitimation.* Oxford: Clarendon Press; New York: Oxford University Press, 1998.

Elliott, Gregory. "Althusser." In *A Dictionary of Cultural and Critical Theory,* edited by Michael Payne with associate editor Meenakshi Ponnuswami and assistant editor Jennifer Payne, 23–26. Cambridge, Mass.: Blackwell Reference, 1996.

Ellul, Jacques. *The Technological Society.* Trans. John Wilkinson. New York: Alfred A. Knopf, 1964.

———. *Propaganda: The Formation of Men's Attitudes.* Trans. Konrad Kellen and Jean Lerner. New York: Alfred A. Knopf, 1965.

———. *Histoire de la propagande.* Que sais-je? no. 1271. Paris: Presses Universitaires de France, 1967.

———. *Perspectives on Our Age: Jacques Ellul Speaks on His Life and Work.* Ed. William H. Vanderburg. Trans. Joachim Neugroschel. Toronto: Canadian Broadcasting Corporation, 1981.

———. *In Season Out of Season: An Introduction to the Thought of Jacques Ellul.* Based on interviews with the author by Madeleine Garrigou-Lagrange. Trans. Lani K. Niles. San Francisco: Harper and Row, 1982.

Elmes, James. *A General and Bibliographical Dictionary of the Fine Arts: Containing Explanations of the Principal Terms Used in Painting, Sculpture, Architecture, and Engraving, in All Their Various Branches. . . .* London: Thomas Tegg, 1826.

Enggass, Robert. "The Altar-Rail for St. Ignatius's Chapel in the Gesù di Roma." *Art Bulletin* 116 (1974): 178–89.

———. *Early Eighteenth-Century Sculpture in Rome: An Illustrated Catalogue Raisonné.* 2 vols. University Park: Pennsylvania State University Press, 1975.

———. "Un problème du baroque romain tardif: Projets de sculptures par des artistes non sculpteurs." *Revue de l'art* 31 (1976): 21–32.

Evans, Jane DeRose. *The Art of Persuasion: Political Propaganda from Aeneas to Brutus.* Ann Arbor: University of Michigan Press, 1992.

Fagiolo dell'Arco, Maurizio. *La festa barocca.* Rome: Edizioni de Luca, 1997.

Falda, Giovanni Battista. *Il nuovo teatro delle fabriche, et edificii, in prospettiva di Roma moderna sotto il felice pontificato di N. S. Papa Alessandro VII.* Rome: Giovanni Giacomo De Rossi, 1665.

Les Fastes du gothique: Le siècle de Charles V. Paris: Éditions de la Réunion des musées nationaux, 1981.

Ferrari, Oreste, and Serenita Papaldo. *Le sculture del Seicento a Roma.* Rome: Ugo Bozzi, 1999.

Ferretti, Silvia. *Cassirer, Panofsky and Warburg: Symbol, Art, and History.* Trans. Richard Pierce. New Haven: Yale University Press, 1989.

Filesi, Teobaldo. *San Salvador: Cronache dei Re del Congo.* Bologna: E.M.I., 1974.

Filipczak, Zirka Zaremba. "'A Time Fertile in Miracles': Miraculous Events in and through Art." In *The Age of the Marvellous,* edited by Joy Kenseth, 192–211. Hanover, N.H.: Hood Museum, Dartmouth College, 1991.

Filiziani, Enrico. *Sul significato delle pitture esistenti nella volta della chiesa di S. Ignazio in Roma.* Rome: "Vera Roma," 1910.

Freedberg, David. *The Power of Images: Studies in the History and Theory of Response.* Chicago: University of Chicago Press, 1989.

Friedlaender, Walter. *Caravaggio Studies.* Princeton: Princeton University Press, 1955.

Fülöp-Miller, René. *The Power and Secret of the Jesuits.* Trans. F. S. Flint and D. F. Tait. New York: Viking Press, 1930.

Fumaroli, Marc. *L'Age de l'Eloquence: Rhétorique et "res literaria" de la Renaissance au seuil de l'époque classique.* Geneva: Librairie Droz, 1980.

———. "Baroque et classicisme: L'*Imago Primi Saeculi Societatis Jesu* (1640) et ses adversaires." In *L'École du silence: Le sentiment des images au XVIIe siècle,* 445–76. Paris: Flammarion, 1998.

———, ed. *Histoire de la rhétorique dans l'Europe moderne: 1450–1950.* Paris: Presses Universitaires de France, 1999.

Gaiffer, Baudouin de. "Une collaboration fraternelle: La dissertation sur S. Ignace par les pères

Jean et Ignace Pinius dan les 'Acta Sanctorum.'" *Archivum Historicum Societatis Iesu* 25 (1956): 179–89.

Gailhabaud, Jules. *Ancient and Modern Architecture: Consisting of views, plans, elevations, sections, and details of the most remarkable edifices in the world.* 3 vols. Trans. F. Arundale and T. L. Donaldson. London: F. Didot, 1846–49.

————. *Monuments anciens et modernes, collection formant une histoire de l'architecture des différents peuples a toutes les epoques.* 4 vols. Paris: F. Didot, 1846–50.

Galassi Paluzzi, Carlo. "La decorazione della sacrestia di S. Ignazio e il loro vero autore." *Roma* 4 (1926): 542–46.

————. *Storia segreta dello stile dei gesuiti.* Rome: Francesco Mondini, 1951.

Gambuti, Alessandro. "Il Gesuita Antonio Possevino, o del come 'costruire e fondare' vantaggiosamente edifici per 'uomini religiosi.'" In *Altari controriformati in Toscana: Architettura e arredi,* edited by Carlo Cresti, 133–41. Florence: A. Pontecorboli, 1997.

Gamrath, Helge. *Roma Sancta Renovata: Studi sull'urbanistica di Roma nella seconda metà del sec. XVI con particolare riferimento al pontificato di Sisto V (1585–1590).* Rome: Bretschneider, 1987.

Ganss, George E., S.J., ed. and trans. *The Constitutions of the Society of Jesus by Saint Ignatius of Loyola.* St. Louis: Institute of Jesuit Sources, 1970.

Gaonkar, Dilip Parameshwar. "Rhetoric and Its Double: Reflections on the Rhetorical Turn in the Human Sciences." In *The Rhetorical Turn: Invention and Persuasion in the Conduct of Inquiry,* edited by Herbert W. Simons, 341–66. Chicago: University of Chicago Press, 1990.

Garber, Klaus, ed. *Europäische Barock-Rezeption.* 2 vols. Wolfenbütteler Arbeiten zur Barockforschung, vol. 20. Wiesbaden: Otto Harrassowitz, 1991.

Gasiorowski, Eugeniusz. "Jan Baptysta Cochii—Architekt Toruński." *Rocznik Muzeum w Toruniu* 8 (1982): 7–26.

Gebauer, Gunter, and Christoph Wulf. *Mimesis: Culture, Art, Society.* Trans. Don Reneau. Berkeley: University of California Press, 1992.

Gelley, Alexander, ed. *Unruly Examples: On the Rhetoric of Exemplarity.* Stanford: Stanford University Press, 1995.

Génin, François. *Les Jésuites et l'université.* Paris: Paulin, 1844.

Gernet, Jacques. *Chine et Christianisme: Action et reaction.* Paris: Gallimard, 1982.

Gilman, Sander L., Carole Blair, and David J. Parent, eds. and trans. *Friedrich Nietzsche on Rhetoric and Language.* New York: Oxford University Press, 1989.

Ginneken, Jaap Van. *Crowds, Psychology, and Politics, 1871–1899.* Cambridge: Cambridge University Press, 1992.

Gioberti, Vincenzo. *Il gesuita moderno.* 1846–47. Reprint, edited by M. F. Sciacca. 6 vols. Edizione nazionale delle opere edite e inedite di Vincenzo Gioberti, nos. 13–18. Milano: Fratelli Bocca, 1940–42.

Goldhammer Hart, Joan. "Heinrich Wölfflin: An Intellectual Biography." Ph.D. diss., University of California, Berkeley, 1980.

Goldstein, Carl. "Rhetoric and Art History in the Italian Renaissance and Baroque." *Art Bulletin* 73 (1991): 641–52.

Göttler, Christine, et al., eds. *Diletto e Maraviglia: Ausdruck und Wirkung in der Kunst von der Renaissance bis zum Barock.* Emstetten: Edition Imorde, 1998.

Grandmaison, Geoffroy de. *Saint Ignace de Loyola: L'art et les Saints.* Paris, 1930.

Griesinger, Theodor. *The Jesuits: A Complete History of Their Open and Secret Proceedings from the Foundation of the Order to the Present Time.* Trans. A. J. Scott. 3d ed. London: W. H. Allen, 1892.

Guibert, Joseph de. *The Jesuits: Their Spiritual Doctrine and Practice; a Historical Study.* Ed. George E. Ganss, S.J. Trans. William J. Young. Chicago: Institute of Jesuit Sources, 1964.

Guilday, Peter. "The Sacred Congregation De Propaganda Fide (1622–1922)." *Catholic Historical Review* 6 (1921): 478–94.

Gurlitt, Cornelius. *Geschichte des Barockstiles, des Rococo, und des Klassicismus.* Vol. 3, *Geschichte des Barockstiles und des Rococo in Deutschland.* Stuttgart: Von Ebner and Seubert, 1889.

Hager, Hellmut. "Johann Dientzenhofer's Cathedral in Fulda and the Question of Its Roman Origins." In *Light on the Eternal City: Observations and Discoveries in the Art and Architecture of Rome,* edited by Hellmut Hager and Susan Scott Munshower, 188–229. University Park: Department of Art History, Pennyslvania State University, 1987.

Hahn, Cynthia. *Portrayed on the Heart: Narrative Effect in Pictorial Lives of Saints from the Tenth through the Thirteenth Century.* Berkeley: University of California Press, 2001.

Hampton, Timothy. *Writing from History: The Rhetoric of Exemplarity in Renaissance Literature.* Ithaca: Cornell University Press, 1990.

Haskell, Francis. *Patrons and Painters: A Study in the Relations between Italian Art and Society in the Age of the Baroque.* 2d rev. ed. New Haven: Yale University Press, 1980.

Hauser, Arnold. *Sozialgeschichte der Kunst und Literatur.* Munich: C. H. Beck, 1953.

Hays, Constance L. "Math Book Salted with Brand Names Raises New Alarm." *New York Times,* 21 March 1999, Section I.

Heffernan, Thomas J. *Sacred Biography: Saints and Their Biographers in the Middle Ages.* New York: Oxford University Press, 1988.

Hinz, Berthold, et al., eds. *Die Dekoration der Gewalt: Kunst und Medien im Faschismus.* Giessen: Anabas, 1979.

Hitler, Adolf. *Hitler's Secret Conversations, 1941–1944.* Trans. and introd. Hugh Trevor-Roper. New York: New American Library, 1961.

Hoffmann, Hermann. *Die Katholische Pfarrkirche Schweidnitz Niederschlesien.* Munich: Verlag Dr. Schnell and Dr. Steiner, 1940.

Holmes, Megan. *Fra Filippo Lippi: The Carmelite Painter.* New Haven: Yale University Press, 1999.

Holub, Robert C. *Reception Theory: A Critical Introduction.* London: Routledge, 1984.

Hood, William. *Fra Angelico at San Marco.* London: BCA; New Haven: Yale University Press, 1993.

Hoog, Anne Hélène. "L'ami du peuple ou 'Le Juif errant' d'Eugène Sue." In *Le Juif errant: Un témoin du temps,* 109–25. Paris: Musée d'art et d'histoire du Judaisme, 2001.

Hope, Thomas. *An Historical Essay on Architecture, Illustrated from Drawings Made in Italy and Germany.* 3d ed. 2 vols. London: J. Murray, 1840.

Horner, Winifred Bryan, ed. *The Present State of Scholarship in Historical and Contemporary Rhetoric.* Columbia: University of Missouri Press, 1983.

Hugo, Victor. *Notre-Dame of Paris.* 1831. Trans. John Sturrock. Middlesex: Penguin, 1978.

Hummel, Edward William, and Keith Huntress. *The Analysis of Propaganda.* New York: Dryden Press, 1949.

Ignatius of Loyola. *Il racconto del Pellegrino: Autobiografia di Sant'Ignazio di Loyola.* Ed. Roberto Calasso. Milan: Adelphi, 1966.

Ijsseling, Samuel. *Rhetoric and Philosophy in Conflict: An Historical Survey.* The Hague: Martinus Nijhoff, 1976.

Incisa della Rocchetta, Giovanni, and Nello Vian, eds. *Il primo processo per San Filippo Neri nel Codice Vaticano Latino 3798 e in altri esemplari dell'Archivio dell'Oratorio di Roma.* 4 vols. Vatican City: Biblioteca Apostolica Vaticana, 1957–63.

Iparraguirre, Ignacio. "Historiografia ignaciana: La figura de S. Ignacio a través de los siglos." In *Obras completas de San Ignazio de Loyola,* edited by Ignacio Iparraguirre, 2:7–48. Madrid: Biblioteca de Autores Cristianos, 1952.

Iusco, Anna Grelle. *Indice delle stampe intagliate in rame a bulino e in acqua forte esistenti nella stamperia di Lorenzo Filippo De' Rossi: Contributo alla storia di una stamperia romana.* Rome: Artemide, 1996.

Jackall, Robert, ed. *Propaganda.* New York: New York University Press, 1995.

Jaskot, Paul B. "Art and Politics in National Socialist Germany." Review of *Auschwitz, 1270 to the Present,* by Deborah Dwork and Robert Jan Van Pelt. *Oxford Art Journal* 22 (1999): 176–84.

Jay, Martin. *Downcast Eyes: The Denigration of Vision in Twentieth-Century French Thought.* Berkeley: University of California Press, 1993.

Jones, Pamela M. *Federico Borromeo and the Ambrosiana: Art Patronage and Reform in Seventeenth-Century Milan.* New York: Cambridge University Press, 1993.

Jowett, Garth S., and Victoria O'Donnell. *Propaganda and Persuasion.* 2d ed. Newbury Park, Calif.: Sage, 1986.

Kaegi, Werner. *Jacob Burckhardt: Eine Biographie.* 7 vols. Basel: Schwabe, 1947–82.

Kagan, Richard L. "Phillip II and the Art of Cityscape." In *Art and History: Images and Their Meaning,* edited by Robert I. Rotberg and Theodore K. Rabb, 115–35. Cambridge: Cambridge University Press, 1988.

Karpowicz, Mariusz. *Matteo Castello Architekt Wczesnego Baroku.* Warsaw: Wydawnictwo Neriton, 1994.

Kaufmann, Thomas DaCosta. "Definition and Self-Definition in Polish Culture and Art." In *Art in Poland, 1572–1764: Land of the Winged Horsemen,* edited by Jan K. Ostrowski et al.; translated by Krystyna Malcharek, 15–25. Alexandria: Art Services International, 1999.

Kemp, Martin. "The Handy Worke of the Incomprehensible Creator." In *Writing on Hands: Memory and Knowledge in Early Modern Europe,* edited by Claire Richter Sherman, 22–27. Carlisle, Pa.: Trout Gallery, Dickinson College, 2000.

Kennedy, George A. *Classical Rhetoric and Its Christian and Secular Tradition from Ancient to Modern Times.* 2d rev. ed. Chapel Hill: University of North Carolina Press, 1999.

Kerber, Bernhard. "Designs for Sculpture by Andrea Pozzo." *Art Bulletin* 47 (1965): 499–502.

———. "Zur Chorgestaltung von S. Ignazio in Rom." *Pantheon* 23 (1965): 84–89.

———. *Andrea Pozzo.* Berlin: Walter de Gruyter, 1971.

Kershaw, Ian. *Hitler, 1889–1936: Hubris.* London: Allen Lane, 1998.

King, Erika G. "Exposing the 'Age of Lies': The Propaganda Menace as Portrayed in American Magazines in the Aftermath of World War I." *Journal of American Culture* 12 (1989): 35–40.

Kircher, Athanasius. *Ars Magna lucis et umbrae, in decem libros digesta. . . .* 2d ed. Amsterdam: Joannem Janssonium à Waesberge, 1671.

Kirwin, Chandler. "Vasari's Tondo of 'Cosimo with his architects, engineers and sculptors' in the Palazzo Vecchio." *Mitteilungen der Kunsthistorisches Institut in Florenz* 15 (1971): 105–22.

König-Nordhoff, Ursula. *Ignatius von Loyola: Studien zur Entwicklung einer neuen Heiligen-Ikonographie im Rahmen einer Kanonisationskampagne um 1600.* Berlin: G. Mann, 1982.

Kowalczyk, Jerzy. "Andrea Pozzo a Późny Barok w Polsce. Cz. I. Traktat i Ołtarze." *Biuletyn Historii Sztuki* 37 (1975): 162–77.

———. "Andrea Pozzo e il tardo barocco in Polonia." In *Barocco fra Italia e Polonia,* edited by Jan Ślaski, 111–29. Warsaw: Państwowe Wydawnictwo Naukowe, 1977.

———. "Ołtarze w Tyczynie a wzory Pozza." In *Podług nieba i zwyczaju polskiego: Studia z architektury, sztuki i kultury ofiarowone Adamowi Milobedzkiemu,* edited by Zbigniew Bania et al., 353–65. Warsaw: Państwowe Wydawnictwo Naukowe, 1988.

———. "Rola rzymu w Późnobarokowej Architekturze Polskiej." *Rocznik Historii Sztuki* 20 (1994): 215–308.

Kracauer, Siegfried. "Propaganda and the Nazi War Film." In *From Caligari to Hitler: A Psychological History of the German Film.* Princeton: Princeton University Press, 1947.

———. *Mass Ornament.* Trans. and introd. Thomas Y. Levin. Cambridge, Mass.: Harvard University Press, 1995.

Krauss, Rosalind. "Welcome to the Cultural Revolution." *October* 77 (1996): 83–96.

Krautheimer, Richard. "Introduction to an 'Iconography of Medieval Architecture.'" *Journal of the Warburg and Courtauld Institutes* 5 (1942): 1–33.

Kruft, Hanno-Walter. *Storia delle teorie architettoniche: Da Vitruvio al settecento.* Rome and Bari: Editori Laterza, 1988.

Krüger, Jürgen. "Das ursprüngliche Grabmal Gregors XIII. in St. Peter zu Rom." *Korrespondenzblatt Collegium Germanicum Hungaricum* 95 (1986): 41–59.

Kugler, Franz. *Handbuch der Kunstgeschichte.* Stuttgart: Ebner and Seubert, 1842.

Lamalle, Edmond, S.J. "Les Catalogues des provinces et des domiciles de la Compagnie de Jesus." *Archivum Historicum Societatis Iesu* 13 (1944): 77–101.

Lane, Barbara Miller. *Architecture and Politics in Germany, 1918–1945.* Cambridge, Mass.: Harvard University Press, 1985.

Lang, Berel, ed. *The Concept of Style.* Rev. ed. Ithaca: Cornell University Press, 1987.

Lankheit, Klaus. *Florentinische Barockplastik: Die Kunst am Hofe der letzten Medici.* Munich: F. Bruckmann, 1962.

Lapresa, Rafael. "La 'Vida de San Ignazio' del P. Ribadeneyra." *Revista de filología española* 21 (1934): 29–50.

Lavin, Irving. "Bernini and Antiquity—The Baroque Paradox: A Poetical View." In *Antikenrezeption im Hochbarock,* edited by Herbert Beck and Sabine Schulze, 9–35. Berlin: Gebr. Mann, 1989.

Lavin, Sylvia. *Quatremère de Quincy and the Invention of a Modern Language of Architecture.* Cambridge, Mass.: MIT Press, 1992.

———. "Re-Reading the Encyclopedia: Architectural Theory and the Formation of the Public in Late-Eighteenth-Century France." *Journal of the Society of Architectural Historians* 53 (1994): 184–92.

LeCoat, Gerard. *The Rhetoric of the Arts, 1550–1650.* Bern and Frankfurt: Herbert Lang, 1975.

Lee, Alfred McClung. *How to Understand Propaganda.* New York and Toronto: Rinehart and Company, 1952.

Lee, Ivy. *Publicity; Some of the Things It Is and Is Not, by Ivy L. Lee, Addresses Delivered Before* the American Association of Teachers of Journalism, Chicago, the Advertising Club of New York, and the Annual Convention of American Electric Railway Association, Including Also Questions and Answers Relating to Principles and Methods. New York: Industries Publishing Company, 1925.

———. The Problem of International Propaganda: A New Technique Necessary in Developing Understanding Between Nations; An address delivered before a private group of persons concerned with international affairs in London, July 3, 1934. Occasional Papers, no. 3. New York, 1934.

Lee, Rensselaer W. Ut pictura poesis: Humanistic Theory of Painting. 1943. Reprint, New York: W. W. Norton, 1967.

Lehmann-Haupt, Hellmut. Art under a Dictatorship. New York: Oxford University Press, 1954.

Leith, James A. The Idea of Art as Propaganda in France, 1750–1799: A Study in the History of Ideas. Toronto: University of Toronto Press, 1965.

Lerner, Daniel, ed. Propaganda in War and Crisis: Materials for American Policy. New York: George W. Stewart Publisher, 1951.

Leroy, Michel. Le mythe jésuite: De Béranger à Michelet. Paris: Presses Universitaires de France, 1992.

Leuschner, Eckhard. "The Papal Printing Privilege." Print Quarterly 15 (1998): 359–70.

Levy, Evonne. "'A Noble Medley and Concert of Materials and Artifice': Jesuit Church Interiors in Rome, 1567–1700." In Saint, Site, and Sacred Strategy: Ignatius, Rome, and Jesuit Urbanism, edited by Thomas M. Lucas, 46–61. Exhibition catalog. Vatican City: Biblioteca Apostolica Vaticana, 1990.

———. "A Canonical Work of an Uncanonical Era: Re-Reading the Chapel of St. Ignatius in the Gesù of Rome (1695–1699)." Ph.D. diss., Princeton University, 1993.

———. "The Institutional Memory of the Roman Gesù: Plans for Renovation of the 1670s by Carlo Fontana, Pietro da Cortona and Luca Berrettini." Römisches Jahrbuch der Bibliotheca Hertziana 33 (1999/2000): 373–426.

———. "Locating the bel composto: Copies and Imitations in the Late Baroque." In Struggle for Synthesis: The Total Work of Art in the 17th and 18th Centuries, edited by Luis de Moura Sobral and David W. Booth, 1:73–84. Lisbon: Instituto Português do Património Arquitetónico, 1999.

———. "The Internationalist Jesuit Style, Evil Twin to National Styles." In Spirit, Style, Story: Essays Honoring John W. Padberg, S.J., edited by Thomas M. Lucas, S.J., 181–202. Chicago: Loyola University Press, 2003.

Lewis, Michael J. The Politics of the German Gothic Revival: August Reichensperger. New York: Architectural History Foundation; Cambridge, Mass.: MIT Press, 1993.

Lichtenstein, Jacqueline. La couleur éloquente: Rhétorique et peinture à l'âge classique. Paris: Flammarion, 1989.

Lincoln, Evelyn. The Invention of the Italian Renaissance Printmaker. New Haven: Yale University Press, 2000.

Lippmann, Walter. The Phantom Public: A Sequel to "Public Opinion." New York: Macmillan, 1927.

Loades, David, and Katherine Walsh, eds. Faith and Identity: Christian Political Experience. London: Basil Blackwell, 1990.

Lorenzetti, Carmen. "Uno stuccatore bolognese a Roma: Luigi Acquisiti." Accademia Clementina. Atti e memorie, n.s., 28–29 (1991): 153–62.

Lothe, José. *L'Oeuvre gravé de François et Nicolas de Poilly d'Abbeville graveurs parisiens du XVIIe siècle*. Paris: Commission des Travaux historiques de la Ville de Paris, 1994.

Lucas, Thomas M., ed. *Saint, Site and Sacred Strategy: Ignatius, Rome and Jesuit Urbanism*. Exhibition catalog. Vatican City: Biblioteca Apostolica Vaticana, 1990.

———. "Le camere di sant'Ignazio a Roma." *La Civiltà Cattolica* 3, nos. 3387–88 (1991): 280–86.

———. *Landmarking: City, Church & Jesuit Urban Strategy*. Chicago: Loyola University Press, 1997.

Lyons, John D. *Exemplum: The Rhetoric of Example in Early Modern France and Italy*. Princeton: Princeton University Press, 1989.

Madonna, Maria Luisa, ed. *Roma di Sisto V: Le arti e la cultura*. Rome: De Luca, 1993.

Mâle, Emile. *L'Art religieux après le Concile de Trente: Étude sur l'iconographie de la fin du XVIe siècle, du XVIIe, du XVIIIe siècle*. Paris: Armand Colin, 1932.

Mandel, Corinne. "Golden Age and the Good Works of Sixtus V: Classical and Christian Typology in the Art of a Counter-Reformation Pope." *Storia dell'Arte* 62 (1988): 29–52.

———. *Sixtus V and the Lateran Palace*. Rome: Istituto Poligrafico e Zecca dello Stato, 1994.

Maravall, José Antonio. *Culture of the Baroque: Analysis of a Historical Structure*. Trans. Terry Cochran. Minneapolis: University of Minnesota Press, 1986.

Marder, Tod. "Renaissance and Baroque Architectural History in the United States." In *The Architectural Historian in America: A Symposium in Celebration of the Fiftieth Anniversary of the Founding of the Society of Architectural Historians*, edited by Elisabeth Blair MacDougall, 161–74. Washington, D.C.: National Gallery of Art, 1990.

———. *Bernini's Scala Regia at the Vatican Palace*. New York: Cambridge University Press, 1997.

———. *Bernini: The Art of Architecture*. New York: Abbeville Press, 1998.

Marí, Bartomeu, Jos ten Berge, and Georg Simmel. *Stimuli: Too much noise, too much movement*. Rotterdam: Witte de With Center for Contemporary Art, 1999.

Marin, Louis. "Le 'Récit,' Réflexion sur un testament." In *Les Jésuites à l'âge baroque, 1540–1640*, edited by Luce Giard and Louis de Vaucelles, 63–76. Paris: Jérome Millon, 1996.

Martin, A. Lynn. *The Jesuit Mind: The Mentality of an Elite in Early Modern France*. Ithaca: Cornell University Press, 1988.

Martin, John R. "Marxism and the History of Art." *College Art Journal* 11 (1951): 3–9.

McGinness, Frederick J. *Right Thinking and Sacred Oratory in Counter-Reformation Rome*. Princeton: Princeton University Press, 1995.

Meissner, W. W., S.J. *Ignatius of Loyola: The Psychology of a Saint*. New Haven: Yale University Press, 1992.

Menestrier, Claude François, S.J. *La Philosophie des Images: Composée d'un ample Recueil de Devises, & du Jugement de tous les Ouvrages qui ont êtê faits sur cette Matiere*. 2 vols. Paris: Robert J. B. De La Caille, 1682.

Michelet, Jules, and Edgar Quinet. *Des Jésuites*. 3d ed. Paris: Hachette, 1843.

———. *The Jesuits*. Trans. C. Cocks. 3d English ed. London: Longman, Brown, Green and Longmans, 1846.

Millon, Henry A., and Vittorio Magnano Lampugnani, eds. *The Renaissance from Brunelleschi to Michelangelo: The Representation of Architecture*. New York: Rizzoli, 1997.

Mitchell, W. J. T. *Iconology: Image, Text, Ideology.* Chicago: University of Chicago Press, 1986.

——. "Iconology, Ideology, and Cultural Encounter: Panofsky, Althusser, and the Scene of Recognition." In *Reframing the Renaissance: Visual Culture in Europe and Latin America,* edited by Claire Farago, 292–300. New Haven: Yale University Press, 1995.

Moisy, Pierre. *Les Églises des Jésuites de l'ancienne Assistance de France.* Rome: Institutum Historicum Societatis Iesu, 1958.

Montagu, Jennifer. *Alessandro Algardi.* 2 vols. New Haven: Yale University Press, 1985.

——. *The Expression of the Passions: The Origin and Influence of Charles Le Brun's "Conference sur l'expression generale et particulière."* London: Yale University Press, 1994.

Montaiglon, Anatole de. *Correspondance des Directeurs de l'Académie de France a Rome avec les surintendants des Batiments.* Paris: Charavay Frères, II, 1888.

Moody, Joseph N. *The Church as Enemy: Anticlericalism in Nineteenth-Century French Literature.* Washington, D.C.: Corpus Books, 1968.

Morolli, Gabriele. "Un saggio di editoria barocca: i rapporti Ferri—De Rossi—Specchi e la trattatistica architettonica del Seicento romano." In *Gian Lorenzo Bernini e le arti visive,* edited by Marcello Fagiolo, 209–40. Rome: Istituto della Enciclopedia Italiana, 1987.

Morrison, Karl. *The Mimetic Tradition of Reform in the West.* Princeton: Princeton University Press, 1982.

Moxey, Keith. *The Practice of Theory: Poststructuralism, Cultural Politics and Art History.* Ithaca: Cornell University Press, 1994.

Muller, Jeffrey M. "Measures of Authenticity: The Detection of Copies in the Early Literature on Connoisseurship." In *Retaining the Original: Multiple Originals, Copies, and Reproductions,* edited by Kathleen Preciado, 141–49. Studies in the History of Art, vol. 20. Washington, D.C.: National Gallery of Art, 1989.

Munson, Gorham. *Twelve Decisive Battles of the Mind: The Story of Propaganda during the Christian Era, with Abridged Versions of Texts Which Have Shaped History.* New York: Greystone Press, 1942.

Nagel, Alexander. *Michelangelo and the Reform of Art.* New York: Cambridge University Press, 2000.

Nava Cellini, Antonia. *La scultura del Seicento.* Turin: UTET, 1982.

Nayrolles, Jean. "Le débat sur les styles dans l'architecture religieuse au XIXe siècle: Le cas de l'Allemagne." *Histoire de l'art* 35–36 (1996): 52–53.

Nochlin, Linda, and Henry A. Millon, eds. *Art and Architecture in the Service of Politics.* Cambridge, Mass.: MIT Press, 1978.

Noehles, Karl. "Rhetorik, Architekturallegorie und Baukunst an der Wende vom Manierismus zum Barock in Rom." In *Die Sprache der Zeichen und Bilder: Rhetorik und nonverbale Kommunikation in der frühen Neuzeit,* edited by Volker Kapp, 190–227. Marburg: Hitzeroth, 1990.

Nolarci, Vigilio. *Compendio della vita di S. Ignatio di Loiola raccolto con fedeltà, e con brevità da quanto n'hanno provatamente stampato in un secolo gravi autori.* Venice: Combi e la Nou, 1680.

Norris, Christopher. *Derrida.* Cambridge, Mass.: Harvard University Press, 1987.

Oechslin, Werner. "*Architectura est scientia aedificandi:* Reflections on the Scope of Architectural and Architectural-Theoretical Literature." In *The Triumph of the Baroque: Architecture in Europe, 1600–1750,* edited by Henry A. Millon, 206–17. New York: Rizzoli, 1999.

———, ed. *Die Vorarlberger Barockbaumeister*. Einsiedeln and Zurich: Benziger, 1973.

O'Malley, John. *The First Jesuits*. Cambridge, Mass.: Harvard University Press, 1993.

O'Malley, John, et al., eds. *The Jesuits: Culture, Sciences, and the Arts, 1540–1773*. Toronto: University of Toronto Press, 1999.

Otto, Almut, Lars Blunck, and Anke Plötscher, eds. *Das XX. Jahrhundert: Ein Jahrhundert Kunst in Deutschland*. Berlin: Nationalgalerie, 1999.

Palladio, Andrea. *I Quattro Libri dell'Architettura*. Reprint, edited by Licisco Magagnato and Paola Marini. Milan: Il Polifilo, 1980.

Panofsky, Erwin. "The History of Art." In *The Cultural Migration: The European Scholar in America*, introduced by W. Rex Crawford, 82–111. Philadelphia: University of Pennsylvania Press, 1953.

———. "Iconography and Iconology: An Introduction to the Study of Renaissance Art." In *Meaning in the Visual Arts*, 26–54. Garden City, N.Y.: Doubleday Anchor, 1955.

———. *Perspective as Symbolic Form*. Trans. Christopher S. Wood. New York: Zone Books, 1991.

———. "What Is Baroque?" In *Three Essays on Style*, edited by Irving Lavin, 19–88. Cambridge, Mass.: MIT Press, 1995.

Parma, Rita. "Su una raccolta di stampe del fondo Barberini della Biblioteca Vaticana: appunti storico-iconografici." In *Culto dei santi: Istituzioni e classi sociali in età preindustriale*, edited by Sofia Boesch Gajano and Lucia Sebastiani, 705–11. L'Aquila and Rome: L. U. Japadre, 1984.

Pascoli, Lione. *Vite de' pittori, scultori, ed architetti moderni*. 1730–36. Reprint, edited by C. Ricci, 2 vols. Rome: E. Calzone, 1933.

Patetta, Luciano. *Storia e tipologia: Cinque saggi sull'architettura del passato*. Milan: Clup, 1989.

Patetta, Luciano, et al., eds. *L'architettura della Compagnia di Gesù in Italia XVI–XVIII sec.: Catalogo della mostra*. Brescia: Grafo, 1990.

Patetta, Luciano, and Stefano della Torre, eds. *L'architettura della Compagnia di Gesù in Italia: XVI–XVIII secolo: Atti del Convegno, Milano, Centro Culturale S. Fedele, 24–27 Ottobre 1990*. Milan: Marietti, 1992.

Patzak, Bernhard. *Die Jesuitenkirche zu Glogau und die Kirche zu Seitsch: Zwei schlesische Barockbaudenkmäler*. Glogow: Hellmann, 1922.

Pavone, Sabina. *Le astuzie dei gesuiti: Le false 'Istruzioni segrete' della Compagnia di Gesù e la polemica antigesuita nei secoli XVII e XVIII*. Rome: Salerno Editrice, 2000.

Payne, Alina A. *The Architectural Treatise in the Renaissance: Architectural Invention, Ornament, and Literary Culture*. New York: Cambridge University Press, 1999.

Pecchiai, Pio. *Il Gesù di Roma*. Rome: Società Grafica Romana, 1952.

Pereira, José. *Baroque Goa: The Architecture of Portuguese India*. New Delhi: Book and Books, 1995.

Perelman, Chaim. "The New Rhetoric." In *The Prospect of Rhetoric; Report of the National Developmental Project, Sponsored by Speech Communication Association*, edited by Lloyd F. Bitzer and Edwin Black, 115–22. Englewood Cliffs, N.J.: Prentice-Hall, 1971.

Peterson, Willard J. "Why Did They Become Christians? Yang T'ing-yüng, Li Chih-tsao, and Hsü Kuang-ch'i." In *East Meets West: The Jesuits in China, 1582–1773*, edited by Charles E. Ronan and Bonnie B. C. Oh, 129–52. Chicago: Loyola University Press, 1988.

Petrucci, Alfredo. "Milesiana." *Studi Romani* 4 (1956): 578–80.

Pevsner, Nikolaus. "The Counter-Reformation and Mannerism." In *From Mannerism to Ro-*

manticism. Vol. 1 of *Studies in Art, Architecture and Design*, 11–33. London: Thames and Hudson, 1968.

Picinelli, Filippo. *Applausi festivi nelle solennità d'alcuni santi*. Milan: Dionisio Gariboldi, 1650.

———. *Il Mondo Simbolico.* . . . 2d ed. Venice: Paolo Baglioni, 1678.

Pinadello, Joannes. *Invicti Quinarii Numeri Series: Quae Summatim a Superioribus Pontificibus et Maxime A Sixto Quinto.* . . . Rome: F. Zannettum, 1589.

Pirri, Pietro. *Giovanni Tristano e i primordi della architettura gesuitica*. Rome: Institutum Historicum Societatis Iesu, 1955.

———. *Giuseppe Valeriano S.I. architetto e pittore (1542–1596)*. Rome: Institutum Historicum Societatis Iesu, 1970.

Pirri, Pietro, and Pietro Di Rosa. "Il P. Giovanni de Rosis (1538–1610) e lo sviluppo dell'edilizia gesuitica." *Archivum Historicum Societatis Iesu* 44 (1975): 3–104.

Plazaola, Juan, ed. *Ignacio de Loyola y su tiempo: Congreso Internacional de Historia (9–13 Setiembre 1991)*. Bilbao: Ediciones Mensajero, 1992.

Polgár, László, S.J. *Bibliographie sur l'histoire de la Compagnie de Jésus, 1901–1980*. Rome: Institutum Historicum Societatis Iesu, 1981.

Polleross, Friedrich. "Architecture and Rhetoric in the Work of Johann Bernhard Fischer von Erlach." In *Infinite Boundaries: Order, Disorder, and Reorder in Early Modern German Culture*, edited by Max Reinhardt, 121–46. Kirksville, Mo.: Sixteenth Century Journal Publishers, 1998.

Ponnelle, Louis, and Louis Bordet. *Saint Philippe Néri et la société romaine de son temps, 1515–1595*. Paris: Bloud and Gay, 1929.

Potts, A. D. "Political Attitudes and the Rise of Historicism in Art Theory." *Art History* 1 (1978): 190–213.

Pratkanis, Anthony, and Elliot Aronson. *Age of Propaganda: The Everyday Use and Abuse of Persuasion*. New York: W. H. Freeman, 1991.

Price, Roy A. "Teaching Students in Social-Studies Classes to Guard against Propaganda." In *Education against Propaganda: Developing Skill in the Use of the Sources of Information about Public Affairs*, edited by Elmer Ellis, 127–33. Philadelphia: National Council for Social Studies, 1937.

Procacci, Ugo. *La Casa Buonarotti a Firenze*. Milan: Electa, 1967.

Quatremère de Quincy, A. C. *Architecture*. 3 vols. Paris and Liège: Panckoucke and Plomteux, 1788–1825.

———. *Dictionnaire historique d'architecture: Comprenant dans son plan les notions historiques, descriptives, archaeologiques, biographiques, théoriques, didactiques et pratiques de cet art*. 2 vols. Paris: A. le Clere, 1832.

Rabb, Theodore K. "Play, Not Politics. Who Really Understood the Symbolism of Renaissance Art?" *Times Literary Supplement*, 10 November 1995.

Rahner, Hugo. *The Spirituality of St. Ignatius Loyola: An Account of Its Historical Development*. Trans. Francis John Smith. Westminster, Md.: Newman Press, 1953.

Ravier, André. *Ignatius of Loyola and the Founding of the Society of Jesus*. Trans. Joan Maura and Carson Daly. San Francisco: Ignatius Press, 1987.

Rayanna, P. *St. Francis Xavier and His Shrine*. 3d ed. Goa: Panjim, 1982.

Raz, Joseph. *Authority*. Oxford: B. Blackwell, 1990.

Récalde, Ignace de. *Les Jésuites sous Aquaviva*. Paris: Libraire Moderne, 1927.

Reeves, Marjorie. *Joachim of Fiore and the Prophetic Future*. London: S.P.C.K., 1976.

Reichardt, Rolf. "Light against Darkness: The Visual Representations of a Central Enlightenment Concept." *Representations* 61 (1998): 95–148.

Rentschler, Eric. *The Ministry of Illusion: Nazi Cinema and Its Afterlife*. Cambridge, Mass.: Harvard University Press, 1996.

Reuterswärd, Patrick. *The Visible and Invisible in Art: Essays in the History of Art*. Vienna: IRSA, 1991.

Reuth, Ralf Georg. *Goebbels*. Trans. Krishna Winston. San Diego: Harcourt Brace, 1993.

Rey, Alain. *Encyclopèdies et dictionnaires*. Paris: Presses Universitaires de France, 1982.

Reynaud, Léonce. *Traité d'architecture: Contenant des notions generales sur les principes de la construction et sur l'histoire de l'art*. 2 vols. Paris: Carilian-Goeury et V. Dalmont, 1850–58.

Ribadeynera, Pedro de. *Vita del P. Ignatio Loiola fondatore della Religione della Compagnia di Giesù*. Venice: Gioliti, 1587.

———. *Flos Sanctorum: O Libro delle Vite de' Santi. . . .* 2 vols. Milan: G. B. Bidelli, 1618–21.

Rice, Louise. *The Altars and Altarpieces of New St. Peter's: Outfitting the Basilica, 1621–1666*. New York: Cambridge University Press, 1997.

Richards, Thomas. *The Dictionary of Architecture*. 8 vols. London: Thomas Richards, 1848–92.

Rickman, Thomas. *An attempt to discriminate the styles of architecture in England, from the Conquest to the Reformation. . . .* 4th rev. ed. London: Longman, Rees, Orme, Green and Longman, 1835.

Riegel, Oscar Wetherhold. *Mobilizing for Chaos: The Story of the New Propaganda*. New Haven: Yale University Press, 1934.

Robertson, Clare. *Il Gran Cardinale: Alessandro Farnese, Patron of the Arts*. New Haven: Yale University Press, 1992.

Robinson, Douglas. "Speech Acts." In *The Johns Hopkins Guide to Literary Theory and Criticism*, edited by Michael Groden and Martin Kreiswirth, 683–87. Baltimore: Johns Hopkins University Press, 1994.

Rosenberg, Alfred. *Der Mythus des 20. Jahrhunderts*. Munich: Hoheneichen, 1930.

Rosengarten, A. *Die Architektonischen Stylarten: Eine kurze, allgemeinfassliche Darstellung der charakteristischen Verschiedenheiten der architektonische Stylarten. Zur richtigen Verwendung in Kunst- und Handwerk*. Braunschweig: Friedrich Vieweg und Sohn, 1857.

Saint-Priest, Count Alexis de. *History of the Fall of the Jesuits in the Eighteenth Century*. Translated from the French. London: Murray, 1845.

Sallmann, Jean-Michel. "Il santo e le rappresentazioni della santità: problemi di metodo." *Quaderni storici* 41 (1979): 584–602.

Salvagnini, Francesco Alberto. *I pittori Borgognoni Cortese (Courtois) e la loro casa in Piazza di Spagna*. Rome: Fratelli Palombo, 1937.

Scaduto, Mario. "La corrispondenza dei primi gesuiti e le poste italiane." *Archivum Historicum Societatis Iesu* 19 (1950): 237–53.

Scamozzi, Vincenzo. *L'idea dell'architettura universale*. Venice, 1615.

Scavizzi, Giuseppe. *The Controversy on Images from Calvin to Baronius*. New York: Peter Lang, 1992.

Schadt, Hermann. "Andrea Pozzos Langhausfresko in S. Ignazio, Rom: Zur Thementradition der barocken Heiligenglorie." *Das Munster* 24 (1971): 153–60.

Schapiro, Meyer. *Theory and Philosophy of Art: Style, Artist, and Society: Selected Papers.* New York: George Braziller, 1994.

Schayes, Antoine Guillaume Bernard. *Histoire de l'architecture en Belgique.* Brussels: A. Jamar, 1849.

Scheller, Robert W. *Exemplum: Model-Book Drawings and the Practice of Artistic Transmission in the Middle Ages (ca. 900–ca. 1450).* Amsterdam: Amsterdam University Press, 1995.

Schieder, Wolfgang, and Christof Dipper. "Propaganda." In *Geschichtliche Grundbegriffe: Historisches Lexikon zur politisch-sozialen Sprache in Deutschland,* edited by Otto Brunner, Werner Conze, and Reinhart Koselleck, 5:69–112. 8 vols. Stuttgart: Klett-Cotta, 1984.

Schiff, Richard. "The Original, the Imitation, the Copy, and the Spontaneous Classic." *Yale French Studies* 66 (1984): 27–54.

Schulte-Sasse, Linda. *Entertaining the Third Reich: Illusions of Wholeness in Nazi Cinema.* Durham: Duke University Press, 1998.

Schulze, Hagen, ed. *Nation-Building in Central Europe.* Leamington Spa and Hamburg, N.Y.: Berg, 1987.

Schurhammer, George. "Der Silberschrein des hl. Franz Xaver in Goa: Ein Meisterwerk christlicher indischer Kunst." *Das Münster* 7 (1954): 137–52.

Schütte, Josef Franz, S.J. *Valignano's Mission Principles for Japan.* 2 vols. Trans. John J. Coyne. St. Louis: Institute of Jesuit Sources, 1983.

Scott, John Beldon. *Images of Nepotism: The Painted Ceilings of Palazzo Barberini.* Princeton: Princeton University Press, 1991.

Scribner, Robert W. "Reformatische Bildpropaganda." In *Historische Bildkunder: Probleme— Wege—Beispiele,* edited by Brigitte Tolkemitt and Rainer Wohlfeil. Zeitschrift für Historische Forschung, vol. 12. Berlin: Duncker and Humbolt, 1991.

———. *For the Sake of the Simple Folk: Popular Propaganda for the German Reformation.* 2d ed. Oxford: Oxford University Press, 1994.

Seidel, Max. "'Castrum pingatur in palatio': Richerche storiche e iconografiche sui castelli dipinti nel palazzo Pubblico di Siena." *Prospettiva* 28 (1982): 17–41.

Seigel, Jerrold E. *Rhetoric and Philosophy in Renaissance Humanism: The Union of Eloquence and Wisdom, Petrarch to Valla.* Princeton: Princeton University Press, 1968.

Sella, Marshall. "The Stiff Guy vs. the Dumb Guy." *New York Times Magazine,* 24 September 2000.

Serbat, Louis. *L'Architecture gothique des Jésuites au XVIIe siècle.* Caen: Henri Delesques, 1903.

Smith, Christine. *Architecture in the Culture of Early Humanism: Ethics, Aesthetics, and Eloquence, 1400–1470.* New York: Oxford University Press, 1992.

Smith, Gil R. "Pompeo Ferrari: A Disciple of Carlo Fontana in Poland." In *An Architectural Progress in the Renaissance and Baroque: Sojourns in and out of Italy,* edited by Henry A. Millon and Susan Scott Munshower, 2:765–99. University Park: Department of Art History, Pennsylvania State University, 1992.

Smith, Ted, ed. *Propaganda: A Pluralistic Perspective.* New York: Praeger, 1989.

Sobral, Luís de Moura, and David W. Booth, eds. *Struggle for Synthesis: The Total Work of Art in the 17th and 18th Centuries.* 2 vols. Lisbon: Instituto Português do Património Arquitectónico, 1999.

Sohm, Philip. "*Maniera* and the Absent Hand: Avoiding the Etymology of Style." *Res* 36 (1999): 101–24.

Sontag, Susan. "Fascinating Fascism." In *A Susan Sontag Reader,* with an introduction by Elizabeth Hardwick, 305–25. New York: Vintage Books, 1983.

Spear, Richard R. *The 'Divine' Guido: Religion, Sex, Money and Art in the World of Guido Reni.* New Haven: Yale University Press, 1997.

Speer, Albert. *Inside the Third Reich: Memoirs.* Trans. Richard Winston and Clara Winston. New York: Macmillan, 1970.

———. *Architektur: Arbeiten 1933–1943.* Foreword by Albert Speer and essays by Jarl Arndt, Georg Friedrick Koch, and Lars Olof Larsson. Berlin and Vienna: Ullstein and Propyläen, 1978.

———. *Architecture 1932–1942,* with essays by Albert Speer, Leon Krier, and Lars Olof Larsson. Brussels: Archives d'Architecture Moderne, 1985.

Speier, Hans. *The Truth in Hell and Other Essays on Politics and Culture, 1935–1987.* New York: Oxford University Press, 1989.

Sproule, J. Michael. *Propaganda and Democracy: The American Experience of Media and Mass Persuasion.* New York: Cambridge University Press, 1997.

Starn, Randolph. "Pleasure in the Visual Arts." In *Meaning in the Visual Arts: Views from the Outside: A Centennial Commemoration of Erwin Panofsky (1892–1968),* edited by Irving Lavin, 151–62. Princeton: Institute for Advanced Study, 1995.

Steele, Richard W. *Propaganda in an Open Society: The Roosevelt Administration and the Media, 1933–1941.* Westport, Conn.: Greenwood Press, 1985.

Stern, Fritz. *The Politics of Cultural Despair: A Study in the Rise of the Germanic Ideology.* Berkeley: University of California Press, 1961.

Stone, Marla. *The Patron State: Culture and Politics in Fascist Italy.* Princeton: Princeton University Press, 1998.

Sue, Eugène. *Le Juif errant.* Paris, 1845.

———. *The Wandering Jew.* London: Routledge and Sons, n.d.

Suleiman, Susan. *Authoritarian Fictions: The Ideological Novel as a Literary Genre.* Princeton: Princeton University Press, 1983.

Sullivan, John Edward. *The Image of God: The Doctrine of St. Augustine and Its Influence.* Dubuque, Iowa: Priory Press, 1963.

Summers, David. *Michelangelo and the Language of Art.* Princeton: Princeton University Press, 1981.

Sutton, Jane. "The Death of Rhetoric and Its Rebirth in Philosophy." *Rhetorica* 4 (1986): 203–26.

Tacchi Venturi, Pietro. "Il fratel Antonio Presutti e i suoi 'ricordi' sopra i festeggiamenti nelle chiese e case della Compagnia di Gesù per la canonizzazione di Ignazio di Loiola e Francesco Saverio." In *La canonizzazione dei santi Ignazio di Loyola, fondatore della Compagnia di Gesù e Francesco Saverio, apostolo dell'oriente,* 87–93. Rome: Grafia, 1922.

———. *La casa di S. Ignazio di Loiola in Roma.* Rome: Casa Editrice 'Roma,' ca. 1924.

———. "Di una mutazione architettonica ideata nel 1692 per la tribuna del Gesù in Roma." *Atti del Primo Congresso Nazionale di Studi Romani* 1 (1929): 641–60.

Tafuri, Manfredo. "J. Barozzi da Vignola e la crisi del manierismo a Roma." *Bollettino del centro internazionale di studi di architettura Andrea Palladio* 9 (1967): 385–98.

Taine, Hippolyte. *Voyage en Italie.* 1866. Reprint, Paris: Julliard, 1965.

Taylor, Brandon, and Wilfried van der Will, eds. *The Nazification of Art: Art, Design, Music, Architecture and Film in the Third Reich.* Winchester: Winchester Press, 1990.

Taylor, Robert R. *The Word in Stone: The Role of Architecture in National Socialist Ideology.* Berkeley: University of California Press, 1974.

Telesko, Werner, and Herbert Karner, eds. *Die Jesuiten in Wien: Zur Kunst- und Kulturgeschichte der Oesterreichischen Ordensprovinz der Gesellschaft Jesu im 17. und 18. Jahrhunderts.* Vienna: Oesterreichische Akademie der Wissenschaften, forthcoming.

Thomson, Oliver. *Mass Persuasion in History: An Historical Analysis of the Development of Propaganda Techniques.* Edinburgh: Paul Harris Publishing, 1977.

Tintelnot, Hans. "Zur Gewinnung unserer Barockbegriffe." In *Die Kunstformen des Barockzeitalters,* edited by Rudolf Stamm, 13–91. Munich: Leo Lehnen, 1956.

Tompkins, Jane P. "The Reader in History: The Changing Shape of Literary Response." In *Reader-Response Criticism: From Formalism to Post-Structuralism,* edited by Jane P. Tompkins, 201–32. Baltimore: Johns Hopkins University Press, 1980.

Trachtenberg, Marvin. "On Brunelleschi's Old Sacristy as Model for Early Renaissance Church Architecture." In *L'Église dans l'architecture de la Renaissance: Actes du colloque tenu à Tours du 28 au 31 mai 1990,* edited by Jean Guillaume, 9–39. Paris: Picard, 1995.

Trottmann, Helene. "La circolazione delle stampe come veicolo culturale nella produzione figurativa del XVII e XVIII secolo." *Arte Lombarda* 98–99 (1991): 9–18.

Vallery-Radot, Jean, and Edmond Lamalle. *Le recueil de plans d'édifices de la Compagnie di Jésus conservé a la Bibliothèque Nationale de Paris.* Rome: Institutum Historicum Societatis Iesu, 1960.

Vaudoyer, Léon. "Études d'architecture en France, ou notions relatives à l'age et au style. . . . Des Eglises au dix-septième siècle." *Magasin Pittoresque* 14 (1846): 105–7.

Verd, Gabriel Maria. "El 'Iñigo' de San Ignazio de Loyola." *Archivum Historicum Societatis Iesu* 45 (1976): 95–128.

———. "De Iñigo a Ignacio: El cambio de nombre en San Ignacio de Loyola." *Archivum Historicum Societatis Iesu* 60 (1991): 113–60.

Vetrocq, Marcia E. "National Style and the Agenda for Abstract Painting in Post-War Italy." *Art History* 12 (1989): 448–71.

Vickers, Brian. *In Defence of Rhetoric.* Oxford: Clarendon Press, 1988.

Vidler, Anthony. *The Writing of the Walls: Architectural Theory in the Late Enlightenment.* New York: Princeton Architectural Press, 1987.

Villoslada, Riccardo G., S.J. *Storia del Collegio Romano dal suo inizio (1551) alla soppressione della Compagnia di Gesù.* Rome: Universitatis Gregorianae, 1954.

Vliegenthart, Adriaan Willem. *De Galleria Buonarotti Michelangelo en Michelangelo il Giovane.* Rotterdam: Bronder-Offset, 1969.

Voss, Hermann. *Die Malerei des Barock in Rom.* Berlin: Propylaen, 1924.

Wallace-Hadrill, Andrew. "Rome's Cultural Revolution." Review of *The Power of Images in the Age of Augustus,* by Paul Zanker. *Journal of Roman Studies* 79 (1989): 157–64.

Warnke, Martin. "On Heinrich Wölfflin." Trans. David Levin. *Representations* 27 (1989): 172–87.

Watkin, David. *Morality and Architecture: The Development of a Theme in Architectural History and Theory from the Gothic Revival to the Modern Movement.* Oxford: Clarendon Press, 1977.

———. *The Rise of Architectural History.* London: Architectural Press, 1980.

Webb, Benjamin. *Sketches of Continental Ecclesiology, or, Church Notes in Belgium, Germany, and Italy.* London: Joseph Masters, 1848.

Weibel, Walther. *Jesuitismus und Barockskulptur in Rom.* Strassburg: J. H. E. Heitz, 1909.

Weisbach, Werner. *Der Barock als Kunst der Gegenreformation.* Berlin: Paul Cassirer, 1921.

Welch, David. *The Third Reich: Politics and Propaganda.* New York: Routledge, 1993.

White, Hayden. "The Suppression of Rhetoric in the Nineteenth Century." In *Rhetoric Canon,* edited by Brenda Deen Schildgen, 21–32. Detroit: Wayne State University Press, 1997.

White, Ralph K. "The New Resistance to International Propaganda." *Public Opinion Quarterly* 16 (1952–53): 539–51.

Wickstrom, John B. "Gregory the Great's 'Life of St. Benedict' and the Illustrations of Abbot Desiderius." *Studies in Iconography* 19 (1998): 31–73.

Wilberg-Vignau, Peter. *Andrea Pozzos Deckenfresko in S. Ignazio.* Munich: Uni-Druck, 1970.

Wilderotter, Hans, ed. *Das Haus am Werderschen Markt: Von der Reichsbank zum Auswärtigen Amt.* Berlin: Jovis, 2000.

Wind, Edgar. *Art and Anarchy.* London: Faber and Faber, 1963.

Wise, Michael Z. *Capital Dilemma: Germany's Search for a New Architecture of Democracy.* New York: Princeton Architectural Press, 1997.

Wittkower, Rudolf. "Il barocco in Italia." In *Manierismo, barocco, rococò: Concetti e termini; Convegno Internazionale, Roma 21–24 aprile 1960,* 319–27. Rome: Accademia Nazionale dei Lincei, 1962.

———. *Art and Architecture in Italy, 1600–1750.* 3 vols. 6th ed., revised by Joseph Connors and Jennifer Montagu. New Haven: Yale University Press, 1999.

Wittkower, Rudolf, and Irma Jaffe, eds. *Baroque Art: The Jesuit Contribution.* New York: Fordham University Press, 1972.

Wolff, Janet. *The Social Production of Art.* London: Macmillan, 1981.

Wölfflin, Heinrich. *Renaissance and Baroque.* Trans. Kathrin Simon. Ithaca: Cornell University Press, 1966.

Wulf, Friedrich, ed. *Ignatius of Loyola: His Personality and Spiritual Heritage, 1556–1956: Studies on the 400th Anniversary of His Death.* St. Louis: Institute of Jesuit Sources, 1977.

Yale French Studies 88 (1995). Special issue on Louis Althusser.

Zanardi, Mario, ed. *I Gesuiti e Venezia: Momenti e problemi di Storia Veneziana della Compagnia di Gesù.* Venice: Giunta Regionale del Veneto, 1994.

Zanker, Paul. *Augustus und die Macht der Bilder.* Munich: C. H. Beck, 1987.

———. *The Power of Images in the Age of Augustus.* Trans. Alan Shapiro. Ann Arbor: University of Michigan Press, 1988.

Zuccari, Alessandro. *I pittori di Sisto V.* Rome: Fratelli Palombi, 1992.

ILLUSTRATIONS

INDEX

Nadal, Jerome, 122

name, of Christ, 17, 150, 177, *fig. 47*

Naples, Casa Professa, 79

nation, as builder, 32, 35

nationalism and architecture, 24, 25, 28, 40

Nazi architecture, 1–2, 9, 12, 65, 233–37, *fig. 1;*
    as art, 233, 236; judgment of, 242n9; as
    Nazism, 234; neutralization of, 234, 236,
    309n7; as politically alive, 5, 233; preserva-
    tion of, 235–36, 309n7; reuse of, 235

Nazi propaganda: analysis of, 59; illegal status
    of, 234

Negroni, Cardinal Gianfrancesco, 90–91

neo-Baroque architecture, 253n92

Nerdinger, Winfried, 233

Neri, Saint Philip, 128, 139, 156, 167–69, 170,
    figs. 39, 63

Neroni, Matteo, 294n16

"New Catholicism," 21

Nietzsche, Friedrich, 37, 66, 67, 256n11, 264n125

Nochlin, Linda, 245n29

Nolarci, Virgilio, 144

Norris, Christopher, 68

Noyelle, Carlo de, 135

Nuvolone, Francesco, 167–69, *fig. 63*

obedience, 54, 80–84, 85, 107, 178, 211, 269n41;
    anti-Jesuit parody of, 23, 32, 269n41; as
    creative principle, 82, 107; and design, 81–
    82, 107; Pozzo's, 98–99, 211–12. *See also*
    under Ignatius of Loyola; Jesuits

"Old Catholicism," 21

Oliva, Gian Paolo, 82, 83, 88, 90, 99, 131,
    296n31

Olivieri, Pietro Paolo, 294n17

Opalińska, Sofia, 217, 221

Oratorians, 167–69

original, 299n61

ornament, architectural, 30–31, 34

Orrigone, Giovanni Battista, 93–94, 272n91

Orta, Pier Francesco, 87, 270n59

Ossoliński, Jerzy, 305n121

Ottone, Lorenzo, *fig. 68*

Paleotti, Gabriele, 49–50, 259n43

Palladio, Andrea, 208

Panofsky, Erwin, 5, 43, 110–11, 146, 183,
    276n6

Papaleo, Pietro, *fig. 76*

Paris: St. Genevieve (Pantheon), 26; St. Paul–
    St. Louis, 251n73

Pascal, Blaise, 22, 28

passions, 50, 53, *fig. 12*

Pastina, Salvatore, 270n51

Patetta, Luciano, 74

patron, representation of, 189, 194, 295n24

patronage: as authorship, 107–9, 194; motiva-
    tions for, 214, 217, 221, 223; responsibilities
    of, 102

Paul, Saint, 116

Paul III, 190, 193, *figs. 25, 82*

Paul V, 294n17

Payne, Alina, 299n63

Pecchiai, Pio, 88, 270n63

Pellegrini, Pellegrino, 208

persuasion, 39, 52, 54

Pevsner, Nikolaus, 39

pharmakon, 44, 68

Philandrier, Guillaume, 196

Philo, 116

photography, 114

Piazza, abbate, 271n73

Picinelli, Filippo, 160, 169

Pirri, Pietro, 266n18l, 300n75

Pius VII, 20–21

Plato, 44, 66, 67–68, 69, 256n11

poesia, 50

Poilly, François de, 303n102

Poilly, Jean de, 303n102

Poland: artistic heterogeneity in, 305n118;
    autonomy from Rome, 305n119; as bulwark
    of Christianity, 214; Catholization of, 214,
    217, 232, 305n121; class and faith in, 217,
    305n122; ecumenical patronage in, 217,
    305n120; political organization of, 216;
    religious heterogeneity of, 214–15; use of
    Italian designs in, 214–32. *See also* churches,
    Jesuit; Pozzo, Andrea; *and individual cities*

Poncino, Tomasso, 306n132

Port-Royal, 47

portraits, of rulers, with buildings, 187–95, *figs.*
    80–85

Possevino, Antonio, 197

Pozzo, Andrea, 17, 31, 64, 80; pupils of, 214,
    218–19; reputation of, 97, 108. Works:
    Chapel of St. Ignatius, 12, 79, 88–109, 118,

Quinet, Edgar, 18, 23, 30, 32, 33, 246n13, 253n88, 269n44

Quintillian, 45, 257nn13,24

Rabb, Theodore, 10

Rainaldi, Girolamo, 74

Ramdohr, F. W. B. von, 26

Rasponi, Cesare, *De Basilica et Patriarchio Lateranensi,* 296n30

Raz, Joseph, 209–11

reception, 13, 184

religion, as condition for art, 26, 249n52

"Renaissance" architecture (term), 29, 31, 33, 34, 55, 249n59, 250nn63,66

Renaissance art, 37, 48–49

repetition, of form, 114

reproductive engravings: audiences for, 205, 209; authorities behind, 204, 207, 209–13; dedications of, 205; institutional control over, 213, 226; Jesuit circulation of, 205–8; types of, 204; uses of, 213, 226

Restori, Luigi, 93, 94, 98

Retz, Franz, 82

revisore (consiliarius aedificiorum), 78, 83

Reynaud, Léonce, 32, 249n61

rhetoric, 42–52; vs. aesthetics, 47, 48, 63, 66, 69; aims of, 45, 49; Asiatic style of, 30, 47; Attic style, 47; audience in, 45, 70; and the Baroque, 43, 48–52, 256n2; as civic tool, 43–44; contemporary views of, 43; demise of, 66; in democracies, 44, 47, 50, 68–69, 256n11; and early modern art theory, 43, 48–49; in education, 45, 68 (in Jesuit schools, 42, 46–47); elements of, 42–43, 45; eloquence, 45, 46; epedeictic, 45, 46, 257n13; ethical basis of, 44, 49, 50, 70; figures of, 48; as form of response, 7–10; as fraudulent, 47; function vs. ends of, 49–50; history of (contemporary, 43, 66–67; Counter-Reformation, 46, 49–50; Greece, 43–45, 50, 67–68, 69, 256n11; humanism and, 46, 50, 69; Middle Ages, 45–46; nineteenth century, 47, 48, 68–69; Rome, 45, 69); and institutions, 11, 43, 44, 46, 52; as interested discourse, 11, 43, 44, 47, 66, 69; Jansenist style, 47; and "Jesuit Style," 30; vs. literature, 47, 66; *logos* in, 44, 45, 67–68; means vs. ends of, 49–50, 52, 70;

as moral argumentation (primary rhetoric), 45, 257n15; passions and, 45, 50; as persuasion, 42, 45, 52, 66, 69, 257n15; vs. philosophy, 42, 44, 49, 66, 67–68, 70, 256n11, 257n18; vs. propaganda, 11, 42–43, 52, 63, 69, 70, 112; in Renaissance theory, 48–49; replaced by propaganda, 42, 55, 69, 70; and spectator, 50; as style (secondary rhetoric), 45, 48, 66, 257n15; as supplement, 67; suppression of, in schools, 47, 68; techniques of, 48; tropes, 66–67; vs. truth-seeking discourses, 48, 66; truth-value of, 44–45, 47, 66, 70; types of, 44–45, 46, 257n13

rhetorical function of images, 49–50

rhetorical turn, 66, 67

rhetoricality, 43, 67, 69

Ribadeynera, Pedro de: engraving of, 123–27, *fig. 26; Flos Sanctorum,* 212, 280n51; Ignatian images supervised by, 121, 125–26 (copies of, 282n71); as image of Ignatius, 126–27; miracles, view of, 281n62; *vita* of Ignatius, 119, 121, 122, 127, 128, 141–44, 176, 280n51

Ricchini, Francesco Maria, 74

Richards, I. A., 66

Richards, Thomas, 249n59, 250n65

Rickman, Thomas, 250n62

Riedel, Johann, 229, 308nn148,150

Riefenstahl, Leni, 113

Riegel, O. W., 59

"Risorgimento" style, 249n59

"Ristretto," 87–88, 93, 271n63

Robertson, Clare, 75–76, 266n11, 267n19

Rockefeller Foundation, 59

Rococo, 29, 249n59, 250nn65,66

Rodchenko, Alexander, 114

"Rodin," 18, 48, *fig. 7*

Roman, Alfonso, 269n37

roman à thèse, 280nn45,46

Roman art, ancient, 64–65

Rome, architecture in: Chapel of St. Ignatius at La Storta, 133, *fig. 30;* Church of il Gesù, 31, 34, 73, 75–76, 118, 127, 131–32, 160–83, 194, 196, 198–99, *figs. 11, 87* (apse, 88, 89; barrel vault, 266n11; barrel vault, decorations of, 88, 90, 99, *figs. 9, 56;* Chapel of St. Francis Xavier, 88, 90–91; churches derivative of, 198–200, 298nn49–51; confessio and crypt designs for, 89–90, *fig. 20;*

TEXT: 9.5/14 Scala
DISPLAY: Scala Sans
COMPOSITOR: Integrated Composition Systems
PRINTER + BINDER: Friesens